DIGITAL SOVEREIGNTY AND THE GREEN TRANSITION

This book is the first investigation of the relationship between EU digital sovereignty and sustainability strategies.

It maps the ambitions and limitations of EU digital strategic autonomy and explores the structural challenges underlying its relationship with its green transition objectives in the context of the ongoing wars in neighbouring European countries and the consequent tensions in the EU energy sector.

The EU is racing to achieve technological independence from third countries and foreign multinational companies to protect its digital sovereignty and preserve its fundamental rights. In the EU, digitalisation and the green transformation are seen as twin transitions. Yet, EU digital sovereignty strategies have a significant environmental cost. Reaching a status of strategic autonomy of the EU at the level of digital infrastructures, products, services and data implies higher energy consumption and exploitation of natural resources. Moreover, the geopolitical tensions following the Russian invasion of Ukraine have provoked an unprecedented energy crisis, which is affecting EU economies and impacting objectives of the twin transitions.

The book offers an interdisciplinary analysis of the major EU regulatory and policy instruments in this field, providing an invaluable guide for academics, practitioners, and policymakers navigating the complex issues of preserving digital sovereignty and addressing climate change in times of war and energy crisis.

Digital Sovereignty and the Green Transition

EU Challenges in Times of War and Energy Crisis

Edited by
Edoardo Celeste
Tamara Alvarez Robles
Gaël Depoorter
and
Tamara Favaro

•HART•
OXFORD • LONDON • NEW YORK • NEW DELHI • SYDNEY

HART PUBLISHING
Bloomsbury Publishing Plc
Kemp House, Chawley Park, Cumnor Hill, Oxford, OX2 9PH, UK
1385 Broadway, New York, NY 10018, USA
Bloomsbury Publishing Ireland Limited, 29 Earlsfort Terrace, Dublin 2, D02 AY28, Ireland

HART PUBLISHING, the Hart/Stag logo, BLOOMSBURY and the Diana logo are trademarks of Bloomsbury Publishing Plc

First published in Great Britain 2025

A catalogue record for this book is available from the British Library.

A catalogue record for this book is available from the Library of Congress.

Library of Congress Control Number: 2025936848

ISBN: HB: 978-1-50998-362-9
ePDF: 978-1-50998-364-3
ePub: 978-1-50998-363-6

Typeset by Compuscript Ltd, Shannon

For product safety related questions contact productsafety@bloomsbury.com

To find out more about our authors and books visit www.hartpublishing.co.uk. Here you will find extracts, author information, details of forthcoming events and the option to sign up for our newsletters.

ACKNOWLEDGEMENTS

This edited volume collects the contributions presented at the inaugural Summer School of the European Master in Law, Data and Artificial Intelligence (EMILDAI), which took place on 8–11 May 2023 at Dublin City University, Ireland. EMILDAI is an international and interdisciplinary joint master programme offered by four partner universities – Dublin City University (Ireland), Avignon Université (France), Universidad de León (Spain), and Università di Pisa (Italy) – and supported by three Research Associate Partners – the ADAPT Centre for AI-Driven Digital Content Technology (Ireland), the Italian National Research Council's Institute of Information Science and Technologies 'Alessandro Faedo' (Italy) and the Centre de Recherche en Droit 'A. Favre' of the Université Savoie-Mont Blanc (France). EMILDAI is funded by the Erasmus Mundus programme of the European Union (2021–2027).

The organisation of the Summer School would not have been possible without the funding of the Erasmus Mundus programme and the help of many colleagues and students from all the involved institutions. In particular, we would like to thank the former EMILDAI officer Dr Daniela Triggiano for her assistance in the organisation of the event. This book also received financial support from the Faculty of Humanities and Social Sciences Book Publication Scheme at Dublin City University. We are particularly grateful to Victor Henriquez Diaz, EMILDAI graduate and current PhD student at Dublin City University, for his strenuous assistance in getting all the contributions ready for production.

Lastly, we would like to sincerely thank the team at Hart Publishing for their continued support, advice and editorial guidance as well as our partners, friends and family members for all their encouragement and patience while completing this project.

Dublin-León-Avignon-Pisa
December 2024

TABLE OF CONTENTS

LIST OF CONTRIBUTORS

Tamara Alvarez Robles is an Assistant Professor of Constitutional Law at the Universidad de León.

Brunessen Bertrand is a Full Professor of Public Law at the University of Rennes 1, where she is head of the European Integration Axis (IODE UMR CNRS 6262) and head of the European Research Centre.

Thibault Carrère is an Associate Professor of Public Law at Avignon Université.

Edoardo Celeste is an Associate Professor of Law, Technology and Innovation at the School of Law and Government of Dublin City University, Ireland, where he is the Programme Chair of the Erasmus Mundus Master in Law, Data and AI (EMILDAI), the Deputy-Director of the Dublin European Law Institute and the Coordinator of the Law and Tech Research Cluster.

Gaël Depoorter is an Associate Professor in Political Science at the Department of Political Science and Economics of Avignon Université.

Francesco Dimichina is a legal officer at the Bank of Italy and a PhD Candidate at the University of Pisa, Italy.

Tamara Favaro is an Associate Professor of Economic Law at the University of Pisa.

Pierre-Henri Morand is a Full Professor of Economics at Avignon Université and a Unit Lead at the French Anticorruption Agency.

Harshvardhan J Pandit is an Assistant Professor at the School of Computing of Dublin City University and a Funded Investigator of the ADAPT Centre for AI-Driven Digital Content Technology, Dublin, Ireland.

Alba Perez Victorio is a Researcher at the Law and Tech Research Cluster of Dublin City University, Ireland.

Cecilia Rasetto is a lawyer and a doctoral researcher at the University of Pisa affiliated with Agritech, the National Center for the Development of New Technologies in Agriculture.

Mauro Santaniello is an Associate Professor of Political Science at the Department of Management & Innovation System of the University of Salerno, Italy, and the director of the Internet & Communication Policy Center (ICPC).

1

The Challenges of the EU Twin Transitions: Socio-Economic and Geopolitical Context

EDOARDO CELESTE, TAMARA ALVAREZ ROBLES, TAMARA FAVARO AND GAËL DEPOORTER*

I. Introduction

In the European Union (EU) regulatory and policy agendas, digitalisation and decarbonisation are seen as 'twin transitions'. 'Twin' not only in the sense that they are occurring at the same time, but also advocating for an integration of the two: digitalisation for decarbonisation and decarbonisation of digitalisation. Indeed, digitalisation possesses a Janus-faced role vis-à-vis the green transition: it can be difficult to achieve efficient decarbonisation without the help of digital technologies, but digital technologies do have environmental implications and their increasingly large-scale use amplifies energy consumption and has an impact on the exploitation of natural resources. For this reason, it also assumed that the EU commitment to achieve no net emissions of greenhouse gases by 2050 should pursue economic growth with a sustainable use of resources.

With the advent of the COVID-19 pandemic, Europe has experienced one of the worst socio-economic crises since the end of World War II, more recently amplified by a stark rise of inflation and a related energy crisis generated by the Russian invasion of Ukraine. Yet, the COVID-19 pandemic has allowed the EU to plan and introduce Next Generation EU (NGEU), an unprecedented economic initiative, given the size and breadth of its ambitions. NGEU's motto 'for a greener, more digital and resilient future' well encapsules the strategic objectives of this measure. Europe aims to recover from the pandemic and foster its economic growth, strengthening at the same time its resilience to climate, energy, health and digital threats. The NGEU recovery plan supports European Member States to achieve the digital and green transitions together. Within the framework of the European

* We would like to thank Victor Henriquez Diaz and Alba Perez Victorio for their research assistance.

Green Deal, the Commission aims to use data, digital infrastructures and AI solutions to inform the decision-making process in the fight against environmental challenges. However, the recent geopolitical tensions following the Russian invasion of Ukraine and turmoil in the Middle East have provoked an unprecedented energy crisis in the EU, which is now affecting Member States' economies and potentially undermining pre-established plans and objectives both in the field of digitalisation and green transition.

On top of these ambitions, the EU is racing to achieve technological independence from third countries and foreign multinational companies with the objective of preserving its fundamental rights and strengthening its position as global leader in the digital sector. The recent EU regulatory and policy frameworks in the digital field have been informed by the notion of 'digital sovereignty', which advocates for increasing strategic autonomy of the EU at the level of digital infrastructures, products, services and data. While this strategy seems to be consistent with the EU objectives and ambitions in light of the current geopolitical and economic context, it might represent an additional obstacle to the process of reconciling the digital and green transitions in the Union. Indeed, essential elements of the EU digital sovereignty strategy, such as reshoring components of the digitalisation process to the EU or incentivising the construction of digital infrastructures within the territories of the Member States, imply higher levels of energy consumption, exploitation of water and rare materials as well as waste generation.

This edited volume aims to trigger an academic reflection on the environmental impact of EU digital sovereignty strategies, analysing to what extent the EU has achieved a level of policy coherence that would take into account other domains of action, as well as the impact of its ambitions not only within the Union, but beyond it. Such an investigation contributes to current research that is exploring how to effectively reconcile the digital and green transition within the EU by stressing that EU digitalisation strategies are no longer geopolitically neutral, but aim to achieve technological independence. In this regard, the choice of the new von der Leyen Commission to appoint an executive vice-president with competence on 'tech sovereignty' confirms the centrality of this objective for the EU.[1]

This book presents a collection of contributions of scholars from law, political science, economics and computing. Its interdisciplinary approach is justified by the complex and multifaceted nature of the context from which the core research question of this work stems. An analysis of the compatibility of EU digital sovereignty strategies with the Union's green objectives cannot be achieved *in abstracto*. It necessarily implies an understanding of the underlying socio-economic and geopolitical context that the Union currently faces. Without aiming to be

[1] EU Commission, 'College of Commissioners', commission.europa.eu/about/organisation/college-commissioners_en#:~:text=The%20College%20is%20composed%20of,for%20a%205%2Dyear%20term.

exhaustive, and considering the fast-paced nature of the developments, section II aims to provide an overview of such a context, highlighting in particular the main elements that are challenging the EU twin transition objectives. In light of the complexities characterising the scenario underlying this research, section III illustrates the rationale for adopting an interdisciplinary approach in the context of this work. Section IV then concludes with an overview of the structure of the book and a summary of its chapters.

II. The Socio-economic and Geopolitical Context

A. The EU after COVID: From the Pandemic to War

The COVID-19 pandemic undoubtedly represented a turning point for the EU. In the aftermath of this health crisis, the then European Commissioner for Economy Paolo Gentiloni convened a High-Level Group on Post-COVID economic and social challenges. In 2022, the Group published a report significantly entitled 'A New Era for Europe'.[2] The pandemic had a profound impact on the EU from a socio-economic perspective,[3] triggering inflation rises, increasing costs of living and affecting public debt, generating fiscal challenges that were possible to face only by suspending standard EU debt rules. COVID-19 exposed the vulnerabilities of European health systems and strained the labour market, creating an overall climate of economic insecurity and declining trust in national and EU institutions.

On the one hand, the pandemic accelerated existing trends, such as the advent of remote and more flexible forms of employment, and amplified existing problems, such as socio-economic inequalities with an higher impact on low-income households, women and migrant workers. On the other hand, COVID-19 prompted the largest institutional reaction at European level since the end of World War II. The EU adopted the €806.9 billion recovery plan NextGenerationEU, whose central instrument, the Recovery and Resilience Facility, aims to fund strategic areas in order to recover after the crisis and enhance the EU's strength and future resilience.[4] The pandemic is thus converted into a unique opportunity to transform and modernise the EU, not only in those fields which were directly affected by the pandemic, such as in the area of preparedness and resilience, but also in

[2] European Commission. Directorate General for Economic and Financial Affairs, 'A New Era for Europe: How the European Union Can Make the Most of Its Pandemic Recovery, Pursue Sustainable Growth, and Promote Global Stability' (Publications Office, 2022), data.europa.eu/doi/10.2765/11297.

[3] See Federico Fabbrini and Christy Anne Petit (eds), *Research Handbook on Post-Pandemic EU Economic Governance and NGEU Law* (Edward Elgar, 2024).

[4] For a critical analysis, see Marco Buti and Sergio Fabbrini, 'Next Generation EU and the Future of Economic Governance: Towards a Paradigm Change or Just a Big One-Off?' (2023) 30 *Journal of European Public Policy* 676.

more general key policy domains, such as research and innovation, digitalisation, common agricultural policy, climate change, biodiversity and gender equality.

As will be examined in more detail in this volume, achieving the twin transitions represents a core objective of the EU post-pandemic. Digitalisation is seen as an unprecedented driver of the green transformation, but there is simultaneously an increasing awareness of the connatural contradictions of these two policy strategies, given the intrinsic environmental impact of the digital sector.[5] On top of this challenge, the underlying geopolitical scenario adds a further layer of complexity. The EU is in the risky position of being dependent upon third countries for supply of digital products, services and infrastructures.[6] Digitalisation for the green transition can no longer be driven by a completely free and open market logic, which would exacerbate the EU's exposure to the ebbs and flows of foreign suppliers. Preserving digital sovereignty – and more generally its strategic autonomy – thus becomes an imperative to guide the EU economic agenda,[7] and two past experiences provide an important warning for the Union. Firstly, the EU has understood the importance of distancing itself from the two major technopoles – the US and China – in order to avoid being subjects to potential reverberations of their politico-economic arm-wrestling.[8] Secondly, the pandemic has taught the EU that there might be major global events that can paralyse global supply chains, regardless of geopolitical factors.

The path to EU recovery, however, does not seem to proceed smoothly. The Union did not have time to 'breathe' after the COVID-19 pandemic before a series of wars started on its doorstep. In February 2022, Russia invaded Ukraine, leading to the most serious conflict on European soil since the end of World War II in terms of number of casualties, both military and civilian.[9] October 2023 then marked the beginning of one of the deadliest war episodes of the longstanding Israeli–Palestinian conflict, which at the time of writing has not ended and is involving other neighbouring countries, such as Lebanon and Syria.[10]

[5] See Edoardo Celeste and Goran Dominioni, 'Digital and Green: Reconciling the EU Twin Transitions in Times of War and Energy Crisis' in Federico Fabbrini and Christy Anne Petit (eds), *Research Handbook on Post-Pandemic EU Economic Governance & NGEU Law* (Edward Elgar, 2024).

[6] See Maximilian Mayer and Yen-Chi Lu, 'Digital Autonomy? Measuring the Global Digital Dependence Structure' (Center for Advanced Security, Strategic and Integration Studies, 2022), www.kas.de/documents/252038/16166715/Digital+Autonomy+-+Measuring+the+Global+Digital+Dependence+Structure.pdf/fb97d384-53fd-b747-908f-2c86e8d0674b?version=1.2&t=1651491803819.

[7] See Edoardo Celeste, 'Digital Sovereignty in the EU: Challenges and Future Perspectives' in Federico Fabbrini, Edoardo Celeste and John Quinn (eds), *Data Protection Beyond Borders: Transatlantic Perspectives on Extraterritoriality and Sovereignty* (Hart, 2021).

[8] Ka Zeng et al, 'Bilateral Tensions, the Trade War, and US–China Trade Relations' (2022) 24 *Business and politics* 399; Xuan-Thao Nguyen, 'Tech Supremacy: The New Arms Race Between China and the United States' (2023) 49 *Articles* 103; Dennis Broeders, Fabio Cristiano and Monica Kaminska, 'In Search of Digital Sovereignty and Strategic Autonomy: Normative Power Europe to the Test of Its Geopolitical Ambitions' (2023) 61 *Journal of Common Market Studies* 1261.

[9] See Paul D'Anieri, *Ukraine and Russia* (Cambridge University Press, 2023).

[10] See 'Israel-Gaza War' *The Guardian*, www.theguardian.com/world/israel-hamas-war.

The Russo–Ukrainian conflict has triggered a severe energy crisis in Europe.[11] As we will explore in more detail in the next section, the EU was heavily dependent on Russian gas, but the EU Commission decided to impose economic restrictions on trade with Russia, which led to price increases and energy instability in Europe.[12] Ukraine also represents a major provider of wheat, sunflower oil and corn in the EU, and commercialisation of these crops has been proceeding intermittently since the start of the war. The threat of a conflict with Russia in an EU neighbouring country also led to major investments in the defence sector as well as to provide military aids to Ukraine.[13] Moreover, the Russo–Ukrainian conflict has triggered a severe humanitarian crisis, with a substantial proportion of the Ukrainian population fleeing the conflict.[14] Similar issues have arisen following the outbreak of the Israeli war against Hamas. Indeed, this conflict is gradually affecting the whole Middle East, generating a climate of uncertainty that affects economic supply to Europe, mainly in relation to oil.

Last, but certainly not least, former President Donald Trump won the US elections in November 2024. Trump's policy is regarded to be commercially hostile both to China and to the EU.[15] At the time of writing, no specific new US economic foreign policies had been announced, but the lessons learned during the 2017–2021 Trump administration reinforce the urgency of the EU implementing its strategic autonomy policy, particularly in the digital sector.

B. The EU Energy Crisis: From Geopolitics to Climate Change

The energy crisis has highlighted the need to reconsider, from a new perspective, the challenges Europe faces in achieving the twin transition. Not only does the European energy market continue to experience significant fluctuations, but the EU also struggles to harmonise immediate energy security needs with long-term objectives of sustainability and digital innovation. The price spikes and uncertainties driven by the energy crisis have created a volatile environment, disrupting both consumer prices and market stability. For instance, gas prices soared by 180 per cent in the early weeks of the 2022 Russo-Ukrainian conflict, with oil and

[11] See, eg, Simone Emiliozzi, Fabrizio Ferriani and Andrea Gazzani, 'The European Energy Crisis and the Consequences for the Global Natural Gas Market' (2024) *The Energy Journal*.

[12] See EU Council, 'EU Sanctions against Russia Explained', www.consilium.europa.eu/en/policies/sanctions-against-russia-explained.

[13] See Igor Pellicciari, *World War Aid: Interventionist Aid and War in Ukraine* (Routledge, 2023).

[14] See Marta Dzhus and Iryna Golovach, 'Impact of Ukrainian- Russian War on Health Care and Humanitarian Crisis' (2023) 17 *Disaster Medicine and Public Health Preparedness* e340.

[15] See Paul JJ Welfens, 'Trump's Trade Policy, BREXIT, Corona Dynamics, EU Crisis and Declining Multilateralism' (2020) 17 *International Economics and Economic Policy* 563.

coal prices also experiencing sharp increases.[16] Although prices have moderated in some areas, the energy market remains highly volatile, influenced by factors such as sanctions, shifting supply chains, and the evolving global demand for liquified natural gas (LNG). The market's sensitivity to external events – such as potential disruptions in LNG supply or extreme weather conditions linked to the current climate change – continues to make energy markets unpredictable.

In response, the EU has implemented measures to mitigate the impact of rising gas prices on consumers and the economy. For example, Regulation (EU) 2022/2576 introduced a 'market correction mechanism', setting a price ceiling to curb excessive volatility and shield businesses and households from unreasonably high costs.[17] Complementary initiatives include energy-saving campaigns, the promotion of renewable energy and the creation of strategic gas reserves to safeguard supply during peak demand.[18] Additionally, the EU has accelerated its diversification of energy sources by increasing LNG imports through terminals in various Member States and securing agreements with reliable suppliers such as the United States (US) and Qatar. Enhanced cooperation among Member States has further strengthened the internal energy market, promoting solidarity through shared infrastructure and cross-border interconnections.

This instability reflects not only the immediate effects of geopolitical events but also the broader challenges of transitioning toward cleaner energy. Governments face the difficult task of balancing security and affordability with sustainability goals. Investments in the energy transition and digital sovereignty are critical, yet funding remains a significant bottleneck. While the Recovery and Resilience Facility initially provided crucial support for climate and digital projects, these resources are now largely exhausted. Moreover, regional and social disparities within the EU have deepened. Southern and Central Eastern Europe, which are more dependent on fossil fuels, encounter greater obstacles in transitioning to renewable energy. Public resistance, exemplified by movements like France's Yellow Vests, highlights the necessity of equitable and inclusive transition strategies.[19]

Challenges such as grid congestion, financing gaps, supply chain disruptions and dependency on non-EU suppliers for critical raw materials – like rare earth elements – further expose the vulnerabilities of clean energy pathways. These systemic issues demand immediate attention, as they not only complicate the present energy crisis but also shape the trajectory of Europe's energy future.

[16] Jakob Feveile Adolfsen et al, 'The Impact of the War in Ukraine on Euro Area Energy Markets' [2022] ECB Economic Bulletin, www.ecb.europa.eu/press/economic-bulletin/focus/2022/html/ecb.ebbox202204_01~68ef3c3dc6.en.html.

[17] Council Regulation (EU) 2022/2576 of 19 December 2022 enhancing solidarity through better coordination of gas purchases, reliable price benchmarks and exchanges of gas across borders.

[18] See Caroline Kuzemko et al, 'Russia's War on Ukraine, European Energy Policy Responses & Implications for Sustainable Transformations' (2022) 93 *Energy Research & Social Science* 102842.

[19] See Mathilde Martin and Mine Islar, 'The "End of the World" vs. the "End of the Month": Understanding Social Resistance to Sustainability Transition Agendas, a Lesson from the Yellow Vests in France' (2021) 16 *Sustainability Science* 601.

C. Digital Sovereignty, Preservation of Democracy and Strategic Alliances

Interest in sovereignty has re-emerged in recent times as a consequence of the geopolitical crises we are experiencing. These crises have a global and technological component as distinctive features and are becoming evident in war conflicts as well as in new concepts, such as hybrid threats, disinformation or grey zone. Sovereignty, which is again coming to the fore, has, however, been transformed into a multifaceted concept encompassing several interrelated aspects: economics, technology, politics and human rights.[20] In the twenty-first century, globalisation, internationalisation and the influence of private powers show a tension that undermines state effectiveness in this context. As a result, international and supranational communities are more successful, as individual states lack the capacity to address and control the challenges posed by globalisation and digitalisation, opting instead to cede part of their sovereignty to institutions such as the EU.

In this context of international, political and diplomatic crises, technological–digital sovereignty emerges as a vital component of geopolitical competition.[21] The rapid evolution of digital technology has a significant impact on the global economy, society and politics, generating key geopolitical implications. Competition between states for technological leadership emerges as a prominent political consequence, as those with a robust technology sector gain competitive advantages, develop new technologies and attract foreign investment. Moreover, the increasing reliance of states on digital technology, essential to the functioning of the economy, society and government, presents another crucial geopolitical implication. States without a robust digital infrastructure become vulnerable to technological threats and attacks, underlining the strategic importance of digital capability.

Digital sovereignty has become a fundamental pillar in the defence of democracy in an increasingly interconnected world dependent on digital technologies.[22] In this sense, digital sovereignty implies the ability of each state to control its own digital space, protect its data and secure its critical infrastructures against cyber threats that cross borders, and guarantee the fundamental rights and freedoms of its citizens. Moreover, the threats to this sovereignty posed by cyber-attacks, disinformation and vulnerabilities in critical or strategic infrastructures underline the need for common policies, such as those promoted by the EU, which seek to achieve both digital self-sufficiency and strategic alliances to face global threats with democratic states.

[20] See Julia Pohle and Thorsten Thiel, 'Digital Sovereignty' (2020) 9 *Internet Policy Review*, policyreview.info/concepts/digital-sovereignty; Broeders, Cristiano and Kaminska (n 8).

[21] On this point, see Santaniello and Alvarez Robles in this volume.

[22] From an EU perspective, see Celeste (n 7); Edoardo Celeste, 'Digital Constitutionalism, EU Digital Sovereignty Ambitions and the Role of the European Declaration on Digital Rights' in Annegret Engel, Xavier Groussot and Gunnar Thor Petursson (eds), *New Directions in Digitalisation: Perspectives from EU Competition Law and the Charter of Fundamental Rights* (Springer, 2024).

It is clear that, by promoting digital sovereignty, the EU advocates technological humanism and the defence of human rights, establishing a normative framework in response to power confrontations between China and the US.[23] Likewise, Europe seeks an alliance with the US in situations involving the defence of human rights or when it perceives threats to its security. This was evidenced by the US–EU Trade and Technology Council in September 2021 denying access to technologies such as artificial intelligence, 5G, chips and certain software to governments that do not respect human rights or pose risks to national security.[24] From an economic perspective, this approach has led to a push towards self-sufficiency and protectionism as countries such as China and Russia develop their capabilities and seek to influence strategic areas for their technological development. Thus, we are confronted with protectionism and self-reliance, strategic alliances and diversification.

In the face of this technological–digital tension, the EU is acting on multiple fronts: strengthening a European digital power by leading its own projects, such as Gaia-X;[25] further developing its digital regulatory framework, focusing on technological humanism; and creating more strategic alliances with democratic states. The ideal vision for Europe involves having its own technologies and capabilities while maintaining links with like-minded states, following what has been called 'open strategic autonomy'.[26]

A further challenge of digital sovereignty lies in the urgency of establishing clear regulations that delimit responsibilities, rights and protocols for action in cyberspace, as well as a coordinated policy commitment in this area. Meeting this objective also means investing in cyber diplomacy: negotiating international agreements and creating cooperation frameworks that guarantee digital security, while respecting the sovereignty of each nation.[27] Cyber diplomacy should promote global standards of protection and ensure a common response to threats, fostering mutual trust and reducing the risks of cyber conflicts that escalate into geopolitical tensions.

III. The Need for Interdisciplinary Research

This complex reality, evident when the theme of the Summer School that inspired this book was first conceived, holds even greater urgency and relevance today.

[23] *cf* Edoardo Celeste and Giovanni De Gregorio, 'Digital Humanism: The Constitutional Message of the GDPR' (2022) 3 *Global Privacy Law Review* 4.

[24] European Commission, 'EU-US Trade and Technology Council Inaugural Joint Statement', ec.europa.eu/commission/presscorner/detail/pl/statement_21_4951.

[25] See Simona Autolitano and Agnieszka Pawlowska, 'Europe's Quest for Digital Sovereignty: GAIA-X as a Case Study' (Istituto Affari Internazionali (IAI), 2021), www.jstor.org/stable/resrep30940.

[26] See Luuk Schmitz and Timo Seidl, 'As Open as Possible, as Autonomous as Necessary: Understanding the Rise of Open Strategic Autonomy in EU Trade Policy' (2023) 61 *Journal of common market studies* 834.

[27] See Amel Attatfa, Karen Renaud and Stefano De Paoli, 'Cyber Diplomacy: A Systematic Literature Review' (2020) 176 *Procedia Computer Science* 60.

In addressing such a complex and evolving issue, it seemed essential to integrate perspectives from diverse disciplines – law, political science, economics and computing – to provide a comprehensive analysis and deepen our understanding of the challenges and opportunities in this critical field.

The legal framework underpinning the EU's twin agenda is multifaceted, and the pursuit of the environmental and social objectives underlying the twin transition has revealed the inadequacy of the traditional economic regulation approach historically adopted by the EU in the energy market. The energy crisis has further emphasised the need for the EU to move beyond its role as a mere regulator and assume a more proactive, strategic stance, requiring not only regulatory reform but also decisive interventions to ensure energy security, foster technological innovation, and address social and environmental equity. This shift also marks the evolution from the European Regulatory State to a new EU industrial policy. This evolution has likely contributed to the growing emphasis on the concept of sovereignty at the European level. Initially discussed primarily in the context of digital sovereignty, the notion of European sovereignty has increasingly expanded to include a more diffuse concept of energy sovereignty. The connection between these two forms of sovereignty – digital and energy – is one of the key issues to be explored in this volume.

Politically, the energy crisis has exposed the fragility of EU solidarity.[28] While mechanisms like the Energy Union aim to promote cohesion and ensure equitable access to resources, diverging national interests often complicate collective decision-making. For instance, debates around the distribution of resources from the Social Climate Fund have highlighted tensions between wealthier and less affluent Member States. Moreover, the crisis has reignited discussions about the role of nuclear energy within the EU's energy mix, with countries like France advocating for its inclusion as a sustainable option, while others remain sceptical.

Economically, the transition demands unprecedented levels of investment in infrastructure, technology and workforce development. The European Investment Bank has estimated that achieving the Green Deal objectives will require annual investments of €350 billion by 2030, a figure that significantly outpaces current spending levels.[29] This financial gap underscores the importance of mobilising private capital, facilitated by instruments like the InvestEU programme and green bonds. However, market fragmentation and regulatory uncertainty pose barriers to investor confidence, necessitating clearer policy signals and enhanced risk-sharing mechanisms.

[28] See Michael Carnegie LaBelle, 'Breaking the Era of Energy Interdependence in Europe: A Multidimensional Reframing of Energy Security, Sovereignty, and Solidarity' (2024) 52 *Energy Strategy Reviews* 101314; Kaisa Huhta and Leonie Reins, 'Solidarity in European Union Law and Its Application in the Energy Sector' (2023) 72 *International & Comparative Law Quarterly* 771.

[29] 'Keynote Address by EIB President Werner Hoyer at B20 Summit Focusing on Climate Finance, "Delivering Climate Finance: No Time to Waste"' (European Investment Bank), www.eib.org/en/press/speeches/delivering-climate-finance-no-time-to-waste-hoyer.

The digital dimension of the EU's agenda is equally critical, given the synergies between technological innovation and energy efficiency. Initiatives like the Digital Europe Programme and the European Chips Act aim to bolster the EU's digital sovereignty, reducing reliance on external suppliers and fostering homegrown innovation. Smart grids, blockchain-based energy trading platforms, and AI-driven optimisation tools are increasingly seen as enablers of a more resilient and sustainable energy system. However, these technologies are not without drawbacks, as they tend to be energy-intensive themselves. Blockchain, in particular, is known for its high energy consumption, largely driven by the computational demands of consensus mechanisms like proof-of-work used in many applications. These mechanisms require significant processing power, contributing to substantial carbon emissions, especially when powered by non-renewable energy sources. Similarly, the computing power required for AI-driven applications in smart grids and other energy platforms often results in considerable energy use, potentially offsetting the sustainability benefits they aim to deliver.[30]

IV. Structure of the Book

The book is divided into three parts. Part I critically assesses the aims of EU digital sovereignty ambitions, examining the issues that the new regulatory framework proposed to address these objectives may have in reaching their full potential, from both a legal and a technical perspective. This analysis will be complemented by multidisciplinary contributions exploring transnational implications of EU digital sovereignty in light of the current geopolitical context. Part II of the book tackles the core research question of this project by assessing the compatibility of EU digital sovereignty ambitions with the green transition agenda. This part aims to challenge the vision of digitalisation and climate change mitigation, seen as harmonious twin transitions, highlighting both points of convergence and existing tensions. The chapter therein explore the environmental impact of EU digital sovereignty ambitions and dive into case studies that simultaneously show the complementary role of digitalisation in the quest for energy autonomy and in achieving a better data-driven policymaking and management of the public good. Part III contextualises the issues analysed in parts I and II by assessing to what extent the integration of disruptive technologies 'made in the EU', which is supported and encouraged by EU digital sovereignty strategies, can strengthen the EU digital economy while having a sustainable impact. The contributions of this part adopt a special focus on the use of blockchain technologies, questioning the compatibility between their sovereign ambitions and their environmental

[30] See Alba Perez Victorio, Edoardo Celeste and Alberto Quintavalla, 'Greening AI? The New Principle of Sustainable Digital Products and Services in the EU' (2024) 61 *Common Market Law Review*.

sustainability. This part also includes an analysis of the new EU Declaration on Digital Rights and Principles, which enshrines a specific chapter on digital sustainability that might inform future regulation of these disruptive technologies. These considerations are further complemented by an examination of the role of the banking system in promoting and stabilising digital sovereignty and environmental good practices in the use of these technologies.

Part I of the book analyses the EU digital sovereignty strategies, focusing on their ambitions, technical challenges and extraterritorial effects. The framework for discussion it sets is developed in the rest of the book. Chapter two, 'EU Digital Sovereignty: Regulatory and Policy Ambitions', by Brunessen Bertrand, opens Part I. 'European digital sovereignty' refers to sovereignty in reverse, ie to the idea that state sovereignty is challenged in many ways by the digital transition, and that only the European scale can limit, and perhaps correct, these attacks. States are faced with digital platforms or foreign powers that have the means to be not only their equal, but perhaps also their superior and competitor. The conceptualisation of European digital sovereignty does not consist of projecting the theory of the state to the European level, but in thinking about the independence, or even the empowerment, of European public power, in a global situation in which it has not been able to find its place: giving back to European states the capacity to act in a world reconfigured by digital technology.

In Chapter three, 'Technical Challenges for EU Digital Sovereignty: Lessons from the GDPR', Harshvardhan J Pandit focuses on the technical feasibility of the current regulatory strategy of the EU in the digital field, which represents the foundation of the quest for digital sovereignty. Several new regulations have been adopted at EU level to address the use of digital technologies and services. While such advances are a positive development, they also raise the broader question of how such EU acts 'fit' or 'work' together – and whether there is a risk of failure to reach their potential. This chapter provides an investigation on this question by utilising the experience of regulating technologies through the General Data Protection Regulation (GDPR) to identify limitations and challenges that are likely to arise individually and collectively in the application of the Data Governance Act (DGA), Digital Services Act (DSA), Digital Markets (DMA) and AI Act. It concludes with the necessity to develop new modalities and mechanisms that complement the existing legal frameworks to also make these laws 'digitally enforceable' through what the author defines a 'reactive techno-regulation' so as to address the scale and scope of progressive technologies.

Chapter four, 'Digital Sovereignty, Cybersecurity and Geopolitical Implications', by Tamara Álvarez Robles articulates three intertwined logical steps. Firstly, she examines the various conceptions and meanings of digital sovereignty in the EU context. In particular, she highlights a divergence of policy and regulatory strategies depending on the notion of digital sovereignty adopted. Secondly, the chapter contextualises EU digital sovereignty claims in the existing cybersecurity regulatory framework, presenting a comparison of the EU and Spanish systems. The third section of the chapter broadens the horizons of the investigation by projecting cybersecurity implications of EU digital sovereignty claims within the global context. The current geopolitical scenario is examined to highlight emerging dependencies and tensions among blocks of states at international level.

Chapter five, 'Digital Sovereignty in the Euro-Mediterranean Region: Protection and Competition in an Interconnected World', by Mauro Santaniello closes Part I. Santaniello analyses how the European discourse on digital sovereignty is affecting EU relationships with its Southern neighbourhood. Building upon constructivist theories of sovereignty, the chapter advances a conceptualisation of digital sovereignty as an adversarial and multiversal discursive resource, and analyses how this framework has been developed by EU institutions in relation to EU's Southern neighbourhood partner countries. The chapter also analyses how the European discourse on digital sovereignty has been received and reformulated by North African countries and by regional organisations operating in the Mediterranean area. The analysis highlights contradictions and tensions between different understandings of digital sovereignty, and their possible implications for the geopolitical relationships between the EU and its Southern partners.

Part II tackles the volume's core research question by assessing the compatibility between EU digital sovereignty ambitions and its green transition agenda. In chapter six, 'Sustainable Digital Sovereignty? Environmental Impact of EU Tech Strategies', Edoardo Celeste and Alba Perez Victorio identify two types of approaches embraced by EU digital sovereignty strategies. The first is called 'centrifugal' and seeks to extend EU standards beyond its borders; the second one is 'centripetal' as it encourages the reshoring of a digital industry to the EU. While the first solution does not seem to negatively affect the environment, the second one de facto implies the creation almost *ex nihilo* of an EU digital sector, generating a significant ecological footprint. The EU is 'duplicating' global digitalisation efforts, leading to higher energy and water consumption, higher exploitation of raw materials and waste generation, with a significant impact not only in the EU, but also at the global level. This chapter thus aims to examine the environmental impact of EU technological strategies, ultimately challenging the idea that the Union is concretely envisaging a really sustainable form of digital sovereignty, in particular, by neglecting the consequences of digital policies beyond its borders.

Chapter seven, 'Fostering the EU Energy Transition through Participatory Digital Sovereignty', by Tamara Favaro, builds on Celeste's contribution by reflecting on the relation between EU energy autonomy strategies and digital sovereignty in the EU. Sections II and III reconstruct the concept of European energy sovereignty considering the evolution of EU energy law, emphasising its implications in the context of public intervention modes within the economy. In contrast, sections IV and V focus on the contribution of emerging digital technologies, and in particular blockchain, to European energy sovereignty, understood as a participatory process aimed at accomplishing the energy transition. Blockchain's potential lies in its ability to decentralise critical sectors like energy, giving local actors more control and reducing reliance on centralised, often foreign-owned systems. This supports the EU's ambition for digital sovereignty by creating more autonomous, transparent and secure digital ecosystems that are not subject to the control of external powers. By enabling decentralised energy platforms, blockchain promises to play a pivotal role in both the energy transition and the broader digital sovereignty agenda of the EU, empowering citizens and local entities while reducing the influence of foreign tech giants.

In chapter eight, 'Government as an Environmental Platform: Digital Sovereignty and Data-driven Environmental Action', Thibault Carrère analyses the emergence of a new type of public environmental action. The purpose of this study is to show how the French 'Government as a platform' policy, through the intermediary of the agency for ecological transition (ADEME) and the state start-up DATAGIR, by producing and disseminating a large amount of environmental data, is attempting to guide the behaviour of individuals and the creation of new services that are key to the ecological transition. This new organisation would make it possible to emancipate Member States from foreign private players and thus strengthen their digital sovereignty. In this context, digital sovereignty, far from being incompatible with the ecological transition, could well be a driving force behind it.

Chapter nine, 'Digital sovereignty and Green Public Procurement' by Pierre-Henri Morand closes Part II, examining the policies and practices of procurement of digital products or services by public administrations. By virtue of EU law and free-trade agreements, public procurement does not allow the pool of companies eligible to bid to be restricted, or the nationality of companies awarded contracts to be controlled. The issue of sovereignty as perceived by public authorities is essentially a matter of domestic protectionism, and environmental criteria are mobilised as an instrument of sovereignty. The strategies proposed by governments to defend digital sovereignty echo those related to the sustainability of public procurement. Morand analyses Tender Electronic Daily data (award notices published in the Supplement to the EU *Official Journal*) to assess the link between digital sovereignty and environmental criteria, and to understand its limitations. The study examines statistical data pertaining to all European public procurement award notices, with a particular focus on France as a case study. The chapter demonstrates how the pursuit of sovereignty in public procurements often involves environmental considerations, although procedures related to digital products and services do not necessarily rely on sustainability requirements to pursue digital sovereignty objectives, rather using other factors related to national sovereignty.

Part III of the book discusses how the production and use of disruptive technologies made in the EU, which is supported and encouraged by EU digital sovereignty strategies, can strengthen the EU digital economy while having a sustainable impact. In chapter ten, 'Bitcoin: a Subversive Model of Sovereignty Undermined by the Climate Challenge?' Gaël Depoorter analyses the sovereigntist ambitions of Bitcoin and its environmental implications. In 1998, John Perry Barlow published a manifesto in which he declared the independence of cyberspace. Ten years later, Bitcoin, backed by blockchain technology, perpetuated this utopia by proposing to take a decisive step towards it. Bitcoin is seen as a currency that can free itself from the social and political constraints of the 'old world' and is commonly presented by its advocates as a genuine alternative to the monetary and political sovereignty of states. However, this chapter questions to what extent the environmental impact of Bitcoin mining makes it truly feasible to realise these cyber-sovereigntist ambitions. The chapter relies on observations from numerous meetings, gatherings and workshops of activists and entrepreneurs during different editions of Surfin' Bitcoin (the most important European event around Bitcoin), as well as on a virtual ethnography of the 'crypto community' on Twitter and Telegram.

Chapter eleven, 'Blockchain for Sustainability: the Case of Agribusiness', by Cecilia Rasetto builds on Depoorter's contribution and focuses on the positive effects on the implementation of blockchain technology in the agri-food sector. It reflects on how risk within agri-food systems compromises sustainable development, with an inevitable impact on integrity and biodiversity in terms of loss of genes, species, habitats, ecosystems and simplification of the landscape, while trying to meet growing global needs. One strategy deemed suitable to limit this phenomenon is adapting blockchain technology to agri-food. Blockchain is a functional tool for acquiring and storing data which, if applied to the agri-food sector, would be able to record and store the entire food production cycle; concretely, it would enable a positive response to the needs for transparency, traceability and certification. However, at the same time, the chapter explores the negative impact of blockchain use on the environment. Since blockchain is also one of the so-called energy-consuming technologies the chapter attempts to offer concrete answers to both questions while keeping in mind the protection of the environment for present and future generations.

Chapter twelve, 'Eco-Digital Products and Services: Towards New EU Sustainability Rights?', by Alba Perez Victorio and Edoardo Celeste examines the contribution of the new EU Declaration on Digital Rights and Principles to shape and recognise new sustainability rights and principles in the digital environment. Perez and Celeste analyse the chapter of the Declaration on digital sustainability, focusing on its legislative history and subsequent amendments. They argue that this new text does not recognise a new right to a healthy environment in the digital society, but rather enshrines a principle of sustainable digital products and services. The novelty of this principle is then examined, positing that the uniqueness of the Declaration lies in making the principle of sustainable products and services explicit through an operation of normative retrofitting that reconstructs a guiding principle of already existing EU and Member State regulatory and policy strategies. Finally, the chapter contextualises this new principle within the EU digital and environmental policy framework, questioning the feasibility of its ambitions starting from the assumption that even a virtuous digitalisation may negatively affect the environment. The authors refer to theories of digital sobriety and degrowth, ultimately arguing that the reconciliation between the twin transitions in the Declaration is unavoidably only partial.

Chapter thirteen, 'Digital Sovereignty and ESG Policies: The Role of the Banking System', by Francesco Dimichina closes Part III. Firstly, with the Banking Union and, secondly, with NGEU, the EU is strengthening its integration in spite of the phenomenon of 'slowbalisation'. NGEU makes it possible for the EU Commission to raise resources to be invested in transnational political priorities, first of all in the green and digital transition. As regards the digital transition, it is necessary to preserve 'digital sovereignty', especially because European data is mostly processed and stored by foreign companies. As this risk also concerns the banking system, in November 2022 the European Central Bank (ECB) joined the European data and cloud network initiative, Gaia-X. Regarding the green transition, environment, social and governance (ESG) policies have become increasingly relevant in the exercise of banking activity. The chapter examines the European Banking Authority (EBA)'s roadmap on sustainable finance and reflects on how the need to preserve digital sovereignty and the ESG policy related to the banking system may promote the success of European integration, despite the Janus-faced role of digital technologies vis-à-vis the environment.

PART I

EU Digital Sovereignty: Ambitions, Challenges and Transnational Effects

2

EU Digital Sovereignty: Regulatory and Policy Ambitions

BRUNESSEN BERTRAND

I. Introduction

'Our stated ambition is more relevant than ever: to pursue digital policies that empower people and businesses to seize a human centred, sustainable and more prosperous digital future.'[1] This conceptual premise at the outset of the 'Digital Compass' presented by the Commission in March 2021 illustrates the ambiguity – or ambivalence, as the case may be – of European Union (EU) policy, which has never been able to choose, or perhaps assume, a priority between the economic and the political, at the risk, perhaps, of carrying neither properly.

Another disruption can be credited to digital technology: the theme of EU sovereignty is making an unexpected comeback in European political discourse, thanks to a redefinition of EU digital policy. More than digital technology itself, it is the ubiquity of digital technology that is at stake, behind the idea of sovereignty: digital sovereignty concerns defence policy, economic policy, trade policy, the defence of democracy and European values, the regulation of the internal market, and cybersecurity. Taken together, these different areas, which in their own way call into question the integrity of European competences and its autonomy, constitute something fundamental and existential for the EU and its Member States: its independence, its ability to retain control over its most fundamental competences and to apply the values that underpin its raison d'être and identity. In these circumstances, it is easy to understand why we have gone beyond a historically taboo idea to demonstrate the urgency of a situation that could, in the long term, annihilate what is at stake.

Added to this is the brutal realisation, perhaps for the first time, of the limits of each state in the face of these challenges. While the rhetoric about being stronger together has always sought to cement a form of EU solidarity, the real awareness

[1] European Commission, Communication from the Commission to the European Parliament, the Council, the European Economic and Social Committee, and the Committee of the Regions, *2030 Digital Compass: the European way for the Digital Decade*, COM(2021) 118 final, para 1.

of the added value of belonging to the internal market has never seemed an unsurpassable horizon either, as Brexit has once again confirmed. Economic advantages have always been weighed against the political constraints of belonging to the EU, and this equation is by no means self-evident in a context of resurgent populism fuelled by the desire to 'take back control'. As far as defence and security issues are concerned, Member States have never been able to dissociate themselves from transatlantic relations, and so they have never been the subject of a truly autonomous European approach. For the first time, digital technology has created a real rupture, with all Member States becoming aware of their individual inability to exist, to defend their values, their model, their economy and their citizens, alone in cyberspace: the economic domination of American and Chinese platforms, the technological power of the United States (US) and China have revealed, in a rather cruel light, the powerlessness of European soft power to exist and defend its choices, and this observation is even more stinging on a national scale. Faced with campaigns of disinformation and manipulation of opinion to destabilise European democracies, cyber-attacks on essential social infrastructures, the powerlessness of economies to fight against the market power of platforms, the capture of EU citizens' and industries' data and a technological backwardness that has become obvious, the sense of individual powerlessness of Member States seems to have shattered the glass ceiling of qualification of the political stakes that are now being played out at EU level. If Paul-Henri Spaak once said that there were 'only two types of state in Europe: the small ones … and those who don't yet know that they are small',[2] digital technology has raised the awareness of states in the latter category.

On a purely legal level, a few introductory clarifications are in order: we are not talking about sovereignty in the sense in which Jean Bodin defined it, which would lead us to apply the theory of the state to the EU.[3] The term 'digital sovereignty' offends jurists and political scientists, who are legitimately attached to the integrity of the concept; linking a microprocessor or rare metals to the power of the state may seem very risky.[4] Instead, digital sovereignty seems to refer to sovereignty in reverse, ie to the idea that state sovereignty is challenged in many ways by the digital transition, and that only the European scale can limit, and perhaps correct, these infringements. States are faced with digital platforms or foreign powers that have the means to be not only their equal, but perhaps also their superior and competitor.

[2] European Council, '"Strategic Autonomy for EU – the Aim of Our Generation" –Speech by President Charles Michel to the Bruegel Think Tank' (European Council – Council of the European Union, 28 September 2020), www.consilium.europa.eu/en/press/press-releases/2020/09/28/l-autonomie-strategique-EUenne-est-l-objectif-de-notre-generation-discours-du-president-charles-michel-au-groupe-de-reflexion-bruegel.

[3] Jean Bodin and Julian H. Franklin (eds), *On Sovereignty* (Cambridge University Press, 1992).

[4] Yet the President of the European Council has stressed that the supply of critical resources, such as rare metals or microprocessors, are 'essential for our digital sovereignty': 'European strategic autonomy is the goal of our generation' Speech by President Charles Michel to the Bruegel think tank (28 September 2020).

The conceptualisation of EU digital sovereignty does not consist of projecting the theory of the state to the European level, but in thinking about the independence, or even the empowerment, of European public power, in a global situation in which it has been unable to find its place: restoring to European states a capacity to act in a world reconfigured by digital technology. So the issue is not European sovereignty, but rather a reversed form of sovereignty: an EU digital sovereignty that would give states back their ability to act and their independence. The EU would be the key to empowering Member States in cyberspace.

The challenges of the digital age are closely linked to those of the sovereignty of EU Member States. Since Carré de Malberg, we know that sovereignty has several meanings.[5] This politico-legal sovereignty of the state, which gives it jurisdiction over its competences and makes it the supreme power with no superior, equal or competitor, could seem to be called into question in a context marked by the extra-territoriality of foreign legislation and global digital surveillance by foreign powers.

Edward Snowden's revelations on the extent of digital surveillance of all the highest European political authorities by US agencies, and the way in which this information may have served American interests, have undoubtedly created a rupture in the European unconscious, which has always been tied to an unalterable transatlantic alliance.[6] The strategy of global surveillance by the main foreign powers, for the purposes of geostrategic manipulation of Europe, is such that it cannot fail to affect the power of the state and its sovereignty-independence to some extent. Moreover, the strategies of certain foreign powers, more specifically China and Russia, target the democratic processes of states through multiple campaigns of disinformation and manipulation of public opinion. On top of all of this, the economic power of digital giants, whose sales sometimes approach state tax revenues, and their accumulation of large volumes of data, making them new geopolitical players on the international stage.

Sovereignty in the politico-legal sense is not really in question, however, as digital issues essentially concern the ability of EU Member States to act, with the advent of cybercurrencies, the circumvention of tax rules, the creation of private 'supreme courts', or security or identification measures proposed by certain digital platforms. The market power of digital giants, which try to capture all value chains and seek to impose their terms, is sometimes edifying, as the tussle between Facebook and Australia at the start of 2021 demonstrated.[7] Their 'systemic' effects set them up as regulators of freedom of expression in the public spaces they have created, rendering all other structures of public debate almost obsolete.

[5] Raymond Carré de Malberg, *Contribution à la théorie générale de l'État* ([1920],[1922] Dalloz, 2003).

[6] David Smith, 'What's Really Changed 10 Years after the Snowden Revelations?' *The Guardian* (7 June 2023), www.theguardian.com/us-news/2023/jun/07/edward-snowden-10-years-surveillance-revelations.

[7] Kerry Flynn, 'Facebook Bans News in Australia as Fight with Government Escalates' (CNN Business, 19 February 2021), edition.cnn.com/2021/02/17/media/facebook-australia-news-ban/index.html.

The fundamental nature and ubiquity of these upheavals have made Europe realise just how impotent it will be if it limits its actions to thinking solely in terms of its internal market. Even if this internal market remains at the heart of the EU's strategy for digital reconquest, through the creation of a European data space or the conditionality of access to citizens' data to the respect of EU rules, the admission of powerlessness is there, and gives rise to a convergent Europeanisation movement.

On the one hand, the Member States accept the Europeanisation of digital policy, even if this is evolving without any real legal basis of its own. Member States also de facto accept the joint exercise of national competencies, which the Commission coordinates with 'toolkits' (for 5G, e-health, digitisation of justice) or 'frameworks' (for filtering foreign direct investment (FDI)). This spontaneous Europeanisation of issues that fall within national spheres of competence should be seen in the light of the importance of the issues at stake, in particular the protection of the European model of liberal democracy. The EU's room for manoeuvre is therefore narrow: faced with the binary structure of the US and China, the Union is still trying to find its place on the world stage, but it has established itself internally as the only possible level of action.

On the other hand, the EU also assumes the need to assert its identity in this digital transformation. The idea of sovereignty is becoming tangible and acquiring the force of evocation: it is gradually asserting itself in political discourse, particularly in the digital domain[8] and, even if it does not take on the politico-legal significance it implies, its appearance in discourse, without being of the performative order, is not neutral either, especially as it is accompanied by highly strategic measures, from cybersecurity to industrial policy, via cyber-defence, platform regulation or data governance. In a way, existence precedes essence: EU digital policy exists and is beginning to address these fundamental issues, regardless of how it may be understood politically and legally.

While the term 'sovereignty' is used, the even more widely evoked 'strategic autonomy' of the EU reflects the reality of the European way of thinking, which is part of an eternal strategy of depoliticisation and technicalisation of the issues at stake. While the demand for independence is part and parcel of sovereignty issues, the quest for autonomy also seems to be a depoliticised way of talking about sovereignty, rather like the case law of the Court of Justice, which defends the autonomy of the EU in relation to external legal orders. Autonomy is nevertheless intended here to be 'strategic', giving the concept a political and, in this case, even geopolitical dimension.[9] Strategy is just as essential as autonomy, in a context where the EU's traditional *soft power* has shown its limits, sometimes even its irenicism. The

[8] 'Over the next few years, the digital transformation will further accelerate and have far-reaching effects. We need to ensure that Europe is digitally sovereign and obtains its fair share of the benefits of this development.': European Council, 'A new strategic agenda 2019-2024' (20 June 2019), www.consilium.europa.eu/en/press/press-releases/2019/06/20/a-new-strategic-agenda-2019-2024.

[9] See Alvarez Robles in this volume.

quest for independence is not enough; perhaps the time has come to assert genuine European power. In the words of the former Internal Market Commissioner Breton:

> We must now be an autonomous and strategic player. And to achieve this, we need to equip ourselves with an arsenal of 'hard power', so that Europe can use its influence to defend its vision of the world and its own interests … These are no longer just words. Today, Europe is equipping itself with the tools it needs to assert itself in defence of its interests and values. This is true in terms of technological defence capabilities, access to our market, disinformation, cybersecurity, hybrid threats and digital sovereignty.[10]

As always, the EU is built on adversity, through crises that make it aware of its weaknesses and impose necessity; this is how the Union always manages to find the political strength and legal resources to defend its values and identity.[11]

Suppose the notion of sovereignty is accepted, despite all that it might imply. In that case, it is because we are talking about EU sovereignty in reverse, reinforcing and protecting the political sovereignty of states. EU digital sovereignty is the condition for state sovereignty. EU digital sovereignty, understood as the defence of the EU strategic autonomy, is not built to the detriment of national sovereignties: it becomes the condition of their integrity.

In this regard, this chapter analyses the implications of the EU digital sovereignty project and how this concept is shaping not only policy-making but also the EU industrial landscape. Section II examines the European Digital Compass as a reflection of the proliferation of policy instruments in quest for digital sovereignty. Section III unfolds the concept of strategic autonomy and its impact on European industrial policy. Section IV discusses the role of cybersecurity in European digital sovereignty. In section V, some concluding remarks are offered.

II. Political Ambition: The European Digital Compass

This Digital Compass, whose name, however outdated, must undoubtedly have some merits that escape us, so much is it beginning to become overused,[12] takes up the fundamentals of European digital policy, as deployed since 2020.[13] At a more granular level, however, a few nuances can be discerned. In this European 'vision' of the digital age, we classically find a defensive aspect, which assumes the objective of 'digital sovereignty', but we also detect an outline of a perhaps more offensive objective, of the geostrategic order no doubt, with the EU even assuming

[10] Thierry Breton, 'Rethinking our security: towards Europe's strategic autonomy' Speech to the European Parliament's Subcommittee on Security and Defence (25 June 2020).

[11] See Santaniello in this volume.

[12] Council of the European Union, Outcome of Proceedings 'A strategic compass for security and defence – For a European Union that protects its citizens, values and interests, and contributes to international peace and security' 7371/22.

[13] European Commission, *2030 Digital Compass: The European Way for the Digital Decade*, COM/2021/118 Final.

a desire to achieve 'digital *leadership*' in the world.[14] If digital diplomacy is to be found in a number of aspects of EU digital policy, the question of connectivity seems to be at the heart of this challenge.[15]

A. A Modest Political Ambition: The European Digital Society

While the political ambition remains modest – it is essentially a question of catching up Europe by anticipating future developments more strategically – it must also be acknowledged that the 'Shaping Europe's Digital Future' strategy adopted by the EU Commission in 2020 has borne some fruit.[16] The perspective, as we have said, has so far been fairly defensive: it was mainly a matter of defending the EU position by opening up digital ecosystems dominated by major platforms (through the Data Governance Act, Digital Services Act, Digital Markets Act and Cybersecurity Act), giving credibility to European industry through public funding (in particular, the 20 per cent of the Recovery and Resilience Facility dedicated to digital transition).[17]

This defensive EU strategy is maintained, but it is coupled with a more marked internal challenge of convergence between Member States in terms of digital transformation, revealing the heterogeneity of national situations. Above all, it is accompanied by a discourse on EU autonomy that seems to have shifted its centre of gravity: through the idea that Europe will achieve digital sovereignty in an interconnected world,[18] we find a form of political realism that no longer seeks to make the EU a separate player in cyberspace, but rather a player in its own right.

The 'European vision' of digital policy is deployed in two points below, covering the 'digital capabilities' of European society (infrastructure and skills) and the digital culture of European society (increased digitisation of businesses and public services).

i. The 'Digital Capabilities' of European Society

First and foremost, it is a question of society as a whole,[19] as well as the creation of cutting-edge sectors, to achieve a sufficient level of expertise. In themselves, there

[14] *cf* the distinction between protective and competitive digital sovereignty presented by Santaniello in this volume.

[15] In the Council Conclusions of 12 July 2021, 'A globally connected Europe', the Council stressed, for example, that the EU must embed connectivity in a geostrategic and global approach.

[16] Alyssia Petit et al, 'Digital Agenda for Europe' Fact Sheets (European Parliament, 31 March 2024), www.europarl.europa.eu/factsheets/en/sheet/64/digital-agenda-for-europe.

[17] European Commission, 'Recovery and Resilience Scoreboard' (13 August 2024), ec.europa.eu/economy_finance/recovery-and-resilience-scoreboard/digital.html.

[18] See Santaniello in this volume.

[19] European Commission, *Digital Education Action Plan 2021–2027 Resetting education and training for the digital age*, COM/2020/624 final.

is nothing very original here: these issues have been identified for years, but it is easy to agree that they are both necessary and far from being achieved. On the first point, the 'Compass' is in line with the European Pillar of Social Rights,[20] which already provided for a broadening of basic digital skills.

The ambivalence of the EU project, which systematically anchors the economic dimension in values, links the worker and the EU citizen, seeing this as a fundamental challenge for society, that of an 'inclusive digital society', which makes access to education enabling the acquisition of basic digital skills a right for European citizens. This right is, quite appropriately, conducive to the internal market, since the citizen protected in this way is also a consumer who will be able to 'trust digital products and online services, identify disinformation and fraud attempts, protect itself against cyberattacks, scams and fraud online'.[21]

The EU digital society we are being promised also needs 'digital infrastructures' – the inverted commas being in order here, as the Commission merges the different layers of cyberspace, in particular the hardware and software layers, behind the idea of infrastructures.[22] While connectivity remains an unalterable constant, the Commission is now adding microelectronics (high-performance computing, quantum technologies) and data infrastructures, which go beyond the question of the cloud, which has long remained central.[23] While the issue of data infrastructures has been heavily influenced by the question of cloud computing, and this remains at the heart of important questions (freedom of choice, cybersecurity, application of extraterritorial laws, environment), it also seems to be moving quite clearly towards the question of *edge* computing and computing at the edge. As a result, EU industrial objectives are now focusing more on the creation of edge nodes than on the Gaia X project, which for a time was the centre of attention.[24]

ii. The Digital Culture of European Society

Classically, we find objectives such as the digital transformation of businesses and the increased, even complete, digitisation of public services, with formulas such as the 'Platform State' or 'Government as a Platform' that will undoubtedly have to be rethought if they are not to become veritable repellents.[25] In counterpoint, as always, an ethical colouring appears in the background, here taking on democratic dimensions. We learn that secure electronic voting would encourage greater public participation in democratic life, with no other argument than the ease of the process. We may remain sceptical about this rather reductive reasoning, but it

[20] European Commission, 'The European Pillar of Social Rights Action Plan' (Publications Office European Commission, 2021), data.europa.eu/doi/10.2767/111056.

[21] European Commission (n 13).

[22] Decision 2022/2481, 'The Digital Decade Policy Programme 2030' [2022] L323/4, Art 3.

[23] ibid.

[24] European Commission, Declaration of the European Alliance for Industrial Data, Edge and Cloud, 1 ff, digital-strategy.ec.europa.eu/en/policies/cloud-alliance.

[25] See Carrère in this volume.

does have the merit of giving the European political 'vision' an air of democracy. This is far from the heart of the European platform state project, which remains the EU digital identity.

B. From Digital Society to Digital Citizenship

Let us be clear from the outset: the European Commission's vision of 'digital citizenship' is more digital than citizen-centric. Without going so far as to evoke *ethical washing*, the challenge seems to be above all pragmatic: to find an ethical concept to bring coherence to this rather heterogeneous assemblage of digital issues for the European citizen–consumer–customer–entrepreneur.

This 'European approach to the digital society' should thus 'underpin and support open initiatives in favour of democracy, contributing to the development of inclusive policies'.[26] In a nutshell, in the EU the 'digital environment' is 'human-centric', but also 'secure and open', 'law-abiding' and must 'enable individuals to assert their rights, such as the right to privacy and data protection, freedom of expression, children's rights and consumer rights'. European digital policy is thus intended to be political, as it defends a certain vision of the individual: we learn that 'the digital technologies and services used must comply with the applicable legal framework and respect the rights and values inherent in the European way of life'.[27] This could be seen as a contradiction in terms since the prevalence of economic considerations is not always compatible with a voluntary political approach centred on rights and values. This can also be seen as a permanent feature, and perhaps also a strength, of the EU discourse, which never assumes to elevate the economy above the individual and a project for society. This complicated European dialectic between economic and political integration will probably never be resolved. Let us call it ambivalence, then, rather than ambiguity. The fact remains, however, that a reading of the project sheds little light on the political and social integration of the individual in this new society that is being heralded, other than to master the rudiments of the Internet.

But let us get back to our 'digital citizen', who we assume will be endowed above all with digital rights. It should come as no surprise, then, that among the most fundamental rights of the digital citizen is the right to have access to affordable, secure and high-quality connectivity, be able to acquire basic digital skills and be provided with other means to enable them to participate fully in the economic and societal activities of today and tomorrow.[28] In a syncretism that has the merit of not trying too hard to create coherence where there is none, they will be able to easily access digital public services, on the basis of a universal digital identity, as

[26] European Commission (n 13) Ch IV.
[27] ibid.
[28] European Commission, European Declaration on Digital Rights and Principles for the Digital Decade 2023, 2023/C 23/01, Ch II.

well as digital health services, benefit from non-discriminatory access to online services and the application of principles such as those relating to safe and reliable digital spaces, work–life balance in a remote working environment, the protection of minors and ethical algorithmic decision-making.[29]

This diversity is also the consequence, no doubt inevitable, of the variability, and sometimes weakness, of the EU competence. While the Commission is well aware of the central importance of media literacy for citizens, and tries to promote it through legislation, declarations and support programmes,[30] its scope for action remains limited. For example, in the Regulation on combating the dissemination of terrorist content online, which provides, among other things, for an injunction procedure for the removal within one hour of online terrorist content, the legislator takes care to specify that regulatory measures to combat the dissemination of terrorist content online should be complemented by Member States' strategies to combat terrorism, including the enhancement of media literacy and critical thinking, the development of alternative and counter-discourses, and other initiatives to reduce the impact of and vulnerability to terrorist content online, as well as investment in social work, deradicalisation initiatives and dialogue with affected communities, in order to achieve sustainable prevention of radicalisation in society.[31]

This global approach remains complicated to implement in EU law, as it is difficult to reconcile with the theory of competencies and the highly sector-based conception of European policies, which results from the variability of legal bases.

i. The European Approach to the Digital Society

This 'European approach to the digital society' is based on full respect for EU fundamental rights. This European approach is sometimes akin to applying fundamental rights to cyberspace, and sometimes to promoting major European laws as the standard-bearers of digital policy. These include freedom of expression, including access to diverse, reliable and transparent information; freedom to set up and run an online business; protection of privacy and personal data, as well as the right to be forgotten; protection of individuals' intellectual creation in the online space.

Added to this is a 'comprehensive set of digital principles', such as universal access to internet services; a secure and reliable online environment; universal digital education and skills enabling citizens to participate actively in society and democratic processes; access to environmentally friendly digital systems and devices; accessible and human-centred digital public administration and services; ethical principles applicable to human-centred algorithms; protection and empowerment of children in the online space; and access to digital health services.

[29] European Commission (n 13), Ch IV.
[30] European Commission (n 17).
[31] Regulation (EU) 2021/784 of the European Parliament and of the Council of 29 April 2021 on addressing the dissemination of terrorist content online [2021] OJ L172/79, Recital 2.

ii. *Thinking about the Individual in the Digital Society*

Thinking beyond fundamental rights to the place of the citizen in a project of political and social integration would be a real break with the methods and reasoning of EU law. This is one of the perspectives that we would have liked to see more clearly behind the Digital Compass and the project for a 'digital decade for Europe' presented in March 2021. Instead of a political integration project, the Commission is proposing a 'framework' of digital principles that are supposed to define a genuine 'European digital citizenship'. Taking up a distinction made by the EU Charter of Fundamental Rights, this digital citizenship would involve the definition of digital rights and principles for European citizens, following public debate and open reflection in the public arena. This framework of digital principles should help to promote and defend the Union's values in the digital space.

Following on from this outline, in December 2022 the EU Commission, the Parliament and the Council adopted a Declaration on Digital Rights and Principles for the Digital Decade, which 'aims to explain common political intentions'.[32] It recalls the most important rights in the context of digital transformation, but also serves as a reference for businesses and other stakeholders developing and deploying new technologies.[33] According to the Declaration, the European vision of the digital transition is centred on citizens, solidarity and inclusion, and asserts the importance of freedom of choice, participation in the digital public space, safety, security and empowerment, and sustainability. Politically, the Declaration affirms the need to increase democratic control of the digital society and economy. Legally, the Declaration is so modest in scope that it is hard to see it as anything other than a summary of the purpose of the various EU laws, which is not very concise, not really coherent and even rather poorly drafted.

The proliferation of compasses, plans, communications, declarations and other strategies increasingly masks a political vision of European digital policy that is, in fact, rather weak. The paradox is as follows: as European digital policy grows in scope and density, the weakness of the underlying political project becomes increasingly apparent. In other words, it could be said that there is no real love, but on the other hand, there are now plenty of proofs of love. The material importance of this policy turns out to be inversely proportional to the political conception behind it. There is undoubtedly a political will, legislative efficiency, legal density and, as a result, a genuine European digital policy. However, we find it hard to be convinced by the existence of an underlying political project that would seek to consider the place of the individual in this transition, in this change of society so announced.

[32] European Commission (n 28).
[33] ibid.

III. Technological Ambitions: European Strategic Autonomy

The Shaping Digital Europe strategy recalls how the ability to guarantee the integrity and resilience of data infrastructures and networks is a premise of EU technological sovereignty.[34] Digital sovereignty requires the development of EU digital solutions and the interoperability of essential digital infrastructures, such as 5G networks.

A. The Dialectic of Law and Technology

The effectiveness of law and the defence of values have become dependent on technological issues. The EU's 'technological sovereignty'[35] depends fundamentally on its industry. Under these conditions, EU digital policy is based primarily on EU industrial policy, which is a policy unlike any other, due to the limits of EU competence, the symbiosis of public and private issues, and the fact that it is less prescriptive than investment-driven. Political will alone is necessary, but it is far from sufficient in this field, where massive investments are required in new technologies whose short-term necessity is not always apparent – *deep tech* remains fairly opaque to many – and which involve risk-taking, for example, in disruptive technologies, which are not always part of the European DNA. The question of investment is therefore central, but so is the definition of a political strategy: the new approach to EU industrial policy is now part of a drive to restore European sovereignty and strategic autonomy. The legal tools for European technological autonomy are to be found in two policies: industrial policy, and research and development policy, which enable public and private interests to be pooled to develop autonomous European technical solutions.

Industrial policy is a limited competence at the EU level, as it corresponds to a supporting and complementary competence of the Union, within the meaning of Article 6 Treaty on the Functioning of the European Union (TFEU). It is also a hybrid and legally atypical policy, which interweaves public and private interests, drawing on the action of national and European public authorities – and private players. In EU law, the cross-cutting nature of this policy[36] calls for consistency with other European policies.

[34] European Commission, *Shaping Europe's digital future*, COM(2020) 67 final.
[35] European Commission, *A European Data Strategy*, COM(2020) 66 final.
[36] Article 173(3) TFEU organises the transversality of European industrial policy, stipulating that all European policies must contribute to achieving the objectives of this policy.

B. Relaying the EU Industrial Policy

The EU industrial strategy proposed in 2020 starts from the observation that 'Europe's future technological sovereignty' depends on its strategic digital infrastructures: beyond the actions undertaken for the security of 5G networks, the objective of European industrial policy will be to develop an essential quantum communications infrastructure, designed to deploy a secure and certified end-to-end infrastructure, based on quantum key distribution to protect the key digital assets of the EU and its Member States.[37] The EU industrial policy also aims to support the development of key generic technologies of strategic importance: robotics, microelectronics, high-performance computing, cloud data infrastructure, blockchain, quantum technologies, photonics, industrial biotechnology, biomedicine and nanotechnologies. Strengthening strategic autonomy thus requires the Europeanisation of the entire digital value chain: data, cloud, next-generation processor technologies, connectivity and 6G networks.[38]

The Recovery Plan adopted in 2020 pays particular attention to 'deep tech'.[39] These technologies mainly concern cloud computing (data processing), quantum technologies (which enable the creation of practical applications) and high-performance computing (which enables data to be processed and analysed much faster than other computers). Certain instruments of the recovery plan are earmarked to finance the development, at the EU level, of the next generation of digital technologies (supercomputers, quantum computing, blockchain, artificial intelligence), to strengthen European capabilities within strategic digital value chains (notably microprocessors) and the deployment of network infrastructures such as 5G.

The technological dependence of states and the EU on the technological resources of foreign companies, subject to the extraterritoriality of US or Chinese law, obviously raises questions about the EU industrial capabilities, and, by capillarity, questions about the integrity of the personal data of European citizens and the industrial data of EU companies. In these contracts, it is indeed the absence of a European cloud capable of offering sufficiently advanced services that has been deplored. Technological dependence is also reinforced by the network effects thus created and the lack of interoperability between storage infrastructures, which makes it difficult to change cloud service providers. The same question that arises today for the cloud will arise tomorrow for deep tech and AI.

The challenge lies in a European cloud infrastructure for the EU digital sovereignty. The weakness of European cloud services makes states and the Union dependent on foreign technical solutions, which limits the effectiveness of

[37] European Commission, *A new industrial strategy for Europe*, COM(2020) 102 final, 13.

[38] European Council, Special meeting of the European Council 1 and 2 October 2020 – Conclusions, EUCO 13/20.

[39] European Commission, *Europe's moment: Repair and Prepare for the Next Generation*, COM(2020) 456 final, 4.2.

fundamental rights protection: difficulties arise whether these companies store data on EU territory (due to the application of foreign extraterritorial legislation) or transfer data abroad, the *Schrems II* case having shown that the data of EU citizens could be transmitted to foreign authorities whose data protection rules do not comply with European requirements.[40] While the cases mainly involve US law, the question will arise a fortiori for Chinese companies (the so-called BATX: Baidu, Alibaba, Tencent and Xiaomi), due to the laws adopted by China in terms of cybersecurity and intelligence, which oblige Chinese companies to cooperate with public authorities. In the absence of a sufficiently efficient European cloud, it would not seem advisable to legally organise data storage that would guarantee immunity from the application of foreign extraterritorial laws. To be effective, certain technologies need to be available, which raises the question of EU industrial policy.

IV. Geopolitical Ambitions: European Cybersecurity

A. 5G and Cybersecurity Issues

Cybersecurity is essential for EU digital sovereignty. According to the European Cybersecurity Act, cybersecurity refers to the actions needed to protect networks and information systems, the users of these systems and other people exposed to cyber threats.[41] Cyber threats are defined as any potential event or action that could harm or damage networks and information systems, users of such systems and other people, or cause interruptions to such networks and systems. Cyber-attacks are carried out by individuals and entities sometimes closely linked to foreign public authorities, and can seriously destabilise democratic functioning (disruption of electoral processes) or services essential to the life of the nation. It can involve classic forms of cybercrime or, increasingly, sophisticated forms of cyber espionage by foreign powers.

The EU's 'future technological sovereignty' depends on its strategic digital infrastructures.[42] 5G networks constitute a strategic digital infrastructure, as they are at the heart of all economic, democratic and societal issues: the cybersecurity of 5G networks is 'essential not only to protect our economies, societies and democratic processes': the 'dependence of many critical services on 5G networks would make the consequences of systemic and widespread disruptions particularly severe'; and

[40] Case C-311/18 *Data Protection Commissioner v Facebook Ireland Ltd, Maximillian Schrems* [2018].

[41] Regulation (EU) 2019/881 of the European Parliament and of the Council of 17 April 2019 on ENISA (the European Union Agency for Cybersecurity) and on information and communications technology cybersecurity certification and repealing Regulation (EU) No 526/2013 [2019] OJ L151/15, Art 2.

[42] European Commission (n 35) 13.

> ensuring the cybersecurity of 5G networks is therefore of strategic importance for the Union, at a time when the number of cyberattacks continues to grow and when these attacks, more sophisticated than ever, emanate from a wide variety of malicious actors, in particular state or state-sponsored actors from outside the EU.[43]

The challenge is to deploy a highly secure 5G network, while 6G networks are already on the horizon.

The EU has little room for manoeuvre when it comes to 5G network security, since national security issues are the sole responsibility of the Member States under Article 4 TFEU. In response to the European Council's call for a 'concerted approach' to 5G network security,[44] the Commission has called on national risk assessments to coordinate this assessment at European level.[45] The 'common European approach' is based on this coordination within the NIS Cooperation Group (made up of representatives from Member States, the Commission and the European Union Agency for Cybersecurity (ENISA)) to analyse the risks and vulnerabilities of 5G networks, which has resulted in a toolkit for 5G cybersecurity in 2020.[46] The toolkit's conclusions recommend that Member States carefully assess suppliers' risk profiles and apply restrictions to high-risk suppliers. These restrictions can go as far as excluding certain suppliers if necessary. Operators are also encouraged to use several suppliers to avoid over-dependence on a single one.

While the Commission can only accompany the implementation of this EU approach to 5G cybersecurity, it remains in a position to act in other areas that have an impact on the security of the 5G supply chain. The 'strategic measures helping to guarantee the EU's sovereignty and technological lead in the future development of network technologies'[47] must maintain a 5G supply and value chain to avoid any form of long-term dependency. To this end, the EU institutions can act by strengthening technical and organisational rules on electronic communications security, or encourage standardisation, and thus promote technical specifications that enable security and interoperability objectives to be met. 5G certification mechanisms can also be envisaged within the European cybersecurity certification framework.

Other tools can complement this strategy of EU autonomy for 5G networks (and encourage the diversification of 5G equipment suppliers), such as the mobilisation of trade defence instruments to combat distortions of the 5G supply market resulting from dumping or subsidies, and the application of competition rules to keep 5G hardware and software supply markets open. Public procurement rules in the field of 5G networks can also contribute to these objectives, by integrating these security requirements when awarding public contracts related to 5G

[43] European Commission, *Security of 5G deployment in the EU – Implementation of the EU toolkit*, (2020) 50 final, 1.

[44] European Council, European Council meeting 21 and 22 March 2019 – Conclusions, EUCO 1/19.

[45] European Commission, Recommendation 2019/534 on cybersecurity of 5G networks [2019] OJ L88/42.

[46] European Commission (n 43).

[47] ibid, 10.

networks. The Commission is also considering applying the EU framework for screening FDI for key 5G assets, controlling it not only on sensitive network assets but, more broadly, across the entire 5G value chain. The other instruments of EU cybersecurity policy, as well as those being put in place in cyber defence policy, can also contribute to the security of 5G networks.

B. The Emergence of a European Cyber Defence Policy

In his 2017 State of the Union address, the President of the EU Commission, Jean-Claude Juncker, asserted that 'cyberattacks are sometimes more dangerous to the stability of democracies and economies than guns and tanks'.[48] Indeed, cyber defence has gradually become the fifth operational field of intervention for European defence.

The EU awareness of cyber defence was somewhat late in coming: it was only in 2007, with the cyber-attack on Estonia, and in 2008, with the conflict between Russia and Georgia, that the magnitude of the challenges posed by cyber-attacks on collective defence issues was revealed, regularly confirmed by attacks on infrastructure in Ukraine. The result of this awareness is an EU cybersecurity strategy proposed in 2013,[49] which established cyberspace as the fifth operational area of defence policy and paved the way for the development of cyber defence capabilities.

Cyber defence has its specific characteristics, in particular the fact that the boundaries between the civilian and military domains become blurred in cyberspace. But the EU's action in the field of cyber defence also comes up against the general difficulties of European defence policy, which remains dependent on national sovereignties and different conceptions of these issues,[50] which make it difficult for a 'European cyber-power' to emerge.[51] The EU is finding it hard to think independently, given that links with the Atlantic alliance remain a strong feature of EU defence.

The stakes for the EU sovereignty are high. The observation is unanimous today:

> [D]ifferent state actors – Russia, China and North Korea among others, but also non-state actors (including organised crime groups) inspired, hired or sponsored by

[48] European Commission, 'State of the Union Address 2017*' (13 September 2017), ec.europa.eu/commission/presscorner/detail/en/SPEECH_17_3165.

[49] European Parliament, European Council, European Economic and Social Committee and Committee of the Regions, 'European Union cybersecurity strategy: an open, safe and secure cyberspace' JOIN(2013) 01 final; see also Council of the European Union, Cyber Defence Policy Framework, 15585/14; see also, European Council, Council Conclusions on Cyber Diplomacy, 6122/15; see also European Commission, *Assessment of the European Union's 2013 Cybersecurity Strategy*, SWD(2017) 0295.

[50] George Christou, *Cybersecurity in the European Union. Resilience and Adaptability in Governance Policy* (Palgrave Macmillan, 2016).

[51] Delphine Deschaux-Dutard, 'L'Union européenne, une cyberpuissance en devenir? Réflexion sur la cyberdéfense européenne' (2020) 117 *La Revue internationale et stratégique* 19.

> states, security agencies or private companies – have been involved in malicious cyber activities in pursuit of political, economic or security objectives that include attacks on critical infrastructure, cyberespionage and mass surveillance of EU citizens, aiding disinformation campaigns and distributing malware (Wannacry and NotPetya, etc.) limiting access to the internet and the functioning of IT systems; whereas such activities disregard and violate international law, human rights and EU fundamental rights while jeopardising democracy, security, public order and the strategic autonomy of the EU.[52]

The Union and its Member States are thus faced with large-scale state threats[53] 'taking the form of state-political cyberattacks': 'offensive cyber-defence capabilities are being used against EU Member States on an unprecedented scale',[54] leading to a situation sometimes described as a 'cold cyberwar'.[55] Alongside more 'ordinary' forms of cybercrime, the challenge to state sovereignty comes from the fact that a large number of cyber-attacks are directed, in violation of international law, by foreign powers or with their support.

The European Commission, which claims to be 'geopolitically minded', is today asserting its desire for a 'paradigm shift' in the EU's strategic autonomy, and for a rethink of Europe's place in the world. Beyond the *soft power* characteristic of a 'naïve' Europe, the Union must become 'an autonomous and strategic player' by adopting a 'hard power arsenal' capable of enabling it to defend its vision of the world and its own interests: technological defence capabilities; the fight against disinformation and hybrid threats; cybersecurity; and digital sovereignty.[56]

Numerous permanent structured cooperation projects deal with cyber defence issues. In December 2020, a political agreement confirmed the creation of a European Defence Fund to finance disruptive military technologies[57] and contribute to the EU's strategic autonomy (although third-party participation in the Fund is possible). The 'cyber-diplomatic toolbox' is designed to define a common EU diplomatic response to cyber-attacks.[58] This response is based on a gradation of

[52] European Parliament, Resolution of 13 June 2018 on cyber defence, 2018/2004(INI) para AE.

[53] 'The number of cyber attacks continues to rise. These attacks are more sophisticated than ever, coming from a wide variety of sources inside and outside the EU, and targeting areas of maximum vulnerability. State-owned or state-backed actors are often involved, targeting critical digital infrastructures, such as major cloud service providers': European Commission, *Communication EU Security Union Strategy*, COM/2020/605 final.

[54] European Parliament (n 52).

[55] This notion of 'cold cyberwar' refers to 'a state of cyberspace in which states equip themselves with a cyber arsenal – both defensive and offensive – and resort – often indirectly, via non-state actors – to cyberattacks as part of destabilization manoeuvres, without crossing the threshold that would characterize an open cyberwar': Deschaux-Dutard (n 51) 18.

[56] Breton (n 10).

[57] Breton (ibid) mentions *edge computing* solutions for aggregating data from military drones, space technologies (military *encryption* satellite positioning receivers using Galileo PRS, military optical sensors for small satellites, Big Data solutions for satellite surveillance), technologies for monitoring and detecting cyber threats, a tactical and military encrypted network.

[58] Council of the European Union, Council Conclusions on a Framework for a Joint EU Diplomatic Response to Malicious Cyber Activities ('Cyber-diplomatic toolbox') 10474/17; see also European Parliament and European Council, 'Resilience, deterrence and defense: equipping the European Union with robust cybersecurity', JOIN(2017) 450 final.

measures ranging from simple diplomatic cooperation and dialogue to preventive measures against cyber-attacks and sanctions. The cybersecurity strategy adopted in December 2020 confirms this diplomatic response to cyber-attacks. It seeks to strengthen cyber defence coordination and cooperation and to build up cyber defence capabilities. European cyber diplomacy also enables the adoption of restrictive measures within the framework of the EU Common Foreign and Security Policy (CFSP), on the basis of a regulation and a Council decision of 17 May 2019,[59] which establish a framework for targeted restrictive measures aimed at deterring and countering high-impact cyber-attacks that pose an external threat to the Union or its Member States. Cyber-attacks are unauthorised actions involving access to information systems, attacks on the integrity of an information system or data, or the interception of data. Such cyber-attacks constitute a threat to Member States if they affect information systems relating to critical infrastructures, services needed to maintain critical social and/or economic activities, critical government functions, the storage or processing of classified information, or emergency response teams set up by public authorities.

The Council took restrictive measures in July 2020 concerning cyber-attacks: the eight individuals and four entities and bodies (Chinese, North Korean and Russian) responsible for cyber-attacks which were included on the list of sanctioned individuals, entities and bodies were subject to a travel ban to the EU and an asset freeze.[60] The EU has thus identified six individuals and three entities or bodies as responsible for cyber-attacks, such as the attempted cyber-attack against the Organisation for the Prohibition of Chemical Weapons (OPCW) and the cyber-attacks known as WannaCry, NotPetya and Operation Cloud Hopper.

Among the individuals sanctioned, it is quite notable, from a sovereignty point of view, that they include members of the Russian intelligence services, identified as human intelligence support officers within the General Intelligence Directorate of the General Staff of the Armed Forces of the Russian Federation.[61] Four Russian agents were thus involved in the cyber-attack against the OPCW in the Netherlands in April 2018.[62] If successful, this cyber-attack would have compromised network security and ongoing chemical weapons investigation work. Sanctioned entities also include the Main Centre for Special Technologies of the Main Directorate of the General Staff of the Armed Forces of the Russian Federation, found responsible

[59] Council Regulation (EU) 2019/796 of May 17, 2019 on restrictive measures against cyber attacks that threaten the Union or its Member States, [2019] OJ L129/1, 1; Council Decision (CFSP) 2019/797 of May 17, 2019 on restrictive measures against cyber attacks that threaten the Union or its Member States, OJ L 129/I, 13.

[60] Council CFSP Decision 2020/1127 of 30 July 2020 amending Decision (CFSP) 2019/797 on restrictive measures against cyber-attacks threatening the Union or its Member States, OJ L 246/12; and Council Implementing Regulation 2020/1125 of 30 July 2020 implementing Regulation 2019/796 on restrictive measures against cyber-attacks threatening the Union or its Member States [2020] OJ L 246/4.

[61] Council CFSP Decision 2020/1127, 2 ff.

[62] Katie Polglase and Laura Smith-Spark, 'Netherlands Officials Say They Caught Russian Spies' (CNN, 4 October 2018), cnn.com/2018/10/04/europe/netherlands-russia-gru-intl/index.html.

for the NotPetya cyber-attacks in 2017 against a Ukrainian power grid,[63] constituting an external threat to the Union or its Member States in that they rendered data inaccessible in a number of Union companies by targeting computers with ransomware and blocking access to data, causing, among other things, significant economic losses. Confirmation of the involvement of Russian entities and agents in these cyber-attacks reinforces the EU digital sovereignty stakes of cyber diplomacy. Digital sovereignty must strengthen 'European resilience', ie the ability to withstand shocks.

V. Conclusion

Digital sovereignty is a complex concept, far more intricate than a political slogan. It touches upon defence, the economy, trade, the protection of European values, the regulation of the internal market, and much more. Rather than simply transferring the theory of state sovereignty to the European level, digital sovereignty is about independence and empowerment. This chapter argues that digital sovereignty works in reverse: by advancing it at Union level, Member States will regain their ability to act independently, with the EU serving as a means to this end.

This ambitious project is reflected in several EU policy initiatives, such as the European Digital Compass, which aims to create an inclusive society where digital skills are considered a right, thus empowering EU citizens. These aspirations place citizens at the heart of the project, granting them digital rights such as access to safe, affordable and high-quality connectivity.

However, a paradox emerges: while policy proliferation is accelerating, the strength of EU digital sovereignty remains limited. Alongside digital sovereignty, the concept of strategic autonomy has gained prominence in the EU discourse. Focus is increasingly placed on the vital role of European industry and the need for investment to compete more effectively in the deep-tech landscape. Current industrial policy highlights the urgent need to redesign strategies and bolster capabilities to secure a stronger position in the global digital supply chain.

Beyond political rhetoric, cybersecurity has been identified as a critical element in achieving European digital sovereignty. It seems logical that in order to regain its independence the EU must secure its strategic digital infrastructure. This has led to the development of EU cybersecurity policies, though they face inherent challenges given that national security traditionally falls under the purview of Member States.

[63] ibid 6.

3

Technical Challenges for EU Digital Sovereignty: Lessons from the GDPR

HARSHVARDHAN J PANDIT

I. Introduction

The European Union (EU) is a *sui generis* supranational entity that has asserted its influence on the globe by virtue of its political and financial prowess.[1] Rather than merely being a political or economic federation, the Union also refers to the establishment of shared rights and freedoms, most prominently described through the Charter of Fundamental Rights.[2] This fact is noteworthy and key to understanding the regulatory regime of the Union, and the enforcement policies prescribed by its executive branch – the European Commission, considering recent rapid technological progress and a new collection of regulations being drafted to shepherd the permeance of digital information and technologies. One of the goals of these new regulations is the strengthening of Europe's digital sovereignty through technological self-sufficiency that promotes 'Europe's ability to define its own rules and values in the digital age' and 'respects our fundamental rights'.[3]

The notion of digital sovereignty has undergone several changes generated by the emergence of new technologies, as have the same meanings of the concept of 'sovereignty' changed when understood through the lens of what is possible in the 'digital' sphere and what can be qualified as non-EU actors.[4] As the EU grapples with the changing meaning of 'sovereignty', it also seeks to understand the emerging nature of 'digital' tools and services which force a reinterpretation of EU values, rights and freedoms in hitherto uncharted avenues.[5]

[1] Cornellia Woll, 'Lobbying in the European Union: From Sui Generis to a Comparative Perspective' (2006) 13 *Journal of European Public Policy* 456.

[2] Charter of Fundamental Rights of the European Union [2012] OJ C 326/02.

[3] European Commission, *Shaping Europe's digital future*, COM(2020) 67 final.

[4] Edoardo Celeste, 'Digital Sovereignty in the EU: Challenges and Future Perspectives' in Federico Fabbrini, Edoardo Celeste and John Quinn (eds), *Data Protection beyond Borders: Transatlantic Perspectives on Extraterritoriality and Sovereignty* (Hart, 2021).

[5] European Commission, 'Operational guidance on taking account of fundamental rights in European Commission impact assessments', SEC(2011) 567 final.

As a broad concept, digital sovereignty explores the extent of control over digital infrastructures and resources. The General Data Protection Regulation (GDPR), as a pan-European binding legal instrument, has an important role in realising digital sovereignty as it regulates personal data, which is a digital resource of increasing value to companies. The GDPR requires data be either stored and processed in EU, or that the EU's rules and regulations regarding data access, security and privacy be applied in other jurisdictions where it is stored. As a consequence of this, several multinational organisations that provide 'cloud technologies and services' have developed technological installations physically located and operated within the EU.[6]

However, having physical storage of data within the EU does not necessarily lead to an expression of EU digital sovereignty, as there is no real technological independence when developing, and maintaining the capability to create, deploy and manage critical technologies still relies on organisations based in foreign nations. Further, the increased presence of non-EU tech multinationals in the EU market threatens the economic competitiveness of native EU entities. To further complicate matters, sovereignty requires the necessity to 'trust' technologies not only when they are being used, but also when assessing how they are being developed and launched on the market; in particular, to ensure that they incorporate the necessary European values and norms as part of their design and operation, and that their use will not negatively affect the society. The recently approved Artificial Intelligence (AI) Act[7] and its enforcement framework utilises a similar argument to regulate the growing concerns of AI technologies being developed and utilised in the EU.

The EU Commission thus has the difficult task of fostering a digital economy through its technological regulations in a way which supports local companies, promotes innovation, ensures fair competition, reduces dependence on foreign tech giants, and boosts national economic growth. To succeed in its vision, the Commission requires robust and comprehensive laws that can effectively regulate technologies, and also ensure their enforcement to drive the technological ecosystem towards its envisioned level sovereign independence.

This chapter explores the effect of the GDPR as the chronologically first – and still one of the most important – in multiple regulations that drive technological sovereignty in the EU Commission's vision. This work is written by a computer scientist from a multidisciplinary perspective, contextualizing EU law within current technological affordances. In particular, the chapter outlines the necessity for closer introspection of the GDPR's enforcement level to understand the key

[6] Brad Smith, 'Answering Europe's Call: Storing and Processing EU Data in the EU' (Microsoft, 2021), blogs.microsoft.com/eupolicy/2021/05/06/eu-data-boundary.

[7] Regulation (EU) 2024/1689 of the European Parliament and of the Council of 13 June 2024 laying down harmonised rules on artificial intelligence and amending Regulations (EC) No 300/2008, (EU) No 167/2013, (EU) No 168/2013, (EU) 2018/858, (EU) 2018/1139 and (EU) 2019/2144 and Directives 2014/90/EU, (EU) 2016/797 and (EU) 2020/1828 (AI Act).

challenges of EU digital sovereignty ambitions that arise due to the nature of digital technologies and their causal origin both within and external to the EU's regulatory enforcement methodologies. Section II explores the current EU regulatory framework in the digital field and argues that there is an urgent need for assessing the closer cooperation of these pieces of legislation and combined enforcement. Section III looks at the current experience of GDPR enforcement and explores key lessons that can inform future policymaking. Section IV compares 'proactive' and 'reactive' enforcement strategies and the effect this has on technological development and application. Section V concludes by discussing the challenges associated with technological progress that outpace existing regulatory processes, and recommending the adoption of a series of anticipatory measures that would enhance their level of synchrony.

II. The EU Digital Regulatory Regime: A Jigsaw Puzzle or a Lego Set?

Consider the current set of regulations governing the development and use of a typical digital service that involves personal data of its users. Any or all of the GDPR,[8] Data Governance Act[9] (DGA), Digital Services Act[10] (DSA) and Data Markets Act[11] (DMA) could be applicable. Further, if AI technologies are involved, then the recently approved AI Act may also apply. Each of these acts defines a set of roles; for example, the role of data controller in the context of the GDPR, the criteria for determining the applicability of that role to an actor involved in the use-case, a series of obligations that result from assuming that role, and a series of corresponding rights and enforcement procedures which are handled by the respective competent bodies. Further, the scope of each regulation also permits it to define specific terms through which digital technologies can be interpreted in the context of these roles and obligations.

Through distinct concepts defined across regulations, the application and utilisation of digital technologies is subject to multiple requirements, which introduce

[8] Regulation (EU) 2016/679 of the European Parliament and of the Council of 27 April 2016 on the protection of natural persons with regard to the processing of personal data and on the free movement of such data, and repealing Directive 95/46/EC (General Data Protection Regulation; GDPA) [2016] OJ L 119.

[9] Regulation (EU) 2022/868 of the European Parliament and of the Council of 30 May 2022 on European data governance and amending Regulation (EU) 2018/1724 (Data Governance Act); GDA [2022] OJ L 152.

[10] Regulation (EU) 2022/2065 of the European Parliament and of the Council of 19 October 2022 on a Single Market For Digital Services and amending Directive 2000/31/EC (Digital Services Act; DSA) [2022] OJ L 277.

[11] Regulation (EU) 2022/1925 of the European Parliament and of the Council of 14 September 2022 on contestable and fair markets in the digital sector and amending Directives (EU) 2019/1937 and (EU) 2020/1828 (Digital Markets Act; DMA) [2022] OJ L 265.

a challenge in their individual as well as combined interpretations and affect how to enforce them effectively across sectors and domains. Thus, a broader question emerges regarding EU's digital strategies: whether these regulations are pieces of a jigsaw puzzle that must fit precisely to create a final picture or a series of building blocks that can be combined to realise multiple structures, but which are prone to mistakes in planning and building. If multiple laws work together in cohesion and harmony, we are more likely to have a clear vision of how to regulate technologies towards achieving digital sovereignty. If, instead, these multiple overlapping laws are not aligned, and each defines a different vision that is not considerate of other legal requirements, then there is a risk of tension and friction in achieving digital sovereignty as each law pulls the ecosystem in a different direction.

For example, the GDPR defines 'processing'[12] as any operation on personal data, and bases its definition of 'controller' based on who determines the 'means' and 'purposes' of the processing.[13] Seen through this lens, a digital technology involving personal data has some processing operations that are conducted under the responsibility of an associated 'controller' who must fulfil appropriate obligations and rights as per the GDPR. Similar definitions for processes involving 'personal data' are also present within the DGA, DSA and DMA along with corresponding roles, legal basis and obligations.[14] Further, the AI Act[15] and the Data Act[16] also contain further criteria that could in the future trigger the application of these regulations in several different ways based on the progress of technologies. For example, the AI Act's definition of how 'artificial intelligence' is developed, deployed and used can include the use of personal data – which would not only bring it within the scope of the GDPR, but also make the use of AI subject to enforcement actions by GDPR's competent authorities.

Thus, we see an emerging pattern where, although the regulations acknowledge and defer to concepts defined in earlier regulations, there is a lack of explicit alignment between these texts in terms of how the roles and obligations arising from the use of shared concepts relate, and how their enforcement is expected to work in practice given the diverse set of competent bodies involved – which each have their own competence, jurisdiction and mandates.

[12] Article 4(2) GDPR states 'processing' means 'any operation or set of operations which is performed on personal data or on sets of personal data, whether or not by automated means, such as collection, recording, organisation, structuring, storage, adaptation or alteration, retrieval, consultation, use, disclosure by transmission, dissemination or otherwise making available, alignment or combination, restriction, erasure or destruction'.

[13] European Data Protection Board, 'Guidelines 07/2020 on the concepts of controller and processor in the GDPR' (2021), www.edpb.europa.eu/system/files/2023-10/EDPB_guidelines_202007_controllerprocessor_final_en.pdf.

[14] For example, the DGA, DMA and DSA identify the use of consent as defined by GDPR as a legal basis for distinct processing operations by entities assuming roles defined in each of the respective regulations.

[15] AI Act (n 7).

[16] Regulation (EU) 2023/2854 of the European Parliament and of the Council of 13 December 2023 on harmonised rules on fair access to and use of data and amending Regulation (EU) 2017/2394 and Directive (EU) 2020/1828 (Data Act) [2023] OJ L 2023/2854.

With each regulation establishing a competent authority, the number of authorities in the EU is likely to increase significantly.[17] The GDPR established the European Data Protection Board (EDPB) for providing consistency and harmonisation in the interpretation of the GDPR as well as resolving disputes arising from disagreements in enforcement among national data protection authorities. However, the recent CJEU ruling in *Meta*[18] raises the question of whether other authorities who wish to interpret and apply the GDPR should also be provided with 'a seat at the table' – and if so then in what roles and which capacities. Such questions have also been raised regarding the inclusion of 'privacy' and 'data protection' authorities within other regulatory areas such as market and competition.[19] These discussions highlight that as technology progresses and permeates more areas of our society, its influence also expands into domains which have conventionally been distinctly regulated, and forces intra-regulatory cooperation.

While it makes for interesting research questions to delve into the overlaps of regulations, such as what determines who is a controller (GDPR) in the development and use of AI technologies (AI Act),[20] it also exposes the uncertainties in how the law applies and should be enforced. Thus we see that the 'fast' technological development is increasingly at odds with a 'slow' enforcement, especially when the model for proliferation of technology is 'move fast and break things'.[21] From this, an important question that must be raised regarding the 'technical enforcement' of a regulation relates to the effectiveness of a legal obligation in regulating technological progress and guiding it towards the intended direction of balancing the economic benefits while upholding rights and freedoms. Measures such as the GDPR's obligation of conducting data protection impact assessments[22] (DPIAs), which require technology developers and operators to ask these questions, are a step in the right direction, but without sufficient guidance and regulatory oversight risk being an empty gesture that does not introduce the necessary changes required for practically implementing EU digital sovereignty. The current state of EU digital regulation is akin to each law in effect creating a 'regulatory silo' where only its norms are defined and where only a particular authority can investigate and enforce its subject matter.

[17] For the GDPR, each Member State has its own national competent authority. For DSA and DMA, the Commission has appointed a competent authority. For DGA, there are competent authorities operating at national as well as EU levels. For the AI Act, each Member State is expected to have its national competent authority, with some Member States likely to utilise their existing GDPR authorities as the AI Act authority, and others, such as Spain, creating a new body to undertake the role of AI authority.

[18] Case C-252/21 *Meta Platforms and Others v German Federal Cartel Office* [2023].

[19] John Ryan and Cristina Cafarra, 'Why Privacy Experts Need a Place at the Antitrust Table' (ProMarket, 28 July 2021), www.promarket.org/2021/07/28/privacy-experts-antitrust-data-harms-digital-platforms.

[20] Jennifer Cobbe and Jatinder Singh, 'Artificial Intelligence as a Service: Legal Responsibilities, Liabilities, and Policy Challenges' (2021) 42 *Computer Law & Security Review*.

[21] Simon Chesterman, 'Move fast and break things: Law, technology, and the problem of speed' (2021) 33 *Singapore Academy of Law Journal*.

[22] GDPR, Art 35.

The previously mentioned landmark judgment in *Meta*, decided by the CJEU in 2023, affirmed that national competition authorities have the power to impose fines for violations of the GDPR.[23] This ruling concerned a case involving the German competition authority, which fined Facebook for abusing its dominant position by collecting and using user data without proper consent. The CJEU clarified that while the GDPR enforcement is a responsibility of the supervisor authorities defined within that law, other authorities such as a competition authority can also address violations that would fall under the GDPR when they also concern competition law violations. This decision highlights the interplay between data protection and competition law, and emphasises how GDPR compliance has a significant implication on market competition (and other laws), thereby expanding enforcement of a 'technical regulation' much beyond its intended scope.

This CJEU judgment, which allows national competition authorities to fine for GDPR violations, significantly impacts digital sovereignty as it provides multiple means for a country to enforce EU regulations in a new way even when such laws were not envisioned to be aligned. This multi-enforcement mechanism enhances national control over digital practices within their borders, ensuring aspects of a nation's sovereignty such as rights (in this case, privacy and data protection) and market regulation (in this case, competition) are upheld without reliance on external entities. By enabling competition authorities to address data privacy issues, the ruling requires companies operating within a country to not only comply with the GDPR, but to also consider the local regulations, thus leading to a potential internal fragmentation of EU digital sovereignty into more sovereign spaces with different levels of enforcement.

By systemising this 'new' regulatory approach through an intended and explicit cooperation between laws and their enforcement authorities, we can safeguard Member States' digital infrastructures, protect citizens' data, and foster a competitive digital economy, all of which are crucial elements of EU digital sovereignty as the pace of technology advances far too rapidly to be regulated by a single law such as the GDPR. Instead, by planning and fostering cooperation across EU digital regulations, each law could build further upon its predecessor and create a multi-pronged approach for governing technologies and digital services. This would allow for an effective strategy to assert digital sovereignty in a methodological manner that is aligned with technological progress. Otherwise, challenges will emerge based on sudden progress in technologies that disrupt the regulatory plan, such as the current situation with 'generative AI' technologies, such as ChatGPT and the need to quickly define and regulate a 'trustworthy AI'.[24]

[23] Case C-252/21 (n 18).

[24] J. Soler Garrido et al, 'AI Watch: Artificial Intelligence Standardisation Landscape Update' (2023) JRC Publications Repository EUR 31343 EN, publications.jrc.ec.europa.eu/repository/handle/JRC131155.

III. Towards a Functional Digital Sovereignty: Brussels Effect and EU Enforcement

To broadly interpret the EU's plan regarding its digital future,[25] its ambition is to apply its values and rights to the ever-growing phenomenon of digital-only environments and services, including technologies such as 'artificial intelligence'[26] and 'virtual worlds'[27] that lack a physical manifestation and rapidly push the boundaries of what is technically feasible. To enforce this vision, the Commission has an arsenal of regulatory mechanisms which range from binding regulations to harmonisation of standards with legal effects to non-binding guidance and recommendations, and for which the Commission relies on a principles-based 'Better regulation toolbox'.[28] Based on these, laws such as the GDPR and the AI Act are drafted following an initial assessment regarding the requirements for aspects to be regulated and their impact on the society and economy.[29]

As a consequence of this desire to reshape and mould the development and use of digital technologies to 'EU' values also at an international level, the so-called 'Brussels Effect'[30] has resulted in a global change both in the way technology companies consider and implement EU digital regulations as well as in how third countries design their laws to mirror or match EU regulatory advancements. Such has been the significance of this effect that not only are the EU's future regulations being analysed through the lens of their extra-territorial effects but the EU digital regulatory regime is being seen as a torchbearer for other similar regulations arising across the globe in response to technological advances such as those for AI.[31]

At the same time, based on a significant political and financial influence, the requirements and obligations for technologies and technology providers have grown increasingly complex and have targeted large market players, most of which are established in non-EU countries.[32] Situated amongst an increasingly globalising 'open market' where the free flow of goods is now being accompanied by calls to free the flow of data,[33] the reach of impacts arising from EU's digital strategy is

[25] European Commission (n 3).

[26] European Commission, *A European approach to artificial intelligence*, COM/2021/205 final.

[27] European Commission, 'Virtual Worlds and Web 4.0 – Factsheet' (2023), digital-strategy.ec.europa.eu/en/library/virtual-worlds-and-web-40-factsheet.

[28] European Commission, *Better Regulation Guidelines*, SWD(2021) 305 final and 'Better Regulation Toolbox' (2023).

[29] European Commission, *Impact Assessment of the Regulation on Artificial intelligence*, SWD(2021) 84 final.

[30] Anu Bradford, 'The Brussels Effect' (2012) 107 *Northwestern University Law Review* 1.

[31] Charlotte Siegmann and Markus Anderljung, 'The Brussels Effect and Artificial Intelligence: How EU regulation will impact the global AI market' (2022) Centre for Governance of AI, doi.org/10.48550/arXiv.2208.12645.

[32] Meredith Broadbent, 'The digital services act, the digital markets act, and the new competition tool' (Centre for Strategic and International Studies, 2020).

[33] United Nations, 'Digital Economy Report 2021' (United Nations Conference on Trade and Development, 2021), unctad.org/publication/digital-economy-report-2021.

only expanding. Thus, an ideal end state of the EU's current strategy would be the development of self-sovereign digital tools and services that reflect its values and rights and which serve to strengthen its economic position. However, two hurdles emerge in the realisation of this dream – first the 'DC effect' where the EU seeks to dictate technologies primarily developed elsewhere and for which the EU has to rely on and adopt its regulations to what is extra-jurisdictionally;[34] second, the Internet is a key part of technologies and the digital future, but is seen as a global neutral jurisdiction for communication of information.[35]

Both challenges are at odds with the idea of 'digital sovereignty'[36] as the EU has to be politically conscious of the impact of regulating foreign technology giants with its relations with other countries who will not necessarily agree with the EU's vision, and because the Internet is a decentralised global network that is both difficult to regulate and to control in a technical sense due to its globally shared infrastructure. Solutions such as those used by China, ie technical controls that enforce the Government's will on people via censorship and restrictions, would represent a manifest violation of EU fundamental rights. A good example of this is the proposal for a 'Chat Control' regulation, which intended to mandate service providers to use automated technologies to scan and monitor private communications for illegal content.[37] It faced significant opposition and ultimately failed due to concerns over violations of EU fundamental rights, particularly the right to privacy and the protection of personal data as enshrined in the Charter of Fundamental Rights of the European Union. The mandatory scanning of private messages constitutes mass surveillance, and undermines privacy and data security. Additionally, the CJEU's prior rulings already emphasised the need for targeted and proportionate measures that respect individuals' privacy rights, which should rule out similar technical measures in the future.[38]

This raises the question of what form and direction 'digital sovereignty' should take when one does not have the effective capability to shape the direction of technological progress and when technical solutions utilised in other jurisdictions cannot be adopted readily. The Brussels effect certainly is a counter to these issues, as changes derived from EU regulations have shaped the direction of technologies globally. For example, the GDPR has provided new rights such as transparency

[34] Michael L Rustad and Thomas H Koenig TH, 'Towards a Global Data Privacy Standard' (2019) 71 *Florida Law Review* 365.

[35] John Perry Barlow, 'A Declaration of the Independence of Cyberspace' (2019) 18 *Duke Law. & Technology. Review* 5.

[36] Celeste (n 4) 211.

[37] European Commission, *Proposal for a Regulation of the European Parliament and of the Council laying down rules to prevent and combat child sexual abuse*, COM/2022/209 final.

[38] Edoardo Celeste and Federico Fabbrini, 'Targeted Surveillance: Can Privacy and Surveillance Be Reconciled?' in Sergio Carrera, Deirdre Curtin and Andrew Geddes (eds), *20 Year Anniversary of the Tampere Programme. Europeanisation Dynamics of the EU Area of Freedom, Security and Justice* (European University Institute, 2020); see also Edoardo Celeste and Giulia Formici, 'Constitutionalizing Mass Surveillance in the EU: Civil Society Demands, Judicial Activism, and Legislative Inertia' (2024) *German Law Journal* 1.

of information[39] and data portability,[40] which empower individuals by increasing accountability and creating an increased competition between digital services. With the Brussels effect, such changes have proliferated outwards from the EU to other jurisdictions through their own legal initiatives and new regulations.[41] However, to understand the limits of the Brussels effect, it is important to not only identify where other jurisdictions are adopting EU regulations such as the GDPR, but also to assess the quality of digital regulation enforcement within the EU as compared to other jurisdictions. Such comparisons are also legally necessary for measures such as 'adequacy decisions'[42] which permit technology and data to be exchanged without regulatory barriers.

The GDPR defines its scope as being limited to 'processing of personal data', and despite most of such processing now taking place through digital technologies and Internet or cloud-based services, it does not only regulate the use of digital technologies, being also applicable to limited cases of non-automated processing.[43] Instead, it defines general obligations regarding consent, transparency and rights which have an explicitly visible impact on the use of technologies. It is undeniable that these increased measures and rights have been a step towards the correct direction in increasing the awareness and implementation of data protection – a fundamental right – and to integrate it within technologies. However, it is also undeniable that the implementation and enforcement of GDPR has been faced with issues – and the aim of this section is to highlight that most of these have been due to technical challenges.

The most notorious examples of these would be the nuisance of 'cookie notices' or consenting dialogues that users find everywhere they go on the Internet.[44] Despite their existence being attributed to the GDPR, most of these notices are found to be in violation of the GDPR.[45] Similarly, smartphones and smartphone applications, which are increasingly the preferred form of interaction in society, also have significant issues when it comes to GDPR violations.[46] The externality of these situations threatens to create a negative societal perception regarding the GDPR and the EU more broadly in terms of digital regulations and their

[39] For example, GDPR Art 12.

[40] See GDPR Art 20.

[41] Christian Peukert et al, 'European Privacy Law and Global Markets for Data' (2020) 1 *Center for Law & Economics Working Paper Series*.

[42] European Commission, 'Adequacy decisions: How the EU determines if a non-EU country has an adequate level of data protection' (2023), commission.europa.eu/law/law-topic/data-protection/international-dimension-data-protection/adequacy-decisions_en.

[43] GDPR, Art 2.

[44] Martino Trevisan et al, '4 Years of EU Cookie Law: Results and Lessons Learned' (2019) 2 *Proceedings on Privacy Enhancing Technologies* 126.

[45] Michael Kretschmer, Jan Pennekamp and Klaus Wehrle, 'Cookie Banners and Privacy Policies: Measuring the Impact of the GDPR on the Web' (2021) 15 *ACM Transactions on the Web* 1; see also Celestine Matte, Cristiana Santos and Natallia Bielova, 'Purposes in IAB Europe's TCF: Which Legal Basis and How Are They Used by Advertisers?' (2020), hal.inria.fr/hal-02566891.

[46] Konrad Kollnig et al, 'Before and after GDPR: Tracking in Mobile Apps' (2021) *Internet Policy Review* 10.

effectiveness,[47] and also create unintended consequences such as concentration of vendors providing 'GDPR compliance'-oriented services[48] – which is at odds with the goal to increase market competition. Similarly, despite the GDPR envisioning its rights to improve the current ecosystem, it has in practice been the subject of challenges in being exercised,[49] and has also led to perils in the implementation of those rights which require technical implementations in privacy enhancing technologies (PETs) for effective remedies.[50]

One of the primary factors in limiting the effectiveness of the GDPR has been its competent bodies – namely the national data protection authorities (DPAs). Findings analysing the decisions undertaken by DPAs across the EU have revealed inconsistencies in the strategies and enforcements, a lack of necessary budgets being allocated, and concluding statements such as the GDPR 'silent failing' and the Commission being 'distracted by the next generation of legislation'.[51] Such factors play into the Brussels effect, where a lack of effective regulation can have negative adoption or dilution whereby technology providers do not deem it necessary to export the EU's requirements into global products and countries no longer see the value in aligning their regulations with EU.[52]

IV. Digital Sovereignty and the Need for 'Reactive Techno-regulation'

In 2021, the EDPB established a task force to address the issues of 'cookie banners' based on numerous complaints filed by the None of Your Business (NOYB) non-governmental organisation (NGO),[53] which published its first report in 2023 providing a list of 'violating' situations in relation to cookie banners.[54] Of note, the report only provides superficial suggestions on the incompatibility of

[47] Joanna Strycharz, Jef Ausloos and Natali Helberger, 'Data Protection or Data Frustration? Individual Perceptions and Attitudes Towards the GDPR' (2020) 6 *European Data Protection Law Review* 407.

[48] Gretta A Johnson, Scott Shriver and Samuel G Goldberg, 'Privacy & Market Concentration: Intended & Unintended Consequences of the GDPR' (2022) SSRN Scholarly Paper 3477686, 2, papers.ssrn.com/abstract=3477686.

[49] Data Protection Law Scholars Network (DPSN), 'The right to lodge a data protection complaint: OK, but then what? An empirical study of current practices under the GDPR' (2022), www.accessnow.org/cms/assets/uploads/2022/07/GDPR-Complaint-study.pdf.

[50] Michael Veale, Reuben Binns and Jef Ausloos, 'When Data Protection by Design and Data Subject Rights Clash' (2018) *8 International Data Privacy Law* 105.

[51] Irish Council of Civil Liberties 'Europe's Enforcement Paralysis: ICCL's 2021 Report on the Enforcement Capacity of Data Protection Authorities', www.iccl.ie/digital-data/2021-gdpr-report.

[52] For an example, see India's development and adoption of the Digital Personal Data Protection Act (2023) *The Gazette of India* – which deviates from its initial use of EU terminology and similarities to GDPR.

[53] European Data Protection Board, 'EDPB establishes cookie banner taskforce' (27 September 2021), edpb.europa.eu/news/news/2021/edpb-establishes-cookie-banner-taskforce_en.

[54] European Data Protection Board, 'Report of the work undertaken by the Cookie Banner Taskforce' (2023), edpb.europa.eu/our-work-tools/our-documents/other/report-work-undertaken-cookie-banner-taskforce_en.

cookie banners with the obligations of GDPR (and the ePrivacy Directive), and does not state other concerns which have been highlighted, such as the necessity of explicit consent for the processing of special categories of personal data. In fact, the most popular use of such banners and notices is to seek consent and to inform users about their involvement in the real-time bidding (RTB) advertising network, which has been highlighted[55] as being incompatible with the GDPR and which was the subject of the recent CJEU judgment in *IAB Europe*.[56] The decision clarified that the technical communications used for advertising on the web are considered personal data and found that the 'standard-setting sectoral organisation' (IAB Europe) is a (joint) controller based on its influence over these data processing operations.

To remedy these issues, the Commission launched in 2022 a plan to 'harmonise some aspects of the administrative procedure' and 'streamline cooperation between national data protection authorities when enforcing the General Data Protection Regulation in cross-border cases' via a new regulation.[57] And in 2023, the EDPB created a task force to address issues related to ChatGPT and similar technologies,[58] for which it provided preliminary views in May 2024, though further details on a concrete position under the GDPR have not yet been finalised. From this, we can ascertain that the Commission and data protection authorities have cognisance of the issues involved, but it is unclear yet as to what steps it will take in reaction and whether they will be accepted by the ecosystem or affected by bureaucratic delays. To give a comparative example of how slow these measures have been, consider how California, a federal state within the US, has rapidly enforced its California Consumer Protection Act[59] (CCPA) through the explicit use of technical tools which were justified based on the state of the art.[60]

It is important to note that the issues highlighted earlier also exist outside of the GDPR's enforcement abilities, and are systemic of the EU's approach to regulations – which requires corresponding changes to enforcement methods in light of rapid technological advancement. Such changes will need to be made from the initiating phase of regulations rather than later during their (late) enforcement. A recent example is the proposal to utilise technical measures to prevent and combat child abuse,[61] which relies on technological innovations which simply do not exist and

[55] Michael Veale, Midas Nouwens and Cristiana Santos, 'Impossible Asks: Can the Transparency and Consent Framework Ever Authorise Real-Time Bidding After the Belgian DPA Decision?' (2022) 2022 *Technology and Regulation* 12.

[56] Case C-604/22 *IAB Europe* (2024).

[57] European Commission, 'Further specifying procedural rules relating to the enforcement of the General Data Protection Regulation' (European Commission, 2023), ec.europa.eu/info/law/better-regulation/have-your-say/initiatives/13745-Further-specifying-procedural-rules-relating-to-the-enforcement-of-the-General-Data-Protection-Regulation_en.

[58] European Data Protection Board, 'EDPB resolves dispute on transfers by Meta and creates task force on Chat GPT' (13 April 2023), edpb.europa.eu/news/news/2023/edpb-resolves-dispute-transfers-meta-and-creates-task-force-chat-gpt_en.

[59] California Consumer Privacy Act (2018) T1.81.5.

[60] Office of Attorney Generals 'Final Statement of Reasons' (2021), oag.ca.gov/sites/all/files/agweb/pdfs/privacy/ccpa-fsor.pdf.

[61] European Commission (n 37).

instead raise grave concerns about legitimacy from a data protection perspective.[62] It also brings into question other regulations related to networking and communications which threatens to create a domino effect in destabilising the regulatory enforcement strategies employed by the EU.[63] Only time will tell whether similar issues arise in the enforcement of the new series of recently adopted data regulations, but it is arguably foreseeable that systemic challenges will only increase in the enforcement of technology without the use of effective remedial steps.

Thus, as technology rapidly progresses, laws become outdated as their requirements need to be reinterpreted in light of the new technological contexts. Further, if the market is resilient to the spirit of the regulation and sees it as a hindrance that must be avoided instead of embraced, it creates radical solutions which not only lengthen the application of the law but also seek to undermine the ability of the law by delaying compliance while continuing malpractices. All of this affects the ambition of EU digital sovereignty by limiting the ability to enforce the laws and achieve the desired effect, while technology continues to create even more complex use-cases whose compliance with existing laws becomes increasingly difficult to ascertain.

The current 'proactive' regulatory methodology must therefore also be supplemented with a 'reactive' regulatory process, where the authorities are given the power through the law to effectively react to new technological outcomes. The GDPR already contains an example of such a mechanism in Article 35(4) which provides national authorities the ability to define processing operations which require a DPIA. However, by itself this provision is not sufficient as it does not enable the authority to also stipulate additional requirements that are contextually relevant to a technology and through which the intended effect of the GDPR can be better achieved. Otherwise, each specific requirement of the GDPR, such as the provision of notice, how consent can be accurately expressed, or how to provide specific rights, must be independently investigated for every use-case – which is time consuming and expensive, and new guidelines must be drafted – which may not be respected until there is a case law established with deterring fines.

V. Conclusion: Syncing Enforcement with Technological Progress

The Commission's current digital strategy[64] diversifies its enforcement mechanisms to combat 'technical challenges'. For example, the DSA and the DMA have specific criteria for determining market dominance and prescribe increased obligations on

[62] Jennifer Cobbe, 'Data protection, ePrivacy, and the prospects for Apple's on-device CSAM Detection system in Europe' (11 August 2021), osf.io/preprints/socarxiv/rhw8c.

[63] Teresa Quintel, 'The Commission Proposal on Combatting Child Sexual Abuse-Confidentiality of Communications at Risk?' (2022) 8 *European Data Protection Law Review* 262.

[64] European Commission (n 3).

actors that fall under a 'large' role. To assist in the interpretation of these laws, the Commission has set up a European Centre for Algorithmic Transparency (ECAT) hosted by the Joint Research Centre (JRC),[65] which will undertake the necessary technical evaluations and conduct research in order to inform the enforcement of the DSA and DMA by the centralised authorities. Such techno-regulatory initiatives are a positive step towards the enforcement of regulations, but also need to be initiated for existing pieces of legislation, such as the GDPR, which have a significant scope and enforcement overlap with upcoming regulations.

In light of difficulties in understanding how technologies work and how regulations should be interpreted for them, a pragmatic approach is to 'embrace foresight and speculative design' where technological trends are anticipated and used to prepare strategic plans for understanding its implications on society, regulatory impacts and relevant of upcoming laws on emerging technologies.[66] Indeed, the European Data Protection Supervisor publishes TechSonar reports on emerging technologies and their relevance to the GDPR[67] as an example of such anticipatory measure. However, its effectiveness is limited in this case without a systemic integration into the larger enforcement stakeholders as well as the policy-making mechanisms. For example, the current series of impact assessments associated with regulations perceive enforcement only in the terms of legal instruments rather than also using foresight on how those measures relate to technological implementations.

Without these anticipatory preparations in the making of a regulation, it is exceedingly unclear whether a legal measure, intended to enforce a certain mechanism, will indeed be successfully adopted, will result in wilful 'mis-compliant' practices, such as cookie banners, or may not be feasible at all. One of the suggestions in response to GDPR's perceived 'slowness' is to propose a 'fast-track process for resolution of selected cases'.[68] By distinguishing between enforcement which requires lesser effort and has more certainty,[69] the effectiveness of a regulation can be vastly improved through more action. This measure also allows a pragmatic and deliberately slowed focus on questions that have larger bearing on the ecosystem – and can act as a filter for which cases should spent more time on.

A second anticipatory measure is to utilise the existence of research environments such as academia and NGOs which have a vested interest in identifying relevant knowledge without conflicts of interest in applying it to their own technical

[65] European Commission, 'European Centre for Algorithmic Transparency' (2023), algorithmic-transparency.ec.europa.eu/what-we-do_en.

[66] Arianna Rossi et al, 'What If Data Protection Embraced Foresight and Speculative Design?' (2022) DRS Biennial Conference Series, dl.designresearchsociety.org/drs-conference-papers/drs2022/researchpapers/248.

[67] European Data Protection Supervisor, 'TechSonar' (European Data Protection Supervisor), edps.europa.eu/press-publications/publications/techsonar_en.

[68] Estelle Massé, 'Five years and counting: GDPR faces a make-or-break moment over enforcement' (Access Now, 2023), www.accessnow.org/press-release/five-years-gdpr.

[69] An example of this is where a privacy notice is absent or a consent interface has one of the violating design patterns heightened in the EDPB's Cookie Task Force report (see n 54).

products and services. Such public consultations are already being utilised by data protection authorities in response to upcoming regulations such as the AI Act. Indeed, the Commission Nationale de l'Informatique et des Libertés (CNIL), the French data protection authority, has launched a sandbox for AI,[70] established a consultation on applicability of 'legitimate interest' as a legal basis in AI,[71] and published an action plan for investigating issues that stem from the use of AI and fall within the scope of GDPR,[72] despite not being formally appointed as an AI regulator. Such measures need to have a wider adoption with the support and initiative of the Commission to be effective across the EU.

Third, the EU envisions the use of standards, especially those related to technology development and management, in the implementation of its regulations, with the AI Act explicitly requiring such standards to exist as part of its enforcement strategy.[73] However, currently, the EU's involvement in standardisation initiatives calls into question the effectiveness of this strategy based on the existence of standards that conform and follow the EU's legal requirements.[74] Rather than merely utilising international standards which are likely to be diluted in terms of EU requirements based on the involvement of other non-EU actors, the EU should develop or extend these to create its own open enforceable standards which would assist in the implementation and evaluation of technologies in light of evolving technological and jurisprudential progress. Such standards would need to be applicable and adoptable to technologies and digital services, and reduce the cost of enforcement. In order to do this, the EU should strategise the involvement of EU experts within appropriate technical standardisation bodies such as Institute of Electrical and Electronics Engineers (IEEE), World Wide Web Consortium (W3C), and Internet Engineering Task Force (IETF) – which currently are dominated by members from the USA.

Fourth, and finally – the evolving nature of digital technologies requires an in-kind response where its enforcement must also be accompanied with digital measures. Such digital enforcement is a novel direction that the Commission must utilise to ascertain the effectiveness of its regulations, as well as to chart the path where technologies are used responsibly. The principle of digital enforcement has

[70] CNIL, '"Sandbox": CNIL launches call for projects on artificial intelligence in public services' (28 July 2023), www.cnil.fr/en/sandbox-cnil-launches-call-projects-artificial-intelligence-public-services.

[71] CNIL, 'Intelligence artificielle: la CNIL lance un appel à contributions sur la constitution de base de données' (27 July 2023), www.cnil.fr/fr/intelligence-artificielle-la-cnil-lance-un-appel-contributions-sur-la-constitution-de-base-de.

[72] CNIL, 'Artificial intelligence: the action plan of the CNIL' (16 May 2023), www.cnil.fr/en/artificial-intelligence-action-plan-cnil.

[73] Demková S, "The EU's Artificial Intelligence Laboratory and Fundamental Rights," Redressing Fundamental Rights Violations by the EU The Promise of the 'Complete System of Remedie' (Cambridge University Press 2024).

[74] Alessio Tartaro, 'Regulating by standards: current progress and main challenges in the standardisation of Artificial Intelligence in support of the AI Acti (2023) 1 *European Journal of Privacy Law & Technologies*.

to be proactively seeking areas where non-compliance is likely or there are gaps in the understanding, and to then be reactive in areas where faults occur despite early guidance and warnings. The principles of digital technologies aiming to automate, increase efficiency and reduce time should also be the aim of developing and using digital enforcement tools and methods. Such measures are in the realm of possibility, and within the capability of the Commission's competencies.[75]

In reality, the situation is always more complicated when it comes to the development of regulations and effectively enforcing them. For example, the proposal for ePrivacy Regulation has been documented as being the target of Google 'slowing down and delaying the process' and 'working behind the scenes hand in hand with the other companies'.[76] It is pragmatic to assume such resistance also occurs after the regulation during its enforcement phase. In light of this, the Commission's digital sovereignty strategy must evolve to consider measures at both *ex ante* as well as ex post phases which seek to use foresight and anticipatory designs to identify how enforcement can and should work in practice. At the same time, the Commission needs to develop its own technical competencies in order to support investigators and authorities in responding quickly to regulatory violations and to utilise mechanisms that can fast-track the enforcement decisions and procedures to match the technological progress and diversity that it seeks to enforce. To end on a note of optimism, the EU has shown the willingness to engage in tackling problems head-on, and this is how it has come to enjoy a leadership position in the world when it comes to regulating digital technologies. The hope is that it continues to do so by considering the new generation of challenges that emerge from technological progress.

[75] For example, the Commission already has several technical initiatives in progress to support its digital strategy, (European Commission, 'European Digital Identity Wallets: Commission publishes first technical Toolbox towards prototypes' (2023), digital-strategy.ec.europa.eu/en/news/european-digital-identity-wallets-commission-publishes-first-technical-toolbox-towards-prototypes.

[76] Google Antitrust Litigation – *State of Texas et al. Vs Google LLC*, Case 1:21-md-03010-PKC, United States District Court – Southern District of New York Document 152 Filed 22 October 2021 63.

4

Digital Sovereignty, Cybersecurity and Geopolitical Implications

TAMARA ALVAREZ ROBLES*

I. Introduction

Recently, the concept of digital sovereignty has been the subject of several news pieces, some of them alluding to regulatory compliance in the domains of personal data protection and/or information security,[1] others in relation to the limitation of certain applications,[2] services or products of some multinational technology companies.[3] In the European Union (EU), the term 'digital sovereignty' is closely related to the area of technological–digital regulation.[4] Meanwhile, within Member States, the emphasis is on strengthening the field of cybersecurity and achieving strategic independence from third parties in the realm of information and communication technologies.[5]

* This chapter has been carried out within the Project: Cyberelections (21/23) 'Cybersecurity in electoral processes. Guarantees against misinformation and other information disorders on platforms', financed within the framework of the TED Projects of the State Plan for Scientific Research, Technical and Innovation funded by the European Union, Reference: TED2021-130876B-100.

[1] An example can be found in María Pía Aqueveque, 'Soberanía digital, poder para el usuario' *Diario Financiero* (25 May 2023), www.df.cl/opinion/columnistas/soberania-digital-poder-para-el-usuario, where the concept of sovereignty is mentioned in relation to the fine imposed on the company META amounting to €1.3 billion for transferring personal data of European users to the US.

[2] See Euronews, 'Which Countries Have Banned TikTok and Why? (7 November 2024), www.euronews.com/next/2024/03/14/which-countries-have-banned-tiktok-cybersecurity-data-privacy-espionage-fears, which states that the EU, US, Denmark, Belgium and Canada have also recently issued orders prohibiting the use of TikTok. Experts fear that sensitive information could be exposed when downloading the application, especially on government devices.

[3] See Ricardo Aguilar, 'Huawei, Eliminada Del 5G En Reino Unido: El Gobierno Prohíbe Por Completo La Utilización de Sus Equipos' (Xataka, 14 July 2020), www.xataka.com/empresas-y-economia/huawei-eliminado-5g-reino-unido-gobierno-prohibe-completo-utilizacion-sus-equipos, which specifies that Huawei will be completely removed from the UK's 5G networks by the end of 2027, a decision taken following a meeting of the National Security Council (NSC) chaired by the Prime Minister, in response to new US sanctions.

[4] See Bertrand in this volume.

[5] *cf* Bertrand and Santaniello in this volume.

This scenario begs the question: are all these spheres or areas related to the concept of sovereignty? Some of them focus on the economic side of technologies, others on the issue of security, and in other cases the concern is fundamental rights, and yet all claim to be related to 'sovereignty'. In short, the same term 'digital sovereignty' is used to reflect different realities, and, furthermore, in the news as well as in scholarly works, the perimeters of this concept are not carefully defined, thus generating greater confusion.[6] In many cases, those who use the term 'digital sovereignty' are trying to point out an absence of that sovereignty, the need to rethink whether and under what conditions such acts of sovereignty exist in the technological–digital realm. In other words, they are seeking to call for the recovery of sovereignty (control) in the digital ecosystem, a domain characterised by globalisation, non-territoriality and fragmentation of public power, as it is traditionally known.[7]

The term 'sovereignty' is complex in its nature and definition. It has been the object of study for centuries and there is no unanimous position on what sovereignty is and what it is not, where it occurs and what its elements are. Rather, there are different visions, schools, as this edited volume also highlights. This complexity is also transferred to the concept of 'digital sovereignty'. In this context, it will be necessary to allude to the subjects and attributes of twenty-first-century sovereignty (technological–digital, economic and political). In this respect, the chapter is structured as follows: section II delves into the historical and theoretical foundations of sovereignty. Section III explores the emergence and significance of digital sovereignty in the modern era. In section IV, the focus shifts to the European Union (EU) and its Member States, examining their roles and interactions in the realm of digital sovereignty. Section V addresses the critical intersection of digital sovereignty and cybersecurity, highlighting the challenges and strategies involved. Finally, section VI discusses the broader implications of striving for digital leadership, particularly in terms of geopolitical dynamics and international relations.

II. Analysing the Concept of Sovereignty

It is not the objective of this chapter to provide a detailed analysis of the concept of sovereignty.[8] We must however mention some of the main ideas at the core of this complex notion. The term 'sovereignty' has its origins in the Middle Ages, when

[6] An example of the ambiguity of digital sovereignty can be found on European Commission, 'Digital Sovereignty: European Chips Act Enters into Force Today' press release (21 September 2023), ec.europa.eu/commission/presscorner/detail/en/ip_23_4518. This analyses the Act but does not define what digital sovereignty is.

[7] Si Chen, 'Research on data sovereignty rules in cross-border data flow and Chinese solution. US-China' (2021) 18 *Law Review* 261, doi.org/10.17265/1548-6605/2021.06.001. See Bertrand in this volume.

[8] See Bertrand in this volume.

it was used to refer to the absolute power of a king or emperor. In the sixteenth century, with the rise of the modern state, sovereignty became a legal concept that defined the exclusive power of the state over its territory and its inhabitants. In the eighteenth century, the French Revolution introduced the concept of popular sovereignty, according to which the sovereign power resides in the people. This concept was consolidated with the development of liberal democracies, in which political power rests with the citizens. Since the twentieth century, sovereignty has faced new challenges, such as the emergence of international organisations, economic globalisation, and the spread of new information and communication technologies.

A. The Attributes of Sovereignty: Authority and Control

From the study of the classical concept of sovereignty,[9] we can deduce that sovereignty is seen as a new form of ordering of a political reality that must be related to an institution or body that represents a true authority exercising or possessing effective power. In this sense, sovereignty is linked to a specific and inalienable way of constructing a supreme power: a power that has no superior, without being political domination, since domination or mere hegemony is not sovereignty. Sovereignty is a voluntary relationship of recognition of authority, not domination, and it is also a public relationship.[10]

From the above we deduce that the attributes of sovereignty are: authority – including the recognition of an authority or authorities by people, citizens, inhabitants – and control – over a territory, people and coercive power (eg defence and security).

B. Sovereignty Fragmentation

The evolution of society and of the state has led to an international system in which we have witnessed a transfer of competences to new supranational institutions (such as NATO or the EU) on occasions derived from the material impossibility of control and effective power in different economic and security fields.[11] In this context, an 'international/supranational paradox' arises: the weakening of the nation-state and the related need for international and supranational communities (such as the EU), to help defend common interests and prevent the disappearance of the state in the face of globalisation. In a very simplified form, we can say that,

[9] As a selection, consider: Jean Bodin, *Les six livres de la république* (1576); Thomas Hobbes, *Leviathan, or The Matter, Forme and Power of a Common Wealth Ecclesiasticall and Civil* (Andrew Crooke, 1651); and Jean-Jacques Rousseau, *Du Contrat social; ou, principes du droit politique* (Marc Michel Rey, 1762).

[10] Ramiro Rico, 'Soberanía' (1952) 66 *Revista de Estudios Políticos* 37.

[11] Benito Aláez Corral, 'Soberanía constitucional e integración europea' (1998) 1 *Fundamentos. Cuadernos monográficos de teoría del estado, derecho público e historia constitucional* 503.

for example, in the EU, the international or supranational authority (originally the European Communities, currently the EU) is recognised by the treaties through which competences are ceded (cession of sovereignty); states maintain the execution of the areas of competences ceded (maintenance of control) and of the ownership of powers that are not ceded. In addition, a regime of sanctions or responsibilities is established for the Member States which fail to comply with the mandates of the international or supranational entity, circumstances that, on occasions, arise when states try to assert their national constitutional identity or their interests in contradiction to those of the respective supranational or international organisation.[12]

The defence of the constitutional national identity is a typical example of how states protect their sovereignty in the supranational framework of the EU. Examples include the Opinion of the Spanish Constitutional Court 1/2004 asserting that 'in any case the Spanish Constitution will prevail'; the reform of the Constitutions of Hungary and Poland, or Brexit.[13] On all these occasions, Member States reinstated their role of masters of the treaties and thus the function of their citizens as sovereigns. An example of the same phenomenon in the international framework is the non-execution of the judgments of the European Court of Human Rights by different states, such as Russia or Turkey.[14]

III. Technological or Digital Sovereignty: Introducing Geopolitics

In a similar way to previous centuries, the concept of sovereignty today is polyhedral and multifaceted. The multiple aspects it touches (economy, technology, politics, human rights, etc) are linked by public relations that respond to the capacities, or 'attributes', of a public *authority* (at the local, state, supranational and international levels) to create *control* mechanisms (through norms, public policies and system of sanctions).

In the current century, we must highlight the importance of the technological–digital component as one of the most significant ecosystems in which a large portion of societal and state life develops. The attributes of sovereignty in this scenario become related to new concepts: authority becomes synonymous with 'leadership' and control is related to 'strategic autonomy'. Moreover, we must bear in mind that technology companies start to be involved in the discussions around digital sovereignty to the extent that they fall under the control of the public authority.

[12] See Javier García Roca, *El margen de apreciación nacional en la interpretación del Convenio Europeo de Derechos Humanos: soberanía e integración* (Civitas, 2010).

[13] Nóra Chronowski et al, 'Hungary: Constitutional (R)evolution or Regression?' in Anneli Albi and Samo Bardutzky (eds), *National Constitutions in European and Global Governance: Democracy, Rights, the Rule of Law* (TMC Asser Press, 2019), doi.org/10.1007/978-94-6265-273-6_31.

[14] Jaume Ferrer Lloret, 'La ejecución de las sentencias del TEDH relativas a la Federación de Rusia y Turquía: ¿Han fracasado las reformas del protocolo 14?' (2018) 61 *Revista de Derecho Comunitario Europeo* 853.

In the early years of the digital age, digital sovereignty focused on protecting telecommunications infrastructure. However, with the advent of the Internet, digital sovereignty has expanded to include the protection of personal data and freedom of expression online. Nowadays, digital sovereignty is a matter of political and legal debate. Some states have taken steps to strengthen their digital sovereignty, for example with the creation of national data centres or the regulation of foreign technology companies; others have opted for a more open stance, arguing that digital sovereignty can limit economic development and innovation.[15]

What is apparent is that, in the current context, digital sovereignty is an important challenge for states, which must guarantee national security, the privacy of citizens and economic sovereignty. This conception is, to some extent, similar at EU level. As Madiega explains:

> The notion of 'technological' or 'digital sovereignty' has recently emerged as a means of promoting the notion of European leadership and strategic autonomy in the digital field. Strong concerns have been raised over the economic and social influence of non-EU technology companies, which threatens EU citizens' control over their personal data, constrains both the growth of EU high technology companies and the ability of national and EU rule-makers to enforce their laws. In this context, 'digital sovereignty' refers to Europe's ability to act independently in the digital world and should be understood in terms of both protective mechanisms and offensive tools to foster digital innovation (including in cooperation with non-EU companies)'[16]

In a similar sense, Cedric Larsen states that:

> Growing mistrust between nations, however, has caused a rise in digital sovereignty, which refers to a nation's ability to control its digital destiny and may include control over the entire AI supply chain, from data to hardware and software. A consequence of the trend toward greater digital sovereignty – which then drives the trend further – is increasing fear of being cut off from critical digital components such as computer chips and a lack of control over the international flow of citizens' data.[17]

In addition, in this scenario, what is interesting is observing the 'theoretical' loss of control by states and supranational and international organisations in favour of tech companies. Calleja-López et al argue that

> the current situation undermines the autonomy and digital sovereignty of their people, reducing them to the status of digital colonies of the great hegemonic powers, in this case the United States and China.[18]

[15] See Paul van den Berg, 'How the CLOUD-Act works in data storage in Europe' (National Cyber Security Centre, 16 August 2022), english.ncsc.nl/latest/weblog/weblog/2022/how-the-cloud-act-works-in-data-storage-in-europe.

[16] Tambiama André Madiega, 'Digital Sovereignty for Europe' (European Parliament Think Tank, 2020), www.europarl.europa.eu/thinktank/en/document/EPRS_BRI(2020)651992.

[17] Benjamin Cedric Larsen, 'The geopolitics of IA and the rise of digital sovereignty' (Brookings, 2022), www.brookings.edu/articles/the-geopolitics-of-ai-and-the-rise-of-digital-sovereignty.

[18] Antonio Calleja-López, Ekaitz Cancela and Marta Cambronero, 'Desplazar los ejes: alternativas tecnológicas, derechos humanos y sociedad civil a principios del siglo XXI' (2022) *Tecnopolítica-UOC* 125 (author's translation).

However, we must demystify this myth of independence from the powers of technology companies, or rather, relativise it. In reality, there are national interests within these companies that are not evident at first glance. Consider the companies that own most of the Internet infrastructure (submarine cables, providers, providers, satellites) or that can condition the technology market with the production of microprocessors; think about the dependencies from companies that collect and process both personal and non-personal data, and consider the cooperation of these companies with their respective states.

If we look at where these tech companies are incorporated, we observe two main loci: China and the US. Neither jurisdiction is driven by the European model of protection, based on the principle of technological humanism, but by economic reasons. Both seek to be strategic technological powers, to create dependencies for the rest of the world; both try to convince the EU that their respective companies do not collaborate directly with their national powers. And yet there is apparent evidence of this company–state collaboration.[19] In addition, both powers try to take over the natural resources of other states (by buying debt, investing or intervening militarily).

This situation brings geopolitics fully into the technological–digital framework, and we begin to see the interlocking of alliances in the international sphere: China is supported by Russia, while the US seeks European complicity.[20] These dependencies, collaborations or alliances have not gone unnoticed in the European framework, which is why the EU is trying to be autonomous or not strategically dependent in the digital field.

IV. EU, Member States and Digital Sovereignty

Across defence, economy, politics, etc, 'digital sovereignty' has different meanings, all of them with an impact on world geopolitics. Here, we seek to delimit the term 'sovereignty', which has been the object of study for several centuries, now with the complication of a technological–digital ecosystem, which affects some of its essential elements: territory, population, power, authority and control.

At this juncture, when we examine the state (public power) as the focal point of the sovereignty discourse, we encounter various forces working in the opposite direction, challenging the preservation of power shares and the effectiveness of state authority, thereby to some extent diminishing its effective control. On the one hand, internationalisation, which is why we look at supranationalism as a

[19] As can be verified from the judgments related to data protection known as Privacy Shield and Safe Harbour. Cristina Vela Marimon, 'Beyond the New EU-US Data Privacy Framework, Privacy and Openness' (Telefónica, 17 July 2023), www.telefonica.com/en/communication-room/blog/beyond-the-new-eu-us-data-privacy-framework-privacy-and-openness.

[20] David Hagebölling, 'La lucha geopolítica por el liderazgo tecnológico' (Política Exterior, 28 April 2022), www.politicaexterior.com/la-lucha-geopolitica-por-el-liderazgo-tecnologico.

response; on the other hand, the development of a technological–digital ecosystem with the pre-eminence of a growing private power that pushes towards an aggregation of interests, again, at the supranational level. In other words, global issues cannot be fought solely and exclusively from the local perspective, within the traditional sovereignty of nation-states.

In this sense, the EU is committed to establishing standards in the technological–digital sphere, in a similar way to what has been happening in the traditional analogue world, in which states have, or maintain, a certain quota of sovereignty. The purpose of this digital regulation would be to protect citizens' fundamental rights and guarantee their security. In this way, the EU tries to lead a digital humanism,[21] focusing not only on economic issues,[22] but also on the protection of rights and freedoms of individuals. It seeks to achieve this shielding through the establishment of a plural regulatory framework that covers different matters (data protection, information security, telecommunications, artificial intelligence (AI), etc) and different actors at the global level (states, companies, citizens).

European institutions thus focus on various levels of action: primary and secondary legislation, public policies, and political positioning in the technological–digital domain.[23] Digital regulation encompasses rights enshrined in EU treaties and secondary legislations, such as the General Data Protection Regulation (GDPR), Digital Services Act (DSA), Digital Single Market (DSM) Directive, Network And Information System (NIS) Directives, e-Privacy Directive and e-Commerce Directive, among others. In the realm of soft law and public policies, the emphasis is placed on recommendations and opinions, as well as guidelines related to standardisation in areas such as the Internet of Things (IoT) and 5G technology, and regarding the use or non-use of certain applications, websites, networks or technologies, such as TikTok. These guidelines play a crucial role in guiding technological development and in user protection. Furthermore, the importance of investing in the development of EU technology is highlighted, by formulating strategies, programmes and projects for both the short and long term. The aim is to achieve an autonomous technological–digital ecosystem with fewer strategic dependencies. Examples of these initiatives include the EU Chips Act, the acceleration of the digitisation of key public services, and the promotion of a digital single market. These collective efforts aim to strengthen technological independence and foster innovation within an effective regulatory framework. Finally, political positioning entails taking important strategic decisions, such as banning suspect technology from other states or forming economic alliances.

[21] See Edoardo Celeste and Giovanni De Gregorio, 'Digital Humanism: The Constitutional Message of the GDPR' (2022) 3 *Global Privacy Law Review* 4.

[22] This is the reason for the creation of the EU itself and the driving force behind the digital single market, which enables competition in regulation and the development of a plurality of public policies in different areas.

[23] See Madiega (n 16).

The scheme of the Union is reproduced at the level of the Member States, where it will be necessary to pay attention to the maintenance of their competences (sovereignty) or to the divergences that occur with respect to the Union, even if there are sanctions that should ensure uniformity between these two levels.[24] If we focus on the regulatory framework of the Member States, it is important to analyse the application and transposition of European legislation to find out if there are divergences between the EU and national legal systems, as well as to investigate the existence of national laws, norms, standards and policies in those technological–digital areas not ceded to the EU. However, we are aware that in the field of digitisation there is a great cooperation agreement between the states and the Union, as was explained above. Regarding national public policies, it is necessary to investigate whether there are projects and programmes that invest in national digital issues or national digital companies, whether they have created intelligence (public and/or private) at the national level, or whether they collaborate with other regions. It is outside the scope of this chapter to analyse these elements in detail from a comparative perspective.

We will now focus on the relationship between digital sovereignty and cybersecurity, mainly looking at the EU and analysing Spain as a case study.

V. Digital Sovereignty and Cybersecurity

We mentioned earlier that several attributes define the concept of sovereignty, among them security and defence. These concepts introduce us to the link between digital sovereignty and cybersecurity, which will be the subject of the remainder of this chapter.

'Digital sovereignty' refers, among other things, to the ability of a country to control its own digital space, including its infrastructure, data and communications. Cybersecurity, on the other hand, aims to protect computer systems, networks and information from cyber threats. Without cybersecurity, states are vulnerable to cyber-attacks that can cause economic, political and social harm.

A. EU Cybersecurity Framework

The EU regulatory framework in the field of cybersecurity is multifaceted, aiming to address a variety of complex and interrelated concerns. These include the absence of a unified European cyberspace, the challenges posed by foreign influence, and the over-dependence on equipment suppliers. Cybersecurity regulations seek to mitigate the risks associated with cyber-attacks and the lack of control over data as well as to address the EU's data dependency. Furthermore, these regulations

[24] For example: Hungary and Poland with fundamental rights regarding LGTBI+.

aim to enhance the EU's competitiveness in new and innovative markets, which is often hindered by a plurality of challenges related to the interplay between regulation and economy of the technological–digital domain.

Additionally, some cybersecurity regulations confront the issue of online disinformation and the dominance of online platforms, many of which are based outside the EU, over entire sectors of the EU economy. This dominance raises significant concerns regarding the sovereignty of EU Member States in critical areas such as copyright, data protection, taxation and transportation. Consequently, regulations in this field are not only about safeguarding cybersecurity but also about ensuring the economic, political and social stability of the EU in the face of these emerging digital challenges.

This response is articulated through a comprehensive and structured approach encompassing various policy areas. Key among these is the implementation of a cybersecurity certification scheme, which aims to standardise and enhance the security features of products and services. Additionally, there is a concerted focus on coordination in matters of cybersecurity, ensuring a cohesive and unified response across different sectors and Member States.

The continuation and strengthening of the data protection and privacy law framework remains a cornerstone of this policy, upholding the rights of individuals and maintaining the integrity of personal data. Furthermore, the formulation of technology policy is firmly rooted in principles of transparency and trust, recognising these as fundamental to the successful adoption and public acceptance of new technologies.

Moreover, security is increasingly recognised as an indispensable element in all public procurement procedures for relevant infrastructure, both at the EU and national levels. This approach underscores the commitment to embedding security considerations in the very foundation of infrastructure development, thereby enhancing the resilience and reliability of critical systems and networks.

We will now illustrate a plurality of regulations that form part of the EU cybersecurity strategy and that respond to the problems seen above.

The EU's cybersecurity policy, comprising regulatory, funding and coordination measures, is outlined in the EU Cybersecurity Strategy for the Digital Decade.[25] This policy has undergone several key revisions and developments over the years. In 2014, Regulation (EU) No 910/2014 (eIDAS) was introduced, providing a framework for electronic identification and trust services in the EU. Subsequently, in 2016, Directive (EU) 2016/1148 (the NIS Directive) was enacted, which requires organisations to improve cybersecurity and establishes a cooperation framework. In 2019, Regulation (EU) 2019/881, the Cybersecurity Act, was approved, introducing a harmonised cybersecurity certification system in the EU. That same year, a proposal for a Cyber Resilience Act was presented, aimed at

[25] European Commission, Communication 'The EU's Cybersecurity Strategy for the Digital Decade', JOIN(2020) 18 final.

strengthening the EU's resilience against cyber threats. More recently, in 2022, Directive (EU) 2022/2555 (the NIS 2 Directive) was adopted, expanding the scope and introducing new requirements regarding cybersecurity.

In terms of public policies, noteworthy are funding programmes such as the Horizon Europe, the European Cybersecurity Competence Center and the Joint Cyber Unit.[26] In addition, we have to consider the Cybersecurity Strategy for the Digital Decade, adopted on 16 December 2020, which stems from the Union's Security Strategy of July 2020.[27]

For the European security strategy, the issue of cybersecurity is recognised as one of strategic importance, leading to the establishment of several key initiatives. Foremost among these is the development of the EU Cybersecurity Strategy, which serves as a comprehensive plan to enhance the cybersecurity posture of the EU. Additionally, there is a recognised need to invest in research, innovation and technological development, which is being addressed through initiatives such as the European Cybersecurity Competence Centre, the Network of National Coordination Centres, and the creation of the EU Innovation Hub for Internal Security.[28] These institutions and networks are pivotal in advancing cybersecurity knowledge, capabilities and technologies. Furthermore, the development of a common regulatory framework is deemed essential for ensuring a harmonised and effective approach to cybersecurity across the EU, thereby safeguarding its digital infrastructure and enhancing the overall security of its Member States. Furthermore, it continues to implement the previously described regulatory framework.

This security strategy is translated into the EU's Cybersecurity Strategy in the Digital Decade, which includes three areas with different lines of action. The first one aims at boosting the security of essential services and connected things, which is a pivotal aspect of enhancing overall cybersecurity. This endeavour includes the revision of rules on the security of network and information systems, ensuring a robust and up-to-date framework to protect vital digital infrastructure. A significant advancement is the development of a European Cyber Shield, which involves a network of AI-enabled Security Operations Centres capable of detecting early signs of a cyber-attack, thereby enabling preventive action to avert

[26] Regulation (EU) 2021/695 of the European Parliament and of the Council of 28 April 2021 establishing Horizon Europe – the Framework Programme for Research and Innovation, laying down its rules for participation and dissemination, and repealing Regulations (EU) No 1290/2013 and (EU) No 1291/2013 [2021] OJ L 170/1; Regulation (EU) 2021/694 of the European Parliament and of the Council of 29 April 2021 establishing the Digital Europe Programme and repealing Decision (EU) 2015/2240 [2021] OJ L 166; Regulation (EU) 2021/887 of the European Parliament and of the Council of 20 May 2021 establishing the European Cybersecurity Industrial, Technology and Research Competence Centre and the Network of National Coordination Centres [2021] OJ L 202/1; European Commission (n 25) 13.

[27] European Commission (n 25), European Commission, *The EU Security Union Strategy*, COM(2020) 605 final.

[28] Regulation (EU) 2021/887 (n 26).

potential damage.[29] Additionally, there is an emphasis on maintaining high standards of cybersecurity for all connected objects, ensuring that the vast array of IoT devices are secure and resilient against cyber threats. Dedicated support to small and medium enterprises is also a key focus, recognising their unique needs and vulnerabilities in the cybersecurity landscape. Attracting and retaining the best cybersecurity talent is crucial to maintaining a skilled and effective cybersecurity workforce. Concurrently, significant investments are being made in research and innovation to stay ahead of evolving cyber threats. Securing 5G networks and their supply chains is also a critical component, given the importance of 5G in future communications and the potential risks associated with its deployment. These comprehensive measures collectively aim to fortify the cybersecurity ecosystem, safeguarding essential services and connected devices against the ever-growing array of cyber threats.

The second line of action aims at strengthening collective capabilities to respond to major cyber-attacks, which is a critical component of enhancing the EU's cybersecurity resilience. This initiative involves providing support to Member States to effectively defend their citizens and national security interests against cyber threats. A key aspect of this effort is the collaboration across various domains, including civilian and disaster response, police and judiciary, as well as in the realms of cyber diplomacy and cyber defence. Such cooperation is essential in preventing, discouraging, deterring and responding to cyber threats in a coordinated and effective manner. Additionally, the establishment of the Joint Cyber Unit stands as a significant development in this endeavour. This platform is designed to significantly enhance the protection of the EU from the most impactful cybersecurity attacks, particularly those that are cross-border in nature. The Joint Cyber Unit serves as a hub for collaboration, information sharing and rapid response, thereby playing a pivotal role in bolstering the collective cyber defence capabilities of the EU and its Member States, ensuring a unified and robust approach to tackling the complex challenges posed by cyber threats.

The last line of action focuses on working with partners globally to ensure international security and stability in cyberspace. Overall, these efforts will lead to the emergence of new strategic initiatives aimed at fortifying cybersecurity across the EU. A notable development is the establishment of an EU-wide Cyber Shield, which is envisioned as a robust protective layer against cyber threats, encompassing advanced monitoring and defence mechanisms.[30] Alongside this, the creation of a Joint Cyber Unit is set to play a pivotal role, acting as a centralised platform for coordination and response against cyber-attacks, enhancing the collective cybersecurity posture of the EU. Furthermore, the focus extends to developing

[29] European Commission (n 25) 6; European Commission, *Proposal for a Regulation of the European Parliament and of the Council laying down measures to strengthen solidarity and capacities in the Union to detect, prepare for and respond to cybersecurity threats and incidents*, COM(2023) 209 final, 9 ff.

[30] ibid.

European solutions for strengthening Internet security on a global scale, acknowledging the interconnected nature of digital threats. There is also an emphasis on regulation to ensure an Internet of Secure Things, which aims to prevent a single poorly protected object from becoming a critical point of failure in the network. Additionally, the implementation of regulation for high standards of cyber and information security in EU institutions, bodies and agencies is planned, ensuring that these entities adhere to the highest levels of cybersecurity practices. These initiatives collectively represent a comprehensive and proactive approach towards establishing a more secure and resilient technological–digital environment within the EU.

B. A Case Study at Member State Level: The Spanish Cybersecurity Framework

Spain, together with Estonia, is one of the leading Member States in the cybersecurity sector, as evidenced in the 2020 Global Cybersecurity Index.[31] Both states have influenced the development of the cybersecurity regulations and policies noted above. Such is the importance of cybersecurity for Spain that it has a plurality of regulatory areas that make up its law of cybersecurity. These can be categorised into eight subjects:[32] 1) national security and cyber threats in the cyberspace; 2) the protection of critical ifrastructure; 3) security regulations; 4) the creation and regulation of a Security Incident Response Team; 5) the discipline of telecommunications and user rights; 6) cybercrime; 7) data protection; and 8) the interaction between government entities and their relation to technological–digital matters. Lastly, the efficient use of information technologies is also a priority, as highlighted by the Royal Decree 311/2022 of 3 May (2022), which regulates the National Security Scheme, ensuring that technology is used effectively and securely in the public sector.

Together, this framework robustly protects Spain's digital landscape and its citizens in the rapidly evolving world of information technology and cybersecurity. Cybersecurity law in Spain is part of the regulation dedicated to defence and security, mainly focused on the field of cyberspace. Its objective is to establish general guidelines for the secure use of cyberspace by promoting an integrated vision that guarantees the security and progress of Spain, involving all public administrations, the private sector and citizens. In this sense, this regulation is based on principles of coordination and cooperation, which are applied vertically (state–EU) and horizontally (public–private and citizen collaboration). Cybersecurity seeks to protect, through this legal framework (with its implementation and development),

[31] International Telecommunication Union, 'Global Cybersecurity Index' (2020), www.itu.int/en/ITU-D/Cybersecurity/Pages/global-cybersecurity-index.aspx.

[32] These eight sections are included in the Cybersecurity Code of Law of Spain.

people, companies, institutions, technology and processes, as evidenced by the cybersecurity strategy.

The Spanish National Cybersecurity Strategy, updated in 2019, regards cyberspace technology and infrastructure as 'strategic elements', while cyberspace vulnerability is understood as a 'major risk' for Spain's development as a nation.[33] Cyberspace security is a priority goal, and cyberspace is seen as vector of strategic communication that influences public opinion and people's way of thinking (manipulation of information, disinformation campaigns or hybrid actions).

In its comprehensive approach to cybersecurity, the strategy delineates five pivotal objectives aimed at fortifying the nation's digital landscape. Firstly, it prioritises the security and resilience of information and communications networks and systems within the public sector, along with essential services, ensuring their robustness against cyber threats. Secondly, it focuses on the secure and reliable use of cyberspace, actively guarding against illicit or malicious activities that compromise digital integrity. Thirdly, the strategy extends its protective scope to the business and social ecosystem, along with individual citizens, emphasising the need for a secure environment conducive to economic and social well-being. Fourthly, it champions a culture of cybersecurity, advocating for a strong commitment to this field and the empowerment of both human and technological capabilities, recognising that people are as crucial as technology in the cyber defence landscape. Lastly, the strategy addresses the security of cyberspace in the international arena, acknowledging the global nature of cyber threats and the necessity for international cooperation and collective security measures. This comprehensive approach underlines the multifaceted and dynamic nature of cybersecurity, highlighting its critical role in safeguarding national security, economic vitality, and the well-being of citizens in the digital age.

The strategy also provides seven lines of action to guarantee a robust framework for enhancing Spain's cybersecurity posture. First, it aims to strengthen capabilities to effectively counteract threats emanating from cyberspace, ensuring a proactive and resilient defence mechanism. Second, it focuses on guaranteeing the security and resilience of Spain's strategic assets, recognising their critical role in national stability and security. Third, the strategy emphasises the need for full implementation of the National Security Scheme and the Critical Infrastructure Protection System, along with ensuring compliance and harmonisation of regulations related to the protection of critical infrastructures and essential services. Fourth, it advocates for the promotion of cybersecurity awareness and practices among citizens and companies, highlighting the importance of collective responsibility in digital safety. Fifth, the strategy underscores the promotion of the Spanish cybersecurity industry, emphasising the cultivation and retention of talent to bolster Spain's digital autonomy and technological innovation. Sixth, it commits to contributing to

[33] National Security Council, National Cybersecurity Strategy of Spain, 2019, Order PCIPCI/487/2019, www.boe.es/buscar/doc.php?id=BOE-A-2019-6347.

the security of cyberspace in the international arena, advocating for a cyberspace that is open, plural, secure and trustworthy, aligning with Spain's national interests. Lastly, it aims to develop a pervasive culture of cybersecurity, recognising that awareness, education and shared responsibility are key to strengthening the nation's overall cyber defence. Together, these lines of action represent a comprehensive and forward-looking approach to securing Spain's digital future in an increasingly interconnected world.

In the Spanish national security governance system, cybersecurity is a key element and is institutionally represented by the National Security Council, which is comprised of two primary components: the Situation Committee and the National Cybersecurity Council. The National Cybersecurity Council itself is an intricate structure, consisting of the Standing Committee on Cybersecurity and the National Cybersecurity Forum. This council brings together various competent public authorities, including the Centro Criptológico Nacional – Computer Emergency Response Team (CCN-CERT), the Instituto Nacional de Ciberseguridad – Computer Emergency Response Team (INCIBE-CERT) and the Computer Emergency Response Team of the Spanish Defence (ESPDEF-CERT), along with the national reference computer security incident response teams (CSIRTs). These entities collaborate to ensure a coordinated and effective response to cybersecurity challenges, reinforcing the national defence against cyber threats and enhancing the overall security of the nation's digital infrastructure. Their joint efforts signify a comprehensive approach to managing and mitigating cybersecurity risks within Spain's national security system.

VI. The Quest for Digital Leadership and Geopolitical Implications

The digital technology field is an area of rapid growth and development, and is having a significant impact on the global economy, society and politics. As a result, the geopolitical implications of digital technology are becoming increasingly important. One of the main consequences is the growing competition between states for technological leadership. States with a strong technology sector have a competitive advantage in the global economy, as they can develop new technologies, products and services, and attract foreign investment. Another important geopolitical implication is the growing dependence of states on digital technologies, which are essential for the functioning of the economy, society and government. Therefore, states that do not have a robust digital infrastructure are vulnerable to threats and technological attacks.[34] All the above informs what is unfolding in the realm of geopolitics and the dynamics of interests among the major powers.

[34] Geopolitical implications of digital technology, in this sense, include the potential for digital technology to be used for propaganda, disinformation, surveillance and control, and to lead to new forms of conflict and warfare (hybrid warfare).

A. Natural Resources, Software and Hardware

The control of the natural resources necessary to develop digital technology is in the hands of few countries in the world. According to Ricart,[35] in 2023 China controlled 36.7 per cent of global rare earth reserves. Brazil and Vietnam, the next countries on the list, together stockpile as much as China does alone (18.3 per cent each). They are followed by Russia, with 10 per cent of the world's total rare metals, and India which detains 5.8 per cent. Furthermore, Ukraine and Russia are the major producers of the gases and heavy metals used to manufacture these products.

Other states, such as the US, have companies that dominate the technological sectors (Apple, Google, Microsoft, Amazon Web Services), as we can observe in Statista's 'Ranking of the 20 leading technology companies in the world in 2022, by brand value (in millions of dollars)'.[36] It is also important to know that, according to the 'Submarine Cable Systems Global Market Report 2023', 97 per cent of global Internet traffic is carried on the submarine cables of a limited number of companies.[37] In this vein, it is relevant to recall the US–China conflict regarding Huawei, ZTE, 5G and TikTok.[38] This technological conflict, which began in 2015, has significantly evolved, driven by economic and political factors. Such a 'technological war' has escalated over time, marked by a series of export control measures imposed by both powers. Under the Biden administration, there has been a strategic shift, with the US aiming to maximise its technological lead over competitors like China through massive incentives, including subsidies and tax benefits.[39] This tactic not only intensifies technological competition but also poses significant challenges for other global players, such as the EU. This approach has created an uneven playing field in the technology arena, where companies like Huawei find

[35] Raquel Jorge Ricart, 'Geopolitical risk: raw materials and technological dependence' (Real Instituto Elcano, 15 March 2023), www.realinstitutoelcano.org/en/blog/geopolitical-risk-raw-materials-and-technological-dependence.

[36] Ranking of the 20 leading technology companies in the world in 2022, by brand value (in millions of dollars), Thomas Alsop, 'Top 20 Technology Brands Worldwide 2023' (Statista, 22 May 2024), www.statista.com/statistics/267966/brand-values-of-the-most-valuable-technology-brands-in-the-world.

[37] Mostly: ZTT, The Okonite Company, TE Connectivity, SubCom, Saudi Ericsson, Prysmian Group, NKT A/S, Nexans SA, NEC Corporation, JDR Cable Systems Ltd., Huawei Marine Networks Co., Ltd., Hexatronic Cables & Interconnect Systems, HENGTONG GROUP CO. Corning Incorporated, Apar Industries, AFL, Alcatel Submarine Networks, Telefonika Kable, Cablel Group, Sumitomo Electric Industries, Norddeutsche Seekabelwerke GmbH, Hesfibel and Leoni Special Cables Gmbh. Companies deploying and owning Internet infrastructure are Google, Microsoft and Facebook (Meta).

[38] TikTok's CEO, Shou Chew, faced over five hours of questioning from lawyers of the House Energy and Commerce Committee, reflecting their distrust of the popular video app over its ties to China, data practices and the app's potential effects on children. David Shepardson and Rami Ayyub, 'TikTok Congressional Hearing: CEO Shou Zi Chew Grilled by US Lawmakers' Reuters (24 March 2023), www.reuters.com/technology/tiktok-ceo-face-tough-questions-support-us-ban-grows-2023-03-23.

[39] The White House, 'President Biden Takes Action to Protect American Workers and Businesses from China's Unfair Trade Practices' Fact sheet (14 May 2024), www.whitehouse.gov/briefing-room/statements-releases/2024/05/14/fact-sheet-president-biden-takes-action-to-protect-american-workers-and-businesses-from-chinas-unfair-trade-practices.

themselves in an increasingly difficult situation to compete on equal terms in the international landscape.[40]

It is clear that the EU advocates for technological humanism and the defence of human rights, establishing a regulatory framework in response to the power confrontations between China and the US. Europe in this sense tries to ally itself with the US when it is in defence of human rights or when it understands that its security is at risk. However, the EU also simultaneously maintains diversification by not closing the door to Chinese companies.[41]

This approach is apparent in a September 2021 report of the Trade and Technology Council (TTC) established by the US and the EU:

> The United States and European Union have significant concerns that authoritarian governments are piloting social scoring systems with an aim to implement social control at scale. These systems pose threats to fundamental freedoms and the rule of law, including through silencing speech, punishing peaceful assembly and other expressive activities, and reinforcing arbitrary or unlawful surveillance systems.[42]

Under the premise that these governments do not respect human rights, and with national security concerns, some states have restricted access to foreign technologies such as AI, 5G, chips, certain software, etc. Therefore, some states develop their own capabilities and try to influence those that are strategic for the development of their technology: both through forms of protectionism/self-sufficiency and strategic alliances (diversification). In other words, this approach has led to self-sufficiency and protectionism in countries such as China and Russia, which are developing their capabilities and seeking to influence strategic areas for their technological development.

In response to the escalating technological–digital tension, the EU decided to pursue a multifaceted solution to establish itself as a significant digital power. Firstly, by spearheading their own initiatives, such as the GAIA-X project, the EU can lead the development of digital infrastructure and services that align with its values and strategic interests. Secondly, the development of a robust regulatory framework is crucial. This includes the implementation and enhancement of regulations that have been previously mentioned like the GDPR, the DSA, DMA and AI Act, among others. These regulations are key to ensuring a secure, fair and competitive digital environment within the EU. Thirdly, the creation of strategic alliances with the US and other democratic states is vital. These alliances would not only bolster the EU's position in the global digital landscape but also facilitate collaboration on shared values and mutual interests in technology and cybersecurity. This comprehensive approach reflects the EU's commitment to shaping a digital future that is secure, equitable and reflective of its principles.

[40] Enrique Feás, 'The US-China Technological War and Its Effects on Europe' (Real Instituto Elcano, 2 February 2023), www.realinstitutoelcano.org/analisis/la-guerra-tecnologica-eeuu-china-y-sus-efectos-sobre-europa.

[41] European Commission, 'Asia-Pacific' (20 November 2024), digital-strategy.ec.europa.eu/en/policies/asia-pacific.

[42] European Commission, 'EU-US Trade and Technology Council Inaugural Joint Statement' (29 September 2021), ec.europa.eu/commission/presscorner/detail/lv/STATEMENT_21_4951.

Nevertheless, the ideal situation for the EU would be to possess their own technologies and capabilities, because this will allow the Union to achieve a status of 'strategic autonomy',[43] and also to diversify partnerships and avoid dependence on any other state, because this would enable it to take 'autonomous technological decisions'.[44] These two concepts – strategic autonomy and the capability of taking autonomous technological decisions – are in fact attributes of digital sovereignty.

B. Digital Wars

In an increasingly digital world, cybersecurity, digital sovereignty and geopolitics are intersecting. Countries that do not take these challenges seriously will find themselves at a strategic disadvantage. The geopolitical landscape is increasingly influenced by the implications of digital technology, as evidenced by several key developments.

One prominent example is the trade war between the US and China, where digital technologies have emerged as a central point of contention. This conflict has highlighted the strategic importance of technological advancements and control over digital infrastructure in global power dynamics. Additionally, there is a mounting concern about cybersecurity, a challenge that transcends national borders, prompting states to collaborate in combating cyber threats. This cooperation reflects a shared recognition of the threats posed by cyber-attacks to national security, economic stability and public safety.

Moreover, the growing regulation of digital technology is another significant aspect, illustrating the divergent interests and values of states. These regulations vary from country to country and are indicative of differing approaches to privacy, data protection, market competition and national security concerns. Each of these examples underscores the profound impact of digital technology on geopolitical relations and the evolving nature of international interactions in the digital age.

Recent developments in the digital technological realm are increasingly coming to the fore, highlighting the growing tensions and their geopolitical implications. Media coverage has been pivotal in bringing these issues to public attention. A notable example is the warning issued by UK's cybersecurity chief regarding China's rapid ascent as a technology superpower,[45] a move that signals growing concerns over China's expanding influence in the tech world. Additionally, Russia's development of computers with their own central processing units (CPUs),[46] as a means to counter Western dominance in technology, is another significant development. The

[43] See n 25.

[44] See nn 20– 25.

[45] Alberto Tejedor, 'La jefa de la ciberseguridad británica da la alerta para frenar el "dramático ascenso de China como superpotencia tecnológica"' (*La Razon*, 18 April 2023), www.larazon.es/internacional/jefa-ciberseguridad-britanica-alerta-frenar-dramatico-ascenso-china-como-first-technological%20superpower_20230418643e3f272f8deb000155ceb6.html.

[46] Juan Carlos López, 'Rusia Ya Tiene Ordenadores Con Sus Propias CPU Para Esquivar a Occidente: Lo Sorprendente Es Quién Se Las Fabrica' (Xataka, 3 March 2023), www.xataka.com/ordenadores/rusia-tiene-ordenadores-sus-propias-cpu-para-esquivar-a-occidente-sorprendente-quien-se-fabrica.

revelation of who is manufacturing these CPUs adds an intriguing layer to this narrative, indicating a strategic shift in Russia's technological independence and resilience.

Furthermore, the US–China chip war has seen new developments, with the Netherlands taking steps to restrict certain exports,[47] a move that underscores the strategic importance of semiconductor technology in global power dynamics. In another development, a US leak has revealed China's efforts in building cyber weapons aimed at hijacking enemy satellites,[48] highlighting the advanced nature of cyber warfare and its potential impact on national security. The threat of cyber-attacks on publicly traded companies has also been a focal point,[49] reflecting the vulnerability of economic institutions to digital threats. In the US, the White House has called upon Big Tech leaders to safeguard the public from the risks associated with AI,[50] emphasising the need for responsible innovation and oversight. Finally, the Biden administration has announced a series of measures to bolster cybersecurity, including the creation of the new Cybersecurity and Infrastructure Security Agency (CISA),[51] a move that reflects the growing prioritisation of cyber defence in national security strategies. These headlines collectively paint a picture of a world grappling with the complex and far-reaching implications of technological–digital advancements.

VII. Conclusion

In light of the evolving nature of sovereignty, it is clear that in the twenty-first century, the concept has become multifaceted, encompassing economic, technological, political and human rights aspects. These elements are interconnected through public relations based on the recognition of public authority at local, state, supranational and international levels. This dynamic involves the creation of control mechanisms through norms, public policies and sanction systems. However, it is crucial that the combination of authority and control ensures the autonomy of communities that voluntarily submit themselves to supranational entities like the EU.

[47] Annabelle Liang, 'US-China Chip War: Netherlands Moves to Restrict Some Tech Exports' (9 March 2023), www.bbc.com/news/business-64897794.

[48] Mehul Srivastava, Felicia Schwartz and Demetri Sevastopulo, 'China Building Cyberweapons to Hijack Enemy Satellites, Says US Leak' (Ars Technica, 21 April 2023), www.ft.com/content/881c941a-c46f-4a40-b8d8-9e5c8a6775ba.

[49] Cyber-attacks on publicly traded companies. For more information see www.fundacionesys.com/wp-content/uploads/2023/03/Policy-Brief-Francisco-Perez-Bes.pdf.

[50] James Clayton and Lucy Hooker, 'White House: Big Tech Bosses Told to Protect Public from AI Risks' BBC (5 May 2023), www.bbc.com/news/business-65489163.

[51] The White House, 'Biden-Harris Administration Announces National Cybersecurity Strategy' Fact sheet (2 March 2023), www.whitehouse.gov/briefing-room/statements-releases/2023/03/02/fact-sheet-biden-harris-administration-announces-national-cybersecurity-strategy.

The central role of state sovereignty is challenged by opposing forces such as globalisation, internationalisation and the influence of private powers. This tension, which undermines state efficacy, suggests that supranational responses might be viable. Individually, states lack the capacity to address and control challenges posed by globalisation and digitalisation, leading to the partial cession of sovereignty to institutions like the EU. This has led to supranational harmonisation efforts, initially focused on the protection of telecommunications infrastructures, and later expanding to the safeguard fundamental rights like personal data protection and freedom of expression in the Internet age, aiming for a form of digital humanism led by the EU.

Digital sovereignty, defined as the capacity to control one's digital space, has led the EU to address concerns such as the lack of a unified European cyberspace, external influences, overdependence on single equipment providers, cyber-attacks, data control, reliance on non-EU data, and the spread of disinformation. In response, the Union has implemented a cybersecurity policy through legislative, funding and coordination measures aligned with the EU Cybersecurity Strategy for the Digital Decade.

In this context, cybersecurity emerges as a vital component in geopolitical competition. The rapid evolution of digital technology significantly impacts the global economy, society and politics, creating key geopolitical implications. The competition between states for technological leadership becomes a prominent political consequence, as those with robust technology sectors gain competitive advantages, develop new technologies, and attract foreign investments. Additionally, states' growing dependency on digital technology, essential for the economy, society and government, presents another crucial geopolitical implication. States without solid digital infrastructure become vulnerable to technological threats and attacks, highlighting the strategic importance of digital capacity.

Examples of digital technology's geopolitical implications include: the US–China trade war; growing concerns over cybersecurity, leading to state cooperation against cyber threats, like police and intelligence agencies' collaboration in the Ukraine conflict; EU-level disinformation campaigns; and increasing regulation of digital technology, reflecting different states' interests and values.

The EU advocates for technological humanism and human rights defence, establishing a normative framework in response to power confrontations between China and the US. Europe seeks alliances with the US in situations involving human rights defence or perceived security threats. In response to technological and digital tensions, the EU's solution involves creating a European digital power, further developing the regulatory framework, and creating more strategic alliances with democratic states. Ideally, Europe should have its technologies and capacities, avoiding exclusive dependence on any state, thus securing 'autonomy in technological decision-making'. In conclusion, the concepts of strategic autonomy and autonomous technological decision-making are indeed the main attributes of European digital sovereignty.

5

Digital Sovereignty in the Euro-Mediterranean Region: Protection and Competition in an Interconnected World

MAURO SANTANIELLO

I. Introduction

One of the most recent evolutions in the digital governance space is the diffusion of digital sovereignty as a policy principle, ie as a principle that conveys political intentions, beliefs and values to policymakers, and provides the whole policy process with general guidance. Once the prerogative of authoritarian regimes aiming at gaining power and authority over Internet governance both at the global and the domestic levels,[1] the principle of digital sovereignty has recently also seeped into the policy discourse and practice of democratic institutions. Particularly in the European Union (EU) and its Member States, digital sovereignty has become a crucial concern of political leaders and public officials over the last few years, and has inspired a set of strategies, policies and proposals for regulations, including the Digital Services Act (DSA),[2] the Digital Markets Act (DMA),[3]

[1] See Jack L Goldsmith and Tim Wu, *Who Controls the Internet? Illusions of a Borderless World* (Oxford University Press, 2006), and Milton Mueller, *Networks and States: The Global Politics of Internet Governance* (MIT Press, 2010).

[2] Regulation (EU) 2022/2065 of the European Parliament and of the Council of 19 October 2022 on a Single Market For Digital Services and amending Directive 2000/31/EC (Digital Services Act) OJ L 277.

[3] Regulation (EU) 2022/1925 of the European Parliament and of the Council of 14 September 2022 on contestable and fair markets in the digital sector and amending Directives (EU) 2019/1937 and (EU) 2020/1828 (Digital Markets Act) OJ L 265.

the Artificial Intelligence Act (AIA),[4] the EU Chips Act[5] and the Cyber Solidarity Act (CSA).[6]

The principle of digital sovereignty has also been used, with various meanings and aims, in several other regions of the world at different governance levels, spanning from national authorities to intergovernmental organisations, from policymakers acting at the municipal level to transnational digital corporations, from global civil society associations to academics and think tanks. However, despite the widespread use of the principle of digital sovereignty in policy circles and in public debates, there is no common definition, nor a shared understanding, of what constitutes sovereignty in the digital ecosystem. As put by Lambach and Oppermann, the protean nature of digital sovereignty 'is not a bug, but a feature', and it has contributed to its diffusion.[7]

The main objective of this research is to probe into the social processes through which different meanings of digital sovereignty are elaborated by different actors, how they are used, and how they interact with particular contexts and political conditions. The object of investigation is the interplay between the production of digital sovereignty claims and the position of the claimant within contingent power relations, both inside and beyond the state. In order to do so, this chapter: (a) elaborates an analytical framework to study digital sovereignty claims, drawing on the combination of available literature on the topic with constructivist theories of sovereignty; and (b) employs this framework to study the policy discourse around digital sovereignty in a wide and heterogeneous geographical area, ie the Euro-Mediterranean region. Section II presents a literature review on digital sovereignty in order to highlight knowledge gaps that this study intends to fill. Subsequently, the chapter delineates the theoretical framework adopted to conceptualise and frame digital sovereignty. Particularly, section III identifies three attributes of digital sovereignty as a policy principle: adversariality; multiversality; and latency. In section IV, methodology, data and results of the analysis are presented, and findings are discussed in light of the theoretical perspective. Section V concludes with a reflection on the limitations of the study and introduces potential avenues for future research, along with a few concluding remarks.

[4] *Proposal for a Regulation of the European Parliament and of the Council laying down Harmonised Rules on Artificial Intelligence (Artificial Intelligence Act) and amending certain Union Legislative Acts*, COM/2021/206 final ('Harmonised Rules on Artificial Intelligence').

[5] Regulation (EU) 2023/1781 of the European Parliament and of the Council of 13 September 2023 establishing a framework of measures for strengthening Europe's semiconductor ecosystem and amending Regulation (EU) 2021/694 (Chips Act), OJ L 229.

[6] *Proposal for a Regulation of the European Parliament and of the Council laying down measures to strengthen solidarity and capacities in the Union to detect, prepare for and respond to cybersecurity threats and incidents*, COM(2023) 209 final ('Proposal').

[7] Daniel Lambach and Kai Oppermann, 'Narratives of Digital Sovereignty in German Political Discourse' (2022) 36 *Governance* 693.

II. The Horizontal Dimension of Digital Sovereignty

This section discusses the main approaches to the study of digital sovereignty, mapping the key themes, perspectives and findings that have emerged from this growing body of analysis. The literature review highlights several underlying trends. Firstly, while theoretical studies on digital sovereignty often adopt a positivist perspective on their research object, a constructivist approach is dominant in empirical research on digital sovereignty. Secondly, there is a growing interest in the principle of digital sovereignty as formulated and implemented in the EU. Thirdly, and most importantly, there is a strong research focus on digital sovereignty in the major world powers of the Global North and on their inter-state relationships, which is referred to here as the horizontal dimension of digital sovereignty.

Theoretical studies on the relationship between state sovereignty and the Internet appeared in the late 1990s.[8] These works have focused on the emergence of new sovereignties in the digital space, and on their relationship with fundamental elements of traditional sovereignty, such as jurisdiction, territoriality and the performance of public functions. More recently, on the same line, Floridi has discussed 'the emergence of a sort of de facto digital corporate sovereignty' over the last two decades, and has advanced the idea of a 'modern-analogue sovereignty' that needs to be complemented by a 'contemporary-digital sovereignty'.[9] Pasquale, reasoning on digital platforms providing public functions, has noted a 'shift from territorial to functional sovereignty [that] is creating a new digital political economy', and has argued that only political institutions can prevent functional (digital) sovereignties from 'further undermining the territorial governance at the heart of democracy'.[10]

Celeste instead has made the point that digital sovereignty may be exercised by state actors without any reference to the territory. Indeed, the EU General Data Protection Regulation, the US Cloud Act and the Chinese 2017 law on national intelligence are examples of extra-territorial sovereignty that 'demonstrate how nation states found alternative ways to exercise their sovereign power, which are not primarily based on the concept of territory'.[11] In line with this reasoning,

[8] See for example James Boyle, 'Foucault in Cyberspace: Surveillance, Sovereignty, and Hardwired Censors' (1997) 66 *University of Cincinnati Law Review* 177; Jack L Goldsmith, 'The Internet and the Abiding Significance of Territorial Sovereignty' (1998) 5 *Indiana Journal of Global Legal Studies* 475; Henry H Jr Perritt, 'The Internet as a Threat to Sovereignty? Thoughts on the Internet's Role in Strengthening National and Global Governance' (1998) 5 *Indiana Journal of Global Legal Studies* 423; Saskia Sassen, 'On the Internet and Sovereignty' (1998) 5 *Indiana Journal of Global Legal Studies* 545.

[9] Luciano Floridi, 'The Fight for Digital Sovereignty: What It Is, and Why It Matters, Especially for the EU' (2020) 33 *Philosophy & Technology* 369.

[10] Frank Pasquale, 'From Territorial to Functional Sovereignty: The Case of Amazon' LPE Project (16 June 2017), lpeproject.org/blog/from-territorial-to-functional-sovereignty-the-case-of-amazon.

[11] Edoardo Celeste, 'Digital Sovereignty in the EU: Challenges and Future Perspectives' in Federico Fabbrini, Edoardo Celeste and John Quinn (eds), *Data Protection Beyond Borders: Transatlantic Perspectives on Extraterritoriality and Sovereignty* (Hart Publishing, 2021) 5.

Ruohonen has highlighted that digital sovereignty, like the often misinterpreted Westphalian sovereignty, has much more to do with state capacity and balance of power than with just territorial sovereignty.[12] On the contrary, Mueller has embedded the issue of territorial sovereignty at the core of his theory of the 'sovereign alignment', which describes governmental efforts to align Internet connectivity with 'the institutions and boundaries of the nation-state'.[13] This approach has been borrowed by Stadnik in her assessment of Internet sovereignty in Russia.[14] Similarly, the analysis of cyber sovereignty in China has highlighted the role of territorialisation as a crucial goal of numerous domestic measures and policies over the past years aimed to enhance governmental capabilities to realise sovereignty.[15]

On a more empirical level, a growing number of researchers are investigating how the principle of sovereignty is adopted and elaborated by multiple actors in the digital governance space. The vast majority of these researchers have inscribed their studies within a constructivist approach, following the 'linguistic turn' in the study of sovereignties advocated by Werner and de Wilde in 2001.[16] This approach is based on the idea that sovereignty is not an object with well-defined attributes. Rather, it is a speech act aimed at legitimising the exercise of power by a specific claimant. As such, it develops in multiple forms as a tangle of various discursive practices. Within this approach, for example, Couture and Toupin have mapped out five categories of discourse on sovereignty in the digital space, which highlight 'the diverse perspectives associated with the notion of "digital sovereignty", and bring to the fore some of the key actors and issues that pertain to each'.[17] Similarly, Pohle and Thiel have identified three discourses on digital sovereignty – states, companies or individuals – according to the subjects for whom digital self-determination is claimed.[18] Hummel, Braun, Tretter and Dabrock have relied on agents, context and values to identify a long list of different understandings of sovereignty in the digital space.[19] Thumfart has highlighted that this multiplicity of

[12] Jukka Ruohonen, 'The Treachery of Images in the Digital Sovereignty Debate' (2021) 31 *Minds and Machines* 439. See also Stephen D Krasner, *Sovereignty: Organized Hypocrisy* (Princeton University Press, 1999).

[13] Milton Mueller, *Will the Internet Fragment?: Sovereignty, Globalization and Cyberspace* (Polity, 2017) 70.

[14] Ilona Stadnik, 'Russia. An Independent and Sovereign Internet?' in Blayne Haggart, Natasha Tusikov and Jan Aart Scholte (eds), *Power and Authority in Internet Governance. Return of the State?* (Routledge, 2021).

[15] Rogier Creemers, 'China's Approach to Cyber Sovereignty' (Konrad Adenauer Stiftung 2020), www.kas.de/en/single-title/-/content/china-s-approach-to-cyber-sovereignty. See also Jinghan Zeng, Tim Stevens and Yaru Chen, 'China's Solution to Global Cyber Governance: Unpacking the Domestic Discourse of "Internet Sovereignty": China's Solution To Cyber Governance' (2017) 45 *Politics & Policy* 432.

[16] Wouter G Werner and Jaap H De Wilde, 'The Endurance of Sovereignty' (2001) 7 *European Journal of International Relations* 283.

[17] Stephane Couture and Sophie Toupin, 'What Does the Notion of "Sovereignty" Mean When Referring to the Digital?' (2019) 21 *New Media & Society* 6.

[18] Julia Pohle and Thorsten Thiel, 'Digital Sovereignty' (2020) 9 *Internet Policy Review*, policyreview.info/concepts/digital-sovereignty.

[19] Patrik Hummel et al, 'Data Sovereignty: A Review' (2021) 8 *Big Data & Society*.

conceptualisations of digital sovereignty implies that 'their meaning changes with the traditions they come from, the contexts in which they are used and the power-relations inherent to those contexts'.[20]

Another common feature of empirical research on digital sovereignty is that it assumes the nation-state as the only unit of analysis. Even when focusing on supranational organisations, like the EU, or on transnational corporations, these organisations are treated as states, compared with other states, or interpreted through state-centric categories. Additionally, empirical analyses tend to concentrate on major powers, mainly China, Russia and, more recently, the EU. This branch of literature includes case studies, comparative analyses and research on international relations among these players.[21] In the case of China, Jiang has shown how the Chinese Government has been successful in using the concept of 'Internet sovereignty' to legitimate its 'authoritarian informationalism', ie 'an Internet development and regulatory model that combines elements of capitalism, authoritarianism, and Confucianism'.[22] Through a discourse analysis of Chinese academic literature, policy documents and public debates, McKune and Ahmed have found that the Chinese Government has developed 'an Internet sovereignty agenda at home and abroad'.[23] Domestically, this agenda has worked to legitimise regime control over the digital experience of the Chinese population. At the international level, the concept of Internet sovereignty has been used to advance a new normative model of global Internet governance based on traditional notions of sovereignty and jurisdiction, supposedly serving the interests of the developing world. Similarly, Hong and Goodnight have demonstrated how the Chinese cyber sovereignty discourses and practices are marked by the tension between global interdependence and national interests. Their analysis of statements retrieved from the website of the Cyberspace Administration of China (CAC) has testified a double-purpose project of the party state: 'to project outwards ideational and material influences and to seek inward-looking power consolidation through techno-economic and ideological steering'.[24] Budnitsky and Jia have showed how the Chinese and Russian Governments, since the early 2000s, have consolidated a sort of cyber alliance in order to 'co-advance the brand narrative of "Internet sovereignty" in opposition to perceived technological and governance hegemony of the United States', and how they have involved their respective business sector (the digital champions) in this endeavour.[25]

[20] Johannes Thumfart, 'The COVID-Crisis as Catalyst for the Norm Development of Digital Sovereignty. Building Barriers or Improving Digital Policies?' 5, www.ssrn.com/abstract=3793530.

[21] See Alvarez Robles in this volume.

[22] Min Jiang, 'Authoritarian Informationalism: China's Approach to Internet Sovereignty' (2010) 30 *SAIS Review* 71, 82.

[23] Sarah Mckune and Shazeda Ahmed, 'The Contestation and Shaping of Cyber Norms Through China's Internet Sovereignty Agenda' (2018) 21 *International Journal of Communication* 3835.

[24] Yu Hong and Thomas G Goodnight, 'How to Think about Cyber Sovereignty: The Case of China' (11 October 2019) 91, ssrn.com/abstract=3467933 or dx.doi.org/10.2139/ssrn.3467933.

[25] Stanislav Budnitsky and Lianrui Jia, 'Branding Internet Sovereignty: Digital Media and the Chinese–Russian Cyberalliance' (2018) 21 *European Journal of Cultural Studies* 594. See also Alexander Gabuev,

Instead, Chin and Li have proposed a comparative analysis of the cyber sovereignty discourse in China and the EU.[26] They have found that, notwithstanding these two great powers share some propositions on the sovereignty of cyberspace due to the common challenges they are facing (cybersecurity, lack of international rules for data flows and the US hegemony), there are fundamental differences between the two approaches. The Chinese one is externally oriented towards a multilateral model relying on intergovernmental cooperation, and internally towards the protection of national security and economic development. On the contrary, the European approach is supportive of the multi-stakeholder model at the international level, which confers policy authority to the private sector rather than governments, and is internally focused on citizens' rights and the bloc's economic interests.

Interesting case studies on Russia are also abundant. For example, Bieniek has argued that the Russian conceptualisation of digital sovereignty shows some specificities compared with Western countries, and that these specificities are rooted in geopolitical and cultural factors that forge the Russian national identity as something distinctive from both the West and the East.[27] Litvinenko has analysed the Russian strategic narrative on Internet sovereignty, whose key elements are control over data flows and infrastructure, and the promotion of a Russian model of global Internet governance.[28] The author has also identified the determinants of this particular strategic narrative, including domestic politics, economic factors, international relations and the specific architectural development of the Internet in the country. The work by Kolozaridi and Muravyov, instead, have reduced the importance of the peculiarities of the Russian contemporary political regime in defining the meanings and the goals of Internet sovereignty in the country. The authors have maintained

> that sovereignty claims are both a reaction to Western-centred Internet governance frameworks, and a reaction to the technology that compels the state to act as a modern state. Both explanations appeal to processes of statecraft, rather than to the results of a particular political regime's policies.[29]

Many of the recent case studies on digital sovereignty are focused on the EU. Pohle, for example, analysing the debate on digital sovereignty in Germany and Europe, has found three main dimensions of the discourse: the governmental; the

'Digital Bromance: The Sino-Russian Partnership Racing Ahead' Carnegie Endowment for International Peace (7 December 2015), carnegiemoscow.org/publications/?fa=62253.

[26] Yik Chan Chin and Ke Li, 'A Comparative Analysis of Cyber Sovereignty Policies in China and the EU' (2021) TPRC49: The 49th Research Conference on Communication, Information and Internet Policy, ssrn.com/abstract=3900752 or dx.doi.org/10.2139/ssrn.3900752.

[27] Otylia Bieniek, 'The Specificity of the So-Called Digital Sovereignty in Russia on the Example of the Russian Segment of the Internet – the RuNet.' (2022) 13 *Public Administration and Security Studies* 235.

[28] Anna Litvinenko, 'Re-Defining Borders Online: Russia's Strategic Narrative on Internet Sovereignty' (2021) 9 *Media and Communication* 5.

[29] Polina Kolozaridi and Dmitry Muravyov, 'Contextualizing Sovereignty: A Critical Review of Competing Explanations of the Internet Governance in the (so-Called) Russian Case' (2021) 26 *First Monday* 13.

economic; and the individual dimensions. The author has also linked the emergence of this multifaceted discourse with three factors, 'including the powerful and central position of a handful of companies, the paradoxical response of democratic states to surveillance revelations, and the search for an alternative normative framework that provides an alternative to the US and Chinese models'.[30] Drawing on the same constructivist approach, Lambach and Oppermann have found

> seven narratives of digital sovereignty in German political discourse: the economic prosperity narrative, the security narrative, the 'European way of life' narrative, the narrative of the modern state, the data protection narrative, the consumer protection narrative and the democratic empowerment narrative.[31]

Moerel and Timmers have detected three main EU conceptual approaches to digital sovereignty: risk management to face cybersecurity issues; strategic cooperation of like-minded parties to face increasing geopolitical tensions and reducing dependence on foreign technology and supplies; and the global common good, which goes beyond the national interest.[32] Framing the European digital sovereignty discourse within the EU quest for global competition vis-a-vis the other great powers, Broeders, Cristiano and Kaminska have identified a process of 'geopoliticisation of EU digital policies', which consists of both the use of trade, competition and foreign policies to exert geopolitical influence, and 'a new generation of intentionally hybrid digital policies in which internal market concerns, fundamental rights concerns and geopolitical concerns are all present, such as the AI-Act and the DSA/DMA'.[33] Furthermore, Burwell and Propp have situated the rising discourse on digital sovereignty in Europe within the context of geopolitical transformations, with EU initiatives mainly 'intended to counter the strong position of US and Chinese digital companies in the European market'.[34] Similarly, Monsees and Lambach have contextualised European digital sovereignty within new geopolitical imaginaries and the attempt to build a new identity for the EU.[35] Farrand and Carrapico have focused on digital sovereignty in the European cybersecurity field, where it manifests the EU's 'desire to "take back control" of the governance of cyberspace and an assertion of its willingness to protect its digital borders from outside competition'.[36]

[30] Julia Pohle, 'Digital Sovereignty – A New Key Concept of Digital Policy in Germany and Europe' (Konrad Adenauer Stiftung, 2020), www.kas.de/en/single-title/-/content/digital-sovereignty.

[31] Lambach and Oppermann (n 7) 6.

[32] Lokke Moerel and Paul Timmers, 'Reflections on Digital Sovereignty' (EU Cyber Direct, 2021).

[33] Dennis Broeders, Fabio Cristiano and Monica Kaminska, 'In Search of Digital Sovereignty and Strategic Autonomy: Normative Power Europe to the Test of Its Geopolitical Ambitions' (2023) 61 *Journal of Common Market Studies* 1261.

[34] Frances G Burwell and Kenneth Propp, 'The European Union and the Search for Digital Sovereignty: Building "Fortress Europe" or Preparing for a New World?' Issue brief (Atlantic Council, June 2020).

[35] Linda Monsees and Daniel Lambach, 'Digital Sovereignty, Geopolitical Imaginaries, and the Reproduction of European Identity' (2022) 31 *European Security* 377.

[36] Benjamin Farrand and Helena Carrapico, 'Digital Sovereignty and Taking Back Control: From Regulatory Capitalism to Regulatory Mercantilism in EU Cybersecurity' (2022) 31 *European Security* 435.

The authors have found that in this field the EU is changing its governance model, with a shift from regulatory capitalism, in which business actors play coregulatory functions no matter of their provenience, toward regulatory mercantilism where only the domestic private sector is considered a trustworthy regulatory partner, while foreign companies are seen more as a threat rather than as a part of the solution in cybersecurity policies. Bendiek and Stürzer have described two directions of European digital sovereignty. One aims at 'externalising European norms by regulating access to the internal market', the other at 'deepening European integration by providing [member States with] guidance on digital challenges'.[37] The authors, just like Burwell and Propp,[38] have also assessed the possible impact of these directions on transatlantic cooperation.

One can clearly detect a horizontal dimension in the research on digital sovereignty, which unfolds along East–West relations at the northern altitudes of global politics. This study, while adopting a discursive approach to analysing digital sovereignty like the vast majority of recent research on the topic, seeks to shift the axis of research, and to explore the interplay among different meanings of digital sovereignty along a north–south route. In the next section of this chapter, theories deployed to analyse discursive practices of digital sovereignty, as discussed in this section, will be combined with the concept of fragmented sovereignty advanced by Kalmo and Skinner.[39] This integration will support the elaboration of an analytical framework marking out the main features of (digital) sovereignty claims, thus providing conceptual orientation for the subsequent empirical analysis.

III. Fragments of (Digital) Sovereignty

A positivist approach to digital sovereignty – looking for the classic features of state sovereignty in the digital space – has the Peace of Westphalia as its historical, and tangible, reference point. As a consequence, this approach tends to overestimate the provisions established by those two treaties,[40] to magnify the dominant contemporary meaning attributed to their texts, and to reify their substance.[41] This study moves

[37] Annegret Bendiek and Isabella Stürzer, 'Advancing European Internal and External Digital Sovereignty. The Brussels Effect and the EU-US Trade and Technology Council' (Stiftung Wissenschaft und Politik, 2022) SWP Comment 2022/C 20, www.swp-berlin.org/publications/products/comments/2022C20_EuropeanDigitalSovereignty.pdf.

[38] Burwell and Propp (n 34).

[39] Hent Kalmo and Quentin Skinner, 'Introduction: A Concept in Fragments' in Hent Kalmo and Quentin Skinner (eds), *Sovereignty in Fragments. The Past, Present and Future of a Contested Concept* (Cambridge University Press, 2011).

[40] The Peace of Westphalia consists of two different treaties, the Peace Treaty of Osnabrück (Instrumentum pacis Osnabrugensis) and the Peace Treaty of Münster (Instrumentum Pacis Monasteriensis).

[41] For a more general criticism of; the Westphalian myth' see Pärtel Piirimäe, 'The Westphalian Myth and the Idea of External Sovereignty' in Hent Kalmo and Quentin Skinner (eds), *Sovereignty in Fragments. The Past, Present and Future of a Contested Concept* (Cambridge University Press, 2011).

from a different historical perspective, which assumes as its focal point not the Peace (of Westphalia), but the war that led to that peace. In other words, instead of looking at the formalised outcome of a long era of armed conflicts, it might be more productive to refer to the use of sovereignty as a discursive resource within those struggles that ultimately ended up with the establishment of the Westphalian system. This choice is supported by the fact that, dealing with digital sovereignty, it is clear that we are not at the end of the conflict, when one, or a few, allied understandings of sovereignty succeed in establishing an ultimate meaning, in such an ordered way that that meaning itself can become an uncontested principle with tangible features and fixed practices. The current situation has much more in common with the Thirty Years War (1618–1648) and the broader period of the European wars of religion (1562–1648), when sovereignty was a concept in use by multiple actors in war against each other. This approach leads us to think about current conflicts and ongoing discursive tussles, to analyse different and contradictory discourses on digital sovereignty as a proxy to understand contemporary political struggles within and beyond cyberspace.

From this perspective, a theoretical contribution is provided by the concept of sovereignty in fragments, developed by Kalmo and Skinner in order to advance a 'pluralist view of sovereignty to capture the contemporary fragmentation of authority',[42] and to 'dispel the illusion that there is a single agreed-upon concept of sovereignty for which one could offer a clear definition'.[43] In line with much of the literature we have already discussed, Kalmo and Skinner maintain that 'sovereignty is not a property that can be analysed in the abstract, separating it from the multiple discursive contexts in which it has been invoked'.[44] They conceive sovereignty as an argumentative resource, as a claim to authority, as 'a multilayered semantic sediment from an accumulation of arguments'.[45] They also stress the fact that this plurality of sovereignty arguments is embedded 'in a rich (but particular) historical setting',[46] and this implies that it is always entrenched in contemporary political conflicts. The authors cite in this regard an enlightening passage from Foucault, where the thinker illustrates how

> at the time of the Wars of Religion, the theory of sovereignty … became a weapon that was in circulation on both sides, and it was both to restrict and to strengthen royal power. You find it in the hands of Catholic monarchists and Protestant antimonarchists; you also find it in the hands of Catholics who advocate regicide or a change of dynasty. You find [the juridico-political] theory of sovereignty being brought into play by aristocrats and *parlamentaires*, by the representatives of royal power and by the last feudalists. It was, in a word, the great instrument of the political and theoretical struggles that took place around systems of power in the sixteenth and seventeenth centuries.[47]

[42] Kalmo and Skinner (n 39) 15.
[43] ibid 5.
[44] ibid.
[45] ibid 11.
[46] ibid.
[47] ibid 8.

If sovereignty is not an object with well-defined attributes, but rather a claim, or a speech act, which is performed by an actor involved in political struggles, then it is possible to investigate the attributes of the claims in order to study these conflicts. Based on our arguments, three attributes of sovereignty claims – in general, and not only with reference to digital sovereignty – can be identified. The first one is *adversariality*. Claiming sovereignty is always an action against someone else. It is explicitly or implicitly an adversarial speech act because it is part of a conflict. As a consequence, in sovereignty speech acts we can always identify one or more adversaries of the speaker, which are brought into the discourse by the means of contradictions (from the latin *contradīcĕre*, composite of 'contra' and 'dicere'; literally 'signify against'). Adversariality as a feature of sovereignty claims is also evident in results from empirical analyses on digital sovereignty in the EU, where 'the US and China are the main actors against which Europe formulates its agenda of digital sovereignty and thereby its identity'.[48] The same evidence comes from the analysis of digital sovereignty in Russia and China, where the dominance of the US Government and American companies, both in terms of normative frameworks and market shares, are perceived as a national security threat.[49]

The second attribute of sovereignty claims is *multiversality*. Since each sovereignty claim aims at legitimising an action – or better – a direction of action, and given the plural and fragmented nature of sovereignty, the sovereignty discourse in a given context typically unfolds along multiple and contradictory directions. Further, since each actor usually pursues multiple aims at the same time, it is not quaint that its own sovereignty claims are contradictory to each other. Multiversality as a feature of sovereignty claims is testified by much of the current literature on digital sovereignty. Pohle, for example, has noted that 'the different dimensions of digital sovereignty often seem to compete against each other'.[50] Lambach and Oppermann argue that digital sovereignty claims 'can be used to justify a multiplicity of policies … and that participants in the debate often switch back and forth between different meanings to suit their particular needs'.[51] The authors make this point even more explicit: 'single texts may well, and often do, include facets of different narratives of digital sovereignty'.[52] Similarly, Ruohonen notes that sovereignty as a concept evolves 'to all directions'.[53]

The third attribute of sovereignty is *latency*. This means that some parts of a sovereignty claim, such as the adversary or the direction, can be hidden or omitted due to particular circumstances or interests, but they still represent an implicit constitutive part of the claim. More importantly, this also means that an entire discourse on sovereignty can be latent, in the sense that it is formally missing, but

[48] Monsees and Lambach (n 35) 378; see also Broeders, Cristiano and Kaminska (n 33), Burwell and Propp (n 34), Farrand and Carrapico (n 36).

[49] Hong and Goodnight (n 24), Budnitsky and Jia (n 25), Chan Chin and Li (n 26).

[50] Pohle (n 30) 19.

[51] Lambach and Oppermann (n 7) 695.

[52] ibid 697.

[53] Ruohonen (n 12) 444.

performatively effective. Indeed, as argued by Werner and de Wilde, 'situations that are closest to the robustness of substantial sovereignty, ie "effective" control over a population on a given territory, "true" political independence and "factual" economic autonomy, are those in which a sovereignty discourse is absent'.[54] In other words, as put by Couture and Toupin, 'it is where authority is weak that the sovereignty discourse appears more strongly'.[55]

This would explain why a discourse on digital sovereignty in the US has never been fully developed. Since American companies and the US Government already have the capacity to exercise sovereignty in the digital world – the argument goes – they don't need to claim digital sovereignty at all. We could say that it is the anti-sovereign, rather than the sovereign, that produces sovereignty as a discourse. And that, as a corollary, it is not the US hegemony that has triggered the emergence of digital sovereignty claims. Rather, from a Gramscian perspective that conceives of hegemony as a form of uncontested power, the digital sovereignty discourse is the breaking point of that hegemony, the point where the US dominion in the digital space comes to be contested. In other words, hegemony is when sovereignty is muted. Finally, latency can also refer to the fact that the same actor can be used to claim sovereignty in one context while not in another, and this difference is meaningful for the analysis too.

Adversariality, multiversality and latency are the attributes of sovereignty claims that will be taken into account in the following empirical analysis of the policy discourse on digital sovereignty in the Euro-mediterranean region, a wide and heterogeneous area crossed by multiple conflicts of authority and conflicting understandings of sovereignty.

IV. Digital Sovereignty in the Euro-Mediterranean Region

This chapter aims to understand how the digital sovereignty principle is formulated and adopted in the Euro-mediterranean region, a geographical area comprising Europe and the Mediterranean Basin.[56] The choice of the Euro-mediterranean region, though unusual in digital sovereignty research, serves two of the aims of this study. The first one is, as already explained, to rotate the axis of research on digital sovereignty, adopting a north–south, vertical perspective on sovereignty instead of a horizontal one to put to the test its plural, controversial and contradictory nature. The second one is that in the Mediterranean area digital sovereignty is only the latest episode of a centuries-old confrontation on sovereignty that has

[54] Werner and de Wilde (n 16).
[55] Couture and Toupin (n 17) 6.
[56] The interconnectedness of this region has led to the establishment of an intergovernmental organisation like the Union for the Mediterranean (UfM), and of several Euro-Mediterranean partnerships (EUROMED) in different policy fields.

forged the relationships between Europe, Africa and the Middle East. Thus, it appears to be fitting the purpose to place the principle of digital sovereignty 'in a rich (but particular) historical setting', and to analyse it as a part of a concrete 'multilayered semantic sediment from an accumulation of arguments'.[57]

Research questions of this study include: who uses the principle of digital sovereignty in the area? Against whom? Towards which directions? When does this principle manifest and when is it latent? Why? Operationally, the research has unfolded through three steps. Firstly, 150 strategic documents in three fields of digital policy – ie digital transformation, data and AI policy, and cybersecurity – drafted by EU's bodies and Member States, by governments of Mediterranean countries, and by intergovernmental organisations working in the area, have been collected and scrutinised. Secondly, 39 documents with an explicit reference to the principle of digital sovereignty have been selected (11 AI and data strategies, 12 digital transformation strategies, 16 cybersecurity strategies), and their claims of digital sovereignty have been qualitatively analysed, according to their adversaries, their directions and their latency. In the third step, results and their interpretations have been triangulated with eight expert interviews, held between June and December 2022 with interviewees from intergovernmental organisations, national authorities, civil society and the private sector.

On a very general level, findings testify that the policy discourse on digital sovereignty in the region is mainly a European discourse. Only five non-EU entities have used the principle in their digital strategies, for a total of nine documents. The Lebanese Government has used it in all three kinds of digital strategies: in the 2019 national artificial intelligence strategy,[58] in the 2019 national cybersecurity strategy[59] and in the 2022 digital transformation strategy.[60] The Government of Turkey has used the principle in the 2020 national artificial intelligence strategy,[61] while Jordan[62] and Morocco[63] refer to 'sovereign capabilities' in their respective cybersecurity strategies. Also, the Commission of the African Union has used the principle in its digital transformation strategy[64] and its data policy framework.[65]

None of the other regional organisations taken into consideration for this study has any kind of reference to digital sovereignty.[66] On the contrary, the EU Commission has systematically used the principle in all its recent digital strategies. For example, digital sovereignty has been used in the EU strategies on digital

[57] cf Broeders, Cristiano and Kaminska (n 33) 11.
[58] Republic of Lebanon, National Artificial Intelligence Strategy in Lebanese Industry 2020–2050 (2019).
[59] Republic of Lebanon, Lebanon National Cyber Security Strategy (2019).
[60] Republic of Lebanon, Lebanon Digital Transformation National Strategy (2022).
[61] Republic of Turkey, National Artificial Intelligence Strategy 2021–2025 (2021).
[62] Government of Jordan, National Cyber Security Strategy 2018–2023 (2018).
[63] Kingdom of Morocco, Strategie Nationale En Matiere De Cybersecurite (2013).
[64] African Union, Digital Transformation Strategy For Africa 2020–2030 (2020).
[65] African Union, Data Policy Framework (2022).
[66] The list of scrutinised documents includes strategies by the United Nations Economic and Social Commission for Western Asia (ESCWA), the Organisation of Islamic Cooperation, the Arab League, the Community of Sahel–Saharan States, the Arab Maghreb Union, the Euro-Mediterranean Partnership (EMP), the Union for the Mediterranean (UfM), and the Euro-Arab Dialogue.

transformation, ie the Digital Compass,[67] 'Shaping Europe's Digital Future'[68] and the strategy on global standards.[69] The Commission has also used the principle in its proposal for an Artificial Intelligence Act advanced in 2021,[70] and in its proposal for a Cyber Solidarity Act issued in 2023.[71] Also, the European Parliament and the Council have used the principle of digital sovereignty in the Digital Decade Policy Programme 2030 co-drafted in 2022.[72] Among the EU Member States, the principle of digital sovereignty has been used in the Austrian, Bulgarian, French, German and Portuguese strategies on digital transformation. It has also been employed in the French, Finnish, German, Dutch, Slovenian, Spanish and Hungarian strategies on data and AI. Finally, it has been variously referred to in the Austrian, Belgian, French, German, Italian, Portuguese, Slovakian, Spanish and Hungarian cybersecurity strategies. The German and the French cases stand out among the EU Member States for the pervasiveness of the principle in all the three kinds of digital strategies.

A. Protective Digital Sovereignty

More detailed analysis of the policy documents suggests that there are two policy principles of digital sovereignty in use in the Euro-Mediterranean region: protective and competitive.

Table 5.1 Principles of digital sovereignty

	Protective Principle	**Competitive Principle**
Posture	Reactive	Proactive
General aim	To shield the state from the Internet	To shape the Internet by the state
Adversaries	Hostile actors Digitalisation itself	Platforms Cyber powers
Directions	Territorialisation Weaponisation	Standardisation Regulation Championisation
Scope	National	Regional

[67] Communication from the Commission to the European Parliament, the Council, the European Economic and Social Committee and the Committee of the Regions. 2030, *Digital Compass: the European way for the Digital Decade*, COM(2021) 118 final.

[68] European Commission, Shaping Europe's Digital Future (2020), commission.europa.eu/system/files/2020-02/communication-shaping-europes-digital-future-feb2020_en_4.pdf.

[69] Communication from the Commission to the European Parliament, the Council, the European Economic and Social Committee and the Committee of the Regions, *An EU Strategy on Standardisation. Setting global standards in support of a resilient, green and digital EU single market*, COM(2022) 31 final.

[70] Harmonised Rules on Artificial Intelligence (n 4).

[71] Proposal (n 6).

[72] Decision (EE) 2022/2481 of the European Parliament and of the Council of 14 December 2022 establishing the Digital Decade Policy Programme 2030.

As visualised in Table 5.1, the protective principle expresses a reactive posture to the development of digital technologies and is aimed at protecting state sovereignty from either malicious external actors or the (often undefined) challenges of digitalisation. A clear formulation of this principle is in the Hungarian cybersecurity strategy of 2013, which

> aims at developing a free and secure cyberspace and protecting national sovereignty in the national and international context, which has undergone a significant change due to the emergence of cyberspace … The protection of Hungary's sovereignty in the Hungarian cyberspace is a national interest.[73]

The principle is also very clear in the African Union Data Policy Framework of 2022:

> To exert control of data to safeguard sovereignty requires both infrastructure and law, but also the technical capacity to do so in a manner that can build trust. … Member States, AUC, RECs, African Institutions and International Organisations shall cooperate to create capacity to enable African countries to self-manage their data, take advantage of data flows and govern data appropriately.[74]

This approach, which mainly focuses on national sovereignty, is common in cybersecurity strategies, and is present both in European documents and in other countries' and organisations' strategies. Two main directions of action seem to be legitimised by this kind of discourse. The first is territorialisation, in the form of data localisation. This prevents the data produced by citizens, the government and companies of a country from flowing abroad and being stored outside the national territory. An example of claims with this direction is provided by the Turkish AI strategy of 2021:

> The development of artificial intelligence technologies and the collection of large-scale data that usually belong to citizens of different countries, cause tensions between big technology companies and countries that own the data, leading to discussions on digital sovereignty.[75]

Other examples are in the digital transformation strategies of the African Union, which claim 'respect for data sovereignty' and envisage the need of 'localization of all personal data of Africa's citizens'.[76] Similarly, the digital transformation strategy of Portugal states that 'information and data security and sovereignty are critical requirements from the outset, which can limit the adoption and type of cloud services',[77] while the digital transformation strategy of Lebanon declares 'that all servers and data centers in Lebanon to be under Lebanon's sovereignty and official institutions only'.[78]

[73] Government of Hungary, Government Decision No 1139/2013 (21 March) on the National Cyber Security Strategy of Hungary (2013) 2.
[74] African Union (n 65) 15, 19.
[75] Republic of Turkey (n 61) 15.
[76] African Union (n 64).
[77] Republic of Portugal, Portugal's Action Plan for Digital Transition (2020) 45.
[78] Republic of Lebanon (n 60) 75.

The second main direction of the protective principle of digital sovereignty as detected in the area is weaponisation. Weaponistion means protecting national sovereignty through the development of cyber capabilities – ie skills, software, devices and vulnerabilities – that enable a state both to defend and attack a digital asset. Examples of this direction are numerous in national cybersecurity strategies. The Austrian strategy, for example, aims at 'coordinating measures to protect sovereignty in the framework of military national defence (cyber defence)'.[79] The Moroccan strategy 'encourages the development of national solutions in the field of cybersecurity'.[80] The French strategy states that 'the answer to this issue of sovereignty requires first and foremost the maintenance of a strong and competitive national and European industry in the specialised field of cybersecurity products and services'.[81] Finally, the Jordan cybersecurity strategy aims at 'establishing the means to develop sustainable sovereign capabilities and corporate entities that can deliver effective cyber security initiatives'.[82]

B. Competitive Digital Sovereignty

The second type of digital sovereignty principle detected by this analysis is a competitive principle. While the protective principle aims to shield the state from the Internet, the competitive principle has a more proactive posture, and aims at shaping the Internet by the state. In other words, the goal is no longer to protect state sovereignty from the negative impacts of digital technologies or from hostile action in cyberspace; rather, it is to take the lead in technological development in order to shape the latter according to one's own interests and values. This competitive principle understands digital sovereignty in terms of strategic autonomy and technological leadership, rather than autarky and ownership. Rather than hostile and malicious actors, digital sovereignty claims are addressed, in this case, against foreign dominant entities, especially private digital platforms and those states that are perceived as dominant cyber powers. A clear formulation of this principle is in the EU Commission's proposal for an Artificial Intelligence Act:

> A solid European regulatory framework for trustworthy AI will also ensure a level playing field and protect all people, while strengthening Europe's competitiveness and industrial basis in AI. Only common action at Union level can also protect the Union's digital sovereignty and leverage its tools and regulatory powers to shape global rules and standards.[83]

[79] Republic of Austria, Austrian Cyber Security Strategy (2013) 11.
[80] Kingdom of Morocco (n 63).
[81] French Republic, French National Digital Security Strategy (2015) 30.
[82] Government of Jordan (n 62) 12.
[83] Harmonised Rules on Artificial Intelligence (n 4) 6.

Another example of this principle is in the 2019 AI strategy of the Netherlands, which warns that 'a "winner-takes-all" or "winner-takes-most" dynamic can arise, with a real chance that the Netherlands will become dependent on other parties. That could potentially damage our economic security, our autonomy and our well-being'.[84] Another instance is provided by the German digital transformation strategy of 2022:

> Technological and digital sovereignty is indispensable if we want to strengthen our capability to act and reduce dependencies. This in turn is essential for competitiveness and innovative capacity as well as resilience. Accordingly, in order to achieve technological and digital sovereignty, we are aiming to promote innovation in a targeted manner, improve expertise in key technologies such as software development and microchips, sensors, artificial intelligence, quantum computing, communication technologies, roll out an advanced digital infrastructure, systematically promote open-source approaches as well as establishing the regulatory framework.[85]

The directions outlined by competitive claims of digital sovereignty are not oriented towards the protection of the nation state, but rather towards the projection of the state's power onto a scenario characterised by increasing global competition. Three main directions can be identified. The first one is standardisation, as exemplified in this EU Commission's formulation from the 2022 global strategy on standards:

> Europe's competitiveness, technological sovereignty, ability to reduce dependencies and protection of EU values, including our social and environmental ambitions, will depend on how successful European actors are in standardisation at international level.[86]

The second direction is regulation, which aims at setting the conditions for technological development by subjecting it to legal requirements. An example of this kind of claims is in the Spanish 2020 artificial intelligence national strategy:

> For Spain to exercise sovereign, effective control over this technological revolution, the appropriate framework for action must be created. … This regulatory framework will allow us to gain global competitiveness and at the same time support European digital sovereignty.[87]

The third direction could be called 'championisation'; that is, the aim to set new conditions for technological development by the means of innovation. This is an advanced version of the neo-mercantilist aim to replace foreign providers of vital technologies with domestic solutions. Here the aim is not to replace foreign technologies, but to develop new technologies that can compete with – and hopefully outcompete – foreign companies. This is clear, for example, in the EU Digital

[84] Government of The Netherlands, Strategic Action Plan for Artificial Intelligence (2019) 10.
[85] Federal Government of Germany, Digital Strategy – Creating Digital Values Together (2022) 2.
[86] See n 69, 1.
[87] Government of Spain, National Strategy for Artificial Intelligence (2020) 65–66.

Decade Policy Programme 2030, where the EU Parliament and the Council set the objective of

> ensuring the Union's digital sovereignty in an open manner, in particular by secure and accessible digital and data infrastructures capable of efficiently storing, transmitting and processing vast volumes of data that enable other technological developments, supporting the competitiveness and sustainability of the Union's industry and economy, in particular of SMEs, and the resilience of the Union's value chains, as well as fostering the start-up ecosystem and the smooth functioning of the European digital innovation hubs.[88]

Another clear formulation of this aim is in the EU Digital Compass of 2023:

> That is the way for Europe to be digitally sovereign in an interconnected world by building and deploying technological capabilities in a way that empowers people and businesses to seize the potential of the digital transformation.[89]

C. Supranational Digital Sovereignty: An EU Feature

It is worth noting that, while protective digital sovereignty is a principle shared by non-EU players in the area, the competitive principle of digital sovereignty seems to be exclusively used by EU institutions and Member States. The only traces of competitive digital sovereignty outside the EU can be found in the African Union's claims for 'politically neutral partnerships' and for 'a digital sovereignty fund'. Indeed, these are attempts to set new conditions for the digital development of Africa. Their aim is to free the continent from other-directed political orientations of technological development. And they are particularly interesting because of their implicit adversary. Considering that EU's southern neighbourhood policy has traditionally conditioned developmental aids and investments in Africa to the accomplishment of political reforms from the side of African partners, a digital sovereignty claim directed to legitimise politically neutral partnerships means the will of the African Union to renegotiate digital partnerships with the EU, detaching them from those commitments towards democratisation and human rights protection that the EU has been used to demand. However, a competitive principle is not fully developed in the African Union's documents, since these initiatives are still discursively framed within a protective approach, with a reactive posture, mainly oriented towards data localisation and territorialisation measures.

The competitive approach to digital sovereignty is a European approach not only because it is embraced only by EU institutions and Member States. It is so also because all the national strategies adopting this kind of principle contextualise it within European strategies, stressing the fact that no individual Member State can face alone the challenges of global competition, and that only a regional initiative

[88] Government of Hungary (n 73) Art 3(1)(c).
[89] European Commission (n 6 7) 1.

can have success.[90] From this point of view, while the protective principle of digital sovereignty was referring to national sovereignty, the competitive principle refers to a sort of *supranational* sovereignty, which fits very well the purposes and the identity of the EU.

These findings suggest that the 'gap of authority', ie the hypothesis that a weak authority produces a strong (digital) sovereignty discourse, needs to be complemented. While it can explain the emergence of a protective principle of digital sovereignty, it is not sufficient for accounting the rise of competitive digital sovereignty. The latter seems to be possible under other conditions. One could be the presence of a sufficient level of state capacity at the supranational level. However, previous studies and empirical evidence suggest that the principle is not formulated in relation to any feasibility assessment, and it is not affected by operational failures, like in the case of the Gaia-X project, or by unattainable objectives, like the European ones on semiconductors market shares.[91] Existing literature rather supports an ideational explanation, which highlights the role of a strong regional political identity. As put by Monsees and Lambach, 'digital sovereignty projects, despite being full of contradictions and tensions, contribute to a distinct EU identity of an agile, future-oriented global player in the digitised economy'.[92] This is a dimension that clearly lacks in the case of the African Union. However, further empirical research is needed to identify the factors that have produced the competitive principle of digital sovereignty as a trait of the EU, and to explain the role of regional political identity. A study on the use of the principle of digital sovereignty by non-state actors in the area could add further insight to this kind of investigation.

In conclusion, it is worth noting that the discourse on digital sovereignty is not free from contradictions and frictions. This feature, which in the theoretical section of this paper has been defined as 'multiversity', is particularly clear in the French case. Despite the fact that, as we have seen, the French Government has been a precursor – and an evangelist – of the European discourse on digital sovereignty, its 2017 digital transformation strategy advances an opposite perspective on digital sovereignty:

> Authoritarian states, eager to assert their digital sovereignty over the world, seek to control the networks, at the expense of the openness that underlies them and at the expense of fundamental rights.[93]

In this case, digital sovereignty is depicted as a claim of authoritarian states rather than a legitimate aspiration of all countries, including the democratic ones. Contradictions, as we have said, occur also within the same text – sometimes even

[90] See Bertrand in this volume.
[91] See Pandit, Perez and Celeste in this volume.
[92] See Monsees and Lambach (n 35) 377. See also Ruohonen (n 12), Moerel and Timmers (n 32).
[93] Gouvernement de France, Stratégie internationale de la France pour le numérique (2017) 4.

in the same paragraph. The Finnish 2021 AI strategy, for example, juxtaposes two phrases with opposing directions:

> The EU's industrial and innovation policy has strengthened the objective of open strategic autonomy and technological sovereignty. Finnish policy has emphasised technological neutrality, meaning that policy guidance does not extend to technological choices.[94]

Finally, there are also claims that deny the adversarial nature of digital sovereignty, like the EU 2020 document 'Shaping Europe's Digital Future', where one can read: 'European technological sovereignty is not defined against anyone else, but by focusing on the needs of Europeans and of the European social model.'[95]

V. Conclusions

The study of digital sovereignty in a wide and heterogeneous area like the Euro-Mediterranean region has helped to sharpen our understanding of this increasingly important policy principle. It has contributed to better focus its controversial and contradictory nature, and to observe how it is formulated in a historically and politically rich context. It has also shown there are at least two different principles of digital sovereignty in the area. The protective principle is a widely shared principle, which legitimises territorialisation and weaponisation measures and as such goes hand in hand with securitisation of digital policies. Its formulations and goals are consistent with the functions and the identity of nation-states, and is fed by the perception of an authority gap. The competitive principle, instead, is a specific EU principle in the area. It is a principle of regional sovereignty, which seems to require a regional capacity and, especially, a regional political identity to be formulated, as it pursues the goals of geopolitical competition. This is a kind of digital sovereignty that goes beyond territorialisation. The competitive principle legitimises a set of policy instruments – regulations, standardisation and championisation – that imply the involvement of very different actors – legislative bodies, technical communities and business sector – who act, or at least aim to act, beyond the territorial boundaries of the nation-state.

The chapter has also highlighted that the formulation and adoption of digital sovereignty principles are embedded within contingent power relations, and as such they may have multiple – also unexpected – consequences. For the EU this means that embracing digital sovereignty does not impact only on Atlantic relations. Rather, it has consequences also on its southern partnerships. Indeed, if partners like the African Union stay on the path of elaborating their own

[94] Government of Finland, Suomesta voittaja kaksoisiirtymässä – tavoitteista käytäntöön (2021) 12.
[95] European Commission (n 68) 3.

competitive principle of digital sovereignty, effective digital partnerships in the area may become unsustainable. Formulations like 'politically neutral partnership', if implemented in a way that seeks to leverage the expansion of Chinese and Russian interests in the African continent in order to detach foreign investments and aids from commitments towards democratisation and human rights protection, may bring to the forth a kind of digital sovereignty that is incompatible with the European one, which has in democratic values and principles its fundamental source of legitimacy. In other words, in its quest for digital sovereignty, the EU should look to the south, as well as to the west and to the east. It is this ability to combine and accommodate different meanings of (digital) sovereignty that will prove to be an asset for EU digital partnerships in the region, rather than the simplistic orchestration of business activities in the name of a new European *raison d'état* like some think tanks seem to suggest.

In order to better understand these processes and their consequences, research should be done with a scope that goes beyond the Mediterranean area, and that includes other areas of Africa (especially the Sahel region), Asia (especially the Middle East), and more in general the Global South. A research agenda able to map and connect the different kinds of digital sovereignties, with their respective forms of adversariality, multiversality and latency, is a much needed step towards a better understanding of ongoing transformations in the global digital governance space.

PART II

Reconciling Digital Sovereignty and the Green Transition

6

Sustainable Digital Sovereignty? Environmental Impact of EU Tech Strategies

EDOARDO CELESTE AND ALBA PEREZ VICTORIO

I. Introduction

The promises associated with digital technologies are manyfold. The 2030 Digital Compass does not only deem them 'imperative' for any professional and educational activities, entertainment and social interactions, the retail sector and for accessing a wide range of services and experiences,[1] but also claims that they will contribute to a 'healthier and greener society'.[2] It is indeed expected that digitalisation will help achieve the European Union (EU) sustainability goals set out in the European Green Deal. The so-called 'digitally enabled green solutions' shall thus play a key role in the transition towards a climate neutral, resource-efficient economy and society.[3] However, despite the EU's intention of linking its digital strategy with its sustainability objectives, one can criticise in practice lack of a coherent, effective and 'twin transitions' policy with a sufficient level of awareness of its global implications.[4]

Indeed, for the promises made by the EU to be fulfilled, the balanced impact of digital technologies on the environment shall be positive, not only in Europe but at the global level. Relying on the digital for a greener society is inherently complex since, although digital technologies may enhance resource efficiency, trace circular economy processes and enable sustainable design, they are also energy intensive.

[1] European Commission, Communication from the Commission to the European Parliament, the Council, the European Economic and Social Committee, and the Committee of the Regions, *2030 Digital Compass: the European way for the Digital Decade 2021*, COM(2021) 118 final, 1.

[2] ibid 1.

[3] See, eg, ibid 3; European Commission, *2022 Strategic Foresight Report – Twinning the Green and Digital Transitions in the New Geopolitical Context*, COM(2022) 289 Final, 3.

[4] *cf* European Commission (n 3); Edoardo Celeste and Goran Dominioni, 'Digital and Green: Reconciling the EU Twin Transitions in Times of War and Energy Crisis' in Federico Fabbrini and Christy Anne Petit (eds), *Research Handbook on Post-Pandemic EU Economic Governance & NGEU Law* (Edward Elgar, 2024).

This challenge has been acknowledged by the Commission,[5] but how the EU digital strategy will implement effective policies to overcome this issue is yet to be determined.

Moreover, while the policy emphasis on twinning the green and the digital transitions is strong, in this chapter we argue that it is not equally clear how the recent focus of the EU digital strategy in achieving a status of strategic independence from third countries may be compatible with the goals of the Green Deal. As illustrated by the contributors to part one of this volume, the concept of digital or technological sovereignty has not received a rigid, univocal definition at EU level.[6] Yet, it is possible to reconduct it to the idea of achieving a strategic independence from foreign actors in the digital field and regaining control on the components of digitalisation process. As we will explain in this chapter, this not only consists in trying to extend EU standards beyond its borders, but also encourages the strengthening of a digital industry made in the EU. While the first solution does not seem to negatively affect the environment, the second one de facto implies the creation almost *ex nihilo* of an EU digital sector through the reshoring of critical components of the digitalisation process from third countries. The ecological footprint of what in this chapter we will define the 'centripetal' approach of EU digital sovereignty strategies is more significant. The EU is 'duplicating' global digitalisation efforts, leading to higher energy and water consumption, higher exploitation of raw materials and waste generation, with a significant impact not only in the EU, but also at the global level.

This chapter thus aims to examine the environmental impact of EU technological strategies, ultimately challenging the idea that the Union is concretely envisaging a really sustainable form of digital sovereignty, in particular, by neglecting the consequences of digital policies beyond its borders. We start in section II by tracing the genealogy of the digitalisation and green strategy in the EU, explaining to what extent they are currently considered as two 'twin' policies. We then focus in section III on EU technology strategies, analysing how digital sovereignty has recently become a guiding principle in the context of a broader EU quest for strategic autonomy from third countries. Despite not being univocally defined, we illustrate how digital sovereignty strategies concretely take a 'centripetal' or a 'centrifugal' approach. Section IV constitutes the core contribution of our chapter, analysing the environmental impact of EU technological policies as oriented by the EU objective of achieving a status of digital sovereignty. We identify the generation of a rebound effect as the symptom of a 'digital insularity' attitude, where the EU still conceives the

[5] European Commission (n 3) 2-3.

[6] See also Edoardo Celeste, 'Digital Sovereignty in the EU: Challenges and Future Perspectives' in Federico Fabbrini, Edoardo Celeste and John Quinn (eds), *Data Protection Beyond Borders: Transatlantic Perspectives on Extraterritoriality and Sovereignty* (Hart, 2021).

digital and green transitions as two siloed policies in terms of effects. We finally introduce the concept of 'environmental sovereignism' to denote the adoption of a 'Europe first' attitude in setting twin transition strategies, which de facto neglects the impact of EU policies beyond its borders. Finally, section V concludes by presenting the theoretical alternative of starting to pursue a more digitally 'sober' approach.

II. Digital and Green: From Siloed Policies to a Tandem Vision

A. Digitalisation with the Human at the Centre

The emergence of the digital field as a top priority of the EU can be traced back to the 1990s. In 1993, the EU Commission adopted the White Paper 'Growth, Competitiveness, Employment – The Challenges and Way Forward into the 21st Century' (the 'Delors White Paper'), in which it identified the emergence of a European 'information society'.[7] The 'dawn of the multimedia world', where digital technologies enable fast transmission of texts, images and sounds, provided unprecedented opportunities to individuals, considered both as consumers and as citizens, in terms of the availability and customisability of products and accessibility to public services.[8] In 1994, the Bangemann Group Report to the European Council proposed a series of strategies to help the European information society thrive in the global context.[9] Liberalisation of the telecommunication sector, major investments in Internet infrastructures, attention to digital education, the development of harmonised regulatory frameworks in the fields of intellectual property, privacy, online security and media ownership, as well as fostering research and development of new technologies, were among the key recommendations in the action plan of the High-Level Group that drafted the Report. Following these guidelines, the EU Commission adopted its first two action plans in 1994 and 1996.[10]

1999 saw the introduction of the e-Europe Action Plan, which aimed to enhance the digitalisation of the life of citizens, schools, public administrations and businesses; boost digital literacy; and increase consumer trust and ensure social

[7] European Commission, White Paper, *Growth, Competitiveness, Employment – The Challenges and Way Forward into the 21st Century*, COM(1993) 700.

[8] ibid 22.

[9] High-Level Group on the Information Society, 'Europe and the global information society. Recommendations to the European Council' (26 May 1994). The High-Level Group took the name from the then EU Commissioner for Industry, Telecommunications, and Information Technology Martin Bangemann.

[10] European Commission, *Europe's Way to the Information Society. An Action Plan*, COM(1994) 347 final; European Commission, *Europe at the Forefront of the Global Information Society: Rolling Action Plan*, COM(1996) 607.

inclusiveness and cohesion.[11] The plan was further endorsed in the Lisbon European Council meeting of March 2020, which set its ambition to make the EU a leading 'knowledge-based' economy,[12] and further complemented by follow up plans in 2001, 2002 and 2005.[13] These policy instruments led to adoption of key regulatory instruments, which laid the foundations of EU digital law, such as the Data Protection Directive, the e-Commerce Directive and the Copyright Directive.[14]

In the aftermath of the 2007–2008 global financial crisis, the EU Commission launched its new Europe 2020 Strategy.[15] Digitalisation represented one of its seven flagship initiatives, leading to the adoption of a comprehensive policy strategy named 'A Digital Agenda for Europe',[16] further detailed in 2015 by the Digital Single Market Strategy.[17] The first EU digital agenda identified seven key areas of intervention: the digital internal market; interoperability and standards; trust and security; fast Internet access; research and innovation; digital literacy and skills; and digital technology benefits for the EU society, including for the environment. Data regulation was certainly one of the distinctive features of the EU digital agenda 2010–2020. Indeed, this decade saw the repealing of the first Data Protection Directive of 1995 with the General Data Protection Regulation (GDPR),[18] the adoption of a directive to protect personal data in the context of law enforcement,[19] a regulation on the free flow of non-personal data,[20] a recast directive on open data and the re-use of public sector information,[21] a directive on

[11] European Commission, *eEurope – An information society for all*, COM(1999) 687 final.

[12] European Council, 'Lisbon European Council 23 and 24 March 2000: Presidency Conclusions', www.europarl.europa.eu/summits/lis1_en.htm#:~:text=PRESIDENCY%20CONCLUSIONS&text=The%20European%20Council%20held%20a,of%20a%20knowledge%2Dbased%20economy.

[13] European Commission, *eEurope 2002: Impact and Priorities A communication to the Spring European Council in Stockholm, 23–24 March 2001*, COM(2001) 140 final; European Commission, *eEurope 2005: An information society for all – An Action Plan to be presented in view of the Sevilla European Council, 21/22 June 2002*, COM(2002) 263 final; *European Commission, i2010 – A European Information Society for growth and employment*, COM(2005) 229 final.

[14] Respectively, Directive 95/46/EC; Directive 2000/31/EC and Directive 2001/29/EC.

[15] European Commission, *Europe 2020: A strategy for smart, sustainable and inclusive growth*, COM(2010) 2020 final.

[16] European Commission, *A Digital Agenda for Europe*, COM(2010) 245 final.

[17] European Commission, *A Digital Single Market Strategy for Europe*, COM(2015) 192.

[18] Regulation (EU) 2016/679 of the European Parliament and of the Council of 27 April 2016 on the protection of natural persons with regard to the processing of personal data and on the free movement of such data, and repealing Directive 95/46/EC.

[19] Directive (EU) 2016/680 of the European Parliament and of the Council of 27 April 2016 on the protection of natural persons with regard to the processing of personal data by competent authorities for the purposes of the prevention, investigation, detection or prosecution of criminal offences or the execution of criminal penalties, and on the free movement of such data, and repealing Council Framework Decision 2008/977/JHA.

[20] Regulation (EU) 2018/1807 of the European Parliament and of the Council of 14 November 2018 on a framework for the free flow of non-personal data in the European Union.

[21] Directive (EU) 2019/1024 of the European Parliament and of the Council of 20 June 2019 on open data and the re-use of public sector information. This directive recast rules in this field following the substantial amendments of Directive 2003/98/EC.

security of network and information systems,[22] and a regulation confirming the role of the EU cybersecurity agency ENISA.[23]

In 2020, the Commission introduced a new policy document to define the objectives of the 'Digital Decade' (2020–2030),[24] further complemented by the communications 'Forging Europe's digital future',[25] 'Europe's digital decade'[26] and 'EU Digital Compass'.[27] These documents present digital technology as having to play a double function: on the one hand, it seeks to boost the efficiency of the internal market, while, on the other hand, it contributes to affirm the EU as a standard-setter in the digital field at global level. The Commission introduced the image of the 'digital compass' to identify the four cardinal points of the EU digitalisation strategy, namely the enhancement of digital skills among the European population, the digitalisation of businesses and the public sector, and the improvement of digital infrastructures. The last few years have seen a new wave of intense legislative activity in the digital field – a phenomenon dubbed as 'actification' by legal scholars – which led to the adoption of seminal normative instruments, mostly in the form of regulations.[28] The list is quite extensive; however, examples include the Data Governance Act on the reuse of publicly held data,[29] a new directive on network and information systems,[30] the Digital Services Act on content moderation by digital platforms,[31] the Digital Markets Act to ensure more competition in the digital single market,[32] and the AI Act, which represents the first

[22] Directive (EU) 2016/1148 of the European Parliament and of the Council of 6 July 2016 concerning measures for a high common level of security of network and information systems across the Union.

[23] Regulation (EU) 2019/881 of the European Parliament and of the Council of 17 April 2019 on ENISA (the European Union Agency for Cybersecurity) and on information and communications technology cybersecurity certification and repealing Regulation (EU) No 526/2013 (Cybersecurity Act).

[24] European Commission, 2030 Policy Programme, *Path to the Digital Decade*, COM(2021) 574 final, para 3.

[25] European Commission. Directorate General for Communications Networks, Content and Technology, 'Shaping Europe's Digital Future' (Publications Office, 2020), data.europa.eu/doi/10.2759/091014.

[26] European Commission (n 13).

[27] European Commission (n 1).

[28] Vagelis Papakonstantinou and Paul De Hert, 'The Regulation of Digital Technologies in the EU: The Law-Making Phenomena of "Act-Ification", "GDPR Mimesis" and "EU Law Brutality"' (2022) *Technology and Regulation* 48.

[29] Regulation (EU) 2022/868 of the European Parliament and of the Council of 30 May 2022 on European data governance and amending Regulation (EU) 2018/1724 (Data Governance Act).

[30] Directive (EU) 2022/2555 of the European Parliament and of the Council of 14 December 2022 on measures for a high common level of cybersecurity across the Union, amending Regulation (EU) No 910/2014 and Directive (EU) 2018/1972, and repealing Directive (EU) 2016/1148 (NIS 2 Directive).

[31] Regulation (EU) 2022/2065 of the European Parliament and of the Council of 19 October 2022 on a Single Market For Digital Services and amending Directive 2000/31/EC (Digital Services Act).

[32] Regulation (EU) 2022/1925 of the European Parliament and of the Council of 14 September 2022 on contestable and fair markets in the digital sector and amending Directives (EU) 2019/1937 and (EU) 2020/1828 (Digital Markets Act).

comprehensive regulatory instrument at global level aiming to govern the development and use of AI systems.[33]

B. From Carbon Emissions Targets to a Just Transition

In 2019, the EU Commission adopted its first green transition comprehensive strategy in a communication entitled 'The European Green Deal'.[34] Enhancing the level of sustainability and contrasting climate change are presented as common objectives that should inform all EU key policy actions. Four are the core directions pursued by the Green Deal: carbon emissions reduction, sustainable energy and mobility, sustainable and circular economy, and just transition.

In terms of carbon emission reduction, the European Climate Law entered into force in 2021 as a legally binding regulation requiring all Member States to reduce by 55 per cent their 1990 carbon emissions levels by 2030 and achieve carbon neutrality by 2050.[35] The Commission further specified the strategy to achieve these objectives in a communication that detailed the so-called Fit for 55 package – '55' representing the percentage of carbon reduction targeted by the EU – a series of legislative reforms focusing on all the key economic sectors.[36] The package included the reform of the EU Emission Trading System (ETS), the cap-and-trade mechanism introduced in 2005 to reduce carbon emissions, with the aim to further lower the overall caps and include new sectors, such as aviation and maritime transport.[37] All the Fit for 55 legislative proposals were adopted by November 2023.[38]

In the field of sustainable energy and transportation, in 2022 the Commission launched the REPowerEU Plan to decrease EU dependency from Russian gas following the start of the Ukrainian war.[39] Also boosted by this development, in 2023 the EU revised the Renewable Energy Directive 2018 seeking to enhance the percentage of renewable energy by 2030,[40] and adopted the Energy Efficiency Directive, which established stricter standards in terms of energy efficiency for

[33] Regulation (EU) 2024/1689 of the European Parliament and of the Council of 13 June 2024 laying down harmonised rules on artificial intelligence and amending Regulations (EC) No 300/2008, (EU) No 167/2013, (EU) No 168/2013, (EU) 2018/858, (EU) 2018/1139 and (EU) 2019/2144 and Directives 2014/90/EU, (EU) 2016/797 and (EU) 2020/1828 (Artificial Intelligence Act).

[34] EU Commission, *The European Green Deal*, COM/2019/640 final.

[35] Regulation (EU) 2021/1119 establishing the framework for achieving climate neutrality and amending Regulations (EC) No 401/2009 and (EU) 2018/1999 (European Climate Law).

[36] European Commission, *'Fit for 55': Delivering the EU's 2030 Climate Target on the Way to Climate Neutrality*, COM(2021) 550 Final.

[37] For more details see Celeste and Dominioni (n 4).

[38] See the timeline at commission.europa.eu/strategy-and-policy/priorities-2019-2024/european-green-deal_en.

[39] European Commission, *REPowerEU Plan*, COM(2022) 230 final.

[40] Directive (EU) 2023/2413 of the European Parliament and of the Council of 18 October 2023 amending Directive (EU) 2018/2001, Regulation (EU) 2018/1999 and Directive 98/70/EC as regards the promotion of energy from renewable sources, and repealing Council Directive (EU) 2015/652.

buildings, appliances and various industry sectors.[41] The Sustainable and Smart Mobility Strategy was presented in 2020.[42] Its objective is to achieve a 90 per cent emission reduction by 2050, boost the production and use of carbon neutral vehicles, and enhance the quality of the European rail network.

Similarly, the Commission introduced three strategies in the area of sustainable and circular economy: the Circular Economy Action Plan, aiming to reduce waste and promote reuse and recycling;[43] the Sustainable Finance Strategy, which seeks to foster private investments in sustainability actions;[44] and the Farm to Fork Strategy, which contributes to limit the environmental impact of the food system.[45]

All these changes have repercussions on the social texture, reason for which the Commission has focused its recent work also on establishing a Just Transition Fund[46] to compensate individuals whose life and jobs had to change following the climate change mitigation measures adopted by the EU, as well as on increasing public participation, social dialogue and skills development.[47]

C. Twinning Digital and Green

Following the COVID-19 pandemic, 2020 saw the adoption of the Next Generation EU (NGEU) Plan: not a further policy strategy, but rather a new mechanism to boost the EU economy following the slowdown dictated by the global spread of coronavirus.[48] NGEU is an unprecedented instrument that provides further funding to core EU policies in order to fill the gap generated by the pandemic and make the EU system more resilient. The Recovery and Resilience Facility (RFF) is the financial engine of NGEU: the motto of the initiative – 'for a greener, more digital

Directive (EU) 2018/2001 at its turn recast the first Renewable Energy Directive (Directive 2009/28/EC).

[41] Directive (EU) 2023/1791 of the European Parliament and of the Council of 13 September 2023 on energy efficiency and amending Regulation (EU) 2023/955 (recast). The first directive on energy efficiency was Directive 2012/27/EU, subsequently amended by Directive (EU) 2018/2002.

[42] European Commission, *Sustainable and Smart Mobility Strategy – putting European transport on track for the future*, COM(2020) 789 final.

[43] European Commission, *A new Circular Economy Action Plan. For a cleaner and more competitive Europe*, COM(2020) 98 final. The first circular economy package was adopted in 2015: see European Commission, *Closing the loop – An EU action plan for the Circular Economy*, COM(2015) 614 final.

[44] European Commission, *Strategy for Financing the Transition to a Sustainable Economy*, COM(2021) 390 final.

[45] European Commission, *A Farm to Fork Strategy for a fair, healthy and environmentally-friendly food system*, COM/2020/381 final.

[46] Regulation (EU) 2021/1056 of the European Parliament and of the Council of 24 June 2021 establishing the Just Transition Fund.

[47] European Commission, *Strengthening social dialogue in the European Union: harnessing its full potential for managing fair transitions*, COM(2023) 40 final; European Commission, *European Skills Agenda for sustainable competitiveness, social fairness and resilience*, COM(2020) 274 final; European Commission, *Conference on the Future of Europe: Putting Vision into Concrete Action*, COM(2022) 343 final.

[48] See Federico Fabbrini, 'The Legal Architecture of the Economic Responses to COVID-19: EMU beyond the Pandemic' (2022) 60 *Journal of Common Market Studies* 186.

and more resilient EU' – well exemplifies the priorities of this plan.[49] Digitalisation and green transition are presented as two transversal policy objectives informing all areas of intervention, from the economy to health and education.[50]

In 2022, the EU Commission published its annual Strategic Foresight Report on the relationship between green and digital transformation, building on a more comprehensive study carried out by the Joint Research Centre.[51] This document marked the official coupling of digitalisation and green transformation in the EU, as these two policies were mostly developed separately beforehand.[52] The report indeed analyses the promises and challenges of 'twinning' climate change mitigation strategies and the digital transformation amidst the complex geopolitical scenario following the Russian invasion of Ukraine and its consequent economic effects in Europe. It is recognised that a comprehensive and contextual analysis of these two parallel transitions is needed, due to their intrinsic 'geopolitical nature'.[53] The different factors pushing for the digital and green transitions are recognised, but the document stresses the need to analyse in more depth how these two policy areas can be 'twinned', in the sense of enhancing the possibility of 'reinforcing' each other.[54] In particular, 10 key areas of intervention are identified.[55]

The main benefits identified by the Commission in deploying digital technologies in the context of the green transition are related to their monitoring, forecasting, reporting and simulating capacity. Digital technologies can help to monitor resource and energy use in a variety of sectors. This element generally enhances efficiency, decreasing environmental impact and contributing to the implementation of a more circular economy. In particular, AI systems processing big sets of data have the potential to produce forecasts and increase efficiency in a broad array of sectors, from smart grids to smart cities.[56] The capability of digital technology to process data and generate reports can foster public participation in innovation and decision-making.[57] Technologies,

[49] European Commission, Directorate General for Economic and Financial Affairs, 'Quantifying Spillovers of next Generation EU Investment' (Publications Office, 2021), data.europa.eu/doi/10.2765/80561.

[50] European Commission, *Review report on the implementation of the Recovery and Resilience Facility* COM(2022) 383 final.

[51] European Commission (n 3); see also European Commission, Joint Research Centre, 'Towards a Green & Digital Future: Key Requirements for Successful Twin Transitions in the European Union' (Publications Office, 2022), data.europa.eu/doi/10.2760/977331.

[52] Celeste and Dominioni (n 4).

[53] European Commission (n 3) 1.

[54] ibid 1.

[55] ibid 12 ff.

[56] See Rajan Jose et al, 'Artificial Intelligence-Driven Circular Economy as a Key Enabler for Sustainable Energy Management' (2020) 2 *Materials Circular Economy* 8; Matthew Wilson, Jeannette Paschen and Leyland Pitt, 'The Circular Economy Meets Artificial Intelligence (AI): Understanding the Opportunities of AI for Reverse Logistics' (2021) 33 *Management of Environmental Quality: An International Journal* 9.

[57] See Joeri Naus, Bas JM Van Vliet and Astrid Hendriksen, 'Households as Change Agents in a Dutch Smart Energy Transition: On Power, Privacy and Participation' (2015) 9 *Energy Research & Social Science* 125; Cuihong Zhang, Ning Liu and Maoling Yuan, 'More Is Better? Stakeholder

such as digital twins – which are 'digital representations' of real products or processes[58] – and quantum computing – new computing systems relying on quantum physics[59] – can generate simulations to design more efficient and sustainable solutions.

At the same time, embedding green objectives into the EU digitalisation strategy first of all means limiting energy consumption and improving its efficiency. Indeed, the current use of digital devices and services has a significant impact on energy consumption, especially if one considers the high energy consumption of data centres and blockchain mining.[60] Furthermore, it also foresees an overall increase in energy use due to technological developments.[61] Secondly, greening digital technologies also implies reducing their environmental footprint in the phases before and after their use. Manufacturing digital devices requires the exploitation of rare metals with a considerable environmental impact associated with mining.[62] Data centres require a significant use of water for cooling off.[63] Moreover, digital development generates problems in relation to waste management.[64]

Finally, twinning the digital and green transitions cannot succeed without a proper societal transformation. Bertrand significantly speaks of the challenges of a 'triple' transition, as digitalisation and climate change mitigation unavoidably impact society.[65] First of all, in terms of employment, by threatening the existence of some types of profession and creating new ones. Secondly, in terms of education, as new technologies and greener solutions require a series of skills. The EU Commission too is aware of this challenge, pledging in its 2022 Strategic Foresight report that 'the twin transitions will be fair or will not be'.[66]

Participation in Regulatory Rule-Setting towards Green Transition' (2024) 349 *Journal of Environmental Management* 119484.

[58] David Jones et al, 'Characterising the Digital Twin: A Systematic Literature Review' (2020) 29 *CIRP Journal of Manufacturing Science and Technology* 36.

[59] See Akshay Ajagekar and Fengqi You, 'Quantum Computing and Quantum Artificial Intelligence for Renewable and Sustainable Energy: A Emerging Prospect towards Climate Neutrality' (2022) 165 *Renewable and Sustainable Energy Reviews* 112493.

[60] See Beth Whitehead et al, 'Assessing the Environmental Impact of Data Centres Part 1: Background, Energy Use and Metrics' (2014) 82 *Building and Environment* 151; Jingming Li et al, 'Energy Consumption of Cryptocurrency Mining: A Study of Electricity Consumption in Mining Cryptocurrencies' (2019) 168 *Energy* 160.

[61] See below section IV on the rebound effect.

[62] See Fraunhofer Institute for Systems and Innovation Research ISI et al, 'Critical Metals in the Path towards the Decarbonisation of the EU Energy Sector: Assessing Rare Metals as Supply Chain Bottlenecks in Low Carbon Energy Technologies' (Publications Office of the European Union, 2013), data.europa.eu/doi/10.2790/46338.

[63] See Whitehead et al (n 60).

[64] See Rashmi Anoop Patil and Seeram Ramakrishna, 'A Comprehensive Analysis of E-Waste Legislation Worldwide' (2020) 27 *Environmental Science and Pollution Research* 14412.

[65] Brunessen Bertrand, 'The Twin Digital and Green Transition Comment la transition numérique s'inscrit-elle dans les objectifs du Green Deal ?' (2022) *RTDEur. Revue trimestrielle de droit européen* 619.

[66] European Commission (n 3) 10.

III. EU Digital Sovereignty as Strategic Autonomy

A. Contrasting Digital Dependence: The EU Quest for Digital Sovereignty

The first two decades of the EU digitalisation process aimed to achieve a smart growth while supporting a liberal idea of an open digital market. This led to an overall condition of structural dependence of the EU from foreign companies for the provision of digital services and goods. The scholarship speaks of 'digital dependence' to denote a status where 'actors in a particular country have to rely on foreign-controlled digital technologies to perform digital activities'.[67] Mayer and Lu proposed a digital dependence index, categorising countries according to their level of digital independence, from absolute autarky to absolute dependence.[68] The bloc of EU countries presents a high level of digital dependence from two 'technopoles'. On the one hand, the EU relies on the US for the provision of digital infrastructures and services. On the other hand, it is dependent on China for the purchase of digital goods. The US conversely emerges as the most digitally independent country, followed by China and South Korea.

The EU status of digital dependence has been perceived as an element of vulnerability, both from an economic perspective, as the EU is unavoidably subject to the ebbs and flows of foreign markets – a risk that has been exacerbated by the recent trade war between the US and China[69] – and, from a legal perspective, as EU institutions, companies and individuals are exposed to threats of espionage, cyberattacks and fundamental rights violations. Also, this is a concrete, and not a purely academic concern. Indeed, the Snowden revelations in 2013 have unveiled a system of mass surveillance put in place by US authorities also vis-à-vis EU individuals.[70] The legal arm-wrestling in relation to the transfer of EU personal data to the US is further evidence of a question that has not yet been fully solved.[71] US law enforcement authorities are legally authorised to access data transferred to US companies, but the conditions of such access violate EU data protection law. Moreover, the 2018 US Clarifying Lawful Overseas Use of Data Act (CLOUD Act)

[67] Maximilian Mayer and Yen-Chi Lu, 'Digital Autonomy? Measuring the Global Digital Dependence Structure' (Center for Advanced Security, Strategic and Integration Studies, 2022) 2, www.kas.de/documents/252038/16166715/Digital+Autonomy+-+Measuring+the+Global+Digital+Dependence+Structure.pdf/fb97d384-53fd-b747-908f-2c86e8d0674b?version=1.2&t=1651491803819.

[68] ibid.

[69] Chad P Bown, 'The US–China Trade War and Phase One Agreement' (2021) 43 *Journal of Policy Modeling* 805.

[70] See Ioanna Tourkochoriti, 'The Snowden Revelations, the Transatlantic Trade and Investment Partnership and the Divide between U.S.-E.U. in Data Privacy Protection' (2014) 36 *University of Arkansas at Little Rock Law Review* 161.

[71] See Maria Tzanou, 'Schrems I and Schrems II: Assessing the Case for the Extraterritoriality of EU Fundamental Rights' in Federico Fabbrini, Edoardo Celeste and John Quinn (eds), *Data Protection Beyond Borders: Transatlantic Perspectives on Extraterritoriality and Sovereignty* (Hart, 2021).

allows US authorities to access data held by companies incorporated in the US, regardless of whether they operate.[72] And the situation on the Chinese front is no more idyllic, China having passed in 2017 a new National Intelligence Law, which, similarly to the US CLOUD Act, authorises intelligence authorities to access data held by Chinese companies operating abroad.[73]

The beginning of the so-called 'digital decade' (2020–2030) has thus witnessed the emergence of a quest for EU digital sovereignty fuelled by these economic and geopolitical risks. In the 2020 Communication, 'Shaping Europe's Digital Future', the EU Commission stressed the need to reduce EU dependence from other global players by enhancing 'technological sovereignty' intended as 'Europe's ability to define its own rules and values in the digital age' combined with an autonomous development and deployment of its own digital capacities.[74] Indeed, the EU standard setting power in the digital field might be undermined if digital infrastructures and devices are provided by foreign actors. However, digital sovereignty is not presented by the EU as determining a closure of the single market, ie as a form of digital protectionism or techno nationalism. The Commission attempts to reconcile its vision of digital sovereignty as strategic autonomy from other countries with the openness that has characterised the digital single market in the previous decades.[75] If, on the one hand, it is recognised that European needs and values are prioritised, on the other hand, such an approach does not aim to penalise foreign actors.[76] This is certainly a vision which might be subject to criticism.[77]

[72] See Steven Smith, 'Clouds on the Horizon: Cross-Border Surveillance Under the US CLOUD Act' in Federico Fabbrini, Edoardo Celeste and John Quinn (eds), *Data Protection Beyond Borders: Transatlantic Perspectives on Extraterritoriality and Sovereignty* (Hart, 2021).

[73] PRC National Intelligence Law (as amended in 2018) 2017, as translated into English via www.chinalawtranslate.com/en/national-intelligence-law-of-the-p-r-c-2017/#_Toc486408897. For an analysis of the Chinese technological reach, see, eg, Edward Schwarck, 'Intelligence and Informatization: The Rise of the Ministry of Public Security in Intelligence Work in China' (2018) 80 *The China Journal* 1; Ausma Bernot and Marcus Smith, 'Understanding the Risks of China-Made CCTV Surveillance Cameras in Australia' (2023) 77 *Australian Journal of International Affairs* 380; Gregory J Moore, 'Huawei, Cyber-Sovereignty and Liberal Norms: China's Challenge to the West/Democracies' (2023) 28 *Journal of Chinese Political Science* 151.

[74] EU Commission, 'Shaping Europe's Digital Future' (2020) COM(2020) 67 final 2, eur-lex.europa.eu/legal-content/EN/TXT/PDF/?uri=CELEX:52020DC0067.

[75] *cf* also 'European Declaration on Digital Rights and Principles' (2022) Recital 6, digital-strategy.ec.europa.eu/en/library/european-declaration-digital-rights-and-principles.

[76] An example of that is the expressed aim to cooperate with non-EU countries through digital partnerships. See European Commission (n 1) 18–20. The impact has also sometimes been considered while drafting legislation. In the Impact Assessment accompanying the Digital Services Act, the Commission took into account the effect of the measure on non-EU legitimate platforms that operate in the UE. See European Commission, *Impact Assessment Accompanying the document Proposal for a Regulation of the European Parliament and of the Council on a Single Market For Digital Services (Digital Services Act) and amending Directive 2000/31/EC 2020*, SWD(2020) 348 final, 58.

[77] See Edoardo Celeste, Victor Henriquez Diaz and Elio Loredo Machado Neto, 'EU Digital Sovereignty as Strategic Autonomy: A Justified Protectionist Model?', Annual International Conference 'International Trade and New Technologies', The governance of digital trade: crossroads of divergent approaches (2023).

The current EU digitalisation strategy is no longer economically and geopolitically neutral. The EU does not aim to achieve a digitalisation *tout court*, but technological sovereignty acts as an orientating principle. The emergence of this new guiding value in EU policy has not been accompanied with a high degree of clarity from a policymaking perspective.[78] The notion of digital sovereignty has not been univocally defined, but has rather been progressively incorporated into EU policy from the political rhetoric of some EU countries – especially France and Germany.[79] Certainly, the difficulty of identifying a scholarly definition of the notion of 'sovereignty' itself, a concept that has significantly evolved over time, does not contribute to shed light on the concept of digital sovereignty.[80] Moreover, the use of this expression was preceded by terms such as 'technological sovereignty', which appears already in the 1960s,[81] and 'data sovereignty', now intended as a subset of the notion of digital sovereignty with specific reference to data.[82] The meaning that the scholarship has given to digital sovereignty claims in the EU context relates to the idea of regaining control over data, digital infrastructures and services, software and hardware. Controlling the digital consists of the possibility to apply EU fundamental rights and value in an autonomous way, thus with an appropriate degree of independence from external influence.

Digital sovereignty claims at EU level emerge from the need to 'control the digital', indented by the ecosystem encompassing data, infrastructures, software, hardware and services which represent the pillars of the digital society.[83] Such 'control' of the digital ecosystem consists – at least in theory – of the possibility to apply EU values and rules to digital assets.[84] However, for that regulatory power to be effective presupposes a status of relative strategic autonomy of the EU in the digital field to progressively attained with a series of policy and regulatory strategies.

[78] *cf* the various discourses surrounding the idea of digital sovereignty in Julia Pohle and Thorsten Thiel, 'Digital Sovereignty' (2020) 9 *Internet Policy Review*.

[79] Celeste (n 6).

[80] See Hent Kalmo and Quentin Skinner (eds), *Sovereignty in Fragments: The Past, Present and Future of a Contested Concept* (Cambridge University Press, 2010).

[81] Stephane Couture and Sophie Toupin, 'What Does the Notion of "Sovereignty" Mean When Referring to the Digital?' (2019) 21 *New Media & Society* 2305.

[82] ibid; on the use of the concept of data sovereignty as an aspect of digital sovereignty see Federal Ministry for Economic Affairs and Energy (BMWi), 'Project GAIA-X – A Federated Data Infrastructure as the Cradle of a Vibrant European Ecosystem' (2019), www.bmwi.de/Redaktion/EN/Publikationen/Digitale-Welt/project-gaia-x.pdf?__blob=publicationFile&v=4. Such an evolution should not surprise as it reflects the perception of technological changes in the contemporary society: see Edoardo Celeste, 'The Scope of Application of Digital Constitutionalism. Output from an Empirical Research' (Nexa Research Papers, 2017), nexa.polito.it/nexacenterfiles/E.%20Celeste%20-%20Research%20Paper.pdf.

[83] See Luciano Floridi, 'The Fight for Digital Sovereignty: What It Is, and Why It Matters, Especially for the EU' (2020) 33 *Philosophy & Technology* 369, 371; Patrik Hummel et al, 'Data Sovereignty: A Review' (2021) 8 *Big Data & Society*, journals.sagepub.com/doi/10.1177/2053951720982012.

[84] Celeste (n 6); See Edoardo Celeste, 'Digital Constitutionalism, EU Digital Sovereignty Ambitions and the Role of the European Declaration on Digital Rights' in Annegret Engel, Xavier Groussot and Gunnar Thor Petursson (eds), *New Directions in Digitalisation: Perspectives from EU Competition Law and the Charter of Fundamental Rights* (Springer, 2024).

B. EU Digital Autonomy Strategies: Centripetal and Centrifugal Tendencies

Digital independence is not a self-standing element in the EU policy agenda. It is tied into a broader strategy aiming at enhancing EU resilience and open strategic autonomy in the current geopolitical framework.[85] As argued in the 2022 Strategic Foresight Report, this includes, for instance, energy efficiency and food security.[86] This document follows the path paved by the 2021 Strategic Foresight Report, which had already identified the 'megatrends' affecting EU strategic autonomy, namely climate change and environmental challenges, the digital and technological transformation, and shifts in global politics including threats to democratic governance as well as demographic changes.[87]

This phase clearly sees the emergence of the defence of EU digital sovereignty as a key policy objective to compete against the superpower of US and Chinese tech firms and, at the same time, preserve EU fundamental rights and liberties.[88] To this end, the second EU digital agenda stresses the importance of investing in a human-centric form of AI that preserves fundamental rights, developing EU digital infrastructures including supercomputing facilities, enhancing the cybersecurity of the whole chain of EU digital systems, ensuring high levels of connectivity through fast broadband, 5G and 6G technologies, as well as controlling the use of semiconductors which are necessary to make chips.[89]

The EU, not being home to digital infrastructure and service providers, nor to manufacturers or suppliers of digital products, has employed a twofold strategy to achieve autonomy in the digital, balancing centripetal and centrifugal tendencies.[90] While centripetal policy measures aim to reshore digital assets such as data or digital infrastructure within the EU physical borders to keep – or gain – control over them, centrifugal measures aim to extend the EU's regulatory influence beyond its borders, namely through the extraterritorial scope of EU law or by acting as a global norm-setter.

The paradigmatic example of how the EU implements digital sovereignty in a centripetal way are data localisation measures.[91] In this regard, the European Strategy for Data envisaged the so-called 'High Impact Project: developing

[85] European Commission (n 3) 12.

[86] ibid 12–13.

[87] European Commission, *2021 Strategic Foresight Report – The EU's capacity and freedom to act 2021*, COM/2021/750 final.

[88] See Celeste (n 6).

[89] European Commission (n 1).

[90] This distinction has been illustrated in Celeste (n 6) and Edoardo Celeste, 'Brexit and the Risks of Digital Sovereignism' in Edoardo Celeste et al (eds), *Data Protection and Digital Sovereignty Post-Brexit* (Hart, 2023).

[91] For examples in Europe, the US and China, see Edoardo Celeste and Federico Fabbrini, 'Competing Jurisdictions: Data Privacy Across the Borders' in Theo Lynn et al (eds), *Data Privacy and Trust in Cloud Computing: Building trust in the cloud through assurance and accountability* (Springer International Publishing, 2021), doi.org/10.1007/978-3-030-54660-1_3.

common European data spaces and interconnecting cloud infrastructures', which aims to establish common and interoperable data spaces in the EU.[92] Other policy measures such as the Gigabit Infrastructure Act[93] and the Chips Act[94] have focused on digital infrastructure localisation. The first aims to promote the use of existing as well as the deployment of new high-capacity fixed and wireless networks across the EU.[95] On the other hand, the Chips Act acknowledges the importance of chips as a strategic asset for key industrial value chains and aims to strengthen the EU's semiconductor ecosystem.[96] To achieve these objectives, this regulation includes the establishment of the Chips for Europe Initiative, which seeks to build extensive technological capacity and support research and innovation activities across the EU semiconductor value chain, enhancing advanced design, systems integration and chip production to boost competitiveness.[97]

Regarding the centrifugal tendency, the extraterritorial effect and de facto influence of EU digital law, and in particular of the GDPR, are well known and have been thoroughly discussed in the literature.[98] In addition, the EU has shown a growing interest in establishing itself as a global norm-setter in the digital field. The Standardisation Strategy argues that the EU's 'strong global footprint' in setting international standards is jeopardised by the current geopolitical context.[99] Therefore, measures shall be taken to uphold such global footprint and to ensure

[92] European Commission, Communication from the Commission to the European Parliament, the Council, the European Economic and Social Committee of the Regions, *A European strategy for data 2020*, COM/2020/66 final. On the status of the common European data spaces, see European Commission, *Common European Data Spaces*, SWD(2022) 45 final, digital-strategy.ec.europa.eu/en/library/staff-working-document-data-spaces and European Commission, *Common European Data Spaces*, SWD(2024) 21 final, digital-strategy.ec.europa.eu/en/library/second-staff-working-document-data-spaces.

[93] Regulation (EU) 2024/1309 of the European Parliament and of the Council of 29 April 2024 on measures to reduce the cost of deploying gigabit electronic communications networks, amending Regulation (EU) 2015/2120 and repealing Directive 2014/61/EU (Gigabit Infrastructure Act) (Text with EEA relevance) 2024.

[94] Regulation (EU) 2023/1781 of the European Parliament and of the Council of 13 September 2023 establishing a framework of measures for strengthening Europe's semiconductor ecosystem and amending Regulation (EU) 2021/694 (Chips Act) (Text with EEA relevance).

[95] Gigabit Infrastructure Act, Art 1.

[96] Chips Act, Preamble (1) and (2).

[97] Chips Act, Preamble (4), Art 1.1.(a) and Arts 3–12.

[98] See, eg, Christopher Kuner, 'The Internet and the Global Reach of EU Law' in Marise Cremona and Joanne Scott (eds), *EU Law Beyond EU Borders: The Extraterritorial Reach of EU Law* (Oxford University Press, 2019); Oskar Josef Gstrein and Andrej Janko Zwitter, 'Extraterritorial Application of the GDPR: Promoting European Values or Power?' (2021) 10 *Internet Policy Review*, policyreview.info/articles/analysis/extraterritorial-application-gdpr-promoting-european-values-or-power; Anu Bradford, *The Brussels Effect: How the European Union Rules the World* (Oxford University Press, 2020); Federico Fabbrini, Edoardo Celeste and John Quinn (eds), *Data Protection beyond Borders: Transatlantic Perspectives on Extraterritoriality and Sovereignty* (Hart, 2021).

[99] See European Commission, Communication from the Commission to the European Parliament, the Council, the European Economic and Social Committee and the Committee of the Regions, *An EU Strategy on Standardisation Setting global standards in support of a resilient, green and digital EU single market 2022*, COM/2022/31 final.

EU competitiveness and the promotion of EU values. More recently, the text of the AI Act pledges EU global leadership in the uptake of 'secure, trustworthy and ethical AI'.[100]

IV. Environmental Impact of Digital Sovereignty Strategies

A. Rebound Effect and Digital Insularity

While implementing digital sovereignty strategies, the EU unavoidably increases the global use of digital technologies. Indeed, the 2030 Digital Compass aims to accelerate Europe's digital transformation, which involves harnessing investments to develop critical technologies that are now mostly developed outside the EU.[101] Although the EU aims to pursue a more sustainable digital future through high environmental standards, the ecological footprint of digital technologies cannot be overlooked. Indeed, as anticipated above, the digital sector requires energy and natural resources, and produces high amounts of waste.[102]

Recent assessments have estimated the energy use of devices, data centres and networks to account for between six and 12 per cent of global electricity use.[103] In the EU, data centres alone used approximately 45 to 65 TWh of electricity in 2022 (1.8 and 2.6 per cent of EU total electricity consumption), with technologies such as AI, blockchain and cryptocurrency being likely to impact this consumption.[104] The total bitcoin energy consumption of 121 TWh in 2023 is evidence of that.[105] While the carbon emissions associated with this consumption have garnered increasing attention, other environmental impacts such as water consumption and noise pollution have been disregarded.[106] For instance, water-based cooling technologies used in data centres placed them among the top 10 water-intensive industries in the US in 2018.[107] Moreover, digital hardware and infrastructure require high amounts of raw materials, namely different types of

[100] Recital 8.

[101] European Commission (n 1) 3.

[102] See, eg, Stefano Bianchini, Giacomo Damioli and Claudia Ghisetti, 'The Environmental Effects of the "Twin" Green and Digital Transition in European Regions' (2023) 84 *Environmental & resource economics* 877. On the nature and scale of the environmental footprint of digital technologies, see United Nations Conference on Trade and Development (UNCTAD), 'Digital Economy Report 2024' (2024), unctad.org/system/files/official-document/der2024_en.pdf.

[103] UNCTAD (n 102).

[104] Joint Research Centre (European Commission), G Kamiya and P Bertoldi, 'Energy Consumption in Data Centres and Broadband Communication Networks in the EU' (Publications Office of the European Union, 2024), data.europa.eu/doi/10.2760/706491.

[105] See 'Cambridge Blockchain Network Sustainability Index', ccaf.io/cbnsi/cbeci.

[106] UNCTAD (n 102) 71.

[107] ibid 83–84.

metals, elements and minerals.[108] Mining activities to obtain them are usually associated with environmental and social negative impacts.[109] Finally, given the short lifespan of information and communications technology (ICT) hardware due to malfunctioning, technical obsolescence, or other reasons, consumers are constantly replacing their devices.[110] This generates a huge annual amount of e-waste, which is predicted to reach almost 75 Mt by 2030.[111]

Despite the promises of using digital technologies to overcome the challenges related to climate change in the EU, the Commission also recognised that digitalisation will unavoidably increase energy consumption if digital technologies are not made more energy efficient.[112] However, even if efficiency improves, rebound effects may hamper the expected reduction in energy consumption.[113] These effects consist of an increase in energy consumption and carbon emissions due to a higher overall use of digital technologies,[114] which counterweigh potential energy savings related to the employment of the latter.[115] Energy efficiency improvements may also contribute to accelerating the accumulation of e-waste, since new digital technologies necessitate replacing hardware that has become obsolete. In this sense, Bertrand argues that 'Moore's Law' explains the increase of digital devices due to increased computing power.[116] Although the latter may contribute to more environmentally friendly technologies, innovation cycles of digital technologies are progressively shortening, leading to more frequent replacement of digital devices and an increase in overall waste.[117]

Following on from the above, the 'highest sustainability standards and innovation' promoted by the European Commission[118] may have a significant (negative) impact on the environment.[119] Rather than minimising the footprint of digital technology, these standards may contribute to increased energy consumption – due to the rebound effect – requiring critical raw materials to manufacture devices

[108] A report from the Geological Survey of Finland distinguishes between 1) high-tech metals, 2) battery metals and minerals, and 3) other metals, elements and minerals. See Jyri Hanski et al, *Digitalization and Natural Resources* (Geological Survey of Finland, 2021) 29.

[109] See UNCTAD (n 102) 59–64.

[110] Hanski et al (n 108).

[111] E-waste is problematic not only because of its volume, but also because of its partly hazardous content. See ibid.

[112] European Commission (n 3) 2. On the promises of green digital technologies, see also European Commission (n 1), 3 and 19.

[113] European Commission (n 3) 3.

[114] Though it may refer to any behavioural response to the efficiency improvement that counterweights the expected savings. See European Commission (n 3).

[115] See Bertrand (n 65) and The Shift Project, 'Lean ICT: Towards Digital Sobriety' (2019) 429 *Futuribles*, theshiftproject.org/en/article/lean-ict-our-new-report.

[116] Bertrand (n 65) 2.

[117] ibid.

[118] European Commission (n 3) 14.

[119] See, eg, Alba Perez Victorio, Edoardo Celeste and Alberto Quintavalla, 'Greening AI? The New Principle of Sustainable Digital Products and Services in the EU' (2024) 61 *Common Market Law Review*, kluwerlawonline.com/api/Product/CitationPDFURL?file=Journals\COLA\COLA2024067.pdf.

that are able to keep up with the latest updates, and generating partly hazardous e-waste. As recognised in the 2022 Foresight Report, the digital transition has thus far not adequately taken into account environmental considerations.[120] The lack of common objectives between the green and the digital in the EU pulls apart the twin transitions, leading to what in this chapter we refer to as 'digital insularity'. The digital transition sails a solo course, prioritising digital sovereignty without considering the green implications in the policies and initiatives implementing it.

B. Environmental Sovereignism

An adequate consideration of sustainable concerns in the digital context would not only imply an effort towards twinning the two transitions in the EU, but also towards measuring and considering its consequences in non-EU countries. We argue that the impact of the digital transition should be taken into account within and beyond the EU, especially given the borderless nature of the environment. Although it seems obvious that high carbon emissions in China will contribute to climate change for the whole planet and not just China, it seems easy to overlook the impact that EU policies have on these emissions. EU climate neutrality policies following the Green Deal only make sense if they do not generate environmental pressures somewhere else. Failing to consider the effects of EU policies and initiatives beyond its borders would make it impossible for the EU to calibrate its strategies towards digital sovereignty, since these effects may have a boomerang impact on the EU's environmental conditions. Global strategies call for a global perspective.

In this regard, digital insularity is not only related to the compartmentalisation between the digital and the green transitions in the EU, but also to the disregard of the global impact of the digital transition: what we could more accurately define as a form of 'environmental sovereignism'. While 'digital sovereignism' has been employed to refer to the adoption by the EU of sovereignist policies that aim to regain digital independence at the expense of third countries, 'environmental sovereignism' would refer to the similar adoption of a 'Europe first' attitude in setting twin transition strategies.

Indeed, the EU does not take into account the environmental effects of its digital policies in non-EU countries. Notably, the EU strategy towards digital sovereignty may create a 'duplication effect': centripetal measures to reshore digital assets to the EU's territory may result in the duplication of data or infrastructure. Indeed, these components of the EU digital infrastructure are not physically moved from other countries to the EU; instead, they are built anew. For example, if data is to be processed in the EU, the establishment of new data centres is required. However,

[120] European Commission (n 3) 1.

even if the EU adopts higher energy efficiency standards, the non-EU data centre where data had previously been processed or stored remains operational, thus increasing the total energy consumption.

This seems to be neglected in the EU agenda. The challenge of data centres has mainly been addressed through a self-regulation mechanism, ie the Code of Conduct on Data Centre Energy Efficiency.[121] The Energy Efficiency Directive adopts a similar approach by outlining solely information disclosure requirements, giving owners and operators of data centres the flexibility to adhere to the Code of Conduct.[122] Although mandatory obligations can be found in the Regulation on ecodesign requirements for servers and data storage products,[123] these regard the efficiency of each single data centre, not considering the overall impact of the data centres network, nor taking into account the potential duplication effect.

V. Conclusion: Sustainable Sovereignty or Digital Sobriety?

Promoting sustainable digital technologies in the EU represents a significant challenge. Advocating for sovereign digital policies that foster sustainability on a global scale adds an additional layer of complexity. Specifically, centripetal digital sovereignty strategies have an environmental impact in the EU – because of the difficult reconciliation between the green and the digital, mainly due to the rebound effect and Moore's Law – as well as in the global economy – due to, for instance, the duplication effect. Although some of these tensions are acknowledged in the EU, they are not concretely considered by digital policies and initiatives. What in this chapter we called digital insularity and environmental sovereignism suggest that, in contrast to the notion of a twin transition, the EU digital sovereignty strategy may not be fully in line with the EU sustainability ambitions.

In response to the issues raised by a non-fully sustainable digital sovereignty in the EU, some have advocated that the turn to the digital should not be automatic. Proponents of digital sobriety suggest that the advancement of the digital transformation should instead be carefully managed, which may imply a voluntary

[121] Mark Acton, Paolo Bertoldi and John Booth, '2022 Best Practice Guidelines for the EU Code of Conduct on Data Centre Energy Efficiency' (European Commission, 2022) JRC128184, e3p.jrc.ec.europa.eu/publications/2022-best-practice-guidelines-eu-code-conduct-data-centre-energy-efficiency. This document is updated annually.

[122] Directive (EU) 2023/1791 of the European Parliament and of the Council of 13 September 2023 on energy efficiency and amending Regulation (EU) 2023/955 2023, Art 12.

[123] Commission Regulation (EU) 2019/424 of 15 March 2019 laying down ecodesign requirements for servers and data storage products pursuant to Directive 2009/125/EC of the European Parliament and of the Council and amending Commission Regulation (EU) No 617/2013 (Text with EEA relevance.) 2019 (OJ L).

abandonment or moderate use of digital technologies.[124] However, integrating such a narrative in the EU context may face significant obstacles. As Bertrand suggested, the EU discourse on the twin transition integrates environmental objectives with a narrative of progress, exactly to avoid triggering fears of regressing to an 'Amish model'.[125]

Finally, the current geopolitical context should not be overlooked. Indeed, the twin transitions are put forward in a complex landscape shaped by multiple wars in neighbouring EU countries and a persisting energy crisis. EU strategies must thus have a variable geometry, adapting their priorities based on the affordances that will be progressively defined by future challenges.

[124] See, eg, The Shift Project (n 115); Antoine Amiel, 'Digital Sobriety: How Can We Adapt Our Uses for a Positive Impact on the Environment?' (Epale, 8 April 2021), epale.ec.europa.eu/en/blog/digital-sobriety-how-can-we-adapt-our-uses-positive-impact-environment; Céline Péréa, Jessica Gérard and Julien De Benedittis, 'Digital Sobriety: From Awareness of the Negative Impacts of IT Usages to Degrowth Technology at Work' (2023) 194 *Technological Forecasting and Social Change* 122670.

[125] Bertrand (n 65) 3.

7

Fostering the Energy Transition Through Participatory Digital Sovereignty

TAMARA FAVARO

I. Introduction

The current conflict between Russia and Ukraine has starkly emphasised the substantial dependence of the European Union (EU) on Russian fossil gas imports. In 2019, approximately three-fifths of the EU's energy consumption originated from net imports. Notably, at the time of the invasion, Russian oil and gas played a pivotal role, underpinning over one-third of Europe's total energy supply.[1] This intricate relationship underscores the critical intersection between the EU's energy market and the geopolitical dynamics surrounding the conflict.

This should not be surprising, as energy has always been a fundamental issue of geopolitical security for Europe. It is noteworthy that, even before becoming a means to assert the increasing strategic autonomy of the EU against third countries, it has been the underlying cause of the European integration process. However, in recent years, the imperative to ensure energy autonomy and achieve the goals underlying the twin transition has significantly transformed the European stance on the energy market, marking the shift from a market-fundamentalist perspective to a new era in EU industrial policy. Nonetheless, this more interventionist approach by the EU, on its own, falls short of achieving the objectives of energy independence and environmental sustainability. Therefore, the latest European legislative acts place citizens, as well as local governments and stakeholders, at the centre of the energy transition, acknowledging the necessity to mobilise all forces to attain the ambitious goals inherent in the energy transition.

In this context, a nascent paradigm takes shape – termed 'European energy sovereignty' – representing an intricate interplay between energy independence,

[1] For a comprehensive view on the issue, see Eurostate, 'Key figures on Europe – 2022 edition', ec.europa.eu/eurostat/web/products-key-figures/-/ks-ei-22-001.

environmental sustainability, EU interventionism, and the empowerment of citizens and communities. Yet, how can the attainment of these seemingly diverse objectives be promoted? Digital technologies, with a particular emphasis on the transformative capabilities of blockchain, appear to play a pivotal role in facilitating this paradigm shift. However, a core dilemma lies in the question of whether blockchain solely reflects neoliberal capitalist principles, as often posited by scholars studying the interplay between blockchain and digital sovereignty, or if it can transcend these limits to become a potent force driving an inclusive energy transition. Blockchain's potential lies in its ability to decentralise critical sectors like energy, giving local actors more control and reducing reliance on centralised, often foreign-owned systems. This supports the EU's ambition for digital sovereignty by creating more autonomous, transparent and secure digital ecosystems that are not subject to the control of external powers. By enabling decentralised energy platforms, blockchain promises to play a pivotal role in both the energy transition and the broader digital sovereignty agenda of the EU, empowering citizens and local entities while reducing the influence of foreign tech giants.

Therefore, this chapter will present pertinent case studies and theoretical underpinnings to deconstruct the role of blockchain as a nexus of energy and digital sovereignty. The final objective is to unravel the transformative capacity of blockchain as a potent force propelling an inclusive energy transition consonant with principles of solidarity and sovereignty.

This chapter will be articulated in two parts. Sections II and III aim to reconstruct the concept of European energy sovereignty considering the evolution of EU energy law, emphasising its implications in the light of the various modes of public intervention within the economy. Sections IV and V focus instead on the contribution provided by blockchain technology to achieve European energy sovereignty, understood as a participatory process aimed at accomplishing the energy transition and contribute to the EU digital sovereignty agenda. In fact, Blockchain technology seems to play a dual role in advancing the EU's energy and digital sovereignty, acting as a critical bridge between these two interrelated objectives. On the one hand, it empowers energy sovereignty by enabling decentralised energy systems such as energy communities and peer-to-peer energy trading. By using blockchain, the EU can facilitate transparent, secure and efficient energy exchanges, reducing reliance on centralised entities or foreign intermediaries and ensuring greater control over its energy resources. On the other hand, blockchain contributes to digital sovereignty by enhancing the EU's ability to independently manage and secure its digital infrastructures, so reducing dependence on foreign technology providers like US-based platforms or cloud services. This aligns with the EU's strategic goals of technological self-reliance and robust governance of digital infrastructures.

In particular, section II briefly traces the legislative evolution of the European energy market, demonstrating how the principle of energy solidarity has evolved from being an instrument of economic integration to progressively becoming a means of social integration and, more recently, a principle of shared administration. Section III endeavours to reconstruct the emerging concept of European energy sovereignty, analysing its potential convergence with the notion of digital sovereignty.

This investigation takes into account that both European energy and digital sovereignty support the twin transition by promoting sustainable, independent energy systems and digitally advanced infrastructure to achieve environmental and technological goals. This perspective aims to highlight the EU's potential to strengthen its role as a global leader by integrating these transitions into a cohesive framework that aligns economic competitiveness, environmental goals and strategic autonomy. Subsequently, we delve into examining how energy sovereignty can actively shape EU industrial policy and empower citizens within the dynamic landscape of the digital era. Section IV unravels the transformative role of blockchain technology in realising European energy sovereignty considering the potential applications of blockchain, from peer-to-peer electricity trading to empowering energy communities and fostering energy democracy. Section V critically evaluates the role of blockchain as a tool for energy and digital sovereignty, questioning its alignment with neoliberal capitalist technology and exploring its potential as a driver for an inclusive energy transition. Finally, section VI synthesises key insights and charts a path forward in the pursuit of a more integrated and sustainable European energy market.

II. Energy Solidarity as the Catalyst for European Integration

A. Solidarity as an Instrument for Economic Integration

It is well known that the roots of the EU trace back to the Second World War, which arose from the rivalry between France and Germany for control over the strategically contested Ruhr and Saar basins, housing coal and steel production sites.

Two of the three original Communities (the European Coal and Steel Community (ECSC) and Euratom) were established with the explicit goal of enabling the joint management of coal and nuclear energy as primary sources. In the words of the renowned Schuman Declaration, the solidarity in pooling coal and steel production aimed to make any war between France and Germany not merely unthinkable, but materially impossible.[2] It is not surprising, therefore, that energy, originally a cause of the conflict, soon became a tool for cooperation

[2] See the 'Schuman Declaration' of 9 May 1950, www.centre-robert-schuman.org/en/robert-schuman-en/robert-schuman-declaration.

and, in the form of coal and nuclear power, gave rise to the process of European integration.

Nonetheless, at that time, energy 'was considered too closely bound up with national sovereignty to be effectively regulated at the European level'.[3] Therefore, energy finds itself under the sign of paradox in the founding treaties of the European Communities.[4] The ECSC and Euratom were wholly devoted to the joint management of coal and nuclear energy, while the original formulation of the Treaty establishing the European Economic Community (EEC) did not include specific provisions for the energy sector.[5] The explicit legitimisation of European energy policy as a concurrent competence of the Union had to wait until the approval of the Lisbon Treaty.[6]

However, the EEC Treaty applied also to the electricity market, as demonstrated by the landmark *Costa v Enel* judgment,[7] which notably established the supremacy of European law. Trivially, during that period, energy security concerns did not appear to also be associated with gas and electricity to the point of requiring the creation of a common market, and they were still perceived as falling under national sovereignty – to such an extent that, in those years, Member States even resorted to nationalising the electrical industry.

It was only in the 1990s, with the rise of the economic liberalisation theory, that the EU began to focus on facilitating the establishment and functioning of the internal electricity market. European energy law aimed to replace the outdated, state-owned and vertically organised energy industry with the new paradigms of global markets, encouraging privatisation and the dominance of horizontally, contractually structured processes within a competitive framework.[8] Consequently, the EU adopted a market-fundamentalist approach, intervening with an economic liberalisation perspective that initiated a phased process of internal competition opening. This was indeed the exclusive goal of the so-called first energy package, adopted between 1996 and 1998[9] and subsequently replaced by the second energy package in 2003,[10] with the objective of allowing industrial and domestic consumers to freely choose their own gas and electricity suppliers from a broader range of competitors.

[3] See Kim Talus, *Introduction to EU Energy Law* (Oxford University Press, 2016) 2.

[4] See Claude Blumann, 'Rapport introductif général' in Claude Blumann (ed), *Vers une politique européenne de l'énergie* (Bruylant, 2012) 3: 'L'énergie se trouve placée sous le signe du paradoxe dans les traités constitutifs des Communautés européennes'.

[5] Herman Vedder et al, 'EU Energy Law' in Martha Roggenkamp et al (eds), *Energy Law in Europe: National, EU and International Regulation* (Oxford University Press, 2016) 187 ff.

[6] Consolidated Version of the Treaty on the Functioning of the European Union [2008] OJ C115/01, Art 4.2. See also Arts 194.1 and 122.

[7] CJUE, Case C-6/64; Rafael Leal-Arcas and Jan Wouters (eds), *Research Handbook on EU Energy Law and Policy* (Edward Elgar Publishing, 2017) 15.

[8] Kim Talus, *EU Energy Law and Policy: A Critical Account* (Oxford University Press, 2013) 270.

[9] Directive 96/92/EC for the electricity market and Directive 98/30/EC concerning the gas market.

[10] It contains two Directives and one Regulation: the second electricity Directive 2003/54/EC, the second gas Directive 2003/55/EC, and Regulation (EC) No 1228/2003 on conditions for access to the network for cross border exchanges in electricity.

However, the European legislator soon realised that ensuring competition among Member States was not sufficient; it would be necessary to establish an integrated market for electricity and gas both within the EU and with third countries. At the same time, but also for this purpose, it was crucial to incentivise the production and consumption of renewable energies. In 2006, due to the impacts in Europe of the gas crisis between Russia and Ukraine, the Treaty establishing the Energy Community was therefore adopted.[11] This Treaty aimed to create a unified regulatory space among the 28 EU Member States and the six European states and territories of the Balkans,[12] with the goal of ensuring supply security and promoting the use of renewable energies. Even in the subsequent period, the EU persisted in its efforts to liberalise the internal electricity and gas market and ensure greater security of supplies, adopting the third energy package in 2009.[13] This was due to the fact that its attempts to exercise geopolitical power had yielded very modest results: indeed, in that year, the effects of the disruption of natural gas supplies to EU Member States caused by the Russo-Ukrainian gas conflict of 2006 were still prevalent.[14] Therefore, the EU employed its regulatory power to promote the liberalisation and integration of national gas markets to influence its energy relations with Russia. For instance, it mandated the separation of ownership between gas production and distribution to challenge monopolistic practices of entities like Gazprom.

Nonetheless, before long, these further regulatory interventions also proved inadequate. The crisis over Russia's annexation of Crimea led to the creation of an 'Energy Union'[15] in 2015 and a proposal the following year of the 'fourth energy package' (colloquially known also as the 'jumbo package' due to the substantial volume of regulatory acts it comprised),[16] which came into effect between 2018

[11] Council Decision of 29 May 2006 on the conclusion by the European Community of the Energy Community Treaty (2006/500/EC).

[12] That is to say Albania, Bosnia and Herzegovina, Kosovo, Montenegro, North Macedonia and Serbia.

[13] The third energy package consists of two Directives and three Regulations: Directive 2009/72/EC concerning common rules for the internal market in electricity and repealing Directive 2003/54/EC; Directive 2009/73/EC concerning common rules for the internal market in natural gas and repealing Directive 2003/55/EC; Regulation (EC) No 714/2009 on conditions for access to the network for cross-border exchanges in electricity and repealing Regulation (EC) No 1228/2003; Regulation (EC) No 715/2009 on conditions for access to the natural gas transmission networks and repealing Regulation (EC) No 1775/2005; Regulation (EC) No 713/2009 of the European Parliament and of the Council of 13 July 2009 establishing an Agency for the Cooperation of Energy Regulators. The package was proposed by the European Commission in September 2007 and adopted by the European Parliament and the Council of the European Union in July 2009. It entered into force on 3 September 2009.

[14] Jonathan Stern, *The Russian-Ukrainian Gas Crisis of January 2006* (Oxford Institute for Energy Studies, 2006).

[15] See European Commission, *A Framework Strategy for a Resilient Energy Union with a Forward-Looking Climate Change Policy*, COM/2015/080 final, www.eur-lex.europa.eu/legal-content/EN/TXT/PDF/?uri=CELEX:52015DC0080. *cf* Annelies Vandendriessche, Angel Saz-Carranza and Jean-Michel Glachant, 'The Governance of the EU's Energy Union: Bridging the Gap?' EUI Working Paper RSCAS 2017/51 (2017) 4.

[16] The package consists of numerous communications, preparatory documents, reports and non-legislative initiatives. The eight main legislative files are: Energy Performance of Buildings Directive (EU)

and 2019. The EU became aware of having been 'A Liberal Actor in a Realist World'[17] and that asserting global leadership was imperative to enhancing energy supply security together with the pursuit of climate neutrality, since the solely pro-competitive approach to energy market regulation did not allow these goals to be achieved. Concurrently, it also needed to address the 'longstanding governance dilemma between European market integration and Member States' discretion'.[18]

The way in which the EU sought to balance these goals is particularly interesting: for the first time, the new governance system placed European citizens, as well as local governments and stakeholders, at the heart of the energy transition, recognising the need to harness all forces to achieve the challenging aims implied by the energy transition. Consumers were no longer merely passive recipients of protection, empowered by new technologies;[19] they could now actively engage in and benefit from the energy market. Indeed, a new regulatory framework allowed 'renewables self-consumers'[20] and 'jointly acting renewables self-consumers'[21] to generate, consume, store and sell electricity, while the possibility of 'peer-to-peer electricity trading' was also introduced.[22]

Additionally, Member States were mandated to ensure that final customers and local authorities (including municipalities) were entitled to participate with stakeholders in renewable energy communities (REC)[23] and citizen energy communities (CEC),[24] to provide environmental, economic or social

2018/844; Renewable Energy Directive (EU) 2018/2001; Energy Efficiency Directive (EU) 2018/2002; Governance of the Energy Union and Climate Action Regulation (EU) 2018/1999; Electricity Regulation (EU) 2019/943; Electricity Directive (EU) 2019/944; Regulation on Risk-Preparedness in the Electricity Sector (EU) 2019/941; and Regulation on the European Union Agency for the Cooperation of Energy Regulators (EU) 2019/942.

[17] *cf* Andreas Goldthau and Nick Sitter, *A Liberal Actor in a Realist World: The European Union Regulatory State and the Global Political Economy of Energy* (Oxford University Press, 2015); Tom Van de Graaf, 'Rule-maker or rule-taker? The EU and the shifting global political economy of energy' in Rafael Leal-Arcas and Jan Wouters (eds), *Research Handbook on EU Energy Law and Policy* (Edward Elgar Publishing, 2017) 165 ff.

[18] Katja Tews, 'Europeanization of Energy and Climate Policy: The Struggle Between Competing Ideas of Coordinating Energy Transitions' (2015) 3 *Journal of Environment & Development* 267.

[19] See below at IV.A.

[20] Article 2(14) Directive (EU) 2018/2001, '"renewables self-consumer" means a final customer operating within its premises located within confined boundaries or, where permitted by a Member State, within other premises, who generates renewable electricity for its own consumption, and who may store or sell self-generated renewable electricity, provided that, for a non-household renewables self-consumer, those activities do not constitute its primary commercial or professional activity.'

[21] Article 2(15) Directive (EU) 2018/2001, '"jointly acting renewables self-consumers" means a group of at least two jointly acting renewables self-consumers in accordance with point (14) who are located in the same building or multi-apartment block.'

[22] As specified by Art 2(18) Directive (EU) 2018/2001, '"peer-to-peer trading" of renewable energy means the sale of renewable energy between market participants by means of a contract with pre-determined conditions governing the automated execution and settlement of the transaction, either directly between market participants or indirectly through a certified third-party market participant, such as an aggregator. The right to conduct peer-to-peer trading shall be without prejudice to the rights and obligations of the parties involved as final customers, producers, suppliers or aggregators.'

[23] See Art 22 Directive (EU) 2018/2001.

[24] See Art 16 Directive (EU) 2019/944.

community benefits for the local areas where they operate, rather than financial profits. Therefore, through a regulation of the internal market for electricity, the EU also imposed upon Member States the duty to recognise and facilitate the establishment of new legal entities tasked with ensuring a new form of shared administration. The aim of this was not only to achieve social cohesion and environmental goals, but also ensure energy self-sufficiency and independence. At the same time, a Regulation on risk-preparedness in the electricity sector was approved,[25] setting rules for cooperation between EU countries with a view to preventing, preparing for and managing electricity crises in a spirit of solidarity.

B. Solidarity as a Means of Social Integration

If, until now, the concept of solidarity among states has primarily revolved around ensuring the security of electricity supply and managing emergency situations, a shift in perspective is imminent. With the CJEU's OPAL judgment in 2021[26] it is clarified that the security of supply principle is just one among various expressions of the principle of solidarity, which evolves into 'the first and only legally binding principle of EU energy law that can be clearly and explicitly identified from EU legal sources',[27] thus encompassing economic and political sustainability, as well as the diversification of supply sources. It entails rights and obligations for both the EU and the Member States, obliging them to consider all interests liable to be affected. Thus, the principle of solidarity is now employed not solely as an instrument for economic integration, as in the Schuman Declaration and subsequent years when it served as an expression of the internal market approach. Additionally, it is a means to protect individuals, households and communities that are most impacted by the energy supply.[28]

In the years immediately following, this change of course became even more radical. The EU swiftly approved a series of legislative acts, all strategically crafted to bolster energy supply security and advance climate neutrality, signalling its willingness to shift from its traditional liberal approach to a more strategic stance.[29] A clear example of this different strategy is represented by the European Green

[25] Regulation (EU) 2019/941.

[26] Case C-848/19 P, *Germany v Poland* [2021] ECLI:EU:C:2021:598. For an analysis of this judgment, see Dirk Buschle and Kim Talus, 'One for All and All for One? The General Court Ruling in the OPAL Case' (2019) *OGEL* 5; Anatole Boute, 'The principle of solidarity and the geopolitics of energy: Poland v Commission (OPAL pipeline)' (2020) 57 *Common Market Law Review* 889.

[27] Kaisa Huhta and Laura Reins, 'Solidarity in European Union Law and its application in the energy sector (2023) 72 *International & Comparative Law Quarterly* 771.

[28] ibid.

[29] *cf* Marco Siddi and Irina Kustova, 'From a Liberal to a Strategic Actor: The Evolution of the EU's Approach to International Energy Governance' (2021) 28 *Journal of European Public Policy* 1076. According to the authors, the EU began to shift towards a strategic stance in the 2000s, in the context of the Energy Charter Treaty negotiations and the growing securitisation of European energy debates.

Deal,[30] which is now widely conceived as an attempt to move beyond the current phase of European integration towards the establishment of a new societal order.[31] With it, the Commission unequivocally assumed a role that goes beyond the mere regulation and promotion of European economic development, to the extent that this act was generally acknowledged as the milestone marking the transition to a new era in EU industrial policy.[32] An additional stride unfolded: the EU pursued not only the enhancement of the social market economy but also a more proactive role. Concurrently, the European Green Deal emerged from the necessity to define a new pact 'to bring together citizens in all their diversity, with national, regional, local authorities, civil society and industry working closely with the EU's institutions and consultative bodies'.[33] Empowering citizens and consumers was viewed as a technique to also mobilise social and economic forces in the field of industrial policy.[34]

C. Solidarity as a Principle of Shared Administration

This innovative approach defines the 'fifth energy package', commonly known as 'Fit for 55%', unveiled in 2021 to align the EU's energy objectives with the European climate ambitions for 2030 and 2050. It not only aims to 'provide a social market economy which delivers good employment prospects, economic growth, environmental protection, and a bit of solidarity on the side',[35] but also acknowledges that achieving these goals requires shared efforts among Member States, ensuring support for those most in need and guaranteeing that the transition positively impacts everyone. To guarantee solidarity, the Social Climate Fund was established, offering dedicated funding for vulnerable citizens and micro-enterprises.

The rapid escalation of the Russo-Ukrainian conflict, leading to the acute energy supply shock caused by the armed incursion in February 2022, then amplified this trend of the Union. Indeed, the so-called REPowerEU[36] was adopted to eliminate all imports of Russian fossil energy progressively and swiftly. This was achieved through the implementation of energy-saving measures, diversification

[30] See European Commission, *The European Green Deal*, COM(2019) 640 final, www.eur-lex.europa.eu/legal-content/EN/TXT/PDF/?uri=CELEX:52019DC0640.

[31] See Edoardo Chiti, 'Managing the ecological transition of the EU: the European Green Deal as a regulatory process', (2022) 59 *Common Market Law Review* 19.

[32] As it has been observed by E Bruti Liberati, 'La strategia industriale europea tra intervento pubblico finalistico e dinamiche di mercato' (2023) *Rivista della Regolazione dei mercati* 252. Kurt Aiginger and Dani Rodrik, 'Rebirth of Industrial Policy and an Agenda for the XXI Century' (2020) 20 *Journal of Industry, Competition and Trade* 189.

[33] European Commission, 'European Green Deal' (Build Up), build-up.ec.europa.eu/en/resources-and-tools/links/european-green-deal.

[34] Chiti (n 31).

[35] Giorgio Monti, 'Editorial Comments' (2021) 58 *Common Market Law Review* 1321, 1339.

[36] See European Commission, *Plan REPowerEU*, COM(2022) 230 final, www.eur-lex.europa.eu/legal-content/EN/TXT/HTML/?uri=CELEX:52022DC0230.

of energy imports, adoption of exceptional and structural measures in electricity and gas markets, and expediting the integration of renewable energies.

Furthermore, the Commission proposed a reform of the electricity market rules in March 2023, consisting of the amending Directive EU/2024/1711 and the amending Regulation EU/2024/1747.[37] This initiative aims to 'secure European energy sovereignty and achieve climate neutrality'.[38] Among various notable aspects, it stands out that the enactment of this energy market regulation is intricately linked to European industrial policy, explicitly referencing the Green Deal Industrial Plan and the REPowerEU Plan. Furthermore, it goes beyond by fostering the active participation of consumers in the market and the development of their demand response. For instance, peer-to-peer trading is concretely regulated as a method for sharing energy, to be promoted even beyond energy communities.

In conclusion, the governance of energy, the catalyst of the European integration process, is currently steering a shift in Europe's approach to intervening in the energy market and, more broadly, in the economy. Within this evolution, the EU is embracing a more dynamic and hands-on role, breaking free from its traditional market-centric approach. To reach this new stage of integration, there is a reinvigoration of the principle of energy solidarity among Member States.[39] It evolves into an ordinary administration rule, legally compelling Member States to weigh all relevant interests in energy matters. Concurrently, citizens and local authorities are assigned a fresh narrative, nurturing innovative models of collaborative administration. This stems from the firm belief that attaining energy independence and navigating the ecological transition demand a united effort from every individual within the EU.

III. The Emerging Concept of European Energy Sovereignty

Amidst this evolution in European policies, the notion of 'European energy sovereignty' emerges prominently, particularly within the political sphere. References to energy sovereignty have been underscored not only in relation to the previously mentioned March 2023 proposal, but also in the endorsement of the European Green Deal, emphasising the pivotal contribution of renewables in reducing fossil fuel imports and affirming the EU's role as a global leader.[40] However, this concept still lacks a widely accepted definition, particularly at the regulatory level.

[37] They were adopted on 21 May 2024 and entered into force on 16 July 2024.
[38] See ec.europa.eu/commission/presscorner/detail/en/ip_24_2261.
[39] Huhta and Reins (n 27).
[40] See www.ec.europa.eu/commission/presscorner/detail/en/ip_23_2061.

A. Defining Energy Sovereignty

At first glance, energy sovereignty seems to imply energy independence, and therefore the EU's efforts to assert its power on a geopolitical level by achieving energy autonomy through the advancement of renewables. However, rather than promoting energy security or prioritising decarbonisation, 'energy sovereignty centres the rights of communities and individuals to make their own choices regarding the forms, scales, and sources of energy as well as the patterning and organization of energy usage'.[41] It is a concept partially inspired by the 'food sovereignty' movement, which advocates for people's right to control their food systems.[42] Since the 1990s, it has been employed in Latin America as a rallying cry for local initiatives asserting the right to determine energy policies, challenging the privatisation of essential services, and opposing the 'corporatization' of state enterprises.[43] More recently, it has been widely adopted in Europe through various campaigns that question the energy oligopoly empowering people and communities to make decisions about energy systems. When they involve local authorities, these initiatives aim also to re-municipalise urban energy utilities and grids to challenge the prevailing energy paradigm controlled by centralised powers.[44] Hence, it is closely intertwined with notions such as 'energy citizenship', 'energy democracy' and 'energy justice' that surfaced in the fourth energy package,[45] adding more support to the idea that this regulation is not exclusively focused on promoting competition. Instead, it suggests that the EU is exploring alternatives to the neoliberal modes of capitalism that have significantly shaped the energy transition thus far.

B. Energy and Digital Sovereignty: A Possible Convergence?

Considering this reconstruction of the energy sovereignty notion, the normative evolution briefly outlined in section II should now assume a more profound significance. The concept of sovereignty appears to reconcile what would otherwise seem to be a triad of opposing forces: the EU's competence to set specific binding targets for renewables across all sectors of the EU economy, asserting its power on a geopolitical level; Member States' freedom to 'determine the conditions for exploiting their energy resources, their choice between different energy

[41] Christopher Schelly et al, 'Energy policy for energy sovereignty' (2020) 205 *Solar Energy* 109.

[42] Mansur Laldjebaev and Benjamin K Sovacool, 'Energy security, poverty, and sovereignty: complex interlinkages and compelling implications' in Lavanya Guruswamy (ed), *International Energy and Poverty* (Routledge, 2015) 102.

[43] See www.newslettereuropean.eu/energy-sovereignty.

[44] ibid.

[45] For a comprehensive understanding of these concepts, especially in the context of the fourth energy package, see Karen RS Hamann et al, 'An interdisciplinary understanding of energy citizenship: Integrating psychological, legal, and economic perspectives on a citizen-centred sustainable energy transition' (2023) 97 *Energy Research & Social Science* 102959.

sources, and the general structure of their energy supply';[46] and the right of citizens and communities to make decisions about the procurement and supply of energy. European energy sovereignty unifies these three dimensions, recognising the significance of a harmonised approach that takes into account the EU's geopolitical ambitions, national freedom (which, however, must be exercised in the spirit of solidarity), and participatory considerations.

Starting from the premise that sovereignty is a 'plastic and evolving' concept,[47] it appears that this interpretation also has the potential to reshape the notion of 'digital sovereignty', a topic still widely discussed by scholars. Indeed, based on our reconstruction, reconciling the three dimensions – European, national and individual – in that context is a challenging task. Digital sovereignty and digital solidarity are still perceived as alternatives.[48] While we are witnessing attempts to implement the principle of solidarity in the digital market – such as the EU Cyber Solidarity Act or the creation of the Common European Data Spaces – solidarity in this context is conceived with a far-from-holistic value, contrary to what is clarified in the energy market according to the CJEU's OPAL judgment. Moreover, harmonising the European dimension of digital sovereignty with the state dimension does not seem straightforward, given that 'a series of unfettered sovereign claims naturally tends toward a state of continuous conflict in the attempt to predominate and possibly establish a scenario of "One Law Rule"'.[49] Additionally, there is a constant risk of nationalistic and protectionist drifts,[50] which could lead to digital colonialism, negatively impacting citizens, especially those who are vulnerable.[51]

Referring to Couture and Toupin's classifications of digital sovereignty,[52] energy sovereignty, as defined here, bears a closer resemblance to 'indigenous' digital sovereignty. However, this concept lacks recognition in the European perspective. Instead, the European viewpoint aligns more with 'personal' digital sovereignty, where individuals wield considerably less authority compared to the energy market context. Digital sovereignty, in this instance, is understood more narrowly as 'data sovereignty', emphasising human-centred autonomy over data, software, etc.[53] Additionally, the role of individual users is markedly diminished. The primary focus is on regaining control over relinquished data, which, when

[46] CJEU, Case C-594/18 P *Austria v Commission*, EU:C:2020:742, para 48.
[47] Milton L Mueller, 'Hague Keynote: Sovereignty in Cyberspace' Internet Governance Project, www.internetgovernance.org/2020/11/13/hague-keynote-sovereignty-in-cyberspace.
[48] See www.lawfaremedia.org/article/toward-digital-solidarity.
[49] Edoardo Celeste, 'Digital Sovereignty in the EU: Challenges and Future Perspectives' in Federico Fabbrini, Edoardo Celeste, John Quinn (eds), *Data Protection Beyond Borders: Transatlantic Perspectives on Extraterritoriality and Sovereignty* (Hart Publishing, 2021) 211, 225.
[50] ibid.
[51] Renata Ávila Pinto, 'Digital sovereignty or digital colonialism?' (2018) 27 *Sur International Journal on Human Rights* 15.
[52] Stephane Couture and Sophie Toupin, 'What Does the Notion of "Sovereignty" Mean When Referring to the Digital?' (2019) 21 *New Media & Society* 2305.
[53] Luciano Floridi, 'The Fight for Digital Sovereignty: What It Is, and Why It Matters, Especially for the EU' (2020) 33 *Philosophy & Technology* 369.

achieved, aligns with purely individual interests. In essence, individuals do not actively contribute to 'assisting' the EU in achieving autonomy and independence from third countries – a right and responsibility acknowledged by the fourth energy package. This is because, in the digital market, the absence of public regulation has not allowed space for individual freedom and self-determination; instead, it has been promptly filled by private big tech entities.[54]

In view of this, what ties together the concepts of energy sovereignty and digital sovereignty? It is the shared recognition that achieving them requires a departure from the conventional tools of market regulation, as defined by the neoliberal approach.

Indeed, recent debates on digital sovereignty signal a change in EU governance – a shift from a more market-liberal stance to a proactive, interventionist approach.[55] For example, regulations on digital services and data protection showcase a growing desire for heightened control over the digital sphere, departing from the traditionally neoliberal approach that characterised the digital single market.[56] Other authors[57] highlight that the AI Act and the DSA/DMA are formulated as a new generation of intentionally hybrid digital policies, encompassing internal market considerations, fundamental rights and geopolitical factors. This contributes to shaping the EU's self-constructed identity as a normative power.

This shift in perspective becomes even more pronounced when delving into the intricate relationship between digital sovereignty and sustainability, as explored in the preceding chapter.[58] Indeed, these initiatives distinguish themselves in legal nature from the regulatory acts typically analysed in studies on digital sovereignty (such as the GDPR, DMA and DSA). In this context, we observe genuine acts of industrial planning, exemplified by initiatives like the RePowerEU Plan, the Net Zero Industry Act, the Important Projects of Common European Interest (IPCEI) and the Strategic Technologies for Europe Platform (STEP), all designed to bolster key technologies and fortify EU sovereignty.

C. Shaping EU Industrial Policy and Empowering Citizens in the Digital Era

Perhaps, the escalating adoption of the sovereignty concept by the European legislator stems from addressing the twin transitions. This notion serves to mark the shift from the European regulatory state to a new EU industrial policy, given that,

[54] Vittorio Bertola, 'La sovranità digitale e il futuro di Internet' (2022) *Rivista Italiana di Informatica e Diritto* 39, 41.

[55] Sebastian Heidebrecht, 'From Market Liberalism to Public Intervention: Digital Sovereignty and Changing European Union Digital Single Market Governance' (2024) 62 *Journal of Common Market Studies* 205.

[56] ibid.

[57] Dennis Broeders, Fabio Cristiano and Monica Kaminska, 'In Search of Digital Sovereignty and Strategic Autonomy: Normative Power Europe to the Test of Its Geopolitical Ambitions' (2023) 61 *Journal of Common Market Studies* 1261.

[58] On this topic, see Celeste and Perez Victorio in this volume.

as observed,[59] the twin transitions themselves constitute the pillars of European industrial policy.

At the same time, though, this increased interventionist approach embraced by the EU is not in itself adequate; it must be complemented by a genuine empowerment of individuals, also within the digital market. Recognition of this principle can also be found in one of the pivotal initiatives dedicated to shaping the new European industrial strategy, namely the new Digital Compass 2030 programme,[60] whose vision is to build a digitalised economy and society based on the principles of solidarity, prosperity and sustainability, achieved through the empowerment of citizens.

However, what is the true essence of sovereignty if it does not merely involve a resurgence of public intervention? Perhaps, the interpretation to attribute to it aligns with Badie's perspective,[61] where, in a 'multicentred world' governed by a 'universe of transactions', sovereignty emerges as a profoundly functional and moral political value, granting societies the ability to make choices. To act as sovereign is to embrace the mantle of responsibility. Consequently, the principle of responsibility becomes the pivotal essence of public policies, with public intervention necessitating the engagement of new entities in the pursuit of public objectives. As recognised by the Digital Compass, facilitating this paradigm shift are digital technologies, particularly the transformative power of key enabling technologies like blockchain, poised to reshape the landscape of public intervention by opening new avenues for engagement and responsibility in the pursuit of public objectives.

IV. Blockchain Technologies for European Energy Sovereignty

The normative reconstruction presented in section II has already foreshadowed how, particularly within the energy market, the European regulator recognises the crucial role of digital technologies in empowering individuals for active contributions to the goals of the energy transition. Notably, blockchain emerges as a key player in unlocking substantial potential in this direction.

A. Blockchain for Peer-to-Peer Electricity Trading

Upon closer inspection, the legislative definition of 'peer-to-peer electricity trading' explicitly invokes blockchain technology. As mentioned earlier,[62] it involves the sale of renewable energy between market participants through a contract with

[59] Michela Passalacqua, 'Green Deal e transizione digitale verso un diritto eventuale' in Michela Passalacqua (ed) *Diritti e mercati nella transizione ecologica e digitale* (Wolters Kluwer, 2022) 3.

[60] EU Commission, *2030 Digital Compass: the European Way for the Digital Decade*, COM(2021) 118 final.

[61] Bertrand Badie, *Un monde sans souveraineté* (Fay, 1999).

[62] Article 2(18) Directive (EU) 2018/2001.

predetermined conditions governing the automated execution and settlement of the transaction, directly between the parties. This definition closely aligns with that of a smart contract, typically associated with blockchain technology, as it is stored and replicated on a blockchain network. Smart contracts, in essence, are self-executing contracts with predefined rules that automatically carry out actions and enforce contract terms, eliminating the need for intermediaries or centralised authorities.[63]

Indeed, for several years now, numerous studies and applied projects have been exploring the use of blockchain in peer-to-peer electricity trading.[64] The earliest application is the 'Brooklyn Microgrid' case, dating back to April 2016. Here, blockchain was employed for the exchange of renewable energy in a community-driven microgrid, facilitating the direct sale of energy generated by photovoltaic panels. Project participants installed smart meters to record the flow of electricity, while blockchain was used to facilitate and record all transactions through smart contracts, eliminating the need for intermediaries. This set-up enables automatic, transparent and real-time tracking of peer-to-peer energy exchanges among neighbours, fostering continuous monitoring of transactions.

B. Blockchain for Energy Communities: Case Studies

Within the framework of the recently introduced energy communities by the European legislator, peer-to-peer trading through blockchain appears to unveil its full potential. We have seen that, through these new legal entities, the aim is to ensure a new form of shared administration between final customers, local authorities and private stakeholders, to provide environmental, economic or social community benefits for the local areas where they operate.

Nevertheless, empirical evidence highlights a persistent lack of active citizen engagement in these communities, suggesting that the economic incentives introduced for this purpose fall short.[65] Several energy communities across Europe are exploring the use of blockchain for peer-to-peer energy trading to address this challenge. In Italy, the energy community of Turano Lodigiano, established in January 2022, connects public administration, citizens and stakeholders via a

[63] European Commission, 'What is a Smart Contract?' (Blockchain Observatory and Forum, 2024), blockchain-observatory.ec.europa.eu/what-smart-contract_en.

[64] See esp Merlinda Andoni et al, 'Blockchain technology in the energy sector: A systematic review of challenges and opportunities' (2019) 100 *Renewable and Sustainable Energy Reviews* 143; Ifigeneia Nai Fovino et al, *Blockchain in the Energy Sector, WP3 – Use cases identification and analysis*, EUR 30782 EN (Publications Office of the European Union, Luxembourg, 2021).

[65] Bernd Bonfert, '"We like sharing energy but currently there's no advantage": Transformative opportunities and challenges of local energy communities in Europe' (2024) 107 *Energy Research & Social Science* 103351; Brendan Lennon, Noel P Dunphy and Ezequiel Sanvicente, 'Community acceptability and the energy transition: a citizens' perspective' (2019) 9 *Energy, Sustainability and Society* 35.

blockchain platform.[66] This platform displays the community's economic revenues and enables real-time monitoring of data related to electricity production, consumption and withdrawal, encompassing individual user metrics. Each user, through a dedicated app, receives advice and valuable information to promote responsible green energy usage and the adoption of increasingly conscientious consumption behaviours, fostering engagement through gaming experiences. Additionally, the platform facilitates the calculation of various environmental sustainability indicators, ranging from reduced c emissions to the equivalent number of trees planted.

Particularly interesting is also the case of GoiEner, an energy community in Spain, which involves payment through a digital currency, Pyloncoin (PYLNC).[67] This currency is created to rewarding the work done by the nodes that validate and maintain the neutral database supported by the blockchain. At the same time, a part of the coins created goes to green energy producers, serving as an incentive and support mechanism for those who invest in renewable energy generation technologies.

C. Empowering Energy Democracy Through Blockchain

Numerous additional examples could be provided. It is worth noting that, in each case, blockchain not only opens up the market to new participants who were previously passive electricity consumers, but also fosters deeper innovation, fully embodying the values of energy citizenship and energy democracy. This dual impact represents progress in the broader liberalisation process and a significant stride toward embracing the fundamental principles of energy sovereignty. Indeed, by engaging within the community, the 'active customer' partakes in the energy market while concurrently exercising citizenship sovereignty. In collaboration with the local entity, he contributes to 'co-producing'[68] the socio-economic and territorial development, benefiting the entire community.

It is well understood that the consumption of goods is also a social act through which human beings communicate, create identity and establish relationships, shaping society in fundamental ways.[69] Within energy communities empowered by blockchain technology users can make decisions not only on whom to buy or sell renewable electricity from based on their price preferences, but also on other criteria reflecting their personal environmental or social values. For instance, consumers may specify the maximum price they are willing to pay for locally produced

[66] For more information see www.sorgenia.it/comunicati-stampa/sorgenia-inaugurata-la-comunita-energetica-rinnovabile-turano-lodigiano.

[67] For more information see www.pylon-network.org/wp-content/uploads/2019/02/TokenPaper_PYLON_ENGLISH.pdf.

[68] *cf* Elinor Ostrom, 'Crossing the great divide: Coproduction, synergy, and development' (1996) 6 *World Development* 1073.

[69] Mary Douglas and Bernard Isherwood, *The World of Goods* (Routledge, 2021).

renewable energy or prioritise the sale or purchase of energy from a particular individual. In this context, the evaluation based on non-price factors is significant for both ensuring the effective functioning of the market through economic regulation and in addressing climate and local development requirements.

These consumers differ from those typically envisioned in liberalist perspectives and align more closely with the concept of 'sovereign consumers' as defined by neoliberal economics.[70] Unlike the liberal view, this concept has strong moral and political implications: for the sovereign consumer, the market becomes not only a space for economic activity but also a platform for participation in sociopolitical processes, essentially evolving into a democratic arena.[71]

In the context outlined so far, blockchain functions primarily as a virtual network with the potential to give rise to new physical networks. Specifically, it facilitates the creation of electricity microgrids, offering alternative infrastructures to the centralised network. Within these microgrids, individuals actively contribute by injecting self-produced renewable energy, assuming personal responsibility within the broader goal of advancing a more sustainable world and achieving energy autonomy. Moreover, these virtual networks appear to be the origin of new 'institutional networks', where connectivity enables innovative collaborations among public entities, stakeholders and civil society, ultimately contributing to the promotion of European energy sovereignty. Thus, the genuine objective for today's regulator should be to champion these evolving relationship possibilities, thereby encouraging practices that empower individuals to leverage technology in actively participating in local socio-economic development.

V. Blockchain as a Nexus between Energy Sovereignty and Digital Sovereignty

Given blockchain technology's potential to advance the public objectives associated with energy sovereignty, it seems possible to undertake a critical reassessment of the current conceptualisation regarding the relationship between blockchain and digital sovereignty. Many scholars[72] view blockchain technology as a force that challenges, to varying degrees, traditional mechanisms of state authority, citizenship and democracy.[73] This potential shift could lead to the general

[70] This particularly refers to the thoughts of Ludwig von Mises, *Bureaucracy* (Yale University Press, 1944).

[71] *cf* Niklas Olsen, *The sovereign consumer: a new intellectual history of neoliberalism* (Palgrave Macmillan, 2019).

[72] See esp Kevin Werbach, *The Blockchain and the New Architecture of Trust* (The MIT Press, 2018); Sarah Manski and Ben Manski, 'No Gods, No Masters, No Coders? The Future of Sovereignty in a Blockchain Word' (2018) 29 *Law Critique* 151.

[73] Marcella Atzori, 'Blockchain Technology and Decentralized Governance: is the State Still Necessary? (2015) *Journal of Governance and Regulation* 45.

disempowerment of citizens and the emergence of a stateless global society,[74] eventually overshadowing both national sovereignties defended by states and international organisations that aspire to acquire sovereignty, such as the EU.[75]

A. Blockchain as a Neoliberal Capitalist Technology?

Conceived within the realm of a libertarian utopia, blockchain is still regarded as a neoliberal capitalist technology,[76] despite the numerous initiatives pursued by the EU to encourage its adoption by public administrations.[77]

It has been argued that blockchain fosters individualism and extensively economises social life, encouraging a form of consumption primarily driven by convenience rather than sustainable considerations.[78] This approach seeks immediate, individual satisfaction without fully considering the long-term or collective implications of consumption decisions. Therefore, 'under the dual banners of "innovation" and "progress" blockchain has become the means *du jour* for the reproduction of capitalist class power'.[79] This is evident in the correlation between blockchain and digital sovereignty, which seems to prioritise enhancing economic self-determination within the framework of neoliberal capitalism rather than recalibrating or invigorating social cohesion.[80]

Indeed, there is a prevalent notion today that digital platforms – including those distinct from blockchain – embody the pinnacle of modern capitalism. Referred to as 'platform capitalism',[81] this concept is fervently endorsed by proponents of neoliberal economics, viewing it as the novel frontier of wealth production. It is an economic model that ends up reproducing, albeit in a digital context, the

[74] ibid.

[75] Riccardo De Caria, 'Blockchain and Sovereignty' in Oreste Pollicino and Giovanni De Gregorio (ed) *Blockchain and Public Law* (Edward Elgar Publishing, 2021).

[76] Robert Herian, 'Blockchain, GDPR, and fantasies of data sovereignty' (2020) 12 Law, *Innovation and Technology* 156.

[77] In 2017, a call for tender was opened by the European Commission to establish a European expertise hub on blockchain and DLTs, leading to the creation of the European Union Blockchain Observatory and Forum in 2018. This initiative aims to accelerate blockchain innovation and ecosystem development in the EU. The Observatory has mapped various blockchain initiatives, organised thematic workshops, and published reports. In 2018, 21 Member States formed the European Blockchain Partnership to create the European Blockchain Services Infrastructure (EBSI) for cross-border services. Additionally, the International Association for Trusted Blockchain Applications (INATBA) was launched in 2019 to enhance public-private cooperation in the blockchain space. As of March 2018, the OECD reported that at least 46 countries globally had initiated over 200 blockchain-related projects in their public sectors. For more information see www.oecd-ilibrary.org/governance/blockchains-unchained_3c32c429-en.

[78] Herian (n 76).

[79] Robert Herian, 'Blockchain and the distributed reproduction of capitalist class power' in Inte Gloerich, Geert Lovink and Patricia de Vries (eds), *MoneyLab Reader 2: Overcoming the Hype* (Yale University Press, 2018).

[80] Herian (n 76) 158.

[81] *cf* Nick Srnicek, *Platform Capitalism* (Polity Press, 2016); Frank Pasquale, 'Two Narratives of Platform Capitalism' (2016) 35 *Yale Law & Policy Review* 309.

well-known extractive paradigm[82] where digital platforms solely aim at value extraction, abusing their dominant position. This model remains deeply rooted in traditional profit and market logics, promoting monopolistic ownership concentration aimed at profit maximisation.

B. Blockchain as a Driver for Inclusive Energy Transition

The preceding argumentation should have illustrated that digital platforms, such as blockchain, are not inherently fitting into this radical view. They also support the assertion of social and productive phenomena grounded in an alternative framework that seeks to promote inclusivity as well as foster new relationships among the public, private and citizens in the creation and distribution of value. In instances like peer-to-peer electricity trading, the aim is not merely to use digital technology to substitute an exchange already feasible in the traditional 'brick and mortar' economy. Rather, it involves establishing transactions that give rise to genuine relationships that would not exist otherwise. This holds particularly true when peer-to-peer electricity trading is conducted within the context of the CEC or REC, given that, by regulatory definition, it must also serve social and environmental purposes. Furthermore, the fact that blockchain enables individual citizens to sell the electric energy produced by their photovoltaic panels to third parties indicates that this emerging form of value creation does not strictly adhere to the traditional principles of capitalism. Indeed, in its original sense, capitalism denotes an economic system in which workers are excluded from capital ownership, which certainly cannot be said in this scenario. Likewise, it does not align with the prevalent manifestation of neocapitalism, where technological advancements and automation contribute to the prevalence of oligopolies, the separation of ownership and management, and the ascendancy of multinational corporations.

The industrial revolution, powered by steam-generated energy, shifted away from natural sources like solar, animal power and wind. Instead, technological advancements favoured the utilisation of substantial fuels such as coal, oil and natural gas, ultimately converting them into electricity. This transformation significantly severed the historical connection between humanity and nature, liberating people from ecosystems that were once their primary sources of sustenance.

Today, we find ourselves in the midst of a new revolution – a process of 'energy transition' that harnesses innovative technologies to develop solutions with a reduced environmental footprint. The move towards sustainability is intertwined with scientific and technological innovation, emphasising the growing social significance of technology, and marking a return of humanity to nature.

[82] *cf* Kinanya Pijl, 'From an Extractive to a Non-Extractive Economy: Disentangling the Building Blocks of Non-Extractive Economic Practices' (2022) 15 *International and Comparative Corporate Law Journal* 13.

This represents a reversal of the trends observed in recent decades – an embrace of renewable energy and locally aggregated energy production, aspects that were dismantled by privatisation and later nationalisation.

VI. Conclusion

In recent years, the convergence of digital transformation and climate change has woven a captivating narrative around the realms of sovereignty and polycentric governance,[83] even at the European level. To justify its expanded role in markets that, until recently, were primarily subject to pro-competitive regulations – such as the energy and digital markets – the EU is increasingly leaning on the concept of sovereignty. The comparison between energy sovereignty and digital sovereignty has allowed us to highlight that the latter is less effective in terms of ensuring solidarity among Member States and enabling inclusivity for individual citizens. European energy sovereignty is instead understood as an inclusive and participatory process aimed at achieving the energy transition. To attain these results, the use of blockchain becomes particularly valuable, as it is already employed to facilitate peer-to-peer electricity trading, empower energy communities, and promote energy democracy. If that is the case, the myth of blockchain as an exclusively neoliberal capitalist technology appears easily debunkable.

Indeed, from a *de iure condendo* prospective, the utilisation of blockchain in energy communities seems to enable not only participatory practices at the local level but even a continuous multilevel dialogue on energy involving the EU, Member States, local authorities and all parts of society. In this regard, Article 9 of Regulation (EU) 2021/1119, establishing the framework for achieving climate neutrality, specifies that the Commission shall actively involve all segments of society, enabling and empowering them to contribute to a fair and socially equitable transition toward climate neutrality. The Commission shall facilitate an inclusive and accessible process, employing all relevant instruments at various levels, involving national, regional and local tiers. This implies engaging them and promoting the dissemination of science-based information on climate change and its social and gender equality dimensions. As observed,[84] the goal should be to shift the centre of decision-making power to promote forms of social mobilisation, ensuring not only ongoing citizen consultations but also genuine co-design processes.

[83] Richard Sturn, 'Digital Transformation and the Sovereignty of Nation States' in Heinz D Kurz et al (eds), *The Routledge Handbook of Smart Technologies. An Economic and Social Perspective* (Routledge, 2022).

[84] See Giuseppe Bellantuono, 'I modelli e gli strumenti della programmazione energetica: un'analisi comparata' in Luigi Carbone, Giulio Napolitano and Andrea Zoppini (eds), *Annuario di Diritto dell'energia 2019 – La strategia energetica nazionale: 'governance' e strumenti di attuazione* (il Mulino, 2019).

This requires starting from the needs of the population to define the tools and objectives of the energy transition.

Perhaps, while allowing new relationships between individuals at the local level, blockchain could also give rise to a decentralised monitoring system among states, further empowering them in reducing emissions or achieving the share of renewable energy consumed. Indeed, as highlighted in the Turano Lodigiano case study (see section IV.B), blockchain not only enables the recording of all electricity transactions but also facilitates the calculation of various environmental sustainability indicators, such as reduced carbon dioxide emissions. By adopting the foundational concept of more traditional platforms like Airbnb and Uber, blockchain could, therefore, promote a more efficient reputational mechanism, enhancing the effectiveness of the existing monitoring system, which currently relies primarily on reports submitted by Member States. In fact, the proposed approach fosters inclusion while cultivating solidarity and mutual oversight among EU Member States, complementing the top-down control exercised by European institutions.

In a recent exploration of the concept of digital sovereignty, Robles-Carrillo suggests that what is fundamentally at stake is how markets, states, and societies should fundamentally interact.[85] Actually, as previously emphasised, sovereign claims inherently lean towards a continuous state of conflict. Nevertheless, in the imperative to delineate roles in reshaping the economy, these may not inherently be antagonistic forces, but rather have the potential to collaborate effectively within a participatory process.

Upon closer scrutiny, the concept of 'participatory regulation by technology' is gaining prominence, extending to digital markets in both the EU and the US. Bassan, for instance, contends that co-regulation and self-regulation give rise to a form of 'participatory regulation', which can be effectively implemented through blockchain.[86] In this context, however, blockchain is conceived solely as a tool for market regulation, while the concept of sovereignty, understood as an approach that goes beyond a market-fundamentalist perspective, is left out.

In conclusion, blockchain is not only emerging as a technological tool for participatory regulation; it is evolving into a transformative force that aligns digital sovereignty with the imperative of energy transition. In this envisioned scenario, the EU could assume the role of a sovereign, not merely adopting a more proactive stance, but also embracing the responsibility for the choices made by individuals. Within this dynamic interplay, blockchain emerges as the linchpin, ensuring an active role for citizens, local governments and stakeholders in steering the energy transition. Together, they create a harmonious blend where the EU's interventionist approach aligns seamlessly with individual agency and technological innovation, forging an exciting path toward a sustainable and participatory future.

[85] Margarita Robles-Carrillo, 'Sovereignty vs. Digital Sovereignty' (2023) 3 *Journal of Digital Technologies and Law* 673.

[86] Fabio Bassan, 'Digital Platforms and Blockchains: The Age of Participated Regulation' (2023) 34 European Business Law Review 1103.

8

Government as an Environmental Platform: Digital Sovereignty and Data-driven Environmental Action

THIBAULT CARRÈRE

Accessible and interoperable data are at the heart of data-driven innovation. This data, combined with digital infrastructure (e.g. supercomputers, cloud, ultra-fast networks) and artificial intelligence solutions, facilitate evidence-based decisions and expand the capacity to understand and tackle environmental challenges. The Commission will support work to unlock the full benefits of the digital transformation to support the ecological transition.

The European Green Deal[1]

I. Introduction

Digital sovereignty has been interpreted in various ways[2] and it can be analysed from three different perspectives.[3] From the viewpoint of sovereign states, digital sovereignty is about asserting control over digital tools and cyberspace.[4] This concept is as much about the establishment of servers on a state's territory as it concerns the state's ability to set the rules governing the services used by its citizens. As Pauline Türk points out, digital sovereignty is not conceived in the same way by all states:

> [A]ccording to an authoritarian and offensive conception, it is based on the right of the State to regain control of digital spaces in order to apply its laws and promote its

[1] European Commission, *The European Green Deal*, COM(2019) 640 final.

[2] Pierre Bellanger, *La souveraineté numérique* (Stock, 2014); Pauline Türk and Christian Vallar (eds), *La souveraineté numérique: la concept, les enjeux* (Mare & Martin, 2017).

[3] We draw upon the work of Pauline Türk on this matter: Pauline Türk, 'Définitions et enjeux de la souveraineté numérique' (2020) *Les Cahiers français: documents d'actualité* 415.

[4] Lawrence Lessig, *Code and other laws in Cyberspace*, 2nd edn (Basic Books, 2006).

> interests; according to a more liberal and defensive conception, it is based on the right of the State to protect its citizens against surveillance and exploitation policies conducted in cyberspace by entities driven by their own interests.[5]

From the point of view of users or groups of users, the concept of digital sovereignty refers to a twofold possibility: that of controlling their personal data, in the face of both private and public operators; and that of organising themselves into a civil society capable of controlling the actions of these operators. Finally, from the viewpoint of private operators, digital sovereignty is a more descriptive concept. It pertains to the ability of these companies to set their rules for the use of cyberspace.

This chapter examines digital sovereignty from the point of view of the sovereign states. It will also address the consequences of the irruption of digital sovereignty issues on state administrative organisation. I will therefore adopt a *legal* definition of digital sovereignty. In 1576, Jean Bodin defined sovereignty as an 'absolute and perpetual' power, including, particularly, the ability to make laws.[6] Today, however, this concept seems outdated. It is not new to assert that state sovereignty is being challenged, in particular by private actors which, because of their dominant position in the market, have the power to set the rules governing cyberspace.[7] Henceforth, the challenge for contemporary states lies in reclaiming their sovereignty and effectively addressing this competition. This challenge has also been taken by international organisations, such as the European Union (EU).[8] This is especially true in the context of ecological transition, which, to say the least, does not always benefit from the monopolistic dominance of private actors.

The relationship between digital sovereignty and environmental protection can be approached from at least two perspectives. The first considers environmental protection as a limit to the development of digital technology. Concepts like 'digital sobriety' or 'digital sustainability', ie the necessity to reduce the environmental footprint of digital technology, are being developed in that respect.[9] The requirements of sobriety or sustainability would call into question digital sovereignty in that they would limit the possible choices made by sovereign states.

[5] Türk and Vallar (n 2) 32.

[6] Jean Bodin, *Les six livres de la République* ([1576], Classique Garnier, 2013).

[7] For instance: Eric Schmidt and Jared Cohen, *The New Digital Age: Reshaping the Future of People, Nations and Business* (John Murray, 2014).

[8] For an overview of this notion in that context, see Nathalie Smuha, 'Digital Sovereignty in the European Union: Five Challenges from a Normative perspective' (Social Science Research Network, 2023), papers.ssrn.com/abstract=4501591.

[9] Hugues Ferreboeuf (ed), *Lean ICT: pour une sobriété numérique* (TheShiftProject, October 2018); Conseil national du numérique, 'Feuille de route sur l'environnement et le numérique' (2020); Sénat français, 'Pour une transition numérique écologique' (Rapport d'information n° 555, Commission de l'aménagement du territoire et du développement durable, mission d'information sur l'empreinte environnementale du numérique, June 2020); BEREC, 'Draft BEREC Report on Sustainability: Assessing BEREC's contribution to limiting the impact of the digital sector on the environment', BoR (22) 35, March 2022. Some countries, such as France, passed several laws to take this issue into account: Loi n° 2021-1485 du 15 novembre 2021 *visant à réduire l'empreinte environnementale du numérique en France*; Loi, n° 2021-1755 du 23 décembre 2021 *visant à renforcer la régulation environnementale du numérique par l'Autorité de régulation des communications électroniques, des postes et de la distribution de la presse.*

This is addressed in several other chapters in this volume.[10] However, the link between digital technology and environmental protection can also be viewed from a different perspective. In this alternative view, digital technology is considered as a means or tool for supporting environmental protection.[11] This chapter will explore this perspective, addressing the question: can digital sovereignty reinforce environmental protection? To answer this, I will develop an analysis based on French public law and administrative science, focusing on how the latter aims to understand the concrete behaviour of the real actors behind the legal personality of administration.

'Government as a Platform' is a concept introduced by Tim O'Reilly, an Irish entrepreneur.[12] In his article of the same name, he develops an innovative conception of modern states. The author uses the Apple App Store as an ideal model for a platform that could serve as a model for organising state administration. In section II, I demonstrate two key points. First, that the notion of Government as a Platform, as it has emerged in France in the past decade, has been a way to defend digital sovereignty; at the cost, however, of a shift in the traditional conception of general interest. In section III, building on this concept, I address the existence of 'Government as an *environmental* platform'. It will show that platform organisation has managed to produce some results and achievements in environmental matters, and I will question the actual or supposed capacity of this new administrative organisation to favour the ecological transition. Finally, I will argue that Government as an environmental platform still raises some challenges concerning data protection and data valuation.

II. Government as a Platform and Digital Sovereignty

The links between Government as a Platform and digital sovereignty reveal a paradox. Indeed, Government as a Platform entails acknowledging that private actors, in the same way as sovereign states, can participate in shaping the general interest. In this respect, the concept can be seen as another manifestation of the erosion of state sovereignty (see section A below). At the same time, in France, Government as a Platform has served as a means to free the state from foreign private actors, thereby keeping it at the forefront of digital public policies. Thus, this concept becomes a vehicle for reaffirming state *digital* sovereignty (see section B below).

[10] See in particular chs 6, 10, 11, 12, 13 of this volume.

[11] Stefano Epifani, *Why Digital Transformation is the Road to Sunstainability?* (Digital Transformation Institute, 2021); Kathryn Sforcina, *Digitalizing Sustainability: The Five Forces of Digital Transformation* (Routledge 2023); Nathalie Hervé-Fournereau, 'Les interférences entre la politique de l'environnement et la stratégie numérique européenne – Pacte vert et boussole numérique: balises juridiques pour une double transition soutenable' in Brunessen Bertrand (ed), *La politique européenne du numérique* (Bruylant, 2023). For institutional writings on this point, see: European Commission, *A European Green Deal*, COM (2019), 640 final.

[12] Tim O'Reilly, 'Government as a Platform' (2011) 6 *Innovations: Technology, Governance, Globalization* 13.

A. Government as a Platform and the Apparent Decline of State Digital Sovereignty

Section i below examines the notion of digital Platform and its application to state organisation, and section II analyses the implications for the French conception of state sovereignty and public action.

i. The Intellectual Roots of Government as a Platform

In the sense used by Tim O'Reilly, a digital platform can be defined as an intermediary structure between service providers and customers. This legal and economic relationship is characterised by an original division of roles. The platform aims to leverage the capacity for innovation of external players, avoiding limitations imposed by its own means of production. To facilitate this, it provides third-party suppliers with tools and data enabling to create new digital services. The suppliers, in turn, can create services that are distributed through the platform and are compensated by the customers who purchase these services. Finally, the role of customers is fundamental, since

> the system is designed to constantly elicit action from its users and integrate them into the production and valorisation processes. This 'activation' is achieved by means of various semio-technical operators: multiple counters that measure 'performance' (displaying the number of 'views', 'subscribers', 'posts', 'shares', 'likes', etc.) but also processes expressly designed to mobilise attention (alerts, notifications, message invitations, etc.). This perlocution is essential because the logic is based on obtaining content from third parties or, at the very least, obtaining their data.[13]

In short, the platform lays out the creation tools, the creators deliver the services, and the customers provide their data. Tim O'Reilly proposed applying this model to government, which is the meaning of the expression 'Government as a Platform'. But what does it mean to consider the Government as a digital platform? In essence, this new concept centres state action around two fundamental missions. Firstly, Government as a Platform suggests opening public data on a massive scale. Government as a Platform and open data are therefore inherently linked. This also involves encouraging the transfer of data and, consequently, the proliferation of application programming interface (API)[14] to enable their reuse: 'Rather than having the government itself build out all of the websites and applications that use that data, providing application programming interfaces to the private sector will

[13] Vincent Bullich, 'La "plateformisation" comme déploiement d'une logique organisatrice: propositions théoriques et éléments de méthode' (2021) 1 *Effeuillage* 9 (author's translation).

[14] An API is software that serves as an intermediary between two applications. It permits different applications to communicate with one another. In that context, an API is used by an administration to support data transfer and to facilitate the creation by private entities of applications which use public data.

allow independent developers to come up with new uses for government data.'[15] Secondly, Government as a Platform entails providing tools that enable private actors to participate in determining general interest and setting up new public services. The underlying idea is that public action could benefit from private innovation.

This new conception of the state had a decisive influence in France, through Henri Verdier, a French entrepreneur. He took up this idea in his 2012 book, *L'âge de la multitude* (literally 'the age of multitude'), written with Nicolas Colin.[16] In addition, he had the opportunity to implement these concepts when he was appointed director of *Etalab*, the French administration department responsible for open data, in 2013. In 2015, he became the head of the Interministerial Direction for Digital Technology (then DINSIC; now DINUM). Therefore, he had the opportunity to implement his ideas within the state apparatus. As a result, Government as a Platform in France has been both a theoretical *discourse* and a concrete *public action*.

ii. The Different Models of Government as a Platform

The consequences of this conception of government are numerous: the promotion of data transparency, a challenge to the bureaucratic organisation of the state based on hierarchical silos in favour of a much more horizontal and transversal organisation, the emergence of state-backed start-ups providing new public services, etc. However, its implementation in France revealed a tension within the notion of Government as a Platform: should it be oriented toward economic actors (such as companies) or non-economic ones (such as associations)? In the mid-2010s, these two major approaches to Government as a Platform came into conflict within the French state. The first approach defended was mostly centred on economic actors. Henri Verdier endorsed such a pro-market version of Government as a Platform. But another approach was advocated by Christian Quest, founder of OpenStreetMaps, first defender of free software and digital commons and, at that time, also member of the French administration. He upheld a version of Government as a Platform centred on private non-economic actors. This approach based on digital commons was also supported at the EU level, by France, during the French presidency of the EU Council and the EU Commission in 2022, outlining the possibility of EU digital sovereignty.[17] In France, for example, these two concepts of Government as a Platform have clashed over the status of the national database listing all addresses in the country.

While the project began with the desire to make this construction a digital commons, as evidenced by the recruitment of Christian Quest and the association with OpenStreetMaps, the choices ultimately made, particularly concerning

[15] O'Reilly (n 12).

[16] Nicolas Colin and Henri Verdier, *L'âge de la multitude. Entreprendre et gouverner après la révolution numérique*, 2nd edn (Armand Colin, 2015).

[17] Digital Assembly, 'Toward a sovereign digital infrastructure of commons' (Report of the European Working Team on Digital Commons, June 2022), www.openfuture.eu/wp-content/uploads/2022/07/220624digital_commons_report.pdf.

the ownership and licence of the database, favoured an open licence that would not allow protection from the exclusive appropriations of the web giants. So, we can see that the pro-market vision of the platform state can also be a springboard for the GAFAMs (Google, Apple, Facebook, Amazon, Microsoft). This helps us understand the path taken by Henri Verdier, who initially defended a rather pro-market vision and who, in order to refocus on the issue of digital sovereignty, converted to the ideology of the digital commons.

Therefore, a more statist conception of Government as a Platform (defended by Henri Verdier) or one more focused on the digital commons (defended by Christian Quest) are, for their part, more attentive to digital sovereignty, understood as resistance to the GAFAMs.[18] What all these approaches had in common, however, was to challenge the classic conception of public action, centred on the idea that public administration is the final guarantor of the general interest. Government as a Platform gave rise to some resistance within the French state, because it was considered a new avatar of neo-liberalism and new public management.[19] The horizontal rather than vertical logic, the questioning of the traditional administrative organisation and the new methods of recruiting agents responsible for this change are often presented as necessary adaptations to modernity. However, they are sometimes perceived both internally and externally as a smokescreen for a profound questioning of the role of public action. Government as a Platform is therefore a new facet of the decline of public administration in favour of the private sector. And, as such, as a decline of state sovereignty.[20] However, this affirmation must be tempered, because Government as a Platform can also be analysed, not as a decline of state sovereignty, but as a simple transformation of it.

B. The Transformation of State Digital Sovereignty

The concept of Government as a Platform has been imported into France in part as a support for digital sovereignty. This can be seen both in the discourse (see section i below) and in the actions (see section ii below) of public players.

i. The Theoretical Reinforcement of State Digital Sovereignty

Government as a Platform can be seen as a way to reassert the role of sovereign states in the global digital competition. In relation to France, two points must be

[18] These two approaches were also complementary. For example, Henri Verdier also defended the idea of digital commons and their capacity to shape France's digital sovereignty. See Henri Verdier and Charles Murciano, 'Les communs numériques, socle d'une nouvelle économie politique' (2017) 5 *Esprit* 132.

[19] Gilles Jeannot, 'Vie et mort de l'État plateforme' (2020) 173 *Revue français d'administration publique* 165.

[20] Jacques Chevallier, 'Vers l'État-plateforme?' (2018) 167 *Revue française d'administration publique* 627.

addressed. Firstly, digital sovereignty was a fundamental concern for the French state since the outset. As a result, the emergence of Government as a Platform has had to accommodate certain requirements relating to sovereignty, which may conflict with its liberal philosophical foundation. For example, the need to protect the security of data, which may be an obstacle to its reuse by private bodies, had to be set against the requirement for open data. Furthermore, the emergence of the platform state does not mean that the public authorities have withdrawn, since they continue to exercise dual control over data: physical control over storage; and oversight of its use through software. The concept of Government as a Platform therefore had to be integrated with the requirements of digital sovereignty from the outset. From that point on, Government as a Platform seems to align with issues long discussed in public economic law concerning the 'strategic state', reflecting a new role for the state, which is less a competitor to the private sector and more its regulator and partner.[21]

Also, in France, Government as a Platform – both in discourse and in practice – was conceived as a tool for achieving independence from major foreign companies. Indeed, the aim was to escape the domination of large non-European private companies through the creation of French digital tools and the emergence of French start-ups.[22] Therefore, Government as a Platform can be considered as a way to put the state back at the centre of general interest in digital matters. Thus, the role of sovereign states is not only to establish legal regulations framing the action of private operators. It is also to provide public services directly or indirectly through those actors. As Pierre Pezziardi and Henri Verdier point out:

> This is a new stance for a State that today sees itself more as a monopolistic service than as a stimulator (or co-producer) of societal initiative. Yet this platform transformation process is not the end of the State, but on the contrary the embodiment of a sovereignty regained at the centre of the digital game.[23]

This new conception of state is not only conceptual; it has been put into concrete actions reinforcing France's digital sovereignty.

ii. The Practical Reinforcement of State Digital Sovereignty

Government as a Platform, in France, resulted in several achievements. Three of them deserve a closer look. First, in less than 10 years, 110 French start-ups have been created, embracing various fields, including public procurement ('*Marché*

[21] Philippe Bezes, *Réinventer l'Etat. Les réformes de l'administration française (1962-2008)* (PUF, 2009); Fabien Bottini, *L'action économique des collectivités publiques. Ses enjeux, son droit, ses acteurs* (Legitech, Institut Louis Joinet, 2020) 483.

[22] Colin and Verdier (n 16) 254256; Pierre Pezziardi and Henri Verdier, 'Des startups d'État à l'État plateforme' (Fondation pour l'innovation politique, Janvier 2017) 32–36; DINUM, 'Une stratégie numérique au service de l'efficacité de l'action publique' (Feuille de route de la direction interministérielle du numérique, March 2023) 14.

[23] Pezziardi and Verdier (n 22) 35 (author's translation).

public simplifié (MPS)'), job search,[24] access to social aid,[25] etc.[26] Similarly, the creation of the 'stopcovid' application enabled the French Government to avoid using a similar application from Apple, thereby preventing foreign private actors from gaining control of COVID-related data. This led to a conflict between the French Government and the tech giants Apple and Google, which blocked part of the 'StopCovid' functions.[27] This episode underscores that, even when it comes to public health, the digital sovereignty of governments in the face of the power of the GAFAMs is a key issue.[28] The second achievement of Government as a Platform is the development of open data and data exchange between administrations. For instance, the service *Dites-le-nous-une-fois* (literally, 'Tell us once'),[29] allows administrations to exchange their data, so citizens can avoid having to repeat the same information to each one of them. In addition, the French Government has opened up a large amount of public data[30] and facilitated its reuse by setting up a large number of APIs.[31]

Finally, the third achievement, and maybe the most important one, is undoubtedly FranceConnect.[32] Initially it was a connexion and identification tool, similar to Facebook Connect or Google Connect, common to many online administrative procedures (eg taxes, social assistance). In addition, FranceConnect now has the ambition, in the long term, to become the 'meta-plaform' of the French state: a central access portal and support for most French administrative processes. While other countries have chosen to authorise the use of Facebook Connect for their administrative procedures, the creation of a sovereign identification tool further demonstrates France's desire to emancipate itself from the tutelage of foreign companies.[33] There is, however, an important point to note. This digital issue should not be seen solely in terms of the public–private divide. Behind digital sovereignty, understood as emancipation from the GAFAMs, there is the desire to emancipate oneself from certain US laws that these companies must comply with. Statutes like the Patriot Act or the Cloud Act, for instance, oblige American companies to transmit all their customers' personal data to the US authorities

[24] www.labonneboite.pole-emploi.fr.

[25] www.mes-aides.gouv.fr.

[26] For an overview of all the services created, see www.beta.gouv.fr.

[27] Gilles Jeannot and Simon Cottin-Marx, *La privatisation numérique. Déstabilisation et réinvention du service public* (Raisons d'agir éditions, 2022) 73–76.

[28] Luciano Floridi, 'The Fight for Digital Sovereignty: What It Is, and Why It Matters, Especially for the EU' (2020) 33 *Philosophy & Technology* 369.

[29] See Loi n° 2018-727 du 10 août 2018 pour un État au service d'une société de confiance; Décret n° 2019-31 du 18 janvier 2019 relatif aux échanges d'informations et de données entre administrations dans le cadre des démarches administratives et à l'expérimentation prévue par l'article 40 de la loi n° 2018-727 du 10 août 2018 pour un État au service d'une société de confiance.

[30] Available at www.data.gouv.fr.

[31] Available at www.api.gouv.fr.

[32] Arrêté du 8 novembre 2018 relatif au téléservice dénommé « FranceConnect » créé par la direction interministérielle du numérique et du système d'information et de communication de l'État.

[33] Marie Alauzen, 'L'État plateforme et l'identification numérique des usagers' (2019) *Réseaux*, n° 213, 211–39.

even though it is not stored on American territory, for national security and 'fight against crime' reasons. It is therefore also the hegemonic power of countries like the US that is targeted by the notion of digital sovereignty, and not just that of tentacular companies.

The emergence of Government as a Platform has therefore created a favourable ground to the development of digital sovereignty. Nevertheless, what about the environment? Can this new conception of state organisation be used to promote an environmental agenda? Or, to put it another way, can digital sovereignty support the green transition?

III. Government as a Platform and Environmental Public Action

Drawing upon this notion of Government as a Platform, we can develop the concept of 'Government as an *environmental* Platform'. Section A below looks at the achievements of Government as an environmental Platform, while section B reviews the tensions still at stake.

A. The Emergence of Government as an *Environmental* Platform

The French Government as an *environmental* Platform is organised around two administrative structures. Firstly, there is the *Agence de la transition écologique* (Ecological Transition Agency) (ADEME). Its role has been to launch cooperation projects between public and private entities in the environmental field. And, secondly, there is what was formerly known as DATAGIR, which depends on the ADEME and is a government start-up responsible for creating and opening environmental databases. DATAGIR has now been replaced by a broader structure, *l'Accélérateur de la transition écologique* ('the ecological transition accelerator'), which still depends on the ADEME and is a state incubator. In this context, section i below asks on what principles those administrative structures are based, and section ii asks what are their concrete creations?

i. The Principles of Government as an Environmental Platform

It is possible to consider two main principles. First of all, Government as an environmental Platform is centred on the ambition to provide *reliable* environmental data. By gathering data and creating databases, the state does not rely solely on data provided by the actors involved in the activities being monitored. This makes it possible to have data from an *impartial* third party; data that is *open* and therefore *open to criticism*. For example, DATAGIR managed to create databases on the environmental impact of food, independently of the data provided by the companies of the agri-food industry. In addition, this first principle is in line with international, European, constitutional and legislative requirements in environmental matters. Two rights can be mentioned here. The right to environmental information, enshrined in Article 1 of the Aarhus Convention, in EU law[34] and, in the case of France, in Article 7 of the Environmental Charter, which has constitutional status, and in Articles L 124-1 and following of the Environmental Code. This right often has a broader scope than the simple right of access to administrative documents, the latter being governed by a formal criterion that does not apply in environmental matters.

Secondly, the ambition of Government as an environmental Platform is to direct both public and private action towards general interest considerations, and more specifically, towards ecological considerations. The underlying idea is that by competing with private platforms, the state can accomplish two things. The primary objective is to diminish the influence of private platforms, which are not known for their environmental consciousness. Furthermore, by organising as a platform, it is claimed that the state can direct the actions of public and private actors (including individuals) in a different way than imposing rules. It is a *softer* way to orient private behaviour. Government as a Platform can therefore be seen as part of an older development in public action and normativity in general. These new forms of state intervention, particularly in economic matters, have been crystallised around the term 'regulatory law'. This form of regulation reflects the state's desire to replace strict regulations that constrain the behaviour of private players with incentives to guide that behaviour. The development of independent administrative authorities or agencies, as well as the use of soft law tools, for instance, leads to a negotiated normativity between public and private players.[35] These tools are particularly used in environmental matters,[36] where governments are still reluctant, for a variety of socio-economic reasons, to impose excessive constraints on private players, constraints that could prove harmful in international economic competition.

ii. The Concrete Creations of Government as an Environmental Platform

For the time being, the French Government environmental Platform is in its infancy, but it is nonetheless a testament to the development of projects involving

[34] European Parliament and Council Directive (EC) 2003/4 on public access to environmental information and repealing Council Directive 90/313/EEC [2003] OJ L 41/26; European Parliament and Council Directive (EC) 2007/2 establishing Infrastructure for Spatial Information in the European Community (INSPIRE) [2007] OJ L 108/1.

[35] Annie Brett, 'Information is Power: Democratizing Environmental Data' (2022) *Utah Law Review* 127.

[36] At the EU level, we can mention, for example, the EU Emissions Trading System. See: Council Directive (EC) 2003/87 establishing a system for greenhouse gas emission allowance trading within the Union and amending Council Directive 96/61/EC [2003] OJ L 275/32.

public actors, private companies and non-profitable private structures. Overall, three sectors of intervention can be highlighted. The food sector is, without a doubt, the leading realm of Government environmental Platform.[37] As such, the ADEME and DATAGIR have participated in the implementation of projects aimed at improving the traceability of agri-food products and questioning the ecological sustainability of certain productions. In concrete terms, this has led to the creation of a database called Agrybalise.[38] This database seeks to measure the environmental impact of agri-food products and agricultural production, relying on multiple factors: use of water resources, use of pesticides, land use, energy use, etc. In collaboration with private operators, this led to the creation of the *eco-score*, a tool for rating food products to assess their environmental impact and deliver this information directly to the consumers.

In addition, ADEME and DATAGIR provide a lot of information on two other sectors: transport[39] and housing. This information is open to the public, and can be integrated to private services or used in scientific research. For instance, regarding housing, they supply information on energy diagnostic data, electricity consumption in households, etc. ADEME's incubator also launched projects on housing renovation and building heating. Concerning transport, they provide information on emissions of carbon per transport, per trip, etc. These are the three primary sectors in which the concept of Government as an environmental Platform is developed. However, other examples could be cited, such as information on EPR channels, which details the obligations of producers to organise sorting for goods like light bulbs and batteries, as well as regional development and planning, where data is provided to support local authorities.

To ensure that all ministerial departments work together, the General Commission for Sustainable Development, an interministerial body, is planning to organise the sharing of data between public and private bodies via the Ecolab innovation laboratory. The creation of these databases is fostered by the EU, which is encouraging Member States to set them up. This is the aim of the Inspire directive for geographical data, for instance,[40] or also the Shared Environmental Information System (SEIS) and the data provided by satellite through the Copernicus programme. The European Environment Agency also has a datahub designed to impart environmental data to all EU citizens.[41] Its most important databases are those on biodiversity, land use and water management. The Agency clearly states that the aim of setting up these databases is the 'exploitation, re-use and recombination of data' as a basis for research projects, in particular. This could take the form of the creation of European Data Spaces, some of which relate

[37] See also Rasetto in this volume.
[38] Available at www.agribalyse.ademe.fr.
[39] Since 2021, public bodies have been required by law to share data relating to transport management and planning.
[40] INSPIRE Directive (n 34).
[41] Available at www.eea.europa.eu/en/datahub.

directly to environmental issues: Green Deal, mobility, energy, agriculture.[42] This logic of open data supporting an environmental platform is therefore at the heart of Europe's environmental strategy. Nevertheless, the emergence of a Government environmental Platform is not without raising some fundamental questions, particularly in terms of data governance.

B. Tensions

The development of Government as an environmental Platform is based on the progress of open data. As such, it brings with it the risks associated with this practice. If open data is based on the dissemination of data, it carries the seeds of major risks for data protection. Indeed, although it may seem counterintuitive, the dissemination of environmental data can raise concerns regarding personal data protection (see section i below). What is more, these data are often treated by administrations, associations or companies as valuable assets and are therefore closely guarded. Yet, to function, Government as an environmental Platform requires the free dissemination of data. As a result, a tension emerges between free access and value-adding, between altruism and budgetary imperatives (see section ii below).

i. Data Dissemination v Data Protection

The first tension is between data dissemination and data protection. The dissemination of data serves an undeniable collective interest, in that it can enhance transparency, foster innovation, and promote societal progress. However, this comes into conflict with data protection, which safeguards individual rights such as privacy and business secrecy. We might think that environmental data has little to do with personal data, but that would be a mistake. The French data protection authority (CNIL) distinguishes between two categories of environmental data: data by nature; and data by purpose. Environmental data by nature is 'for example, geographical data and metadata directly produced for the purpose of understanding and analysing the territory'.[43] In contrast, environmental data by purpose is 'data collected and processed initially for uses that are not directly related, but which may provide information on aspects of human activity',[44] such as mobility data or water and energy consumption data. While environmental data by nature has very little to do with personal data, the same cannot be said of environmental data by purpose, which focuses on the behaviour and uses of individuals.

[42] European Commission, *Common European Data Spaces*, SWD(2022) 45 final.

[43] CNIL, 'Données, empreinte et libertés. Une exploration des intersections entre protection des données, des libertés et de l'environnement' Cahiers Innovation & Prospective, No 9 (June 2023) 51, www.cnil.fr/sites/cnil/files/2023-07/cnil_cahier_ip9_0.pdf (author's translation).

[44] ibid.

From this perspective, some environmental data may fall within the scope of the GDPR. Consequently, the sharing of such data for the public interest must be balanced with the respect of individual rights. At a time when the EU is advocating for *data altruism*, ie the sharing by private actors of data considered useful to the general interest, the European Data Protection Board (EDPB) has warned of the risks of this practice for the protection of personal data within the Union. First, it has pointed out that 'general interest' is not inherently a sufficient legal basis under the GDPR. Second, it emphasised that consent cannot be presumed or universally applied in such cases.[45] For example, the opening up of certain data relating to the use of pesticides by farmers could eventually lead to their identification by environmental activists; these farmers and their plots could then run significant risks. Obviously, this cannot be the purpose of opening that kind of data. Government as a Platform aims to implement global public policies, not to punish individual behaviour. But this shows the limits of data dissemination. The paradox is that the more data is opened up, the more cross-checking will be possible and personal protection will be in danger. That can be an obstacle to open data for administration, which is often irrationally afraid of the GDPR. This balancing act between the need to open data and the need to protect individuals is sometimes difficult for civil servants. In particular, this results in a kind of self-limitation, upstream, for fear of violating the requirements of the GDPR, even in risk-free situations. Moreover, this balancing act is not made any easier by the wide range of data categories and related legal regimes: health data, data of general interest, personal data, etc. As environmental data does not, for the moment, have any real legal characterisation, this leads to major difficulties in setting up a genuine environmental platform.

ii. Data Valuation v Free Data

The second tension that emerges is that between data valuation and free data. This double imperative weighs on the agents of the French state. The initial idea of Government as a Platform was to provide data for free, so that private operators can create value. It is a very neoliberal idea: states must bear the cost of innovation whereas the value created by innovation should be collected by the private sector.

However, this is about to change. In fact, two ideas have arisen since the development of the concept of Government as a Platform. The first idea that is starting to gain ground is that certain data may no longer be free. In principle, open data implies that data should be free of charge. This is part of the very spirit of the phenomenon, as well as the legal rules governing it. However, there are already some exceptions to this principle of free access. Some data may have to be paid for: access and reuse may be subject to the payment of a fee.[46] This is already the

[45] EDPB, 'Statement 05/2021 on the Data Governance Act in light of legislative developments' (2021), www.edpb.europa.eu/our-work-tools/our-documents/statements/statement-052021-data-governance-act-light-legislative_en.

[46] Article L 324-1 French Code of relations between the public and the administration.

case for certain environmental data,[47] such as meteorological data or information relating to the physical marine environment and its evolution, and for certain geographical data. There is nothing to prevent the authorities from establishing several licences for the same data, for example by imposing a paying licence for commercial use and a free licence for non-commercial use.

These possibilities result from the transposition into Member State law of the 2019 Open Data Directive.[48] However, the payment of a fee remains the exception, and state law tends to reaffirm this forcefully. The logic of Government as a Platform is that these provisions should be maintained as they stand, insofar as the cost of exploiting data falls on private individuals. Moreover, free access is supposed to encourage innovation and enable all players, even the smallest, to participate in this wealth creation.[49] The introduction of an entry fee would have the effect of favouring Big Tech enterprises to the detriment of small companies, which is the opposite of the desired objective. However, given the reality of European governments' finances, and at a time when they are doing their utmost to create value from their movable and immovable assets, can they deprive themselves of the financial windfall that public data could represent? The balances in this area seem precarious, but the idea of making more data subject to a charge is already gaining ground in policy and among legal scholars.[50]

The second idea that is emerging is that individuals and private actors should also be obliged to share certain data for free, in particular environmental data. In France, for example, the obligation to provide environmental data is also imposed on private operators, as long as they are in charge of a public service mission.[51] Also, at the EU level, since the passing of the Corporate Sustainability Reporting Directive, implemented in France with the Ordinance No 2023-1142 on December 6, 2023, certain companies (approximately 50.000 in the EU) are obliged to publish certain environmental data.[52] It was already the case for public companies and data originating from public research.[53] Moreover, this logic also seems to arise from the Data Governance Act.[54] This directive, adopted in May 2022 and applicable from September 2023, enshrines the notion of 'data altruism'. This notion is defined as

[47] Article D 324-5-1 French Code of relations between the public and the administration.

[48] European Parliament and Council Directive EU 2019/1024 on open data and the re-use of public sector information [2019] OJ L 172/56.

[49] O'Reilly (n 12) 35.

[50] Mohammed Adnène Trojette, 'Ouverture des données publiques. Les exceptions au principe de gratuité sont-elles toutes légitimes ?', (Rapport au 1er ministre, 2013) 90–98, www.medias.vie-publique.fr/data_storage_s3/rapport/pdf/134000739.pdf.

[51] Article L 124-3 of the Environment Code.

[52] European Parliament and Council Directive EU 2022/2464, amending Regulation (EU) No 537/2014, Directive 2004/109/EC, Directive 2006/43/EC and Directive 2013/34/EU, as regards corporate sustainability reporting [2022] OJ L 322/15.

[53] European Parliament and Council Directive EU 2019/1024 on open data and the re-use of public sector information [2019] OJ L 172/56.

[54] European Parliament and Council Regulation EU 2022/868 on European data governance and amending Regulation (EU) 2018/1724 (Data Governance Act) [2022] OJ L 152/1.

> the voluntary sharing of data on the basis of the consent of data subjects to process personal data pertaining to them, or permission of data holders to allow the use of their non-personal data without seeking or receiving a reward that goes beyond compensation related to the costs that they incur where they make their data available for objectives of general interest as provided for in national law, where applicable, such as [...] combating climate change.[55]

Environmental data by nature or purpose may well correspond to the requirements of this text,[56] that is fully in line with the principles set out above. The introduction of data-sharing intermediaries demonstrates the desire to guarantee confidence in data sharing. As for the introduction of a register of altruistic organisations, this is part of a rationale of encouragement rather than coercion.

What is more, the notion of the altruism of data is reminiscent of Henri Verdier's concept of the multitude. For Verdier, the hallmark of a platform is the ability to use all individuals to create value, which in the digital age means essentially to create data. From this perspective, the capture of environmental data will also rest on the shoulders of a very large number of associations and individuals. Added to this is the fact that the environment is the major political cause of the twenty-first century, Government as an environmental Platform could benefit from a form of activism by and through data. However, mastering this multitude once again presents the state with major challenges in terms of personal data protection, since citizens often collect environmental data via their individual smartphones.

There is a third option concerning the economics of environmental data: the appeal to digital commons.[57] In this hypothesis, environmental data would fall neither within the scope of public data, managed by the public authorities, nor within that of the market. The data produced and its use would be the result of joint management and control. The ADEME already launched a series of initiatives concerning digital commons in environmental matters. A number of calls for commons projects have been launched to encourage innovation, particularly in the fields of energy efficiency and regional resilience. This has led to the creation of many different digital commons, such as the COASTWARDS application, which aims to monitor rising sea levels in a decentralised way, by asking users of the application to take photographs as they walk along the coast.[58] Although, as we have already seen, both the EU and France are committed to this approach, which is perfectly compatible with the logic of Government as a Platform, it would appear to be a complementary option that is not yet intended to replace the role of the state or the market.

All of this is interesting because it seems to deepen the logic of Government as a Platform. Thus, by imposing free dissemination of data to both public and private operators, the cooperation is strengthened, and the creation of value does

[55] Article 2(16).
[56] CNIL (n 43) 57.
[57] Digital Assembly (n 17).
[58] See www.coastwards.org.

not depend solely on the state. But in France, problems arise in particular for associations responsible for public service missions. This kind of association collects data but has no real interest in opening them, as these databases constitute the basis of their expertise. We can see that these operators implement avoidance strategies so as not to have to provide their data. Cooperation appears to be an easy word, but a complex realisation.

IV. Conclusion

This chapter has led to two key findings. Firstly, the concept of Government as a Platform has emerged as a pivotal framework for safeguarding digital sovereignty. It has facilitated the development of numerous national digital services, partially reducing reliance on foreign corporations and advancing the goal of technological independence. At the conclusion of this analysis, it becomes evident that while the concept of Government as a Platform has been presented as a significant innovation, it does not result in a drastic transformation of the state or its organisational structure. However, it has facilitated the development of new tools for public action. Moreover, this reimagined approach to governance proves particularly valuable in advancing environmental public action.

This chapter has defended the existence of Government as an *environmental* Platform. In this way, alongside traditional methods of state-led environmental public action – such as subsidies (for example, for the purchase of electric vehicles), economic planning (the direction of industrial production), direct intervention, basic regulation, taxation, etc –sovereign states are developing a new approach: data-driven environmental action. Sovereign states intervene in ecological matters *through* data by adopting the logic and codes of digital platforms. It is a way to encourage and develop environmental public and private action by other means. This implies to admit that effective environmental action depends on the collaboration between the public and private sectors, particularly through the shared use of environmental data. As such, Government as a Platform can be a powerful structure favouring this cooperation. The postmodern state, often deemed outdated, demonstrates remarkable agility in adapting and integrating new concepts, thereby preserving or reinvesting its sovereignty.

9

Digital Sovereignty and Green Public Procurement

PIERRE-HENRI MORAND

I. Introduction

Addressing the connection between digital sovereignty and sustainable development through the lens of public procurement may seem unexpected, especially when the analysis is carried out by an economist. However, we will see how the strategies proposed by governments to defend digital sovereignty echo those related to the sustainability of public procurement. We will also look at how the Tender Electronic Daily (TED)[1] data (award notices published in the Supplement to the *Official Journal of the European Union* (OJEU) can be used to objectify this link, and to understand its limitations. In this chapter, we will examine the statistical data pertaining to all European Union's (EU) public procurement award notices, with a particular focus on the French example.[2] Furthermore, we discuss how the concept of sovereignty through public procurement markets is raised in specific terms, and we will study how this approach is relevant to the study of digital sovereignty issues in the context of public procurement. We will argue that, when it comes to digital procurement contracts, the interplay between digital sovereignty and environmental concerns is highly specific.

Public procurement is a significant contributor to the economy, with the state, local authorities and public bodies making substantial purchases in services, works and supplies. In Western countries, public procurement accounts for

[1] This is the online version of the 'Supplement to the Official Journal' of the EU dedicated to European public procurement: see ted.europa.eu/en/simap/european-public-procurement.

[2] All the calculations and maps relative to the French case are formulayed by the author from the data available in the FOPPa database: see Lucas Potin et al, 'FOPPa: an open database of French public procurement award notices from 2010–2020' (2023) 10 *Scientific Data* 303. This dataset was funded by ANR (French NSF) Grant ANR-19-CE38-0004.

almost 15 per cent of the gross domestic product (GDP).[3] When awarding a public contract, a decision is made, within the legal constraints of public procurement law, as to which company will carry out the contract and, to some extent, how it will be provided. As Carrier notes:[4]

> It is difficult to envision a more sovereign, trade-related act than the purchase of goods, supplies, and services by a government with monies collected primarily from its citizens for the purpose of funding government operations and public welfare generally. The relationship between sovereignty and government procurement is an intimate one, and, as one scholar has quipped in relation to domestic protectionism generally, '[d]iscrimination in favor of local products sometimes seems to be one of the basic human urges'.[5]

Carrier distinguishes between internal and external sovereignty. While the former concerns the relationship of the governmental purchasing entity to its nationals (and is out of the scope of this chapter), the latter

> concerns the relationship between the contracting sovereign to the nationals (including corporations and enterprises) of other countries. In such cases, there is an extra consideration related to sovereignty, ie, how any acts or decisions possibly involving external suppliers of goods, supplies and services affect the interests of the country and its nationals.[6]

Therefore, addressing the question of sovereignty in public procurement contracts is, from the point of view of the governments, essentially questioning the buyer's ability to ascertain (or to favour) the nationality and/or the location of the winning company, its potential subcontractors or suppliers.

In the same vein, green public procurement (GPP) is defined as 'a process whereby public authorities seek to procure goods, services and works with a reduced environmental impact throughout their life cycle when compared to goods, services and works with the same primary function that would otherwise be procured'.[7] In order to ascertain the sustainability of public procurement, it is necessary to examine the influence of the public buyer on the environmental quality of acquisitions and the environmental impact of their purchases. In essence, the issue of sovereignty in public procurement can be reduced to a question of 'who': who wins the contract, who owns the winning firms, and who participates in the supply chain of the contract. In contrast,

[3] OECD, *Reforming Public Procurement: Progress in Implementing the 2015 OECD Recommendation* (OECD Publishing, 2019), doi.org/10.1787/1de41738-en.

[4] Paul J Carrier, 'Sovereignty under the Agreement on Government Procurement' (1997) *Minnesota Journal of International* Law 78.

[5] Original footnote: John H Jackson, *World Trade and the Law of GATT* (Bobbs-Merrill, 1969) 274.

[6] Carrier (n 4) 84.

[7] European Commission, Communication from the Commission to the European Parliament, the Council, the European Economic and Social Committee and the Committee of the Regions, *Public procurement for a better environment*, COM/2008/0400 final 2008, para. 3.1.

the issue of environmental sustainability in public procurement can be reduced to a question of 'how'. However, determining the 'how' will inevitably impact the 'who'.

Nevertheless, such opportunities to express specific preferences during public procurement are not subject to individual discretion. They must respect legal constraints, in particular those that prohibit unequal treatment of competitors and those that limit the scope of criteria that a public purchaser is entitled to choose as the basis for its selection.

II. Public Procurement in the EU and Free Trade Agreements

Within the EU, the award of public procurement contracts must adhere to the principles of the Treaty on the Functioning of the EU. These principles include the free movement of goods, freedom of establishment and the freedom to provide services, as well as derived principles such as equal treatment, non-discrimination, mutual recognition, proportionality and transparency. In simpler terms, the winner is determined through the open and transparent process of public procurement bidding. It is imperative that considerations of protectionism not be imposed as an a priori constraint that would limit the pool of companies eligible to compete, particularly with regard to the nationality of potential winners.

On a worldwide scale, this principle of non-discriminatory treatment is echoed in the 2012 World Trade Organization Government Procurement Agreement (WTO GPA) that also ensures open, fair and transparent conditions of competition in the public procurement markets.[8]

Behind these general principles of non-discrimination, set as a prior condition for the proper functioning of public procurement markets, the practice is more nuanced. Specifically, global trade agreements are mandatory only for contracts above certain thresholds. Additionally, certain sectors identified as strategic by the parties may be exempt from the agreements.

[8] Article IV GPA reads: '1. … each Party, including its procuring entities, shall accord immediately and unconditionally to the goods and services of any other Party and to the suppliers of any other Party offering the goods or services of any Party, treatment no less favourable than the treatment the Party, including its procuring entities, accords to: (a) domestic goods, services and suppliers; and (b) goods, services and suppliers of any other Party. 2. … a Party, … shall not: (a) treat a locally established supplier less favourably than another locally established supplier on the basis of the degree of foreign affiliation or ownership; or (b) discriminate against a locally established supplier on the basis that the goods or services offered by that supplier for a particular procurement are goods or services of any other Party.'

Last, but not least, preferential public procurement policies do exist. These preferential policies can result from an explicit 'buy local policy', when the government offers a specified preference for domestic suppliers.[9] It can also be implicit when the government uses policies based on discriminatory product quality standards.[10]

Outside the EU, the most famous illustration of explicit preferential public procurement is the United States (US) 'Buy American Act'.[11] It is applicable to all purchases of goods by US Federal Government agencies valued over the US micro-purchase threshold, which is currently set at $10,000.[12] For goods purchased by federal entities for public use under the Act, there is a requirement for these goods to be produced in the US. In order to qualify as being produced in the US, the goods must be manufactured domestically, and at least 50 per cent of the cost of their components must be derived from US sources.[13] Obviously, Buy American requirements do not apply to EU countries for US federal purchases covered by the revised WTO GPA, to which the EU countries are parties. When bidding on US federal procurements covered by these agreements, EU suppliers benefit from the same treatment as American suppliers. But none of the US's WTO GPA commitments apply to procurements at the municipal level.

In early 2021, the then US President Joe Biden issued an executive order stating that the 'Government should [procure goods] materials, and services from sources that will help American businesses compete in strategic industries'.[14] On 7 March 2022, the US Federal Acquisition Regulatory (FAR) Council published the final rule containing changes to the Buy American Act relative to domestic preference requirements. This final rule is a significant step towards the implementation of a policy to enhance domestic preferences announced by President Biden just a few days after taking office. The FAR Council previously issued a proposed rule that contemplated: 1) phased increases in domestic content thresholds; 2) enhanced preferences for critical products and components; and 3) post-award reporting requirements for critical products and components.

The second option available to buyers to avoid detrimental competition for national businesses in the context of full-frontal competition is through

[9] Florance Naegelen and Michel Mougeot, 'Discriminatory public procurement policy and cost reduction incentives' (1998) 67 *Journal of Public Economics* 349.

[10] Michel Mougeot and Florence Naegelen, 'A political economy analysis of preferential public procurement policies' (2005) 21 *European Journal of Political Economy* 483.

[11] The Buy American Act (Title 41 of the United States Code titled 'Public Contracts', enacted on 4 January 2011, consists of federal statutes regarding public contracts USC §§ 8301–8305) required the US Government to give preference to US-made products in its purchases.

[12] Federal Acquisition Regulation 2.101 – Definitions.

[13] Federal Acquisition Regulation 52.225-1 – Buy American-Supplies.

[14] Exec Order No 14005, 86 FR 7475 (25 January 2021).

the selection criteria they are allowed to use. Social and environmental objectives have become increasingly important in procurement practices. As noted by Saussier and Tirole, 'the significant amounts at stake in the public procurement system make it a potential lever for achieving social, environmental and innovation-related objectives, in which case the public authority must incorporate these criteria at the contractor selection stage.'[15] This represents a major evolution in the technical considerations deemed acceptable under international trade law. The United Nations Commission on International Trade Law (UNCITRAL) Model Law on Public Procurement, approved on 1 July 2011, integrates the possibility of selecting contractors based on their ecological characteristics. This same rationale is explicitly present in Article X (Technical Specifications and Tender Documentation) of the Revised Agreement on Government Procurement as of 13 December 2010. Article X-1 articulates the general principle of free trade:

> A procuring entity shall not prepare, adopt or apply any technical specification or prescribe any conformity assessment procedure with the purpose or the effect of creating unnecessary obstacles to international trade.

Article X-6 allows for environmental considerations to be incorporated into technical specifications:

> For greater certainty, a Party, including its procuring entities, may, in accordance with this Article, prepare, adopt or apply technical specifications to promote the conservation of natural resources or protect the environment.

In the same vein, the current EU Procurement Directive (2014) provides new opportunities for promoting sustainability through the public procurement process.[16] In France, as early as 2004, the French Public Procurement Code allowed social and environmental considerations to be taken into account in the procurement process.[17]

Section III below explores how sovereignty and sustainability can be linked in the context of public procurement. We will see how, in public discourse first, sustainable public procurement practices and sovereignty come to be interlaced. This coupling transforms the aim of sustainable procurement into an implicit means of protectionism or defence of external sovereignty as previously defined. In Section IV, we will empirically verify and question the reality of this link using European and French data relative to public procurement. In doing so, we will highlight that the connection is less clear-cut concerning digital services and supplies (see section V). We will argue that the issue of digital

[15] Stéphane Saussier and Jean Tirole, 'Strengthening the efficiency of public procurement' (2015) 22 *Notes du conseil d'analyse economique* 1.

[16] Directive 2014/24/EU of the European Parliament and of the Council of 26 February 2014 on public procurement.

[17] Décret No 2004-15 du 7 janvier 2004 portant code des marchés publics, Art 53.

sovereignty in public procurement may need to be addressed through alternative approaches.

III. Localism, Protectionism, Sovereignty and Environmental Concerns

Three recent written questions to the French Government, asked by representatives, two deputies and one senator respectively, underscore the desire to break away from the principles of total free competition in public procurement in order to favour national, or even local, enterprises and to strengthen national sovereignty.[18] Moreover, the Government's responses subtly outline the connection made between protectionism, sovereignty, digital sovereignty and environmental considerations.

The written question from Deputy Benoit Potterie to the French Minister of Finance inquires about the feasibility of instituting a local preference mechanism in the awarding of public contracts.[19] It is worthy of note that the Deputy does not include the term 'sovereignty' in the question he has written. The Deputy's argument is based on what he sees as a contradiction between the Government's sustainability goals, which aim to encourage short supply chains and invigorate local economies, and the counterproductive effects of excessively open public procurement. He points out the 'absurdity of local municipalities and public inter-municipal cooperation establishments not having the means to prioritize locally established companies when awarding contracts'.[20] In light of this, he proposes that the legislation on public contracts be reviewed to potentially include geographic criteria in the awarding of public procurement contracts, illustrating an implicit link between sustainable development and the intention to bypass the principle of non-discrimination in public procurement by incorporating criteria of localism. He emphasises the fact that the promotion of local purchasing also responds to environmental and ecological concerns. He posits that those who are sensitised to sustainable public purchasing seek to reduce the ecological footprint of their purchases by limiting transportation and emissions of pollutants during the execution of their contracts.

In response, the minister outlines the legal obstacles that would prevent such a practice.[21] He states that the constitutional principles of public procurement and the principles of non-discrimination and freedom of movement of persons, capital

[18] Marchés publics, Préférence locale pour l'attribution de marchés publics, Débats Parlementaires, *Journal Officiel* (19 November 2019) 24584; Débats Parlementaires, *Journal Officiel* (25 February 2020) 1485 and Souveraineté économique européenne et commande publique, *Journal Officiel* (4 May 2023) 2894.

[19] Débats Parlementaires (19 November 2019) (n 18).

[20] ibid.

[21] ibid.

and services set out in the EU treaties present an obstacle to taking into account a geographical criterion in the award of public contracts. He notes that the European judge and the French administrative judge frequently censure performance conditions or award criteria based on the origin of products or the geographical location of companies. Consequently, any modification of public procurement law in this regard would be unconstitutional and unconventional. Nevertheless, he acknowledges the potential for establishing or even exploiting a connection between the selection of local businesses and environmental considerations. This could occur when the latter are pursued for objectives divergent from the original intent of such selections.

The French Public Procurement Code already provides buyers with the necessary tools to facilitate access to their markets for local companies. At the stage of awarding contracts, buyers can base themselves on criteria such as the development of direct supplies or performance in terms of environmental protection. It is thus possible, for example, to assess the quality of bids with regard to the effort to reduce greenhouse gas emissions, particularly for the transportation of supplies or staff travel. It is enlightening to contrast the Government's response with that provided several months later to the written question from Deputy Christophe Naegelen.[22] Unlike the previous question, Naegelen's considerations do not touch on environmental aspects, but focus solely on digital sovereignty and its potential defence through public procurement regulation.

Mr Naegelen draws the attention of the Minister of the Economy to the concrete measures required to build and defend genuine French and European digital sovereignty. He begins by stating that, for over two decades, major countries have implemented assertive industrial policies to defend their digital sectors. These include reserved or preferential public purchasing policies. In France, despite record fundraising by French start-ups, some of which were sold to non-European funds, the Government does not appear to be taking a stance to prevent the administration's data from being exploited by foreign entities. Nor is it supporting the emergence of national digital players. The deputy defines sovereignty as the capacity to enable domestic digital enterprises to avoid reliance on foreign companies, and in terms of handling national data. He suggests that the geographical criterion in public procurement should be strengthened so that the state can more substantially support digital companies established in France or Europe, thereby contributing to the creation and distribution of national wealth. One example of this would be to reserve 50 per cent of public purchases for European companies.

In the Government's reply, the minister reiterates the legal constraints impacting public procurement.[23] The Government is aware of the necessity to foster the

[22] Débats Parlementaires, *Journal Officiel* (10 November 2020) 7897.
[23] ibid.

relocation of strategic purchases. But, in doing so, it must adhere to the bounds set by international treaties and European law, which prohibit discrimination against candidates on the basis of nationality. Furthermore, it must comply with the conditions set forth by public procurement law, which requires the enactment of measures that will create the conditions for an increase in the French share of the state's purchases. In order to achieve this objective, purchasers are encouraged to utilise all available tools, with particular emphasis on the promotion of non-price competitiveness criteria and the incorporation of demanding conditions of execution in terms of the environment, social inclusion and traceability within their contracts. Nevertheless, they argue that reserving a percentage of public purchases for European companies is not a viable option in light of France and the EU's international commitments, particularly the Agreement on Government Procurement concluded within the framework of the WTO. Further addressing the issue of data sovereignty, the reply specifies:

> Regarding the data of the administration and the support to cloud computing industrialists, the reflection around digital sovereignty is at the heart of the national cloud strategy unveiled on May 17, 2021. This strategy is based on three pillars: The first creates a framework to identify solutions that meet our criteria of sovereignty and security, associating them with the term 'trusted cloud'. The second requires that the State's information system uses trusted cloud solutions whenever sensitive data are handled, ensuring that the sensitive data of our citizens and companies are out of reach of any foreign interference. … The currently implemented cloud strategy precisely provides answers to the questions raised: to protect the data of our citizens and companies.[24]

The end of the Ministry's response therefore includes a specific consideration relating to digital sovereignty. It is understood here as sovereignty over data. And the demand for sovereignty over data gives rise to a number of specific concerns.

In the last question,[25] Senator Sylvie Robert draws the attention of the Minister for the Economy, Finance and Industrial and Digital Sovereignty to the application of Article L 2112-4 of the French Public Procurement Code, which states that

> a public purchaser may require that the resources used to carry out all or part of a contract, or to maintain or modernise the products acquired, be located within the territory of the Member States of the EU in order, in particular, to take account of environmental or social considerations or to ensure the security of information and supplies.[26]

[24] ibid, author's translation.

[25] Written question n 06613 – 16e legislature, *Journal Officiel du Sénat*.

[26] The article was introduced into French law as a consequence of the transposition into French law of Article 23 of Directive 2009/81/EC of 13 July 2009 on defence or security contracts.

The text highlights the potential of this provision as a powerful instrument for the reindustrialisation and economic sovereignty of Europe. However, it notes that this potential is not being fully realised, as purchasers have not been adequately informed of the circumstances under which they can make use of it.

Furthermore, the document cites the sole instance of invocation of this particular article of the public procurement code: the French Directorate for Healthcare Provision (DGSOS) recommended its utilisation for the acquisition of personal protective equipment (PPE) in December 2021, on the grounds that it was incumbent upon the public authorities to

> contribute to the development of European production capacities for healthcare masks in order to strengthen their sovereignty and thus secure the supply chain in the long term for the benefit of players in the healthcare system, by putting in place an appropriate public procurement mechanism.[27]

The relationship between sovereign procurement and environmental considerations is clearly established. It now appears in specific instruction on healthcare products:[28] the current European legal framework makes it possible to encourage the emergence of production sectors, particularly for the production of PPE, medical devices and critical medicines in Europe, through public procurement. Several levers can be used to this end:

- requiring part of the production to be carried out in Europe to ensure the security of strategic supplies for the proper functioning of the healthcare system;
- include performance and environmental protection clauses and conditions, and include a significantly weighted selection criterion;
- make compliance with equipment quality standards a condition for the admissibility of bids, and heavily weight the technical merit criterion when awarding the contract, while symmetrically reducing the weight of the financial criterion;
- providing for heavy financial penalties in the event of a significant deterioration in the quality of supplies or delivery conditions for orders placed.

[27] Instruction N° DGOS/PF/PHARE/2021/254 du 15 décembre 2021 relative à la sécurisation du processus d'achat de fournitures et équipements critiques, www.achatpublic.info/sites/default/files/document/documents/bulletin_officiel_sante_-_protection_sociale_-_solidarite_ndeg_2021_24_du_31_decembre_2021.pdf.

[28] Instruction N° DGOS/PHARE/2024/36 du 20 mars 2024 relative à la sécurisation du processus d'approvisionnement souverain en fournitures, produits de santé et équipements critiques, www.preventioninfection.fr/wp-content/uploads/2024/04/2024_Instruction-Securisation-approvisionnements_MNSTR.pdf.

As specified in these instructions, these techniques do not guarantee that the most competitive bid will come from a company based in Europe, but if they are used to best effect, they could significantly increase the likelihood of this happening.

In fact, Article L 2112-4 of the French Public Procurement Code permits purchasers to stipulate, in their specifications, the location of the resources used to carry out all or part of a public contract on the territory of the Member States of the EU (including for the maintenance or modernisation of the products acquired). Nevertheless, this stipulation must not impede the implementation of the guarantee of equal access to public procurement afforded by the EU to certain third countries under trade agreements. Consequently, purchasers are permitted to invoke this clause only if they can demonstrate that it is justified by the purpose of the contract, and is both necessary and proportionate to the objective of ensuring the proper performance of the contract. It thus falls upon the purchaser to demonstrate that the objective of the contract can only be achieved by requiring the location of all or part of the resources in question, particularly in terms of information security and supply chain resilience, or in consideration of social or environmental factors. It is crucial to highlight that, in the context of digital sovereignty, the environmental issue no longer serves as a means of exercising sovereignty, in contrast to other aspects of sovereignty in public procurement. The intrinsic connection between sovereign public procurement and environmental sustainability is no longer evident.

By way of illustration, the Ministry's response refers to the need to guarantee the security of information, which, in addition to the specific guarantees linked to compliance with the rules set out in the GDPR,[29] would require the establishment of computer servers within the territory of the EU, whose data could not be extracted remotely by companies based in third countries that do not provide guarantees equivalent to those required by this regulation.[30]

IV. Local, Sovereign and Green Purchasing in Statistics

While the regulatory framework depicted in sections II and III imposes stringent constraints on states to not allow a priori restrictions on the access of all companies to public procurement, what about the contracts that are concluded? The mere possibility for a company of any nationality and location to bid for

[29] Regulation (EU) 2016/679 of the European Parliament and of the Council of 27 April 2016 on the protection of natural persons with regard to the processing of personal data and on the free movement of such data, and repealing Directive 95/46/EC (General Data Protection Regulation).

[30] Written question (n 25).

a public contract does not necessarily mean it will do so, nor does it ensure its success in winning the contract. To objectively measure the real openness of European public markets to foreign companies, we analysed all the available data relative to procurement contract award notices in the EU. This open data is freely available online on the TED, the digital version of the supplement to the OJEU, enabling a relatively straightforward examination of the reality of some 3,000,000 public contracts advertised in the OJEU from 2010 to 2021, specifically those exceeding the European publicity threshold and thus more likely to attract large foreign enterprises.[31]

The implicit connection made between environmental clauses or criteria and sovereignty may be based on the following reasoning: distance – and the transportation it entails – constitutes an environmental externality associated with public procurement; moreover, compliance with local environmental standards provides a comparative advantage to companies established in the public buyer's territory. Explicitly considering the environmental impact of a public contract tends so to favour local businesses, which in turn could enhance sovereignty induced by public procurement. Let us test this hypothesis against the observed data.

Two statistics allow us to examine the impact of environmental criteria on the awarding of public contracts. Let us first observe the effect of these criteria on the distance between the public purchaser and the awarding company. Collecting the national ID of all public buyers and all winning firms, we can geolocate both entities and compute the distance between buyers and suppliers. Table 9.1 below provides the mean distance for all public procurement contracts with award notices published in the TED from 2010 to 2020, with a French public buyer. By collecting all the award criteria present in the electronic award notices and analysing them automatically in terms of semantics, we determined which of the contracts included environmental criteria (regardless of the weight given to the criterion).

Table 9.1 Average distance between buyers and suppliers

Type of contract	All contracts		Contracts with environmental criteria	
	Distance (km)	No of observations	Distance (km)	No of observations
Supplies	195	676,033	139	48,815
Utilities	315	646,149	251	84,893
Works	103	316,999	102	26,948

[31] Most of the calculations and all the maps are made by the author from the data available in the FOPPa database: see Potin et al (n 2).

Thus, in line with intuition and whatever the type of contract, the distance between buyer and supplier is statistically smaller for contracts incorporating environmental criteria.[32] It could be objected that what is true for contracts in general is less relevant in the digital domain: the distance (from client to server, from software development to deployment on a specific site, etc) is by its very nature less involving, as the digital space is ubiquitous.

In order to focus on public procurement contracts which, by their very nature, involve the most considerations linked to the digital dimension, let us now restrict our attention to specific public procurement contracts such as IT services (consulting, software development, internet and support, cloud storage) software package and information systems. In order to do so we limit our data to contracts with specific Common Procurement Vocabulary codes.[33]

By a pure sampling effect (as the market concentration of companies operating in the digital sector is inherently lower than that of markets as a whole), we can expect the distance to increase. Besides, the environmental impact of the distance between the place of acquisition and the place of production (which is one of the negative environmental externalities of a distant procurement market in terms of transport and the resulting greenhouse gas emissions) is probably lower in the digital sector: it does not matter whether your data is hosted 100 or 10,000 km away; for the vast majority it is the environmental quality of the infrastructure that matters, not its distance.

Nevertheless, we observe similar results. Using an environmental criterion during the award process reduces the distance between the selected suppliers and the public buyers.

Table 9.2 Average distance between buyers and suppliers for IT services, software and information systems

Type of contract	All contracts		Contracts with environmental criteria	
	Distance (km)	No of observations	Distance (km)	No of observations
Supplies	228	30,353	209	734
Utilities	334	5,031	190	204
Works	231	118	251	5

[32] For a more detailed discussion, see Pierre-Henri Morand and François Marechal, 'Achats publics responsables et achat local: enseignements des données ouvertes françaises' (2023) 3 *Revue d'Économie Régionale & Urbaine* 387.

[33] The Common Procurement Vocabulary establishes a single classification system for public procurement aimed at standardising the references used by contracting authorities and entities to describe the subject of procurement contracts.

But while the link between environmental criteria and proximity seems empirically established, this is a rather crude approach to the problem.

If we consider the concept of sovereignty in its original sense, ie the concepts of supremacy of power over a territory and independence,[34] it is perhaps more relevant to study the territorial impact of environmental criteria rather than the sole variable of distance. As we saw earlier, the issue of sovereignty in public procurement is, in public discourse, akin to the desire to increase the likelihood of a contract being awarded within a country's borders. Proceeding in a similar way, we therefore present in the following tables the share of public contracts awarded within the same administrative territory. Three geographical scales are proposed: regional (France is divided into 13 regions); departmental (France is divided into 96 departments); and local (France counts for 1243 intercommunal subdivisions). Table 9.3 contrasts the result considering specifically contracts with environmental criteria.

Table 9.3 Proportion of local purchasing

Type of contract	**% same region**		**% same department**		**% same local area**	
	All	**Env crit***	**All**	**Env crit**	**All**	**Env crit**
Supplies	49.45	58.7	32.05	40,4	18.64	21.4
Utilities	27.86	33.9	17.54	19.3	8.7	10.0
Works	62.2	67.3	49.0	51.9	24.9	25.5

* Environmental criteria.

It is clear that (whatever the administrative perimeter considered) there has been an increase in the award of contracts to companies located in the same territory as the public purchaser.

Once again, let us check that this result remains valid in the field of digital public procurement:

Table 9.4 Proportion of local purchasing for IT services, software and information systems

Type of contract	**% same region**		**% same department**		**% same local area**	
	All	**Env crit***	**All**	**Env crit**	**All**	**Env crit**
Supplies	37.5	58.4	14.5	28.3	12.1	24.9
Utilities	28.9	44.1	8.2	5.9	5.4	0
Works	62.2	14.3	49.0	14.3	24.9	0

* Environmental criteria.

[34] See Andrew Keane Woods, 'Litigating Data Sovereignty' (2018) 128 *Yale Law Journal* 328.

There indeed exists an empirical link between so-called green public purchasing and the attribution of contracts to companies belonging to the purchasing territory. However, the relevant perimeter for studying issues of intra-border versus cross-border procurement is likely that of the country rather than its administrative divisions. Let us broaden our analysis for a moment to consider the results of public procurement at the scale of the EU as a whole.

The initial observation that can be drawn is the extraordinary localism of these markets. Out of 7,245,028 referenced contracts during the period, 98 per cent were awarded to companies located in the contracting country. The proportion even rises to 99.6 per cent for contracts awarded by an EU country to a European company. At first glance, therefore, public procurement markets do not escape national companies, even though they are subject to a regulatory framework that mandates openness and the absence of discrimination. The map in Figure 9.1 presents the share of public purchases made by a company belonging to the buyer's country.

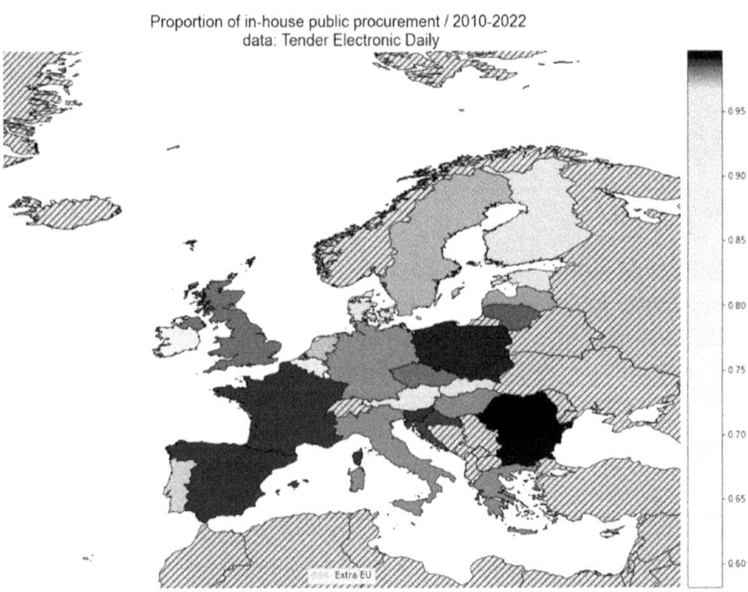

Figure 9.1 Percentage of public purchases made by a company belonging to the buyer's country
Source: TED.

Of course, what is true on average for all works, services and utilities that can be procured through public tenders does not necessarily hold for digital contracts. Nonetheless, we can replicate the analysis by focusing exclusively on digital services and goods. The resulting map in Figure 9.1 appears to be quite equivalent:

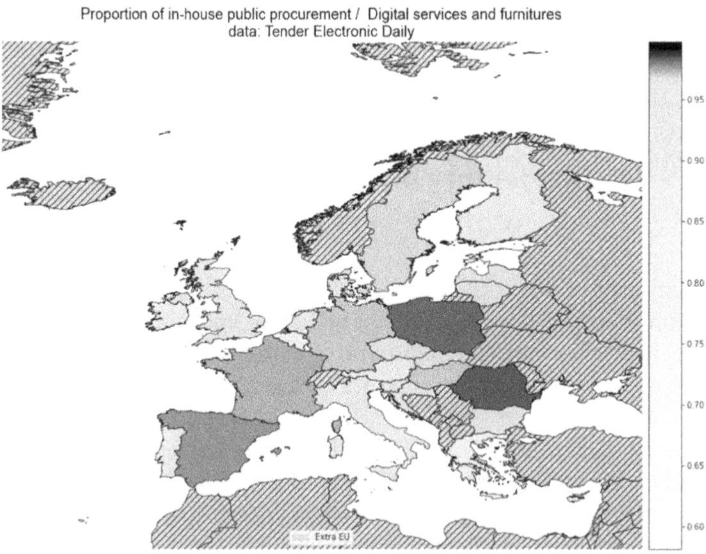

Figure 9.2 Percentage of public purchases of digital goods and services made by a company belonging to the buyer's country
Source: TED.

The greatest heterogeneity observed stems from the very nature of the national offering in these types of products or services. This accounts for the tendency of 'smaller' countries to more extensively engage non-national providers for such contracts. Nevertheless, the mean proportion of digital public contracts awarded to companies located within the national territory remains particularly high, standing at 98.4 per cent.

Conversely, as Figure 9.3 illustrates, it is possible to identify non-European countries that sometimes win some of these contracts.

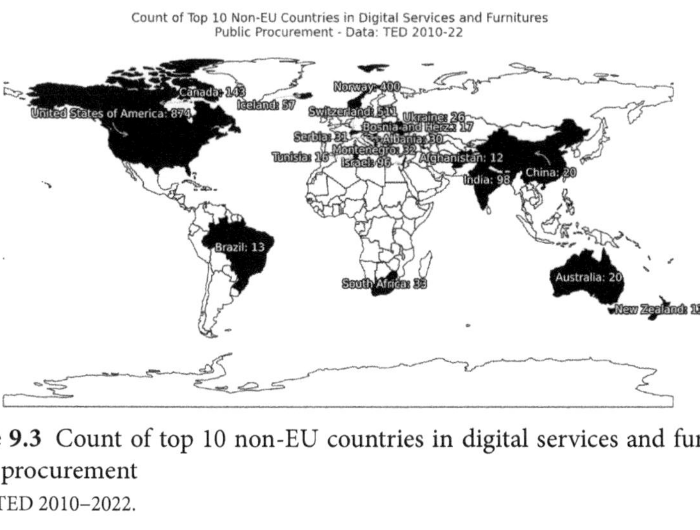

Figure 9.3 Count of top 10 non-EU countries in digital services and furnitures public procurement
Source: TED 2010–2022.

Thus, several thousand contracts have been won by companies from Switzerland, the US, Norway, Canada, India, Israel, etc. However, they represent only a very small minority of the total number of contracts in question.

V. Sovereignty on Data: The Challenges of the Sovereign Cloud

Does this mean that, when examining the data of European public procurement, the question of sovereignty that it might uphold or endanger does not ultimately arise, especially when considered in terms of European sovereignty? The data, in reality, are deceptive and do not allow for a clear distinction of different mechanisms. What we have been able to demonstrate so far pertains to so-called direct cross-border procurement: this occurs when firms operating from their home market bid and win contracts for invitations to tender launched in another country. The picture would be very different when considering indirect cross-border procurement, which arises when:

- firms bid for contracts through subsidiaries, ie when their foreign affiliates bid for tenders launched by authorities of a country different from the home country where the firm has its headquarters or where the parent company is located;
- domestic bidders (prime contractor) include foreign subcontractors;
- foreign bidders submit offers in consortia with local firms in order to participate in competitive procurement;
- a domestic firm imports goods in order to supply them to a contracting authority or entity.

The sole analysis of data from the TED does not allow for the illustration of these various situations. A study (unfortunately now somewhat dated) from the European Commission – DG Internal Market and Services – provides us with interesting elements.[35] During the years 2007, 2008 and 2009, a share of 1.6 per cent direct cross-border procurement was identified. Note that this share is quite similar to the one we identify during the period 2010–22. During the same period, 11.4 per cent indirect cross-border procurement through affiliates was identified. For computer and related services, the direct cross-border accounts for 2.8 per cent, while the indirect through affiliates account to 41 per cent: the direct cross-border/indirect ratio appears to be much higher in the digital sector. Even if European digital public procurement markets are only slightly more open to cross-border sourcing, the potential impact of dependence on non-European companies is significant. In this case,

[35] European Commission, DG Internal Market and Services, 'Cross border procurement above EY threshold', Final Report (March 2011).

sovereignty is not an issue so much of the location of the winning company as of the nationality of the parent company. Since the implicit link between sovereignty and environmental concerns in public procurement is based on the effects of localism induced by the latter, it must be reconsidered in the perspective of this specificity. Let us consider two illustrations using the TED 2010–22 data.[36]

Take first the case of Microsoft Corporation. An analysis of the period from 2010 to 2022 reveals that Microsoft secured 536 contracts, amounting to a total of €4,670,743,396. In approximately 82 per cent of these cases, the contract was awarded to a subsidiary of Microsoft located in the purchasing country. Only one of the 536 contracts was won by the American parent company; the remaining 18 per cent of contracts not allocated to a national subsidiary in the purchasing country were awarded to European affiliates of Microsoft.

The case of Google presents a somewhat different scenario. Over the same period, 77 public procurement awards were identified, with the firm Mountain View securing more than €763,054,342 in public procurement. Remarkably, all of these contracts were won by Google Ireland Limited. This accounts for only 2.6 per cent of the contracts awarded to a company located in the purchasing country. However, it represents 100 per cent of the contracts awarded to a European subsidiary of Google.

In a speech given on 12 September 2022 in Strasbourg to mark the inauguration of a new OVHCloud data centre, Bruno LeMaire, the French Minister for the Economy,[37] said:

> I listened to the engineers and I understood one simple thing: if we want to be sovereign, we can't allow any power to steal our data. I'm opposed to the principle of American extraterritoriality. I have always fought against it and will continue to do so. I don't see why, in whose name we would accept that the American justice system could seize data that is essential to our sovereignty and independence.[38]

LeMaire refers here to the US CLOUD Act. In fact, the CLOUD Act is not an extraterritorial law, but only a law that applies to any company within the jurisdiction of the US in the meaning of US law, which is actually quite extensive (more than 25 per cent of shares). Therefore, the CLOUD Act applies to any company within the jurisdiction of the US that controls computer data

[36] Tenders Electronic Daily (TED) (csv subset) – public procurement notices (3.6) (2024) [Data set] (European Commission, Directorate-General for Internal Market, Industry, Entrepreneurship and SMEs), data.europa.eu/88u/dataset/ted-csv (original work published 2015).

[37] It is worth noting that the official denomination of the French Minister for the Economy is Minister for the Economy, Finance and Industrial and *Digital Sovereignty*.

[38] Déclaration de M Bruno Le Maire, ministre de l'économie, des finances et de la souveraineté industrielle et numérique, sur la stratégie nationale pour le Cloud et la souveraineté numérique, à Strasbourg le 12 septembre 2022, www.vie-publique.fr/discours/286403-bruno-le-maire-12092022-souverainete-numerique (author's translation).

entrusted to it by its customers, regardless of the customers' nationality and regardless of the physical location where such data is transmitted or stored. All the GAFAM are companies within the jurisdiction of the United States, as are their subsidiaries.

Hence, the use of environmental criteria to defend sovereignty may appear less effective in the case of digital services than in other sectors of the economy. Governments may use procurement-specific criteria to achieve data sovereignty by favouring digital service suppliers that are isolated from the legal authority, or technological control of foreign governments and other actors. Selective procurement in these ICT sectors can complement data localisation measures because domestic suppliers' operational approaches and deployment of their business models often involve some degree of de facto data localisation. Governments may attempt to leverage this by designing procurement practices so that only domestic suppliers with sovereign data practices are selected for contracts with government agencies. In this vein, France has released its National Cloud Strategy,[39] which mandates that all public projects be built on public clouds and introduces a *cloud de confiance* (trusted cloud) certification that protects cloud providers from laws like the US CLOUD Act.

However, European sovereign cloud providers are still collaborating with foreign multinationals. For instance, the French companies Capgemini and Orange have announced a joint partnership with Microsoft to deliver a platform suitable for *cloud de confiance* certification. Similarly, Deutsche Telekom from Germany is partnering with Google Cloud to deliver a German sovereign cloud for both government and private enterprises. It is difficult to judge the consistency of these national policies with international trade rules as they are not yet fully developed. However, without a targeted focus on government data, these measures may lack the stronger justificatory basis that would support a purely government sovereign data framework. Furthermore, the US legislation providing for these data communication injunctions was recently revised, following the judgment of the Court of Justice of the EU of 16 July 2020 (C-311/18), known as *Schrems II*, to provide a better framework for them and more effective remedies. This legislation was declared compliant with European data protection standards, enabling the European Commission to adopt a new adequacy decision on 10 July 2023, recognising that the new framework for transfers of personal data between the US and the EU, the Data Privacy Framework, provides an adequate level of protection.[40]

[39] 'Stratégie Nationale pour le Cloud', press release (May 2021), www.numerique.gouv.fr/uploads/Strategie-nationale-pour-le-cloud.pdf.

[40] See EU–U.S. Data Privacy Framework (EU–U.S. DPF), www.dataprivacyframework.gov/Program-Overview; Commission implementing decision of 10.7.2023 pursuant to Regulation (EU) 2016/679 of the European Parliament and of the Council on the adequate level of protection of personal data under the EU–US Data Privacy Framework, C(2023) 4745 final.

Until now, we have considered the link between sovereignty and environmental concerns in one way only: when buyers implicitly seek to meet a sustainability objective in public procurement, they can increase the proportion of sovereign purchases they make. But the relationship can also be seen in the other direction: seeking sovereignty means taking into account the environmental impact of public procurement. If digital sovereignty can be promoted in the context of public procurement through mechanisms that do not involve environmental considerations, the link between digital sovereignty and sustainable development needs to be re-examined. The effect of re-localising activities awarded in public procurement contracts can be seen as a 'positive externality' of environmental concerns. In turn, this promotes the widespread use of environmental criteria. In the case of public procurement of digital services, if the desired effect of sovereignty is achieved through other instruments, environmental considerations may be relatively less present than in other markets. Figure 9.4 below shows the evolution of the proportion of public contracts including environmental criteria over the period 2010–22, for all contracts and specifically for digital service and supply markets in France.

Figure 9.4 Public contracts for digital service and supply markets in France including environmental criteria over the period 2010–2022

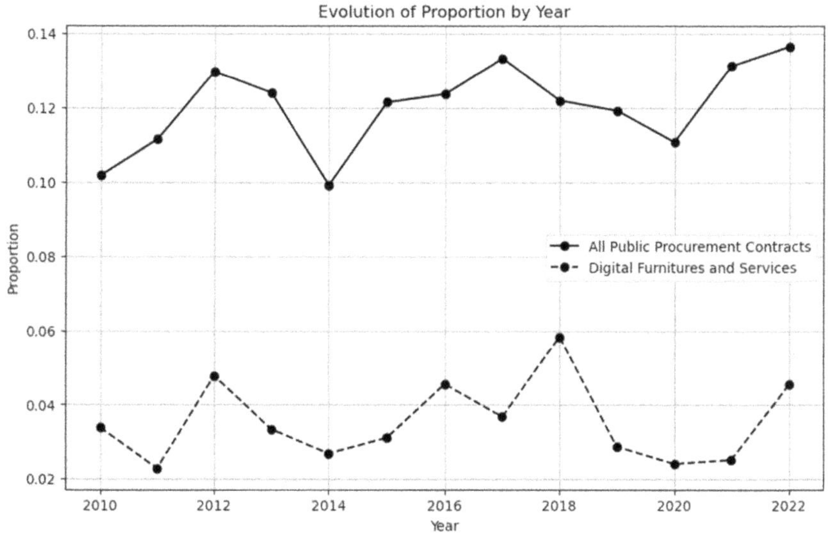

Source: TED.

Although this analysis could benefit from more detailed elaboration, data suggest that the integration of environmental considerations within public procurement processes, through the application of award criteria, is comparatively less prevalent in the digital sector than in the broader spectrum of public procurement contracts in

France, with negligible progression observed over time. Contrary to the Ministry's responses to the written questions of the three parliamentarians studied above, the pursuit of digital sovereignty seems to conflict with environmental concerns, which may appear somewhat counterintuitive. This is in fact the whole problem of using environmental considerations in public procurement for purposes other than what they are supposed to be, ie as a process by which public authorities seek to achieve the appropriate balance between the three pillars of sustainable development – economic, social, and environmental – when procuring goods, services or works at all stages of a project, and not as a mere protectionist tool.

VI. Conclusion

By virtue of EU law and free trade agreements, public procurement does not allow the pool of companies eligible to bid to be restricted or the nationality of companies awarded contracts to be controlled. The issue of sovereignty as perceived by public authorities is essentially a matter of domestic protectionism, and we have shown, using the French case as an illustration of the situation in EU countries, how the environmental objective is mobilised as an instrument of sovereignty. It is presented as a means of increasing the likelihood of a contract being awarded to a national (or European) company. The question of digital sovereignty, however, is framed differently. It is essentially a question of sovereignty over the data (produced and stored). Consequently, increasing the possibility of awarding contracts to a national company does not ensure that the objective of sovereignty is achieved, which seems to be much more independent of the location of the company awarded the public contract. On the other hand, other technical specifications can be included in the award criteria to ensure a form of digital sovereignty. An analysis of the data illustrates this perfectly: green public procurement meets the objective of purchasing more locally and less open to international competition, but in public procurement with a digital dimension, environmental concerns seem to be little used.

PART III

Towards a Sustainable and Sovereign EU Digital Economy?

10

Bitcoin: A Subversive Model of Sovereignty Undermined by the Climate Challenge?

GAËL DEPOORTER

Bitcoin is a shitty shitcoin.

Nouriel Roubini[1]

I. Introduction

For many official observers, it is a foregone conclusion: Bitcoin has absolutely no value and will collapse at any moment, dragging in its wake millions of naive investors hoping for quick financial gains. The most redundant criticisms generally focus on three aspects: its speculative nature, the threat to monetary sovereignty and its energy consumption. Firstly, as Nouriel Roubini points out in the quote above, Bitcoin is a purely speculative, worthless monkey currency. But at the same time, it would undermine the monetary basis of state sovereignty. For John Lipsky, number two at the International Monetary Fund (IMF), cryptocurrencies as a whole 'can threaten the monetary sovereignty of any country'.[2] It is surprising that a 'crap currency' should be able to undermine the monetary sovereignty of all countries so quickly. A final stream of criticism has been emerging since 2021 around Bitcoin's energy consumption. Alex de Vries, Bill Gates and Elon Musk have all spoken out about Satoshi Nakamoto's cryptocurrency, which is said to be a threat to the climate. According to the Cambridge Bitcoin Electricity Consumption Index,[3] by 2022 the Bitcoin blockchain would have consumed more

[1] Nouriel Roubini, Twitter (9 March 2020), x.com/Nouriel/status/1236850934355046401.

[2] Cecilia Barría, 'Bitcoin: qui est qui dans la guerre des crypto-monnaies (et comment cela peut vous affecter)' BBC News Afrique (13 June 2021), www.bbc.com/afrique/monde-57346994.

[3] Available at www.ccaf.io/cbnsi/cbeci.

energy than Argentina.[4] In 2017, Newsweek headlined 'Bitcoin Mining on Track to Consume All of the World's Energy by 2020'.[5] Greenpeace followed suit and commissioned the artwork *Skull of Satoshi* at the beginning of 2023 to condemn Bitcoin's consumption and encourage it to switch from proof of work (PoW) to proof of stake (PoS), which consumes much less energy.[6] However, its creator, Canadian artist Benjamin Von Wong, has since indicated that he does not believe Bitcoin to be the environmental disaster it has been portrayed to be,[7] a small victory for the Bitcoin community.

More generally, cryptocurrencies seem to feed just about every fantasy, and to be the receptacle of the hopes and fears of our time. On the one hand, they would destabilise states,[8] accompany far-right populism,[9] reinforce rogue capitalism,[10] lead to post-colonialism,[11] a form of technological neo-Messianism,[12] and deliver the environmental *coup de grace* by consuming an aberrant amount of fossil fuel.[13] On the other hand, this technology would emancipate individuals, promote the development of developing countries, protect privacy,[14] and repair

[4] Cristina Criddle, 'Bitcoin consumes "more electricity than Argentina"' BBC (10 February 2021), www.bbc.com/news/technology-56012952. If there is to be any comparison, it should be noted that in 2022 the market capitalisation of Bitcoin reached $800 billion, while Argentina's GDP was $630 billion at the same time.

[5] Anthony Curtbertson, 'Bitcoin Mining on Track to Consume All of the World's Energy by 2020' *Newsweek* (11 December 2017), www.newsweek.com/bitcoin-mining-track-consume-worlds-energy-2020-744036.

[6] Gujari Singh, 'Artist Benjamin Von Wong & Greenpeace Unveil Giant Skull to Highlight Bitcoin's Climate Impact (Greeepeace, 23 March 2023), www.greenpeace.org/usa/artist-benjamin-von-wong-greenpeace-unveil-giant-skull-to-highlight-bitcoins-climate-impact. PoW and PoS are two of the most common 'consensus mechanisms'. These mechanisms are a set of ideas, computer protocols and economic incentives designed to secure and organise the various stakeholders in a distributed blockchain. They aim to resist attacks seeking to take control (the so-called 'Sybil attack') and to select the authors of blocks by establishing a solid, automated system of trust. These two models rely on different proofs of objective and sincere involvement on the part of the 'miners' (called 'validators' for the PoS). To achieve this, PoW relies on a race to solve complex mathematical puzzles that require significant investment in computer hardware and therefore energy consumption. PoS, on the other hand, requires possession of a large number of tokens on the blockchain in question, and therefore requires much less energy to validate legitimate blocks.

[7] Von Wong, Twitter (25 March 2023), www.twitter.com/thevonwong/status/1639691433811615744?ref_src=twsrc%5Etfw.

[8] Martin Chevalier and Benjamin Vignolles, 'Le bitcoin : défi à la souveraineté monétaire des États et ressource pour le blanchiment d'argent' (2014) 14 *Regards croisés sur l'économie* 122.

[9] David Golumbia, *The Politics of Bitcoin: Software as Right-Wing Extremism* (University of Minnesota Press, 2016); Stephen Diehl, Jan Akalin and Darren Tseng, *Popping the Crypto Bubble* (Consilience Consulting UK, 2022).

[10] Joshua Dávila, *Blockchain Radicals: How Capitalism Ruined Crypto and How to Fix It* (Repeater, 2023).

[11] Olivier Jutel, 'Blockchain Humanitarianism and Crypto-Colonialism' (2022) 3 *Patterns*.

[12] Nastasia Hadjadji, *No Crypto: Comment Bitcoin a envoûté la planète* (Editions Divergences, 2023).

[13] Alex de Vries et al, 'Revisiting Bitcoin's Carbon Footprint' (2022) 6 *Joule* 498.

[14] Ariel Shapira, 'Blockchain is the only viable path to privacy and censorship resistance in the 21st century' (Cointelegraph, 7 December 2022), www.fr.cointelegraph.com/news/blockchain-is-the-only-viable-path-to-privacy-and-censorship-resistance-in-the-21st-century.

democracy and freedom of expression,[15] but also envisage a socialist society by weakening the institutions of capitalism while providing the tools for an inclusive and democratic alternative,[16] while still others project themselves into a form of crypto-communism.[17] So how do we untangle and understand this imbroglio of contradictory and exuberant analyses? Why does Bitcoin frighten some people and hold out the magical promise of a better world to others? Why take an interest in it now when the die seems to have been cast? How can Bitcoin be seen as a subversive model of sovereignty?

Unanimity, whether on the part of its supporters or detractors, is often suspected of bias, particularly when research seeks to determine the true meaning, the definitive 'truth',[18] of a social phenomenon, and in so doing homogenises it. It is as if, by peeling back the layers of thought in a social phenomenon, we could find at its heart the definitive, written and necessary essence. But, as Wittgenstein says, 'words have no meaning, they only have uses'.[19] And usages vary over time and according to context. It is to this task of clarifying usage that we wish to contribute here, starting from the point of view of the players, the *Bitcoiners*, and the meaning they give to Bitcoin. This interim report is based on ethnographic fieldwork carried out over the last three years, both online by following the crypto community on Twitter (now X) and Telegram, and offline, during the last three editions of Surfin' Bitcoin in Biarritz, France. This is an opportunity to conduct participant observation, to analyse the discourses, to identify their argumentative tropisms, the dividing lines or, on the contrary, the points of agreement, to grasp their diversity and their points in common, to meet the protagonists of this social world, and to interview them. The aim is to get to grips with Bitcoin through practice.

In section II, we will attempt to clarify what Bitcoin is. To do this, we will answer the question of where the innovation lies in Bitcoin, its value proposition. In fact, in the second half of the 2010s, a craze around blockchain technology invaded both the media and investor circles. They thought they could extract the innovative essence of Bitcoin, while leaving aside the sulphurous dimension of the king of cryptocurrencies (see section II.A). But Bitcoin is first what some people use it for, and we will analyse some reports to understand the scale of its adoption. Despite attacks and warnings, Bitcoin's particularly powerful adversaries have not managed to stop it. So, whatever we may think, what we are seeing is first and foremost the emergence of a segment of the social world that is gradually becoming autonomous, with its own players, practices, principles, and internal struggles (see section II.B).

[15] See 'Alex Gladstein: Bitcoin fixes democracy' Youtube (19 February 2023), www.youtube.com/watch?v=IZ7jhQQMcBQ&t=375s.

[16] Joshua Davila, theblockchainsocialist.com/what-can-blockchain-give-to-the-left-part-3.

[17] Mark Alizart, *Cryptocommunisme*, Perspectives Critiques (PUF, 2019).

[18] Stephen Diehl et al (2022), www.poppingthecryptobubble.com.

[19] Ludwig Wittgenstein, *Philosophical Investigations* ([1953], Wiley-Blackwell, 2009) §43.

Once we have established that Bitcoin has become a genuine social fact, section III then explores the way in which it recomposes the question of sovereignty through the way in which the Internet's 'thurifers' have sought to define the contours and substance of the emerging social world. This notion of sovereignty has been profoundly challenged by the deployment of digital technologies. By presenting itself as a philosophy of the social contract in the age of cyberspace, hacker epistemology updates the methodological fiction of the state of nature.[20] In this context, it holds out the promise of a social world recomposed from individuals freed from all social discipline (see section III.A). But this first stage of development, of which open source is the standard-bearer, does little more than maintain the 'new informational man'[21] in oblative relationships of gift and counter-gift.[22] This is where Satoshi Nakamoto takes over from the social philosophy promoted by hackers, giving them access to a new 'stage' in their development. First and foremost, Bitcoin promises to do away with the archaic contract of the gift as a principle of organisation and distribution of roles. Instead, he proposes to bring cyberspace into the age of modernity by means of a digital currency, and through it into a rationalised world made up of agents who now have the tools to maximise their economic interests. It is at this price that Bitcoin proposes to fulfil the hacker project of sovereignty redistributed to each individual (see section III.B).

Finally, in section IV, we will explore how Bitcoin, to implement the principles outlined in the prolegomena of cyberculture, has had to move away from cyberspace and reconnect with the physical world, commonly referred to as 'meatspace', a term John Perry Barlow used to describe the domain of 'tired giants of flesh and steel'.[23] This return to reality is fraught with difficulties, and particularly the thorny issue of climate change. Because of the way it works, both socially and technologically, Bitcoin consumes, and must consume, a great deal of electricity. Indeed, this consumption is in fact the tool of its security, an attribute of its power and thus the guarantee of its strategic autonomy (see section IV.A). However, this consumption increasingly goes hand in hand with low-carbon energy projects. Counterintuitively, Bitcoin seems more likely to become a decisive ally in the ecological conversion of our societies than its imperative rival (see section IV.B).

[20] Gaël Depoorter, 'Le « bal des hackers ». Sociologie critique d'un exotisme postmoderne. La « communuauté » du Libre, entre tropisme individualiste et processus d'institutionnalisation' (Doctoral thesis, Université Picardie Jules Verne, 2018).

[21] Nicolas Auray, 'Politique de l'informatique et de l'information : Les Pionniers de La Nouvelle Frontière Électronique' (Doctoral thesis, EHESS, 2000).

[22] Marcel Mauss, *Essai Sur Le Don. Forme et Raison de l'échange Dans Les Sociétés Archaïques* (PUF, 2012).

[23] See John Perry Barlow, 'A Declaration of the Independence of Cyberspace' (1996), www.eff.org/cyberspace-independence.

II. Bitcoin: The King of Crypto

Bitcoin is now the leading cryptocurrency, or crypto asset as the IMF and G20 prefers to call it.[24] However, relatively little is known about how it works, so our understanding of it is still very remote. But every technical choice implements a certain type of social organisation (see section A below). Over the past 15 years, increasing numbers of people around the world have invested in Bitcoin, turning it into a social phenomenon (see section B below).

A. Social Issues and Technical Choices

Satoshi Nakamoto developed Bitcoin during the subprime crisis in 2007. He published the white paper for the project on 31 October 2008, mined the first block[25] (the 'genesis' block[26]) on 3 January 2009, and published a first version of the Bitcoin software as open source a month later. Little is known about the creator other than that it is not his real name and that his last message dates from 10 December 2010. Bitcoin's value proposition[27] is to deploy an independently certified electronic transaction system, ie one that relies on cryptographic evidence rather than the trust of a third party. Satoshi Nakamoto is proposing to meet two challenges at once: one economic and political; the other technical. Firstly, during the banking crisis, public confidence was severely tested by the financial manipulations of a few institutions, some of which were saved at the last minute by the United States (US) Government (thanks to money printing). Secondly, we know that nothing is more easily reversible and reproducible than dematerialised information or a computer operation. The marginal cost of copying digital information (a 'bit') is close to zero, which is why Chris Anderson says that 'bits want to be free'.[28] A new free economy has flourished since the 2000s, based on two models: open source (the 'digital commons') on the one hand; and (increasingly targeted) advertising on the other.

The question Satoshi Nakamoto set out to answer was how to produce a computerised exchange of information, in this case a monetary transaction, which we can be sure will not be duplicated or subsequently modified. In other words, how can we do away with the ctrl+C, ctrl+V and ctrl+Z functions that are so

[24] Financial Stability Board, 'G20 Crypto-asset Policy Implementation Roadmap' (22 October 2024), www.imf.org/-/media/Files/Research/imf-and-g20/2024/imf-fsb-g20-crypto-asset-policy-implementation-roadmap.ashx.

[25] Satoshi Nakamoto uses the front page headline of that day's *Times*: 'The Times 03/Jan/2009 Chancellor on brink of second bailout for banks'.

[26] The value of the first bitcoins mined by the *genesis* block was $0.001 in October 2019, the estimated cost of the electricity needed to produce them.

[27] If Bitcoin (with a capital letter) is a payment system, then bitcoin (with a lower case letter) is the system's currency.

[28] Chris Anderson, *Free: The Future of a Radical Price* (Hyperion, 2009) 288.

central to our daily computing practices? From a technical point of view, the difficulty can be broken down into two cumulative problems: (a) the 'double spending' problem; and (b) the 'Byzantine generals' problem. To be more precise, it is a question of (a) deploying a technical architecture that ensures that the same unit of currency cannot be spent several times, thereby artificially increasing the quantity of currency, in an uncertain ecosystem (b) where information can be lost, and the various parties involved can change their minds at will or maliciously. So how can we have confidence in information that is reliable and definitive?

It was to answer these questions that Satoshi Nakamoto created Bitcoin, a protocol for moving value securely. As software, it is presented as a protocol, ie a set of explicit rules organising its governance, compiled in its open-source code, and therefore auditable by anyone with the necessary skills. In concrete terms, it is a 'peer-to-peer distributed time-stamping server that uses computer calculations to generate proof of the chronology of transactions'.[29] This network is therefore organised without centralised control, adding each bitcoin transaction (compiled in a 'block') to a public and open distributed register, thus progressively constituting a 'blockchain'. Consensus on the validity of transactions by 'users' and their entries in the blockchain is ensured by proof-of-work technology carried out by 'miners', whose role is to provide the computer hardware and energy needed to 'validate' each block using a cryptographic calculation.[30] Miners are rewarded with transaction fees and the creation of new bitcoins. The protocol stipulates that there cannot be more than 21 million bitcoins (BTC).

As of 1 February 2024, 19,614,875 BTC had already been mined, according to the CoinMarketCap website. Bitcoin's rules stipulate that a transaction block containing 2MB of transaction data[31] is validated or 'mined' every 10 minutes (the difficulty of the mathematical calculations involved is adjusted to this requirement, regardless of the performance of the hardware or the number of machines used). The reward is currently made up of transaction fees and the creation of new bitcoins. The remuneration in new bitcoins was originally 50 BTC per block and is halved every 210,000 blocks (ie approximately every four years), a process known as 'halving'. The last one took place on 20 April 2024 and saw the reward drop to 3,125 BTC. By 2140, all the bitcoins will have been mined, so the reward will come from transaction fees alone.

The idea of a decentralised, independent currency, organised without state or bank control, was not new and emerged in the 1980s in the cypherpunk movement.

[29] Satoshi Nakamoto, 'Bitcoin: A Peer-to-Peer Electronic Cash System' (bitcoin.org, 2008).

[30] We will return to this point in more detail in the final section of this chapter.

[31] Since 1 August and the 'New York compromise', blocks have contained 2MB of transactions, after an event pitting developers, users and miners against each other. This has been dubbed the 'civil war of the blocks'. Until then, the blocks had been 1MB in size. The developers managed to keep the block size small in order to preserve the decentralised nature of the Bitcoin blockchain. The larger the block size, the larger the blockchain, and the more the infrastructure needed to host it distances individuals from participation in the network, reinforcing its centralisation in the hands of a few major players in the ecosystem.

But if the principles are not recent, neither are the technologies used. Asymmetric cryptography[32] emerged in the late 1970s and was widely deployed in the 1990s. Blockchain technology first appeared in 1982 in David Chaum's doctoral thesis[33] to organise transactions between players without trust. The idea of certifying digital documents by time-stamping dates to 1991.[34] In 1997 Adam Back used proof-of-work technology[35] to propose HashCash, which made it possible to limit spam and denial-of-service attacks. 1999 saw the launch of Napster, the first software application to use peer-to-peer file-sharing technology. In 2002, the first block systems for storing data on a network appeared. In 2005, Nick Szabo developed 'bit gold', the first decentralised currency whose value is not based on any underlying asset (such as gold in the case of 'e-gold', Douglas Jackson's centralised currency launched in 1996).[36]

As is often the case when it comes to innovation, most of the technologies used by Bitcoin already existed, and most of the time had for a long time. The 'revolution' that some see as Bitcoin's standard-bearer is not based on one key word: 'blockchain'. What makes Bitcoin different lies more in the way Satoshi Nakamoto has interwoven the various available technologies (peer-to-peer network, timestamping, blockchain, PoW, asymmetric cryptography). Sometimes used separately in other sectors, with Bitcoin they are combined to solve a specific problem (that of the trust and security of decentralised monetary transactions). The novelty brought by the anonymous creator of Bitcoin is also that, to cement the whole, he has added a social organisation based on the alignment of the interests (mainly economic) of the various stakeholders. Following one's personal interest should help to produce the collective interest. This alignment is achieved by setting a maximum number of bitcoins, producing them on a regular basis,

[32] Asymmetric cryptography makes it possible to ensure the confidentiality of an exchange and to authenticate users without having to go through a central authority. This technology is based on the production of two types of key that respond to each other and work together: one encrypts in a specific way, the other is the only one that can decrypt the first. The first is public and can be transmitted. If an individual wishes to make contact, they must use it to encrypt their message in a way that only the second (private) key can decrypt. The second (private) key is therefore highly critical and must be carefully preserved to ensure the security of the exchange.

[33] David L. Chaum, 'Computer Systems Established, Maintained and Trusted by Mutually Suspicious Groups' (Doctoral thesis, University of California, 1982).

[34] Stuart Haber and W Scott Stornetta, 'How to Time-Stamp a Digital Document' (1991) 3 *Journal of Cryptology* 99.

[35] The concept was first developed by Cynthia Dwork and Moni Naor in 'Pricing via Processing or Combatting Junk Mail' in Ernest F Brickell (ed), *Advances in Cryptology – Crypto'92* (Springer, 1993), while the term 'proof of work' was coined a little later in 1999 by Markus Jakobsson and Ari Juels in their article 'Proofs of Work and Bread Pudding Protocols' in Bart Preneel (eds), *Secure Information Networks* (Springer, 1999).

[36] Other more or less centralised digital currency initiatives had already been launched: Arthur Budovsky's Liberty Reserve in 1996, Wei Dai's b-money in 1998, and Jim and Pamela Fayed's e-Bullion in 2001, for example. In the early 1990s, David Chaum launched the eCash system, offering an anonymous digital currency (cyberbucks) at a relatively decentralised floating price, but relying on banks as trusted third parties.

setting up profit-sharing schemes, deflating the currency,[37] the choice of proof method, and so on. Together, these technical and socio-economic choices form what is known as the 'Nakamoto consensus'. So Bitcoin's innovation is less technological than social, and lies more in the choices and linkages between these two dimensions.

To address the problems of 'double spending' and 'Byzantine generals', the Nakamoto consensus is based on several key elements, which we will summarise briefly below. Firstly, decentralising and opening participation in the network to all avoids a political problem, which can be translated into a technical problem: doing without any central control authority, which can also prove to be a single technical point of failure. This dimension enables the system to be resilient to failures and thus tolerant of breakdowns, whether arbitrary or malicious, thanks to the redundancy and replication of the public register. These characteristics are made possible by the peer-to-peer network, the open-source code and the fact that the true identity of the creator is unknown.

Then, to get the whole network to agree on the order of valid transactions, the 'miners' compete to solve a complex mathematical, cryptographic, equation selected at random. They compete with each other and invest their computing power (ie computer hardware and electricity) to be the first to obtain the correct answer and produce the secure cryptographic link between the validated block and the previous one. The first to succeed is rewarded with transaction fees and bitcoins created with each block. Once the equation has been solved, the transaction is confirmed, recorded and made public on the blockchain. So, the winner obtains the right to propose the next block of transactions to be added to the register. The timestamp of the previous block is included in its imprint to form a chain (each timestamp reinforcing the solidity of the previous one). For their part, the participants (network nodes) verify (using cryptographic key signatures) and validate the proposed block. This mining process is known as proof-of-work technology and is based on asymmetric cryptography.

The third key element is that the various nodes in the network follow the longest blockchain, since this is the one that contains the greatest number of puzzles solved, and therefore blocks validated. This principle ensures that each node tends towards one and the same verified, time-stamped version of the history of the Bitcoin blockchain. This characteristic could have been a source of vulnerability in the early years of development. Indeed, the energy required to redo or break the cryptographic calculations from the beginning and produce a corrupted blockchain, longer and masquerading as the authentic one, might have been attainable. Today this is no longer the case, and this characteristic is one of the strengths of the Bitcoin blockchain, which has been in uninterrupted service since 2009.

[37] Deflationary because, while there will never be more than 21 million bitcoins, there will never be 21 million bitcoins in circulation. A certain number have been and will be lost for good: owners die without having been able to transfer them, loss or damage to property retaining the keys to access the wallet, etc.

The fourth decisive dimension of Nakamoto's consensus is the economic incentive for miners to follow the rules of the protocol. The PoW seeks to ensure their loyalty by requiring them to invest in computing power. The theory behind this system is that a miner who invests so many resources and is only paid later has no reason to be malicious because he runs the risk of losing the value of his payment. Furthermore, any attempt to produce an invalid block is increasingly costly and uncertain, given the number of participants in Bitcoin 'mining' and the large amount of energy required to solve a puzzle (or to resolve all the puzzles carried out since the block added that you wish to modify).[38] As the entire network holds the complete history of the blockchain – 'the public history of transactions'[39] – the malicious block would be identified and rejected fairly quickly. So, the strength of the Bitcoin blockchain asserts itself month after month. The initial objective of ensuring secure, irreversible transactions with no centralised third-party control is reinforced and assured as more blocks are added, burying the transactions made ever deeper under a heavy layer of cryptographic calculations.

What we see emerging here behind the gleaming shadows of the staging of different technologies is a real social relationship, an organisation of interactions. While we are unable to determine once and for all what *Bitcoiners are* (anarchists, hyper-capitalists, defenders of freedom, extreme right-wingers, communists, avowed polluters, etc), what they are trying to do seems more accessible. Bitcoin is not so much a network without trust[40] as a network that redistributes trust to everyone. One of the axioms of the crypto community is the expression 'do your own research' (DYOR), which refers to the need to reinvest individually in the conditions that make trust possible, rather than delegating them to a third party. Is there a response to this project? What is the state of adoption of Bitcoin?

B. The Bitcoiner: A Picture of Gradual and Significant Adoption

When we generally hear about Bitcoin, it is very rarely to inform the public about how it works, or the project behind it, but mainly to relay flashy information. Here we hear about very high prices (BTC has risen to $66,000 in 2021), there about

[38] PoS works differently. The 'validator' who registers the transaction is drawn at random from all those who have bet, staked or immobilised part of their tokens. He or she is remunerated solely by the transaction fees. Most of the time, there is a minimum stake to take part in the draw (32 ETH for Ethereum). In addition, the chance of being chosen depends on the total percentage of the currency held, which tends to favour centralisation of the system, but does not involve any specific electricity consumption. The more tokens you have, the greater your chances of being selected. The rule for selecting the legitimate chain here is to choose the 'heaviest' chain, ie the one that required the largest stake from the validators. The theory behind this model is that anyone who owns and invests a sufficiently large number of tokens has no interest in validating malicious transactions, as they would jeopardise their own capital.

[39] Nakamoto (n 29).

[40] Kevin Werbach, *The Blockchain and the New Architecture of Trust* (The MIT Press, 2023).

dizzying falls in price (during COVID it fell to $5,200). Although the Theranos affair reminded anyone who had forgotten that frauds were not confined to the world of cryptocurrencies, it is this type of news that is spread first, such as the one operated by Sam Bankman-Fried through his centralised cryptocurrency exchange platform FTX. Comparisons are tricky because the control mechanisms are so different, but money laundering in traditional currencies ('fiat' currency) represents two to five per cent of global GDP according to a UN agency[41] (between $800 and $2,000 billion), while illicit crypto transactions represented 0.15 per cent of the total volume (nearly $15 billion) in 2021 according to the extremely detailed report by the crypto data analysis website Chainanalysis.[42]

However, despite this sulphurous news, an increasing number of people have been buying cryptocurrencies, particularly the largest of them all: Bitcoin. In February 2024, its market capitalisation alone represented $936 billion (at its peak on 21 October 2021, it had risen to $1,240 billion), ie half the total capitalisation of all cryptocurrencies.[43] MicroStrategy has been investing almost all its cash in Bitcoin for several years, and BlackRock, one of the world's largest asset management companies, managed to get the US regulator to approve the launch of exchange-traded funds (ETFs) tracking the price of Bitcoin in early January 2024, making it the best ETF launch in 30 years.

Despite this, the image of Bitcoin remains extremely negative in the media, and among many political and economic figures. On a regular basis, patent oracles predict the end of Bitcoin and the wrath of regulation announcing its demise. Despite this climate of anxiety, in 2024 there were more than 1.2 billion addresses on Bitcoin,[44] according to the blockchain data analysis platform Glassnode.com, and more than 10 million have been created every month for the past six years. 80 million of them hold bitcoins[45] or 'satoshis'.[46] These are not necessarily individual addresses – the same person or entity may hold several – but it gives us an order of magnitude. More than 65 million of these addresses hold less than $1,000, and 96 per cent less than 1 BTC. Since 2017, 10 to 22 million addresses have carried out Bitcoin transactions at least once a month.

[41] See United Nations, Office on Drugs and Crime, www.unodc.org/unodc/en/money-laundering/overview.html#:~:text=The%20estimated%20amount%20of%20money,goes%20through%20the%20laundering%20cycle.

[42] Chainalysis, 'The Chainalysis 2022 Crypto Crime Report' (2022).

[43] According to CoinMarketCap, there will be almost 10,845 cryptocurrencies in February 2025.

[44] Data available at www.studio.glassnode.com/metrics?a=BTC&category=Addresses&ema=0&m=addresses.Count.

[45] Addresses are a kind of bitcoin 'wallet'. Each address has a double key (public and private) so that secure transactions can be carried out. These addresses can be individual or represent a collection of individuals (for example, addresses belonging to exchange platforms, which group their customers' assets together in a few addresses). An individual can hold as many addresses as they wish. However, many users of centralised exchange platforms leave their cryptocurrencies there against Bitcoin's recommendations of caution and principles, which encourage them instead to create their own address and repatriate their cryptocurrencies there.

[46] One bitcoin can be divided into 'satoshis', or 'sat'. One bitcoin represents 100,000,000 sats. The satoshi is therefore the bitcoin cent.

At the same time, there are an estimated 130 million users of cryptocurrency exchange platforms.[47]

In Europe between 10 and 14 per cent of Europeans according to the European Central Bank (ECB)[48] hold cryptocurrencies (of which 66 per cent have less than €5,000, and six per cent more than €30,000), and more than 50 per cent of these holders are between 18 and 35 years old. In France, of the 10 per cent of the population who own cryptocurrencies, 23 per cent declare an annual income of less than €18,000 and 24 per cent more than €60,000, according to a study by KPMG in 2023.[49] This study also indicates that more than 60 per cent of French people who own cryptocurrencies have bitcoin, and at least one in seven has already held a crypto asset.

Beyond Europe, Chainalysis published a report in October 2023 on the global geography (155 countries analysed) of cryptocurrencies according to the level of adoption.[50] The countries with the highest adoption rates, in order of ranking, are India, Nigeria, Vietnam, the US, Ukraine, the Philippines, Indonesia, Pakistan, Brazil and Thailand. So, we see that cryptocurrencies, as a whole, are a long way from being a technology used by people in Western countries. This global diversity of adoption is often likened by crypto enthusiasts as a way for users to protect themselves from particularly high inflation rates, but we would need more precise work to describe the diversity of contexts (economic, political and social) of use. If we compare the world's major regions, we find North America at the top (24.4 per cent of total volume), followed by Central and South Asia and Oceania (19.3 per cent), Western Europe, North and Central Europe (17.6 per cent), Eastern Europe (8.9 per cent), East Asia (8.8 per cent), South America (7.3 per cent), the Middle East and North Africa (7.2 per cent) and Sub-Saharan Africa (2.3 per cent).[51]

Finally, in a relatively short space of time (15 years), with no institutional support and despite regular attacks and threats, as well as being mocked, Bitcoin has managed to unite a surprisingly large number of users-investors across the planet, culminating in its becoming a legal tender in El Salvador in 2021. It should be remembered that the euro, benefiting from all the institutional strength of powerful states and European structures, took 20 years to develop between the time it was voted for (1992), adopted (2002), and then the only currency in circulation (2012). There are many reasons to invest in Bitcoin: to protect yourself from inflation (which is becoming exponential in some countries) and an uncertain economic future; to escape the control of central banks; to put cypherpunk ideas

[47] Data available at www.insights.glassnode.com/bitcoin-supply-distribution.

[48] Lieven Hermans et al, 'Decrypting Financial Stability Risks in Crypto-Asset Markets' (2022).

[49] KPMG and ADAN, 'Web 3 and Crypto in France and Europe. Adoption by the General Public and Applications in Industries' (2023), www.adan.eu/wp-content/uploads/2023/09/ETUDE-KPMG-x-ADAN-2023-EN.pdf.

[50] Chainalysis, 'The 2023 Geography of Cryptocurrency Report' (October 2023). The adoption index is calculated from the amount of value received, weighted by the size of the country's population, the level of purchasing power, etc.

[51] We use the Chainalysis breakdowns here; see ibid.

into practice; to discover an innovative technological and economic environment; to participate in a world that is being created; the hope of future gains; access to the world of investment (on exchange platforms the smallest stake is generally around $10); etc. At the same time, this multiplicity of possible converging reasons increases the type of social profiles interested in Bitcoin. Its social base is thus expanding, becoming more structured and more complex, gradually making Bitcoin a genuine social fact.

III. Bitcoin, the Next Stage in Hacker Sovereignty?

Bitcoin was not created *ex nihilo*. It is part of the cybernetic utopia[52] that it completes, and of the 'hacker epistemology'[53] that it extends (see section A below). Through Bitcoin, the hope of institutionalising a 'hacker sovereignty' seems to be asserting itself (see section B below).

A. Cyberspace: Building a Territory and Promoting a Model of Individual Sovereignty

Since the 1990s, the promoters of cyberspace have been developing a performative narrative about what the Internet is, in order to legitimise its existence. This mythology of cyberspace partly feeds into the debates around digital sovereignty, through which states are now trying to position themselves. Since the challenge is to characterise this space, we will approach the question of sovereignty here primarily from the angle of criticism of a hacker ethnology that is, in some respects, somewhat caricatured. Hacker ethnology has sought to describe a social world emerging from individuals freed from all social constraints. To do this, it updates the methodological fiction of the state of nature and describes and maintains hackers (as 'pioneers') in a tribal or communal stage of development. The way in which cyberspace was conceived by its pioneers was intended to provide fertile ground for Internet users to reappropriate their individual sovereignty. Rebuilding society from below, through individuals, rejecting all forms of social rules, means first and foremost challenging the process by which traditional social and political institutions have captured these scattered sovereignties.

Several journalistic and scientific works, an ethnological lexicon is often used to describe the space created by the Internet. Once all the lands of the globe had been promised, conquered and consumed, it was mental space that was occupied. Cyberspace thus takes over from this history of conquests and political hopes of

[52] Fred Turner, *From counterculture to cyberculture: Stewart Brand, the Whole Earth Network, and the rise of digital utopianism* (University of Chicago Press, 2006).

[53] Depoorter (n 20).

rebuilding new social links, and in so doing a new society purified of the dross of the past. In this way, the fable of cyberspace sustains the fantasy of a magical return to a state of nature as a way of dissolving the constraints of the social. Unlike Hobbes or Rousseau, the anthropology employed here is neither negative nor positive, but liberal. Man 'by nature' is neither good nor bad, but free. And it is society that binds him. A new society could be rebuilt based on free individuals, emancipated from the constraints of 'meatspace' (as Gibson calls it in *Neuromancer*)[54] and fully autonomous. A true 'new man' of the information age, the hacker becomes the new 'savage' of this mysterious territory. The term 'hacker' is gradually becoming a veritable ethnonym, but at the same time a caricature of what sociologist Norbert Elias called 'homo clausus'.[55]

An epistemology of the very latest modernity unfolds, inscribing the radicality of contemporary transformations primarily within individuals who are weightless in the social world. This new exoticism is based on an individualist reading of the social world and a mentalist reading of behaviour. The ethnography of cyberspace makes hackers into veritable 'pioneers' of a 'frontier' that is now electronic. They will soon be giving birth to 'digital natives' whose characteristics are reminiscent of the outdated ethnographies of the nineteenth century. They would be endowed with a slang, a somewhat mysterious quasi-language compiled in Eric Raymond's 'Jargon File'.[56] He also identifies an 'implicit mental model' for these individuals, who essentially feed off 'bandwidth'. They are said to have characteristic physical features, and their folkloric get-ups have long been mocked in TV series such as *The IT Crowd* and *Geeks and Freaks*. They are said to live in charming mansions ('virtual communities'), haunted by evil spirits ('trolls'). What is more, hackers, like all good 'savages', are also said to have a particularly fetishist esoteric religion. In the same way that Bitcoiners are sometimes portrayed as devotees of blockchain technology, hackers are said to be fascinated by the source code of which they are the servants and mere spokespersons, and in which is inscribed the story of a new form of freedom. But for both tribes, the reason for their strong attachment is not because the object is all-powerful (as a neophyte might think), and that the human element is absent. It is precisely the opposite: because it's full of them. What they see is above all crystallised, organised human labour.

Finally, hackers are said to be resistant to any form of authority, living in virtual anarchy. Contracts and other forms of rationalisation, particularly economic, are inaccessible to them. Their interactions are therefore governed by the social rules that organise the archaic exchange of the 'gift'. What's more, like the 'savages' described in outdated nineteenth-century ethnographies, hackers do not work; they play. As such, they are the bearers of a work ethic that is presented as

[54] William Gibson, *Neuromancer* (Ace Books, 1985).

[55] See Norbert Elias, *The Civilizing Process: The History of Manners and State Formation and Civilization* ([1939] Blackwell, 1994).

[56] Eric S Raymond, *The New Hacker's Dictionary* (MIT Press, 1993).

revolutionary, likely to consign the one described by Weber[57] to an outdated past. It would no longer be dictated by any constraint, neither by money nor by interest, but motivated exclusively from within, by pleasure and play. Yet, as Isabelle Kalinowski reminds us, the process that Weber uncovers is first and foremost 'the constitution of an individualist ideology leading to a completed form of internalisation of constraint, which pushes the agent to see in the maximum exploitation of himself the expression not of his subordination but of his freedom'.[58]

This painstaking work of compilation, refinement, complexity and unification of scattered behaviours builds otherness, homogenises a group of individuals and develops what is now known as the 'hacker culture'. However, observers are divided on whether hackers are 'selfish'[59] or 'altruistic',[60] or even 'hybrid'.[61] This radical dispersion of analyses highlights the impasse and the errors of a culturalist approach that seeks to determine not what people 'do', as sociology proposes by observing practices, but what people 'are', by seeking to explore the depths of their souls. On the one hand, the wonderful world of meaning; on the other, the chaotic space of practices, at the centre of these new ethnologists. They magically hope to discover an unaltered 'mental programme' that necessarily determines behaviour.

At this stage, we have an 'imagined territory', and individuals artificially singled out by the refined elaboration of a culture producing otherness. This erases the familiar face of the other and reveals the disturbing but fascinating face of the other, often spelt with a capital 'O', as if to emphasise everything that distances us from them. But in 1996 John Perry Barlow added a decisive stone to this edifice of empowerment by making an act of sovereignty with his declaration of independence for cyberspace.[62] At the time, it was difficult for this position to be truly effective, as hackers seemed to remain hopelessly on the fringes of history, a 'people' that Nicolas Sarkozy, President of the French Republic, wanted to 'civilise'.

B. Bitcoin or the Achievement of Hacker Sovereignty

It is this story that the mysterious Satoshi Nakamoto, the invisible hero of cyberspace, is extending and perhaps completing. From an epistemological point of view, the story of a society of emancipated individuals can continue. From an anthropological point of view, with Bitcoin, cyberspace is moving away from the archaism of

[57] Max Weber, *The Protestant Ethic and the Spirit of Capitalism* (Stephen Kalberg tr, rev 1920 edn, Oxford University Press, 2010).

[58] Isabelle Kalinowski, 'Le capitalisme et son « éthique » : une lecture de Max Weber' [2005] *Agone* 253.

[59] Michel Gensollen, 'Économie non rivale et communautés d'information' (2004) 124 *Réseaux* 141.

[60] Benjamin Grassineau, 'La Dynamique Des Réseaux Coopératifs. L'exemple Des Logiciels Libres et Du Projet d'encyclopédie Libre et Ouverte Wikipédia' (Doctoral thesis, Université de Paris Dauphine, 2009).

[61] Christophe Lazaro, *La liberté logicielle : une ethnographie des pratiques d'échange et de coopération au sein de la communauté Debian* (Bruylant, 2008).

[62] Barlow (n 23).

the digital 'gift' embodied by open source[63] to take a great leap forward and enter a society of money. Elias and Weber have shown how this is a determining factor in the complexification and rationalisation of societies. The Bitcoin blockchain uses technology to instrument (and experiment with) a link between individuals freed from the shadow of the constraints of social rules. Marcel Mauss detailed precisely how oblative exchange unfolds through the triptych: giving–receiving–giving back. Giving is thus a social rule that requires learning to discipline and conform behaviour. It aims to create and maintain a social bond, and in so doing, the norms that frame and nurture it. This is what pushes us, incites us and compels us to 'give back' when we have received a gift (known as the gift and counter-gift): a smile, a meal, kind words, an object, etc.

On the contrary, money should enable us to free ourselves from these rules. Monetary exchange frees us from social constraints by closing the link and depersonalising it. Once I have paid the merchant for the item, I feel under no obligation to continue the relationship. The ties mediated by money are thus presented as purely 'contractual' ties that we can close and open as we see fit. They would thus be the result of our one and only individual will, and not the consequence of the quasi-automatic reproduction of a learned rule, like 'social' ties in the strong sense of the term. Faithful in this respect to the hopes born after the century of horrors and its two world wars, Bitcoin would make it possible to envisage a society without social ties, made up of free, enlightened and responsible individuals. Instead, the links are no longer 'social', but 'inter-individual', unfolding in the delights of pure and perfect game theory. They feature rational, autonomous individuals rather than agents disciplined by meatspace and its categories.

It is not so much the technology that is new, as the way it is supposed to be organised, without intermediaries, and therefore without institutions, without trusted third parties; in other words, without delegating individual sovereignty. But without that to perpetuate this social space, it is the trust of each individual in the network and this reconfiguration of relationships that must be mobilised and maintained, and which gives it its value. As in any social space that becomes institutionalised, the value is placed on maintaining belief in and participation in this 'imagined society', whatever the cost. Participants are encouraged to 'hodl', ie hold on to bitcoins, despite the sometimes-dizzying ups and downs of the market. The DYOR axiom already mentioned is a way of soliciting permanent individual validation. If we have to accept rules, then they have to come from us. Everything must happen as if we were re-founding them individually. Finally, any social space in the process of becoming autonomous produces a tautological doxa that justifies its own existence ('art for art's sake' for the literary field; 'business is business' for the economic field; 'free software liberates' for the FOSS world, etc). For Bitcoin, this takes the form of a formula regularly reproduced on social networks: 1BTC = 1BTC. The 'bear markets' experienced by Bitcoiners (when the market

[63] Jacques T Godbout, 'Une « nouvelle frontière » pour le don' (2010) 35 *Revue du MAUSS* 497.

collapses without any certainty that it will one day recover), which are remembered and which command the respect of newcomers, are all events transformed into initiation rites that test the solidity of the miners' motivations. The model of sovereignty that is unfolding takes the form of a loose coalition of a multitude of distributed, instrumented individual sovereignties, constituted by the Bitcoin blockchain.

As Mark Alizart points out, the way Bitcoin is organised aims to balance and separate the powers of the various players: miners, developers and users.[64] The miners can be seen as the executive power that implements the decisions taken. By operating computers to validate transactions and mine bitcoins, stopping others that impact transaction speed and costs, updating their computers with the latest version of the Bitcoin code, or refusing to do so or threatening not to do so, they bring Bitcoin's legislation into existence for all in daily practices, choices and directives. This legislative power is implemented by the Bitcoin Core developers, who repair and improve the software, adopt a conservative or transformational approach to software, making strategic and political choices in their technical developments, give the general orientations after having deliberated collectively. Users, for their part, represent the judicial power, exercising its power of sanction through their participation ('loyalty') or defection ('exit') in the network. The third type of behaviour in Hirschmann's triptych,[65] 'voice', thus takes the form of 'fork', that inalienable right of the open-source field, as was the case in 2017 with 'Bitcoin Cash' following the 'civil war of the blocks'.

This conflict gradually escalated between 2016 and 2017. It pitted the miners against the developers of Bitcoin Core on an interesting issue, one that we no longer ask ourselves in our old contemporary societies: that of the political dimension of time. The miners wanted to increase the size of the blocks to improve the speed of transactions and increase their earnings. The developers, however, in keeping with Satoshi Nakamoto's white paper (Bitcoin's 'constitution'), were against the idea because it would have made the Bitcoin blockchain much heavier – the larger the blockchain, the more difficult it is for any user to participate by hosting the common register. The risk against which the developers wanted to protect themselves is a high degree of centralisation of the network, which could jeopardise its independence. They therefore decided to reject speed and accept relative slowness to preserve Bitcoin's autonomy, model of justice, organisation of power and decentralisation.

Reaffirming Bitcoin's principles has been a way of controlling its development and strengthening the network's independence and sovereignty in the face of interference from external injunctions from other fields, such as economics. Despite the decisive role and influence of the miners, they have not succeeded in imposing their preference. Although they have the machines, for them to have any value they still need to be used by Bitcoiners and updated by Bitcoin developers.

[64] Alizart (n 17) 102.

[65] Albert O Hirschman, *Exit, Voice, and Loyalty: Responses to Decline in Firms, Organizations, and States* (Harvard University Press, 1970).

There will be other conflicts, and it is by aligning everyone's interests that Bitcoin's defenders believe social order can be maintained. Of course, there are winners and losers, but above all the Bitcoin organisation has shown that it can settle and overcome dissent.

This story shows that despite not winning, the 'losers' still feel they have everything to gain. On both sides of the conflict, beyond their opposition, everyone agrees, and thus validates, the rules of the game defined by Bitcoin. Of course, this is a far cry from traditional sovereignty and the level of crystallisation in the organisation of contemporary nation-states. But Bitcoin is gradually evolving into a social world that is becoming institutionalised and structured. It is managing to maintain a level of control over its development and borders with other fields, deploying a set of shared rules that produce a Bitcoiner ethos and promoting a form of economic isolationism: '1BTC=1BTC'. This last point, combined with the stock market valuation, suggests to maximalist Bitcoiners that Bitcoin is gradually gobbling up billions of dollars, not in order to multiply them when the price of Bitcoin rises, but to destroy the dollar and fiat currencies, by taking them out of circulation so that they can simply accumulate more and more of tomorrow's currency.

IV. Bitcoin and the Climate Challenge: A Risk or an Opportunity?

The strength of sovereign nations is expressed in their ability to produce and control infrastructure, particularly that for energy. Europe has based part of its power on coal, the US on oil. What about electricity? Bitcoin's energy consumption is significant, but does not appear to be a weakness for Bitcoiners. On the contrary, it is a sign of its power (see section A below). However, on closer examination, some analyses tend to show that, counterintuitively, this energy consumption is not necessarily opposed to the climate challenge but, on the contrary, supports it (see section B below).

A. Electricity Consumption: An Attribute of Power

Bitcoin consumes a lot of electricity. In 2009, Satoshi Nakamoto himself raised this issue in a discussion.[66] But for him, this had to be set against the usefulness of his programme. So electricity is not a secondary issue for Bitcoin. It is not just a matter of running the computers to mine Bitcoin, it is the *ultima ratio*. In fact, energy is consubstantial with Bitcoin's very infrastructure, and is the reason why

[66] 'Re: Bitcoin minting is thermodynamically perverse', bitcointalk.org/index.php?topic=721.msg8114#msg8114.

Bitcoin is probably no longer attackable. With PoW, the electricity needed to mine the blocks does not disappear as if the window of a room had been opened; it changes form and crystallises, adding up to the blockchain and making it secure. Block by block, patiently, first in total anonymity, then in contempt, and now in broad daylight, Bitcoin is becoming stronger and stronger thanks to the energy it uses. Its autonomy and sovereignty are asserted through the inviolability of its blockchain. Today, no one seems able to stop it, except by turning against its users. Moreover, the reaffirmation that Bitcoin is and has been developed so that it cannot be censored is a recurring theme at conferences. For them, even if the legislator were to turn against Bitcoin and its users, it would be very difficult to ensure that his decision was effective. The infrastructure has given itself the means to counter attacks. Bitcoin has never been hacked and has been operating without interruption for 15 years, which is quite an achievement. It is probably the only example of this in the IT world. From a technical point of view, to modify or corrupt Bitcoin, you would have to redo all the cryptographic calculations needed to validate the existing blocks. This means that we would need to be able to mobilise as much energy as has been required since 2009 to date to deploy it. Suffice to say that this is impossible at the moment. The total cost of securing Bitcoin since 2009, if we consider that it is equal to the remuneration of miners, was estimated at nearly $30 billion in 2021,[67] a level that is probably unprecedented.

As we have seen, with PoW, to 'mine' bitcoin a processor (central processing unit (CPU), graphic processing unit (GPU), or now Asics) has to make a multiplicity of propositions until it manages to find the one that solves the riddle. Each proposition is called a 'hash'. The computing power of a computer network is thus expressed in 'hashrate'. On 8 February 2024, the Bitcoin network reached an exceptional level of 609 exahash per second (EH/s), with a three-day peak of 617 EH/s, increasing by more than 300 EH/s in the space of a year. These levels of computing power are difficult for humans to understand. An exahash corresponds to one quintillion calculations per second, with one quintillion corresponding to one billion trillion. This computing capacity makes the Bitcoin network the most powerful on the planet, ahead of any of the GAFAMs (Google, Apple, Facebook, Amazon, Microsoft), further defining the boundaries of its sovereignty and the scope of its security.

But PoW mining is also a distributed consensus system, a majority decision-making process. This is because the decision is determined by the longest blockchain, ie the one with the highest PoW invested. The participants (in this case the 'nodes') 'vote', Satoshi Nakamoto tells us, 'with their CPU power, expressing their acceptance of valid blocks by working to extend them and rejecting invalid blocks by refusing to work on them'.[68] If a traditional voting system had been chosen, using one IP address=one vote, for example, the process could have been

[67] Saifedean Ammous, *The Fiat Standard: The Debt Slavery Alternative to Human Civilization* (The Saif House, 2021).

[68] Nakamoto (n 29).

fraudulent, with a multiplicity of addresses being created, explains the anonymous creator. As for the choice made, it is in line with a common digital principle: do-ocracy. It is the doer who has the power. Participation is a way of validating, of voting, it being understood that no one is forbidden to stop contributing or to fork the project. However, from now on, the value in terms of electrical power, network stability, bitcoins or dollars makes a defection or fork a potentially costly project. The PoW and the electricity it consumes is therefore both a security instrument and a governance tool.

Bitcoin's autonomy is based on its ability to capture, collect and transform energy. As a currency backed by an energy source, it is able to move value through space and time and make it available to its users. It is therefore worth noting here that it is precisely by moving out of cyberspace and into the physical world that the cybernetic utopia is giving itself the means to assert real independence, more than 10 years after the declaration of independence of cyberspace. But what is the price of Bitcoin's power? Does not it come at the expense of the climate, by consuming increasingly scarce fossil fuels?

B. Bitcoin to Support the Climate Challenge

The Bitcoin network, through the PoW, consumes a lot of energy to produce, store, move and secure value within the world's largest computer network. It is estimated that the network consumes between 80 and 110[69] terawatt hours of energy per year (Twh/year),[70] or 0.55 per cent of global consumption. This is a far cry from the alarmist predictions that Bitcoin would consume all the energy it produces. However, even if we have clarified the role of this consumption in the operation of the network, we need to come back to the way in which it is deployed.

The war in Ukraine has led to fears in Europe of an energy shortage. Yet on a global scale there is no shortage of energy, and a significant proportion of it is wasted. The mining sector is highly competitive, and the fluctuating Bitcoin market encourages miners to look for the lowest possible electricity prices. This situation is leading more of them to turn to certain types of energy production, in particular methane and renewable energy.[71] Bitcoin thus tends to consume energy that has been produced but that no one wants.

Renewable energies are opening the way to low-carbon energy, but one of their characteristics is that they are not controllable: we cannot decide when it is windy

[69] Michel Khazzaka, 'Bitcoin: Cryptopayments Energy Efficiency' (Social Science Research Network, 20 April 2022); KPMG, 'Bitcoin's Role in the ESG Imperative' (2023).

[70] By way of comparison, the traditional banking system consumes 2206 Twh/year. Of course, the uses and volumes of transactions are not the same. We need to compare their energy efficiency per transaction. On this point, see Khazzaka (ibid).

[71] See Bitcoin Mining Council, bitcoinminingcouncil.com/bitcoin-mining-electricity-mix-increased-to-59-5-sustainable-in-q2-2022/andbitcoinminingcouncil.com/wp-content/uploads/2022/05/Bitcoin_Letter_to_the_Environmental_Protection_Agency.pdf; KPMG (n 69).

or when it is sunny. This means that we need to build production capacity that is greater than that of other controllable energy sources to meet demand. The result: overproduction peaks that jeopardise the infrastructure when not consumed, and force producers to sell off this energy, or even to pay customers to consume the electricity so as not to jeopardise the electrical installations. In 2023, France's Réseau de Transport Électrique estimates that these negative prices will affect more than 1.5 per cent of annual electricity production time, compared with more than 3.5 per cent in the Netherlands, for example.[72] Tepco, Japan's largest electricity producer, has announced that it will mine Bitcoin in 2022 to avoid wasting electricity that exceeds demand.[73]

Bitcoin miners can simply set up and provide an easily controllable solution for relieving the grid or monetising low-cost electricity residues when demand is low. When demand increases and prices rise again, miners can quickly disconnect from the network and restore energy. Many initiatives are moving in this direction, so it is not surprising that 59 per cent of the hash rate produced in the US is generated in Texas, the US state that produces the most renewable energy. Bitcoin's ability to go with and support the development of renewable energies was highlighted in an article by the World Economic Forum in 2022.[74]

Several developing countries, not only in Africa but also in Asia and South America, are seeking electrification as a means of development. The construction of hydroelectric dams has therefore been underway for several years. This type of installation is based on estimated demand over the next 50 years. At the start of the project, the dams are in overcapacity and the economic balance is precarious. Bitcoin miners can come and plug in their machines to help make the project profitable. This is what Sébastien Gouspillou's French company BigBlock GreenService is doing in the Virungas park, or in Paraguay with the Itaipu dam,[75] whose overcapacity is estimated at 5,000 megawatts, the equivalent of five nuclear power stations. Making these projects viable is essential to avoid traditional practices that use carbon-based energy and enable miners to benefit from a sufficiently low cost of electricity (around five cents per kilowatt-hour) to make their activity of securing the Bitcoin network profitable.

Today we are still largely dependent on oil extraction. This activity releases large quantities of methane into the atmosphere. This gas is one of the main causes of climate change, 80 times more harmful than carbon dioxide. This gas is generally not used: either it is released as it is into the atmosphere, or it is burnt directly

[72] Data available at www.analysesetdonnees.rte-france.com/bilan-electrique-2023/prix#Prixnegatifs.

[73] Thomas Pontiroli, 'Pourquoi l'électricien japonais Tepco se met à miner du bitcoin' (LesEchos, 12 September 2024), www.lesechos.fr/finance-marches/marches-financiers/pourquoi-lelectricien-japonais-tepco-se-met-a-miner-du-bitcoin-2118589.

[74] World Economic Forum, 'Cryptocurrency Can Retire Fossil Fuels for Good. Here's How' (10 August 2022).

[75] See www.cleansatmining.com/csm-beta; Raphaële Karayan, 'BigBlock Datacenter, Le Français Qui Chasse l'énergie Verte Pour Miner Du Bitcoin' (23 February 2022), www.usine-digitale.fr/article/bigblock-datacenter-le-francais-qui-chasse-l-energie-verte-pour-miner-du-bitcoin.N1787012.

on the wells in the form of flares to convert it into carbon dioxide. As oil wells are generally far from residential areas, the gas released by each well is often too small to justify the construction of recovery infrastructures. The World Bank estimates that by 2022, nearly 140 billion square metres of methane will have been released, with an evaporated value of nearly $16 billion.[76] Bitcoin miners such as Crusoe Energy can set up in these facilities, use and monetise the methane and thus reduce its impact on the environment. In 2021, a study revealed that capturing the energy from gas burned in this way in the US and Canada would be enough to power the entire Bitcoin network.[77] Companies such as Vespene Energy are making the same kind of use of waste collection areas.

So, as counterintuitive as it may seem today, Bitcoin is in a position to make a positive contribution to the energy transition. The proportion of green energy used to run the network is steadily increasing, and now exceeds the level of many industries. Today, the Bitcoin Mining Council estimates that it is around 58 per cent[78] and growing every year. They are probably doing this not so much out of environmental ethics but because it meets their economic interests in a context of increasing scarcity and rising prices of fossil fuels. Of course, Bitcoin alone will not solve the challenge we face. The figures we have are not yet truly exhaustive, nor are they easy to check and cross-reference. However, by understanding it not as a speculative tool but rather as a tool that can be combined with energy production, it seems to be able to play its part in meeting the climate challenge we face by supporting the development of renewable energy infrastructures and by recovering the value of electricity that is produced or extracted but not used. In addition to the battle over Bitcoin consumption figures, it is interesting to note that mining and Bitcoin players have taken up the environmental issue and the climate challenge. They are convinced that the environmental transition will have to include Bitcoin if it is to achieve its goal.[79]

Energy consumption must therefore be weighed against the social utility of the phenomenon observed. Of course, if we keep Bitcoin in the distant image of a gadget for graduate students, its interest and energy consumption will always seem disproportionate. But if we take seriously, as we have tried to do in this chapter, the promises of decentralisation, collaborative governance, network security, independence, individual and collective autonomy, and its positive impact on climate change made by Bitcoiners, then the point of view changes, or at least becomes more complex.

[76] Riccardo Puliti, 'Limiter les rejets de gaz torchés pour renforcer la sécurité énergétique et réduire les émissions de méthane' Banque Mondiale Blog (6 October 2022), blogs.worldbank.org/fr/voices/limiter-les-rejets-de-gaz-torches-pour-renforcer-la-securite-energetique.

[77] Nic Carter, 'How much Energy Does Bitcoin Actually Consume' *Harvard Business Review* (5 May 2021).

[78] See Bitcoin Mining Council, www.bitcoinminingcouncil.com/bitcoin-mining-council-survey-confirms-year-on-year-improvements-in-sustainable-power-mix-and-technological-efficiency.

[79] This is particularly the case for Alexis Stachtchenko, one of the key players in the French ecosystem. See A Stachtchenko, 'Bitcoin : Une Solution Contre-Intuitive Au Changement Climatique' Medium (25 April 2023).

V. Conclusion

Bitcoin has made a dramatic entrance into public debate over the last decade or so. Many politicians have criticised the risk it poses to the monetary sovereignty of states, and its environmental cost. With its hacker and cypherpunk origins, the software and the community that deploys it dream of producing another form of sovereignty. They hope that the millions of Bitcoiners will be the protagonists of a new society built around truly autonomous individuals, freed from any form of social control. They are seeking to update and transform the forms of collaboration, solidarity and governance that can be objectively organised through technology. Technology is thus at the heart of some fairly intense socio-political negotiations that mark out and guide its development. The example of Bitcoin highlights the idea that a technology is permeated, irrigated and shaped by social struggles and choices. Bitcoin's stated aim is to guard against any form of instrumentalisation or misappropriation of the capacity to act that has hitherto been entrusted to collective institutions. This political interpretation is translated and converted into IT development guidelines. But by relying on technology to reclaim individual power, these Bitcoiners are helping to extend and deepen the rationalisation of the social world, the principle of which is to produce predictability and reduce the uncertainty associated with human behaviour.

As Bitcoin's territory grows, its uses develop and its adoption spreads, so does its authority. Initially, this authority is made visible by the solidity of its technology. But, as is the privilege of sovereigns, its reliability and durability are strongly correlated with its ability to monopolise, redirect and gobble up vast amounts of energy. In order to legitimise this capture and make it viable (both economically and politically), a growing number of players are seeking to link Bitcoin, with some success, to the central challenge of modernity: the climate challenge.

11

Blockchain for Sustainability: The Case of Agribusiness

CECILIA RASETTO

I. Introduction

For several years, we have been witnessing global digitalisation. This phenomenon is a direct consequence of the development of digital platforms and the use of new ways of communicating, selling and purchasing products or services. It is part of the broader process of globalisation that has hit our planet in recent decades and has found its realisation through the new immaterial and delocalised dimension, without borders, generated by digital commercial platforms conveyed through electronic communication net.

If we want to restrict the territorial boundaries of the phenomenon to the geographical perimeter of the European Union (EU), we can highlight that, within the EU institutions, this subject has been studied and deepened in the European Digital Agenda for the decade 2020–2030, which was specifically dedicated to these issues.[1] The Digital Agenda focuses on creating secure digital spaces and services, establishing a level playing field in digital markets with large platforms, and addressing the technological gap between the United States (US) and China. There is a strong awareness that Europe cannot fully realise its potential in terms of digital leadership without these measures, and one of the most significant and immediate consequences of digitalisation is the real need for states to regulate the use and management of data. How a state regulates and exercises the governance of technology and services used in various ways within its national territory is defined as 'digital sovereignty'.[2] This concept concretely means managing and ensuring the protection of data, allowing companies, organisations and individuals

[1] United Nations, Transforming our world: the 2030 Agenda for Sustainable Development (adopted 25 September 2015) A/RES/70/1. The 2030 Agenda for Sustainable Development is an action programme for people, planet and prosperity, signed by the governments of the 193 Member Countries of the UN, and approved by the UN General Assembly. The Agenda is composed of 17 Sustainable Development Goals (SDGs) framed within a broader action programme consisting of 169 targets.

[2] For a definition of the concept of digital sovereignty, see the contributions to part I of this volume.

to take advantage of all the opportunities related to the digitalisation of information, while maintaining control of where data resides, where it flows and who has control over it. When it comes to digital sovereignty, therefore, the social and regulatory implications are broad and diverse.

In parallel, there is a global growing interest in achieving a more sustainable economy. This implies the optimisation of natural resources to foster economic growth and development while keeping consumers and users at the core. It is apparent that such concerns have permeated recent EU law and policymaking, which is now steering towards a 'green transition'.[3] Thus, in the wake of the EU quest for digital sovereignty, sociologists, economists and legal scholars are faced with the dilemma of how to use technologies for common good in order to deliver the digital and green transition, also named as the 'Twin Transition'.[4]

Against this backdrop, special attention is given to the use of disruptive technologies to reduce the environmental impact of traditional industry sector. This chapter addresses the question of how the application of blockchain technology could enhance sustainability in a particularly relevant area of EU policy, the agribusiness sector, and analyses the challenges it poses. To answer these questions, section II reviews the origin of sustainability and food sovereignty, and how they have become a primary objective in the EU agricultural policy; section III illustrates the main components of the agrobusiness sector and analyses its regulation in the EU; section IV explores how the digital transformation is having an impact on agribusiness; section V discusses the suitability of blockchain as a response for the needs of this industry and reconstructs the main challenges of greening blockchain applications in the agribusiness sector; section VI offers some final remarks.

II. Sustainability and Food Sovereignty in the EU Agricultural Policy

Throughout the course of evolution, humans exploited the earth's resources without worrying about the consequences that their often-destructive activity would generate. However, the international environmental community has demonstrated through its efforts that the limits of the planet are real and effective, and that there is an urgent need for a new model of development based on environmental, social and economic sustainability.[5] Such a renewed interest in environmental sustainability is leading to a significant reduction of the intensive exploitation of

[3] See Celeste and Perez Victorio in this volume.

[4] See, eg, Edoardo Celeste and Goran Dominioni, 'Digital and Green: Reconciling the EU Twin Transitions in Times of War and Energy Crisis' in Federico Fabbrini and Christy Anne Petit (eds), *Research Handbook on Post-Pandemic EU Economic Governance & NGEU Law* (Edward Elgar, 2024).

[5] United Nations, The Paris Agreement (adopted on 12 December 2015). This is a legally binding international treaty on climate change which entered into force on 4 November 2016.

land, paving the way for a new development model which prioritises the planet's resources.

A commonly accepted definition of environmental sustainability is mentioned in the 1987 Brundtland Report presented at the meeting of the UN World Commission on Environment and Development.[6] The Brundtland Report describes sustainable development as a system that ensures the satisfaction of the needs of the current generation without compromising the needs of future generations. Over the past decades, the importance of sustainability has grown and now has taken on a central role in global initiatives such as the 2030 Agenda presented at the United Nations (UN) conference containing the 17 Sustainable Development Goals (SDG).[7] They have global validity, concern all countries, and involve all components of society – from private companies to the public sector, civil society, and information and cultural operators. The SDGs address a series of important issues for the economic, social and ecological development of states, including digitalisation, connectivity and high technology in the agri-food sector.[8]

The new role attributed to digitalisation as a tool for sustainability is reflected through various initiatives, also at EU level; for instance, the EU Common Agricultural Policy (CAP) adapted over the years to follow the requirements of the new economic context. Today, support for farmers and rural stakeholders in EU countries is based on the modernised legal framework of the CAP 2023–2027 and the choices specified in the CAP Strategic Plans, approved by the European Commission.[9]

[6] Gro Harlem Brundtland, 'Our Common Future: World Commission on Environment and Development (WCED)' (1987) United Nations A/42/427. This report formulated a guideline for sustainable development that is still valid today. The Brundtland report found that global environmental hotspots and problems are mainly due to extreme poverty in the South and unsustainable production and consumption patterns in the north. It highlighted the need to implement a strategy that integrates the needs of development and the environment.

[7] United Nations, 'United Nations Conference on Sustainable Development, Rio+20', sustainabledevelopment.un.org/rio20. The World Conference on Sustainable Development 'Rio+20' was Agricultural Policy for 2023–2027 aimed at building the strategic framework following the Millennium Development Goals (MDGs), which was set to end in 2015.

[8] United Nations (n 1).

[9] European Commission, 'CAP 2023–27' (13 December 2024), agriculture.ec.europa.eu/common-agricultural-policy/cap-overview/cap-2023-27_en. CAP 2023–2027 is a modernised policy with a strong focus on results and performance. The agreement on the reform of the CAP was formally adopted on 2 December 2021. The new legislation, which entered into force on 1 January 2023, paves the way for a fairer, greener and more results-based CAP. It aims to ensure a sustainable future for European farmers, provide more targeted support to smaller farms and offer more flexibility for EU countries to adapt measures to local conditions. Agriculture and rural areas are at the heart of the European Green Deal, and the 2023–2027 CAP will be a key tool to deliver on the ambitions of the Farm to Fork Strategy and the Biodiversity Strategy. On 1 March 2017, as a contribution to the debate on the new EU project launched on the occasion of the 60th anniversary of the signing of the Treaty of Rome, the European Commission published the White Paper on the Future of Europe (European Commission, 2017). It is a document, as the subtitle states, of reflection and scenarios for the EU27 towards 2025.The new Common Agricultural Policy (CAP 2023–2027) makes EU agriculture fairer, greener and more results-oriented.

Another example that highlights the instrumentalisation of technology for sustainability purposes is the European Green Deal.[10] This emphasises data-driven innovation while underlines the importance transparency, accessibility and interoperability features, all of which is the core of precision agriculture. Digital transformation will act as a catalyst for a sustainable economy, enabling the sharing of information needed for environmental protection, improved use of natural resources, monitoring the implementation of climate policies, and creating greener mobility, agriculture and food systems.

The European Green Deal has also developed strategic actions to address the phenomena that have affected agriculture, which are of a climate, demographic and technological nature. Among these, the most significant is the From Farm to Fork strategy,[11] which is a policy focused on traceability as a tool to implement a sustainable system. Its aim is to safeguard a European agricultural model that integrates all stakeholders, starting with the most vulnerable, who play an important role in protecting the territory and the environment, alongside other objectives of health and environmental protection. This Commission's strategy contributes to achieving climate neutrality by 2050 by steering the current EU food system towards a sustainable model to achieve the objectives of food sovereignty. These goals include: (a) ensuring food supply and food security; (b) guaranteeing nutritious food in sufficient quantities and at affordable prices within planetary boundaries; (c) promoting the sustainability of food production; and (d) encouraging more sustainable and healthy consumption and dieting. In addition, the latest document drafted by the European Commission's Standing Committee on Agricultural Research (SCAR) outlines a framework for future development strategies and transition towards healthy and resilient food systems, which can be achievable through the circularity of product information, healthy and sustainable diets, and respect for biodiversity.[12]

Finally, two different projects developed within the EU have also provided specific and unprecedented tools for the implementation of the CAP plan.[13] These are the longstanding European Agricultural Fund for Rural Development

[10] European Commission, *The European Green Deal*, COM(2019) 640 final. On 11 December 2019, the European Commission adopted the European Green Deal which is a strategy to define climate and environmental engagement and transform the EU into a fair and prosperous society with a modern, resource-efficient and competitive economy that will not generate net greenhouse gas emissions in 2050 and where economic growth will be decoupled from resource use.

[11] European Commission, *A Farm to Fork Strategy for a fair, healthy and environmentally-friendly food system*, COM(2020) 381 final.

[12] European Commission, 'Resilience and Transformation: Report of the 5th Expert Group of the SCAR Foresight Exercise: Natural Resources and Food Systems: Transitions to a "Safe and Fair" Operational Area' (2020).

[13] European Parliament, 'The Common Agricultural Policy – Instruments and Reforms' (30 September 2023), www.europarl.europa.eu/factsheets/en/sheet/107/the-common-agricultural-policy-instruments-and-reforms. The reform of the CAP in June 2003 and April 2004 focuses on rural development by introducing a single financing and programming instrument: the European Agricultural Fund for Rural Development (EAFRD). This instrument, established by Regulation (EC) No 1290/2005 on the financing of the common agricultural policy, aims to strengthen the Union's rural

(EAFARD), dating back to 2005, and the most recent Horizon 2020 framework programme.[14] Overall, any analysis on the future of the agri-food sector, must acknowledge the profound intersection with digital technologies which, as demonstrated by EU interventions, have favoured the advent of a new form of agriculture: *smart agriculture* or precision agriculture, which will be discussed below.

Now, the most pressing matters of sustainability revolve around intensive farming and breeding livestock practices to meet the growing demand for meat and fish in human nutrition, the excessive consumption of electricity not derived from renewable sources, food waste, and environmental exploitation which disregards biodiversity. From the analysis of the initiatives referenced above, it becomes apparent that food security and sovereignty are of primary importance within the EU. Nonetheless, this concern goes beyond European borders, reflecting a global interest.

In 2007, the Nyéléni Forum for Food Sovereignty was held in Mali.[15] During this event, the six principles of food sovereignty were built and adopted, also defining 'the right of peoples to a healthy and culturally appropriate diet'. Subsequent meetings followed this direction. For instance, in 2011 the Nyéléni Forum adopted the Food Sovereignty Declaration, and in 2016, its European network also extended its reach to Central Asia, becoming the most important pan-European articulation for food sovereignty.[16]

In implementing these principles, each community is given the opportunity to define and execute its own agricultural policies, protect and regulate production and the local market, and pursue sustainable development adjusted to its needs and livelihood. Food sovereignty favours the local and national economy and markets, promotes family farming, traditional fishing and livestock practices, and encourages the production, distribution and consumption of food based on environmental, social and economic sustainability. It also involves decentralised governance, where decisions are made at the local or national level, allowing communities to influence agricultural policies and practices.

Faced with the growth of global population and the challenge of malnutrition, food sovereignty addresses how individuals can access a safe, culturally appropriate and balanced diet. Small-scale farmers have the skills and knowledge to maximise crop yields through diversified and locally adapted production. Conversely, agricultural societies and large farms tend to follow the monoculture model, which

development policy and simplify its implementation. In particular, it improves the management and control of the new rural development policy for the period 2007–2013.

[14] European Commission, 'Horizon 2020', research-and-innovation.ec.europa.eu/funding/funding-opportunities/funding-programmes-and-open-calls/horizon-2020_en. Horizon 2020 is the EU's seven-year programme dedicated to research and innovation. With a budget of more than €77 billion (in current prices), Horizon brings together all European funding in the sector in a single framework to facilitate the transformation of new scientific knowledge into innovative products and services.

[15] For more information, see www.fao.org/agroecology/database/detail/en/c/1253617.

[16] See, respectively: viacampesina.org/en/food-sovereignty-a-european-answer-to-the-crisis and www.fao.org/family-farming/detail/en/c/449337.

on average yields less per hectare than that of small farms with the diversified agricultural system implemented by small-scale farmers. For locally adapted cultivation methods to be possible in the long term, fair food prices are required. It is not enough for consumers to buy locally; policymakers must also design laws and subsidies in favour of small-scale diversified agriculture and its regional commercialisation. In addition, policy instruments must enable direct co-determination by consumers and producers.

In this context, the question arises as to whether and how technologies can contribute positively to achieving sustainability and protection of the right to food. In an increasingly connected world, technologies play a crucial role in the implementation of food sovereignty. Thus, digital technologies work as enablers of a new agri-food model, oriented towards data usage, collaboration with supply chain actors, and a focus on the end consumer.

Digital transition in this sector mainly involves digital tools that have been developed for other industries, such as finance. Among such innovative technologies, distributed ledgers, and particularly blockchain, seem most adaptable to the agri-food context. In particular, due to features like disintermediation and decentralisation, blockchain may offer promising solutions to the challenges of transforming food systems towards sustainability.[17] Thanks to its characteristics, the blockchain can work as a system for storing and exchanging data – for instance, information regarding a product, including food – in a way that prevents counterfeiting, fraud and food waste. At the same time, it provides the consumer with certainty about the origin of products as well as information on their organoleptic characteristics.[18] The application of blockchain to the agri-food sector promotes environmental sustainability by creating synergy between the digital and the food sectors. It guarantees sustainable production and consumption models while promoting the adoption of accurate information for the consumer and to combat food waste and fraud.

III. Agribusiness and its Regulation in Europe

Agribusiness encompasses the various economic systems involved in the production and distribution of agricultural and food products. Its structure is influenced by the economic, socio-cultural and institutional environments.[19] There are two main trends currently affecting agribusiness. Firstly, the adaptative responses to the changes in Western economy, historically influenced by the need to address

[17] Joachim Von Braun et al, *Science and Innovations for Food Systems Transformation* (Springer International Publishing, 2023).

[18] Herwig Winkler, *Blockchain-Based Digitalisation of Logistics Processes – Innovation, Applications, Best Practices* (Basel MDPI Books, 2022).

[19] Roberta Paltrinieri, Stefano Spillare and Francesco Svoia, *Circular Economy in the Agrifood Sector: The SinCE-AFC ebook* (FrancoAngeli, 2022).

food demands and mass distribution; and, secondly, the interactions with environmental factors, land resources and overreaching effects of climate change.

In addition to the aforementioned elements, agri-food systems are impacted by globalisation, modernisation and technological progress in agricultural and food practices. In its current stage of development, the agri-food sector is looking for new forms of integration within the entire economic and socio-cultural system of countries. Most importantly, agribusiness is experiencing an evolution driven by: (i) innovations in the field of information and communication; (ii) advancements in bioengineering; (iii) changes in food consumption; and (iv) modernisation in the industrial framework. The agri-food sector also includes, in a broader sense, catering and commercial intermediaries specialised in food supply, as well as providers of fresh and prepared products tailored to the particular demands of costumers in terms of shape, size and packaging. Its multifaceted nature and complex internal structure require a differentiated legal discipline, distinct from non-agricultural and non-food economic activities.

The importance of the individual components of the agri-food system is closely linked to internal and external factors affecting it, which may be variable and unpredictable. The main internal factor is represented by the natural, hydrological, forestry, rural and wildlife characteristics of a given production location. In contrast, external factors include regulatory policies, the use of natural resources, product marketing, dietary habits of a given population, historical periods, stages of industrial development, and socio-economic conditions of a country. Additionally, economic crises, energy shortages, wars and pandemics can have relevant impacts on the sector.

Agricultural matters are regulated both at the national level, within the individual Member States, and at the European level. In the EU, the agri-food sector has been the subject of a process of harmonisation to minimise regulatory asymmetries inherent to internal markets.[20] When the Treaty of Rome established the common market in 1958, agriculture in the six founding Member States was characterised by strong state intervention. To include agricultural products in the free movement of goods while maintaining public intervention in the agricultural sector, it was necessary to abolish national intervention mechanisms incompatible with the common market and transpose them at the Community level: this is the fundamental reason for the birth of the CAP.

The Treaty on the Functioning of the European Union (TFEU) is the relevant EU legislation applicable to this sector. Article 4 TFEU refers to the list of shared competencies of the EU, agriculture and fisheries, while Articles 38–44 contain the discipline of the CAP, regulating the Community legislative competence (Article 38); the objectives of the CAP (Article 39); and competition policy and state aid (Article 42). In particular, Article 38 states that, for the purposes of the

[20] European Union, 'Application of European Union Rules for the Agri-Food Chain' (13 April 2023), eur-lex.europa.eu/IT/legal-content/summary/enforcing-eu-rules-for-the-agri-food-chain.html.

internal market, there is no mere regulation of agricultural and fishery products by the Union, but a real common policy for the entire agricultural and fisheries sector. This grants the EU the competence to carry out policy and regulatory interventions affecting both production and market.

In this area, EU interventions are guided by specific objectives that define and legitimise the Union's legislative actions. These objectives shape all initiatives, actions and programmes developed by EU institutions within the agri-food sector. In sections below we will focus in particular on the application of digital technologies in this domain.

IV. Digital Transformation in Agribusiness: Towards 'Digital Agriculture'

The agri-food sector is pursuing the challenge of including the use of technological tools in production chains. Data collection and analysis inform both production activities that take place in protected environments, such as greenhouses and agro-industry, and in open environments, such as those agricultural activities that are subject to climate variability and territorial elements like weather or soil conditions.[21] Technological innovation and digitalisation have impacted agribusiness enabling sustainable practices, increasing the productive capacity of the land, while reducing the use of non-renewable resources. It is no coincidence that in recent years there has been an increasing use of digital tools, especially to achieve environmental sustainability and the modernisation of agriculture.[22]

Technological development and the spread of digitalisation have fostered the evolution of an integrated agricultural management model, whose applications can be considered tools for the study of environmental variables and allow the most appropriate decisions to be made in terms of sustainability, efficiency and respect for the territory. Precision agriculture – and its most recent evolution that defines it as 'digital agriculture' – finds its strength in information management systems which integrate the expertise of the farmer with information from digital sources. The goal is to manage space, time and quality variability present in all primary production systems, which were almost impossible to address in an efficient way until the advent of precision agriculture.[23] Thanks to the solutions

[21] AIDA-IFLA, *Italian Food Law Association, Italian Food Law Association, Innovation in agri-food law between technology and comparison* (Wolters Kluwer, 2019).

[22] Karim Marini Thomé, Michael Bourlakis and Patricia Guarnieri, *Food Supply Chain through Ongoing Evolution: Lessons from Continuous Transformations* (Multidisciplinary Digital Publishing Institute, 2022); Rachel Bezner Kerr et al, *Rethinking Food System Transformation* (Springer Nature Switzerland, 2023).

[23] Elsayed Said Mohamed et al, 'Smart farming for improving agricultural management' (2021) 24 *The Egyptian Journal of Remote Sensing and Space Science* 2; Hossein Azadi et al, 'Rethinking resilient agriculture: From Climate-Smart Agriculture to Vulnerable-Smart Agriculture' (2021) 319 *Journal of Cleaner Production*.

offered by precision agriculture, this sector has become one of the most important priorities of the EU for innovation and sustainable growth.[24]

From an operational point of view, precision agriculture is divided into three phases: 1) monitoring and recording of geodata; 2) analysis, elaboration and planning of operations according to specific needs; and 3) regulation and control of operations. In addition, it is based on four main technological pillars: (a) geographic positioning systems based on satellite constellations (GPS); (b) geographic information systems (GIS); (c) remote sensors and actuators for variable dosing and control of sections or guidance systems; and (d) systems for connectivity and interoperability.[25]

Of course, the use of technologies in agribusiness involves a wide range of legal areas that require the attention of Member States' legislators as well as the EU. Think, for example, of the use of drones, GPS, driverless vehicles, worker safety, civil liability, legislation on water, nitrates, plant protection, animal welfare, soil degradation, environmental exploitation and measures to incentivise agricultural activities, but above all the protection of data transfers. To date, the most delicate legal area concerning the digitalisation of the world of agriculture is the use of data. The European General Data Protection Regulation (GDPR) provides an answer for the processing of personal data during agricultural activities, whether they relate to the farmer, to the workers employed in agricultural activities or to other individuals involved in them. However, it is necessary to recognise several gaps concerning raw data generated by machines that cannot be classified as personal data or the conditions of their economic exploitation and marketability.[26]

This leads to a new vision of the agricultural supply chain according to which, thanks to the implementation of digital technologies in all its individual segments, the entire sector is able to support resilient and sustainable models, to respect more the environment and – last but not least – to increase its competitiveness on the market. To address the difficulties of the sector, the European Commission has carried out, as part of the European Industrial Strategy, a public consultation project to define common objectives for the green and digital transition of agri-food companies by 2030.[27] The project document outlines some of the most critical points in the sector, covering seven different sections: sustainable competitiveness,

[24] The European Commission has planned the following programmes for the implementation of workers' skills and for the creation of new jobs in the agri-food sector: Horizon 2020 programme; cohesion policy; national co-financing; rural development; business plan; national policies.

[25] European Parliamentary Research Reservice, 'Precision Agriculture and the future of farming in Europe' Scientific Foresight Study (2016) 581.892. We also remember expressions such as smart farming, digital farming, Internet of farming and agriculture 4.0, which, however, are not always understood as synonyms of precision agriculture but are used in the literature to underline an evolution of precision agriculture towards forms of farm management in which greater importance is given with the latest technologies, in particular to big data.

[26] Pamela Lattanzi, 'L'agricoltura di precisione, una sfida anche per il diritto' (2018) 14 *Agriregionieuropa*.

[27] European Commission, *Updating the 2020 New Industrial Strategy: Building a stronger Single Market for Europe's recovery*, COM(2021) 350 final.

regulation and public governance, social dimension, techniques and technological solutions, infrastructure, skills, investments and financing.

Also, this vision will include efficient data collection on progress made in different areas, monitoring of greenhouse gas emissions, water and land use, energy production, waste production, use of renewable energy and recycled materials, private investment in circular solutions and adoption of new technologies. The European Commission's objective is to develop, on the one hand, an operational framework of data on food chains in the EU managed by the European Food Safety and Supply Organisation (EFSCM), and, on the other hand, a mapping study of the EU Code of Conduct on Responsible Food Marketing and Business Practices.[28] This study examines the commitments and activities of the different signatories of the Code to identify areas where additional efforts are needed.

Digitalisation promises to increase the effectiveness and efficiency of value chains and production processes (eg smart agriculture, industry 4.0), improve adaptability and forecasting (eg Big Data and business intelligence), and enable interaction with end consumers (web technologies and market intelligence). By improving processes across the entire supply chain and leveraging the data generated in each area of the value chain, digitalisation has the potential to reduce the industry's carbon footprint. Conversely, the green transition appears urgent for at least three reasons: the non-postponement of the reduction of the effects of human activities on the climate; growing consumer demand for environmental and social sustainability from companies; and the strong orientation of the financial system (public and private) to integrate accessibility and sustainability, with a preference for companies with an advanced ESG profile.[29]

V. Blockchain Technology as a Tool for Creating Smart and Sustainable Agrifood Systems

Applications that use the blockchain protocol have become increasingly common over the past few years. Blockchain is a distributed ledger technology (DLT).[30] Based on the so-called chain of custody, it guarantees complete traceability of the actions and behaviours of the different operators in a network of exchanges and relationships. Blockchain is indeed a decentralised distributed database, structured as a chain of blocks, containing transactions that are related to each other according to a chronological principle and whose integrity is ensured by a system of algorithms and cryptographic rules.

[28] More information is available at food.ec.europa.eu/horizontal-topics/farm-fork-strategy/sustainable-food-processing/code-conduct_en.

[29] See Dimichina in this volume.

[30] For an accurate reconstruction, see Depoorter in this volume.

In the agri-food sector, blockchain takes the form of a set of technologies with recognised potential both for controlling global production, marketing and consumption chains of agri-food products, and for creating and consolidating knowledge and skills.[31] Within a blockchain platform, each player in the supply chain can record traceability information regarding their business, thus making it immutable and at the same time visible to all other nodes in the network.

Consumer information is a fundamental dimension of agri-food law, especially within the EU regulatory framework. Over time this area has evolved into an elaborate system of rules and instruments aimed not only at protecting consumers' health but also at certifying products, allowing consumers to make informed choices based on characteristics such as origin or environmental sustainability.[32] In the examination of the applications of blockchain technology to the agri-food sector, its objectives and the main fields of use are key areas of interest which require further analysis.

The main objectives of blockchain technology applied to the agri-food sector range from promoting sustainability to protecting and guaranteeing food safety and consumer health. This involves ensuring sustainable food production and safety, and promoting a sustainable food supply chain from start to finish, meaning from processing to sale (both wholesale and retail) including as well ancillary services, such as hospitality and catering. In addition, blockchain supports, sustainable food consumption and the transition to healthier dietary habits, fighting food fraud along the supply chain and reducing food waste. It is also worth highlighting that, through a blockchain platform, data can be collected, secured against tampering and be made accessible to certifiers and consumers, who would thus have the opportunity to know the entire journey taken by the product along the supply chain.

At the national level, the research carried out by the CREA Research Centre and the Blockchain Observatory of the Politecnico di Milano, a centre of excellence in Italy, is moving in this direction.[33] An analysis of the data collected over the last two years has shown that the projects applying blockchain to traceability and certifications have enabled monitoring compliance with quality standards in the fishing industry. This provides safeguarding to natural reserves, detects the

[31] Ching Fu Li, 'Blockchainizing Food Law' (2019) 74 *Food and Drug Law Journal*; Giorgio Remotti, 'Possible auxiliary functions of blockchain technologies for brands and indications of origin: traceability of the food supply chain, competitive dynamics and merchant mechanics' (2022) *Revista di Diritto dei Media*.

[32] Examples include Regulation (EU) No 1169 of 2011 of the European Parliament and of the Council of 25 October 2011 on the provision of food information to consumers, amending Regulations (EC) No 1924/2006 and (EC) No 1925/2006 of the European Parliament and of the Council.

[33] The Council for Research in Agriculture and Analysis of Agricultural Economics (CREA), an Italian research body dedicated to agri-food supply chains with legal personality under public law, supervised by the Ministry of Agricultural Policies, Food Sovereignty and Forests (Masaf).

presence of allergens and allows the withdrawal of compromised batches with a view to food safety.[34]

The use of blockchain is particularly relevant in implementing measures to control and preserve the path of food products. For instance, in the event that health hazards for humans or animals emerge, blockchain plays a crucial role in the activation of the Rapid Alert System (RASFF) developed within the EU.[35] In this case, timely communication of risks to consumers plays a central role in mitigating potential and actual adverse effects on human and animal health and welfare, while also limiting the permanence of dangerous products on the market. In essence, the relationship between science and law, consumer awareness and the strengthening of trust with producers can be improved through the application of innovative systems. This system can promote greater consumer awareness by providing empirical and tangible knowledge of the life cycle and chemical composition of a product, beyond mere probabilistic evaluations.

For real transparency in the agri-food sector, the quintessential communication tool is labelling which,[36] like traceability, represents a main area for the application of blockchain technology. Consumers increasingly require a range of nutritional information and, blockchain seems to be able to offer the best answer to meet this need, since it is a tool that promotes the accessibility of traceability-related information. With the introduction of the mandatory nutrition declaration on the label,[37] it has been possible to respond to the emerging needs for greater transparency for health prevention, greater identifiability of data relating to the nutritional aspects of products, and greater environmental sustainability. Manufacturers are obliged to report all the information regarding the identity, composition, properties and other characteristics of food, including also shelf life, methods of use and harmful effects.

To quickly convey information, smart labels have also been introduced. These labels can automatically identify and track goods by detecting alterations or health risks, related to alterations in the correct storage temperature or contamination of the environment. In addition, they provide optional valuable information related to the product's life cycle reflecting the EU commitments to create an environmentally friendly, resilient and sustainable system.

[34] Giuseppe Spoto, 'Gli utilizzi della blockchain e dell'Internet of Things nel settore degli alimenti' (2019) *Rivista Di Diritto Alimentare* 25; and Arianna Di Conno, 'Agriculture 4.0., blockchain and certifications' (2022) *Rivista di Diritto Alimentare*.

[35] The early warning system (RASFF) is defined in Art 50 et seq of Ch IV of Regulation (EC) No 178/2002 and consists of a network system linking all Member States' national authorities, the Commission and EFSA.

[36] Regulation (EU) No 1169/2011 of the European Parliament and of the Council of 25 October 2011 on the provision of food information to consumers, [2001] OJ L 304/18. The definition of a label is provided by Art 1(1) and (2)(i), which states: 'any trade mark or trademark, sign or image or other graphic representation written, printed, stamped, marked, embossed, embossed or imprinted on the packaging or container of a food or accompanying such packaging or container'.

[37] The mandatory nutrition declaration entered into force on 13 December 2016 and is governed by Arts 2 and 30 Regulation (EU) 1169/2011.

Blockchain can make a positive contribution to verifying the veracity of labels. These smart labels are characterised by the presence of barcodes and QR codes or equipped with more sophisticated systems such as radio frequency identification (RFID) or near field communication (NFC) tags.[38] The adoption of smart labels as a useful tool for greater transparency and communication of information has strengthened the relationship between operator and consumer while ensuring greater traceability of agri-food products throughout the supply chain. This is also valuable in combating counterfeiting phenomena and with a view to promoting the conveyance of information relating to ethical choices, increasing transparency in this sector.

A. Blockchain for Food Traceability and Sustainability

Despite traceability being theoretically a neutral tool, it has different meanings, and the term is often used interchangeably with 'retrievability'. Nonetheless, traceability may map the journey from raw materials to the finished product (ascending traceability), to retrace the path taken by the product (descending traceability). Through food traceability, it is possible to trace the paths followed by foods in the supply chain, find all the specific information on the safety and quality of the products, and implement, if necessary, recall plans for food products already placed on the market.

Traceability has been defined by Regulation (EC) No 178/2002. In Article 3(15), traceability is defined as 'the possibility of reconstructing and following the path of a food, feed, animal or substance intended or likely to become part of a food or feed through all stages of production, Transformation and Distribution'. Likewise, Article 18 then deepens the definition in terms of objective and expected result, and establishes the obligation for all operators in the sector to provide information on the origin of products and all the subjects involved in the individual stages of production along the entire supply chain. Article 18(2) provides:

> Food and feed business operators must be able to identify who has supplied them with food, feed, food-producing animals or any substance intended for or likely to be incorporated into a food or feed. To that end, those operators must have systems and procedures in place to provide information to competent authorities upon request.

In summary, the agri-food system outlined by Regulation (EC) No 178/2002 – which still represents the reference legislation for traceability– highlights that traceability does not make a product safe in itself, but serves as a tool to mitigate actual food safety risks.

The institution of food traceability has been the subject of intervention under the new CAP adopted by the European Council for the period 2023–2027, for a

[38] RFID can be used to receive and transmit radio waves over distances of 100m or more (for active tags, equipped with their own battery); NFC is limited to no more than 20cm in the best cases.

more sustainable system. This includes Regulation (EU) 2021/2115 establishing rules on support for strategic plans to be drawn up by Member States under the CAP ('CAP Strategic Plans') and financed by the European Agricultural Guarantee Fund (EAGF) and the European Agricultural Fund for Rural Development (EAFRD), as well as the repeal of Regulations (EU) No 1305/2013 and (EU) No 1307/2013.

Article 47(1) of Regulation (EU) No 2021/2115 provides that for each objective of the CAP Strategic Plans, Member States may choose a type of intervention, including 'the implementation of traceability and certification systems, in particular with regard to the quality control of products sold to final consumers. Article 84 of the same Regulation provides for a specific delegation of powers to the European Commission to establish additional requirements regarding the types of rural development interventions, including support for traceability. Moreover, Article 100 of the Regulation empowers the European Commission to assess the contribution of policy to the achievement of climate change objectives through a simple and common methodology: the traceability of climate-related spending.

Traceability has also been a strategic objective of the main international organisations and associations carrying out activities in the agri-food sector. Thanks to the International Standardization Organisation (ISO) standard UNI EN 22005:2008, the main actors involved in the agri-food supply chain system – such as the Codex Alimentarius Commission, the International Association of Hotels and Restaurants, the Global Food Safety Initiative (GFSI) and the Confederation of Agri-Food Industries of the European Union (CIAA) – can identify and track every aspect of the activity of the operators involved in the process, from farms to the consumer's table. In such a structured context, in which transparency and knowledge about the phases of food production process constitute critical vulnerabilities of the agri-food sector, operators are naturally looking for tools capable of streamlining this process. Above all, they look for systems capable of containing, store and managing a huge amount of information related to the entire food supply chain.

For operators in the sector, having a software for food traceability has significant advantages in terms of: (a) transparency; (b) sustainability; and (c) savings. Traceability allows products to be identified with regard to details related to weight, allergens, type of packaging, specifications, expiration dates and dates of manufacture, which are all recorded and transferred together with the product to facilitate identification. The same benefits can also be found on the consumer side. In fact, knowing the path taken by products (from their origin to the marketing of the finished product) allows consumers to keep track of the time, storage and conservation conditions, controls carried out and the product's journey along the supply chain throughout its life cycle, to be able to guide their choices in an informed way.

Ultimately, blockchain technology would act as a tool that makes it possible to ensure the effectiveness of consumer rights in the agri-food industry. In this scenario, the blockchain – by virtue of its advantageous properties – allows precision monitoring, encourages virtuous behaviour by denouncing and sanctioning illegitimate actions. It is also able to create a transparent traceability and communication system aimed at combating civil and criminal offences. By leveraging the characteristic of 'disintermediation', or decentralisation of control, the sharing, reuse and recycling of materials are encouraged, therefore environmental sustainability and the circular economy are favoured in a related way so as to facilitate industrial symbiosis with the establishment of a promoted communication and certification system.

B. Potential and Risks of Blockchain for Agribusiness

The functioning of the blockchain in the case of food products is varied. Carrefour was the first large-scale retailer in Italy to apply blockchain technology to the traceability of food, in particular to the supply chain of free-range and antibiotic-free chicken, in a transparent manner so that this information can also be consulted by the end consumer. Through a QR code, it is possible to access the information related to the purchased product and examine the mapped data thanks to a very intuitive interface that is easily accessible to everyone. Blockchain technology guarantees the immutability of the recorded data and of the history of the supply chain product information. Each component of the food supply chain (producers, processors and distributors) can provide traceability information on each batch of product, which can never be changed by anyone. The advantages are easily perceived in terms of transparency and fast circulation of nutritional and commercial information; however, the system is exposed to risks.

In the face of the multiple and diversified forms of use of blockchain technology in the agri-food sector, there are inevitable risks to which the technology, by its nature, is exposed, including: (i) the violation of cybersecurity (a problem, moreover, closely related to digital sovereignty); (ii) the civil liability profiles of operators in the sector, (iii) the complex interaction of man with technology; and (iv) the significant impact that the exploitation of these technologies has on the environment. Certainly, real awareness and more accurate scientific diagnosis have yet to mature about the negative implications deriving from the application of blockchain to the agri-food sector. However, it is already possible to delimit the perimeter of the critical issues and disadvantages that blockchain experiences in its current form.

The intersection between the user and the network requires the implementation of ad hoc procedures and adequate training of the various actors involved in order to have the digital culture and technical skills necessary to operate consciously and correctly in the blockchain environment. This would ensure the fundamental trust between the various actors involved. Thus, it becomes crucial for every company to make sure that the other partners in the network have the space, technical resources and dedicated staff to fulfil their shared responsibilities.

It is also necessary to monitor the risks inherent to new blockchain technology, as well as taking into account that the incidence of bugs is very frequent during the early stages of the evolution of any technology – blockchain is certainly not immune.

Blockchain networks can differ in the role of who can participate and who has access to the data. Networks are typically labelled as public or private, to highlight who is allowed to participate, with or without permission, and to highlight how participants gain access to the network. There are risks strictly related to cybersecurity, such as the risk of data back-up and the theft of public and private keys by hackers, which must therefore be stored outside the blockchain securely so that they do not become an easy target for hackers who use fishing, routing and sybil.[39]

The issue of civil liability in relation to the protection of digital content is always alive in every area and context in which technology is used for the exchange of goods and/or services. Since it is not possible to reconstruct the entire evolutionary and regulatory framework of civil liability of the subjects involved, we will limit ourselves to listing the emerging liability profiles. In general terms, the main forms of civil liability involve digital platforms for infringement of intellectual and industrial property rights and for unlawful processing of personal data.

The most critical issues related to the use of blockchain in agribusiness, however, are found in terms of ethical contradictions of a technology at the service of the environment, but at the same time energy intensive. Blockchain can only work through the exploitation of energy. It is therefore necessary to also evaluate the phenomenon under consideration in relation to this aspect, which is closely connected with the issue of the energy crisis analysed in this volume.[40] This is partly related to the type of blockchain and the block validation system. The environmental impact of blockchains is felt especially in the Bitcoin and cryptocurrency sector, where it can be very high due to PoW mining, which involves a large expenditure of energy and carbon dioxide emissions. The processors of these machines consume large amounts of energy and in particular fossil fuels, which are an important source in the generation of electricity. However, not all blockchains pollute in the same way, and it is also possible to talk about eco-sustainability in this case. Indeed, the blockchain itself does not necessarily have an energy-consuming connotation.

Among the virtuous examples, there is that of the Ethereum Foundation, the organisation behind the Ethereum cryptocurrency, which is working on a new way to verify transactions, switching to a different method (called Proof of Stake, or PoS) that could reduce the energy cost of each transaction by 99.95 per cent. At the same time, many players in the industry want to ensure that the energy consumed

[39] Maddalena Castellani et al, *Blockchain: guida pratica tecnico giuridica all'uso* (GoWare, 2019); Daniel T Stabile, Kimberly A Prior and Andrew M Hinkes, *Digital assets and blockchain technology: US law and regulation* (Edward Elgar, 2020).

[40] Kushankur Dey and Umedsingh Shekhawat, 'Blockchain for sustainable e-agriculture: literature review, architecture for data management and implications' (2021) 316 *Journal of Cleaner Production*.

by industry is completely carbon-free. In April 2021, three major organisations (the Energy Web Foundation, the Rocky Mountain Institute and the Alliance for Innovative Regulations) formed the Crypto Climate Accord, which is supported by organisations spanning the climate, finance, non-governmental organisations and energy sectors.[41] The goal of the Agreement is to decarbonise the crypto industry in record time and achieve net-zero emissions by 2030.

A further form of containment of energy consumption is represented by the mining operating protocol, which can generate great savings in terms of energy. The PoS model, for example, does not reward computational racing, but requires that the nodes participating in the blockchain are randomly selected, consuming in this way significantly less energy. Moreover, there is also a form of 'green blockchain' that is characterised by low energy consumption, whose operation is mainly based on renewable sources and capable of producing no waste. This model is being monitored within the UN, as blockchain's potential to protect the environment is being tested in a number of international projects.[42] For example, an ad hoc solution has been developed in collaboration with the World Wide Fund for Nature (WWF), to combat and reduce the scale of fish fraud and protect the environment and consumers of the tuna industry. In particular, WWF New Zealand has used blockchain to track the supply chain of longline tuna in Fiji.[43] This is also why the UN supports blockchain and reminds us not to generally extend the negative aspects of cryptocurrencies to the underlying technology, which can conversely make a great contribution to sustainable development.

VI. Conclusion

Having adopted a functional-axiological perspective on the incidence and influence of digital technologies in the agribusiness sector, some conclusions can be drawn. First, it is necessary to recognise the design of an evolved digital society, in which every economic sector must coexist with digital technologies. In order to progress, each sector can only 'exploit' these tools in its favour. Progress and digital innovation in the agri-food sector have generated great enthusiasm among

[41] See cryptoclimate.org.

[42] 'UN Study Reveals the Hidden Environmental Impacts of Bitcoin: Carbon Is Not the Only Harmful By-Product' (United Nations University, 24 October 2023), unu.edu/press-release/un-study-reveals-hidden-environmental-impacts-bitcoin-carbon-not-only-harmful-product. UN scientists assessed the activities of 76 bitcoin mining nations during the period 2020–2021 and found that the global bitcoin mining network consumed 173.42 terawatt hours of electricity.

[43] In addition, in 2021, the coalition of NGOs, The Environmental Justice Foundation, Oceana, Pew Charitable Trusts and WWF (IUUW) submitted to the European legislator a proposal to amend Regulation of the European Parliament and of the Council amending Council Regulations (EC) No 1224/2009, (EC) No 768/2005, (EC) No 1967/2006 and (EC) No 1005/2008 and Regulation (EU) 2016/1139 of the European Parliament and of the Council on controls in the fisheries sector with a view to sustainable fishing and the fight against illegal fishing.

scholars and operators in the sector. The application of digitalisation to this field is destined to evolve again, as the technology underpinning it evolves.

Thanks to the capacity to make agricultural activities more efficient, competitive, resilient and sustainable, the application of modern digital technologies to the agri-food sector brings with it a radical change to pre-existent food models. However, a comprehensive examination of the topic cannot ignore the deep limitations and dilemmas inherent to blockchain. From a legal perspective, it is necessary to overcome systemic issues, such as the fragmentation of the regulatory discipline, which, to date, despite European attempts of harmonisation, remains disorganised. In this context, while the implementation of digital technology is a source of great benefits and innovations, it also entails high costs, risks and responsibilities. The issues that arise encompass technical, legal, social and environmental aspects.

Blockchain is a relatively recent technology, especially in its applications, and it is yet to be understood which areas of societal application will be most effective and useful. What is certain is that it is essential to understand its dynamics in order to better identify the levers that can be used to build sustainable models. The coming years will be crucial to continue delving into the practical implementation of blockchain-enabled solutions for agribusiness as well as to study how the regulatory framework of the EU will react to these developments.

12

Eco-Digital Products and Services: Towards New EU Sustainability Rights?

ALBA PEREZ VICTORIO AND EDOARDO CELESTE

I. Introduction

The European Commission envisioned the adoption of a framework of digital rights and principles as an element of the 2030 Digital Compass strategy.[1] The first draft of the European Declaration on Digital Rights and Principles for the Digital Decade was published on 26 January 2022, following a heated period of discussions within the European institutions.[2] On 23 January 2023 the Declaration was solemnly adopted by the Commission, the Parliament and the Council.[3] Although this instrument is not legally binding, both the European Union (EU) and its Member States should refer to the Declaration within their respective competences using it as a guidance document.[4] European values permeate the Declaration, putting people at the centre, supporting an autonomous and sovereign role of the EU in the digital field, with a commitment to a secure, safe and sustainable digital transformation.[5]

Compared with the EU Charter of Fundamental Rights, the Declaration represents a step forward in terms of environmental protection in the digital context. While in the Charter only one article guides EU policies by establishing a general

[1] European Commission, *2030 Digital Compass: the European way for the Digital Decade 2021*, COM/2021/118 final.

[2] *European Declaration on Digital Rights and Principles for the Digital Decade 2022*, COM (2022) 28 final.

[3] European Declaration on Digital Rights and Principles for the Digital Decade 2023/C 23/01. For a commentary, see Edoardo Celeste, 'Digital Constitutionalism, EU Digital Sovereignty Ambitions and the Role of the European Declaration on Digital Rights' in Annegret Engel, Xavier Groussot and Gunnar Thor Petursson (eds), *New Directions in Digitalisation: Perspectives from EU Competition Law and the Charter of Fundamental Rights* (Springer, 2024).

[4] ibid Preamble.

[5] See Celeste (n 3). For an analysis of EU digital sovereignty strategies, see Edoardo Celeste, 'Digital Sovereignty in the EU: Challenges and Future Perspectives' in Federico Fabbrini, Edoardo Celeste and John Quinn (eds), *Data Protection Beyond Borders: Transatlantic Perspectives on Extraterritoriality and Sovereignty* (Hart, 2021).

need to protect and improve the quality of the environment,[6] Chapter VI of the Declaration is entirely devoted to digital sustainability.[7] It calls out specific measures related to the mitigation of the negative impact of digital products and services in the environment, by promoting circular economy and by empowering users to make environmentally responsible choices. In addition, Chapter VI lists the efforts that the EU commits to make at that level. By doing so, the Declaration provides clearer guidelines for EU institutions and Member States to integrate sustainability in their policies.

Sustainability – or, more specifically, sustainable development – is a general principle of EU law, which has been recognised in the Charter of Fundamental Rights of the EU and in the TFEU.[8] In particular, the EU sustainable development strategy is very much related to the United Nations (UN) 2030 Agenda and the 17 Sustainable Development Goals (SDGs).[9] One of the most cited definitions of sustainable development is the one given by the Brundtland Report of 1987, named after the Chairwoman of the World Commission on Environment and Development (WCED) and which was sponsored by the UN.[10] The Brundtland Report provided a broad definition that puts the emphasis on technology and social organisations meeting the needs of present generations without prejudicing the needs of future ones.[11] With this definition, the promotion of a 'balanced and sustainable development' as an objective of the EU in the Preamble of the Charter is to be interpreted in the sense that there are environmental limits to economic growth and these have to be considered from a long-term perspective. In the same line, Article 37 of the Charter requires the principle of sustainable development to be used to incorporate a 'high level of environmental protection

[6] EU Charter, Art 37.

[7] See Alba Perez Victorio, Edoardo Celeste and Alberto Quintavalla, 'Greening AI? The New Principle of Sustainable Digital Products and Services in the EU' (2024) 61 *Common Market Law Review* 1019, which analyses the contribution of this chapter in the context of EU AI policies.

[8] While the concept of sustainability is often used to refer to *ecological* sustainability, sustainable development is usually defined as encompassing three interdependent components: economic, social and ecological. See Jennifer A Elliott, *An Introduction to Sustainable Development* (Routledge, 2006); Carlos Alberto Ruggerio, 'Sustainability and Sustainable Development: A Review of Principles and Definitions' (2021) 786 *Science of The Total Environment* 147481. However, these terms are used indistinctly in this chapter. On sustainable development in EU law, see András Jakab, 'Sustainability in European Constitutional Law' in Marie-Claire Cordonier Segger, Marcel Szabó and Alexandra R Harrington (eds), *Intergenerational Justice in Sustainable Development Treaty Implementation: Advancing Future Generations Rights through National Institutions* (Cambridge University Press, 2021).

[9] European Commission, 'Sustainable Development Goals', commission.europa.eu/strategy-and-policy/sustainable-development-goals_en; UN Department of Economic and Social Affairs, 'Transforming Our World: The 2030 Agenda for Sustainable Development' (2015) A/RES/70/1, sdgs.un.org/2030agenda.

[10] Michelle E Jarvie, 'Brundtland Report, Publication by World Commission on Environment and Development' *Britannica* (2023), www.britannica.com/topic/Brundtland-Report; United Nations General Assembly, 'Report of the World Commission on Environment and Development: Our Common Future' (1987), www.are.admin.ch/are/en/home/medien-und-publikationen/publikationen/nachhaltige-entwicklung/brundtland-report.html.

[11] ibid para 27.

and the improvement of the quality of the environment' into EU policies, a point reiterated in Article 11 TFEU.

However, the Charter does not explicitly enshrine a right to a healthy environment. This has been object of discussion at EU level, especially in the EU Parliament. On 9 June 2021, the Parliament published a Resolution which addressed and reviewed the EU Biodiversity Strategy for 2030 adopted by the EU Commission.[12] Among the several points that are considered, paragraph 143 of the Resolution recalls that the principle of environmental protection is recognised in the Charter and argues that the right to a healthy environment should also be explicitly enshrined in this document. Moreover, the Parliament claims that the EU should not only promote the right within the borders of the EU but also at the international level.

Within this context and given the focus of the recently adopted Declaration on Digital Rights and Principles on digital sustainability, this chapter examines whether and to what extent this document is shaping or recognising new sustainability rights in the digital environment. Section II analyses the content of Chapter VI of the Declaration, focusing on its legislative history and subsequent amendments. We will argue that Chapter VI has not recognised a new right to a healthy environment in the digital society, but rather enshrines a principle of sustainable digital products and services. The novelty of this principle is then examined in section III, which looks in more detail at EU and Member States law as well as at existing digital bills of rights. The chapter will posit that the uniqueness of Chapter VI lies in making explicit the principle of sustainable products and services through an operation of normative retrofitting that reconstructs a guiding principle of already existing EU and Member State regulatory and policy strategies. Finally, section IV contextualises Chapter VI within the EU digital and environmental policy framework, questioning the feasibility of its ambitions starting from the assumption that even a virtuous digitalisation may negatively affect the environment. We will refer to theories of digital sobriety and degrowth, ultimately arguing that the reconciliation between the twin transitions in the Declaration is unavoidably only partial.

II. New Sustainability Rights?

Although the theme of sustainability was not addressed at the very beginning of the genealogy of the Declaration, it was quickly incorporated during the legislative process. Indeed, sustainability was not included in the set of digital principles and rights as originally envisioned by the European Commission in its first

[12] European Parliament, Resolution of 9 June 2021 on the EU Biodiversity Strategy for 2030: Bringing nature back into our lives 2021, 2020/2273(INI).

Communication on the topic.[13] The European Commission proposed 'digital systems and devices that respect the environment' – what in this chapter we define as 'eco-digital'– as an area of principles to enshrine in the Declaration during the public consultations that preceded the adoption of this document.[14] That concern has been a constant element during the legislative process and in both versions of the Declaration. Indeed, Chapter VI ('Sustainability') was included in the first version of the Declaration. However, some amendments were subsequently made. While comparing these two versions, this section first analyses the content and nature of Chapter VI. Second, it answers whether Chapter VI follows the Parliament's 2021 Resolution on the EU Biodiversity Strategy for 2030 and recognises a right to a healthy environment in the digital context.

For clarity, the chapter will hereinafter refer to the 'initial draft', 'first version' or 'previous version' for the version of the Declaration published in 2022, and to the 'second version', 'final version' or simply the 'Declaration' for the final text of the Declaration published in January 2023.

A. Digital Sustainability in the Declaration

The title of Chapter VI of the Declaration ('Sustainability'), well depicts its substantive content. It is divided into Article 23 and Article 24, and further includes a series of commitments that the EU undertakes in order to protect the accomplishment of the mentioned provisions. The core element of Chapter VI, which is present in both versions of the Declaration, can be identified in the promotion of eco-digital products and services to prevent significant harm from being caused to the environment. The latter is to be achieved by means of circular economy and of increased awareness of the users.

From a more formal point of view, the sequence of articles succeeded by commitments is the *modus operandi* followed by each chapter in the Declaration. Besides commitments, Celeste argued that the Declaration includes three other groups of articles: rights and two types of principles.[15] Rights are recognised by the use of the expression 'everyone has the right to', and principles generally adopt the present or the conditional tense. In this case, Articles 23 and 24 are formulated by using the conditional tense 'should'. Therefore, they are part of the second category of principles, which gives them a softer normative character.[16] From synthetising the content and type of articles present in Chapter VI in the context of the

[13] It was not included in the set of digital principles and rights to be declared in the declaration envisioned by European Commission, *2030 Digital Compass: the European way for the Digital Decade 2021*, COM/2021/118 final.

[14] See European Commission, 'Public Consultation on a Set of European Digital Principles | Shaping Europe's Digital Future' (12 May 2021), digital-strategy.ec.europa.eu/en/consultations/public-consultation-set-european-digital-principles.

[15] Celeste (n 3).

[16] ibid 6.

Declaration, this chapter claims that they merely declare a principle – and not a right – of sustainable digital products and services.

Article 23 aims to prevent harm to the environment, while Article 24 envisions responsible choices at the user level. Therefore, the principle is composed of a substantial element and a procedural element. The final version of Article 23 states that the design, production, use, reparation, recycling and disposal of digital products and services should be done in such a way as to mitigate their negative impact on the environment and on society. In addition, it shall avoid premature obsolescence. Indeed, this article puts an emphasis on the implementation of circular economy methods, where materials and products are reused, either in their original form (eg by repairing the product), or in a new one (eg by transforming them and making other products). It is also to be noted that the level of protection has been lowered throughout the legislative history of the Declaration. While in the first version Article 23 aimed to 'minimise' the environmental and social impact, in the final text it now simply seeks to 'mitigate' it. From a literal interpretation of this article, 'minimisation' implies reducing something to the least possible level. On the contrary, 'mitigation' only requires making it less harmful. Therefore, the guidelines given by the Declaration call for reducing the environmental and social impact of digital products and services, but without it being necessary to limit their impact to the least possible level.

Moreover, the final version of Article 24 establishes the possibility to access accurate and easy-to-understand information about the environmental impact and the energy consumption of digital products and services, their reparability and lifetime. As set out by the Declaration, this would enable people living in the EU to make responsible choices.[17] In comparison with the first version of this provision, the second one is more specific on which type of information shall be accessible. Indeed, the initial draft only referred to information on environmental impact and energy consumption, while the second one included information about reparability, lifetime and premature obsolescence of the product. This evolution reinforces the role of users by adding an additional 'choice period' once the product is already in use. In other words, while information about environmental impact and energy consumption enables a responsible choice when buying the product, information about the reparability and lifetime of the product enables a responsible choice when the product is being used – the so-called after-sales context. In addition, the power to decide whether to repair or update the product or service once it has deteriorated or is out of date lies not only in the hands of the user but also in those of the manufacturer.[18] Indeed, the user can only decide whether to repair it if such a service is available. Thus, the second version also reinforces the role of the

[17] Article 24 uses the expression 'everyone', but the Declaration is consistent in using the expression 'people living in the EU'. Therefore, 'everyone' is here interpreted as limited to people living in the EU, being this comprehensive of EU citizens and non-EU citizens that live in the EU.

[18] 'Manufacturer' is understood in broad terms and may also encompass the producer, importer, seller, or any other person which intervenes in the value chain of the product or service.

corporate sector, since manufacturers may, for instance, offer convenient reparation services themselves, manufacture the product in a way in which pieces can be easily changed, or design robust products that do not become rapidly obsolete and that allow for the incorporation of updates if required.

Finally, in relation to the commitments established in Chapter VI of the Declaration, while the first version included two aspects in which the Commission engages, the second version adds up to four. The first two commitments, only slightly amended in the second version, include the support of the development and use of digital technologies that are sustainable, in the sense that their negative environmental and social impact should be minimal.[19] They also include the promotion of the 'development, deployment and active use' of digital technologies that are innovative, in the sense that their impact on the environment and climate is positive as it stimulates the green transition.[20] Although these commitments already referred to technologies that have a positive effect on the environment, the specific mention to the green transition was only added in the second version. The two undertakings that are incorporated in the second version are the encouragement of consumers and businesses to make sustainable choices, as well as the enhancement of responsible corporate conduct, including not only environment-related behaviours but also with a view to prevent forced labour attitudes, in worldwide value chains.[21] Last, the EU also pledges to promote standards and labels that show the sustainability levels of digital products and services.[22]

The clarification of the first two commitments and the inclusion of two additional ones implies an extension of the scope of Chapter VI in relation to the engagement of EU institutions, and it may allow for more tangible actions. Notably, by explicitly adding the mention to the so-called green transition, the second version makes explicit the link between eco-digital products and services, on the one hand, and the green transition, on the other hand. The link between digital and green is in line with the EU Commission's Strategic Foresight Report 2022.[23] Moreover, both additional commitments put the emphasis on the user and on the corporate sector. The aim of the EU is to drive the latter towards sustainable and responsible choices. Their function is further highlighted by the promotion of standards and labels, which indicate that the corporate sector shall place them on their products and services, and the user shall take them into account when effectuating a purchase.

In sum, on the one hand, despite the use of the word 'mitigate' instead of 'minimise' in relation to the negative impact of digital products and services in the

[19] Chapter VI(a).

[20] Chapter VI(c). For a deeper analysis of the relation between the digital and the green transition in the EU, see section IV of this chapter.

[21] Chapter VI(b).

[22] Chapter VI(d).

[23] European Commission, *2022 Strategic Foresight Report Twinning the green and digital transitions in the new geopolitical context 2022*, COM/2022/289 final. See section IV of this chapter for a deeper analysis of this link.

environment, the scope and characteristics of the principle of sustainable digital products and services are further elaborated in the second and final version of the Declaration. There seems to be an aim to broaden the effects of the Declaration in the second version and to make it more inclusive.[24] Proof of that is, for instance, also the fact that the holders of the rights and principles extend from 'Europeans', to 'people living in the EU'.[25] On the other hand, there is an increased attention to the responsibilities of the user, also in line with the promotion of 'consumer's ability to make autonomous and informed choices' enshrined in Chapter III of the Declaration (Freedom of choice).

B. Towards a Right to a Healthy Environment in the EU?

Putting the above in relation to paragraph 143 of the EU Parliament's Resolution of 9 June 2021,[26] two preliminary remarks can be made. First, the Resolution was published before both the first and the second versions of the Declaration. Therefore, it has not directly influenced the amendments made from one version to the other. Second, the Resolution argues in favour of the recognition of the right to a healthy environment in the EU Charter of Fundamental Rights and Principles, as well as internationally.[27] Thus, the resolution is very specific as to in which particular instrument should the right be enshrined in the EU. The Declaration of Digital Rights and Principles is formally independent from the Charter. However, both proclaim European values, and the Declaration explicitly states that it builds on the rights enshrined in the Charter, and which are thus articulated in the context of the digital environment.[28]

The 'right to a healthy environment' was declared for the first time in the 1972 Stockholm Declaration,[29] on occasion of the first world conference on the environment.[30] Principle 1 of the Stockholm Declaration states that 'Man has the fundamental right to freedom, equality and adequate conditions of life, in an environment of a quality that permits a life of dignity and well-being'.[31] This right has since been progressively endorsed at both the national and the regional level, and is now widely recognised around the world.[32] Different expressions are used to

[24] Celeste (n 3).
[25] eg in the section 'Fair and just working conditions', four commitments are added.
[26] European Parliament Texts adopted – EU Biodiversity Strategy for 2030 (n 12).
[27] Resolution, para 143.
[28] Celeste (n 3) 6.
[29] United Nations, 'United Nations Conference on the Human Environment, Stockholm 1972', www.un.org/en/conferences/environment/stockholm1972.
[30] See Aguila Yann, 'The Right to a Healthy Environment' (29 October 2021), www.iucn.org/news/world-commission-environmental-law/202110/right-a-healthy-environment.
[31] Declaration of the UN Conference on the Human Environment. UN Doc A/Conf.48/14/Rev.1 (1972).
[32] For an empirical analysis of the implementation of the right to a healthy environment, see David R Boyd, 'Catalyst for Change: Evaluating Forty Years of Experience in Implementing the Right

describe the right to a healthy environment, such as 'healthy environment', 'clean', 'safe', 'favourable', 'wholesome' or 'ecologically balanced', alongside many means to protect the right.[33] Nonetheless, the right to a healthy environment is often seen as a safeguard that allows for the effective enjoyment and preservation of other human rights,[34] and that is intrinsically related to the right to life.[35]

As argued above, the Declaration limits itself to establish the principle of sustainable digital products and services. The Declaration does not incorporate a right or a commitment to a healthy environment in the digital context nor a *right* to sustainable digital products and services. Yet, it can be argued that the recognition of a principle promoting the sustainability of digital products and services is, in the digital decade, a necessary condition to preserve a healthy environment. Indeed, because of the rapid development of digital technologies and its weight in today's society, it is necessary to mitigate their negative consequences if the environment is to be protected.

It can also be argued that the principle of sustainable digital products and services is a specific articulation of the right to a healthy environment. According to the Special Rapporteur of the Human Rights Council, the right to a healthy environment implies the recognition of both procedural and substantive rights.[36] The first refers to, for instance, the right to access information or to take part in environmental decision-making processes. An example of the second group of rights is the right to breathe unharmful air.[37] In this case, the aforementioned principle articulates a procedural element of that right: it defines how digital technologies should be used (Article 23 of the Declaration) and which information shall be accessible (Article 24).

Ultimately, however, this may not be the only procedural condition that shall be met in order to guarantee a right to a healthy environment: the digital may jeopardise the environment in other ways that are not prevented through implementing the principle of sustainable digital products and services. For example, even sustainable products and services may promote other less sustainable choices. This phenomenon can be explained through the so-called 'rebound effect', which will be further elaborated in section IV.

to a Healthy Environment' in John H Knox and Ramin Pejan (eds), *The Human Right to a Healthy Environment* (Cambridge University Press, 2018) and Human Rights Council, 'Report of the Special Rapporteur on the Issue of Human Rights Obligations Relating to the Enjoyment of a Safe, Clean, Healthy and Sustainable Environment' (UN, 2018) A/73/188, digitallibrary.un.org/record/1639368.

[33] See Human Rights Council (n 32) and Yann (n 30).

[34] It is seen as such in the Declaration of the UN Conference on the Human Environment. UN Doc A/Conf.48/14/Rev.1 (1972), Ch I, 1; Human Rights Council (n 32) and Yann (n 30). On the relationship between environmental protection and human rights, see Amedeo Postiglione, 'Human Rights and the Environment' (2010) 14 *The International Journal of Human Rights* 524.

[35] David R Boyd, 'The Implicit Constitutional Right to Live in a Healthy Environment' (2011) 20 *Review of European Community & International Environmental Law* 171 considers that because of this relation, the right to a healthy environment is implicitly recognised in constitutions.

[36] See Human Rights Council (n 32).

[37] ibid.

III. Sustainable Digital Products and Services: A New Principle?

The Declaration on digital rights and principles for the digital decade illustrates the political purposes of the EU in the digital context, with a focus on individual rights, and the commitments taken to achieve them.[38] The Declaration asserts that it expands previous EU legislation.[39] In particular, it adapts fundamental rights and European principles applicable in offline situations to the digital context.[40] This is coherent with the claim presented in the previous section, according to which the Declaration does not recognise a right to a healthy environment. Otherwise, the Declaration would be formulating *ex novo* a right in EU law.

However, following this line of arguments, if the Declaration is only translating existent EU values and fundamental rights, the principle of sustainable *analogue* products and services should already be present in an offline context. This section discusses whether this is the case or, in other words, whether the principle of sustainable digital products and services adds something new to the existing law.

A. Sustainable Products and Services in the 'Analogue' World: An Implicit Principle

Although, as established above, sustainable development is a general principle in the EU, the principle of sustainable products and services in an 'analogue', ie non digital, context, is not explicitly recognised in the EU Charter or in the Treaties. From empirical research of CJEU decisions on the topic,[41] the judgments analysed do not explicitly refer to a similar principle, nor is it possible to conclude it is implicit in their decisions. The Court referred to other principles such as the 'waste hierarchy principle'[42] or 'the general environmental protection principles of precaution and sustainability, technical feasibility and economic viability, protection of

[38] Declaration, Preamble 7.

[39] Declaration, Preamble 10. See Celeste (n 3).

[40] Declaration, Preamble 3.

[41] The methodology involved a search using the CJEU search engine (curia.europa.eu) of decisions from January 2019, year of publication of the EU Green Deal, up to September 2023. The criteria selected was 'Environment' as the subject matter, and different searches combining one, some or all the following words: 'sustainable product', 'sustainable products', 'product sustainability', 'ecodesign', 'ecolabel', 'products', 'product', 'sustainability' and 'sustainability of products'.

[42] This principle is enshrined in Art 4 Directive 2008/98/EC of the European Parliament and of the Council of 19 November 2008 on waste and repealing certain Directives [2008] OJ L 312/3, which reads as follows: '1. The following waste hierarchy shall apply as a priority order in waste prevention and management legislation and policy: (a) prevention; (b) preparing for re-use; (c) recycling; (d) other recovery, e.g., energy recovery; and (e) disposal.' See Case C-305/18 *Verdi Ambiente e Società – Aps Onulu and others* [2019].

resources as well as the overall environmental, human health, economic and social impacts',[43] access to information, public participation in decision-making and access to justice in environmental matters.[44]

EU regulations that may recognise the principle of sustainable analogue products and services can be found in the clean and circular economy framework. The European Green Deal represents the EU agenda for sustainable growth.[45] Although not formulating the principle as such, the Green Deal does refer to the potential of promoting sustainable products and services policies for a clean and circular economy.[46] The EU adopted the Circular Economy Action Plan (CEAP) as one of the main blocks of the European Green Deal.[47] The CEAP outlines different initiatives that affect the entire lifecycle of products and aims to ensure that the design of products takes into account circular economy processes, encourages sustainable consumption and prevents waste. Indeed, it aims to make sustainable products the norm in the EU.[48] The CEAP also establishes, for instance, that the EU Ecolabel, which is the EU official voluntary scheme for environmental excellence of products and services, shall be based on the environmental performance of the product.[49] Moreover, the New Consumer Agenda 2020 aims to empower consumers for the green transition by making sure that they have the information to make decisions that are environmentally conscious when buying products, and to protect them from misleading 'greenwashing' practices.[50] Thus, the regulation proposes to amend the Consumer Rights Directive and to create a new right for information on the durability and reparability of products.[51]

Another example is to be found in the recently adopted Sustainable Products Initiative,[52] aiming to make the EU more efficient in terms of resources use and climate-neutrality, within the broader aim of achieving a free of pollution circular economy. In this context, the Ecodesign for Sustainable Products Regulation (ESPR) entered into force.[53] This regulation establishes the requirements for

[43] These principles are enshrined in Art 4(2) Directive 2008/98/EC (ibid). See Case C-305/18 *Verdi Ambiente e Società – Aps Onulu and others* [2019] and Case C-487/17 *Criminal proceedings against Alfonso Verlezza and Others* [2019].

[44] See Case C-432/21 *Commission v Poland (Gestion et bonne pratique forestières)* [2023] and Case T-9/19 *ClientEarth v EIB. External relations – international agreement.*

[45] European Commission, *The European Green Deal*, COM/2019/640 final, Ch 1.

[46] ibid Ch 2, section 2.1.3 ('Mobilising industry for a clean and circular economy').

[47] European Commission, *A new Circular Economy Action Plan For a cleaner and more competitive Europe*, COM/2020/98 final.

[48] ibid Ch 1 ('Introduction').

[49] ibid Ch 2 ('A Sustainable Product Policy Framework').

[50] European Commission, *New Consumer Agenda Strengthening consumer resilience for sustainable recovery*, COM/2020/696 final.

[51] European Commission, 'Circular Economy: Commission Proposes New Consumer Rights', ec.europa.eu/commission/presscorner/detail/en/ip_22_2098.

[52] European Commission, *On making sustainable products the norm*, COM/2022/140 final.

[53] Regulation (EU) 2024/1781 of the European Parliament and of the Council of 13 June 2024 establishing a framework for the setting of ecodesign requirements for sustainable products, amending Directive (EU) 2020/1828 and Regulation (EU) 2023/1542 and repealing Directive 2009/125/EC.

product reparability at the production phase and, particularly, for product design and for the availability of spare pieces. For instance, the requirements refer to product durability and reliability, reusability, upgradability, reparability, maintenance, recyclability, carbon footprint and expected generation of waste.[54] In addition, the EU adopted the Directive on empowering consumers for the green transition (ECGT).[55] This legislation further elaborates on the New Consumer Agenda, and provides the consumer with better information regarding the durability and reparability of goods when buying them. That shall allow for sustainable purchasing decisions.

Last, the EU also adopted a Directive on common rules promoting the repair of goods,[56] which puts the focus in the after-sales context. Likewise, referring to consumers, the Proposal for a Green Claims Directive[57] shall make green claims reliable, comparable and verifiable across the EU, and prevent 'greenwashing'. It is to be noted that, particularly regarding the ESPR, the ECGT and the Directive on the repair of goods, the European Commission has argued that these regulations jointly recognise the so-called 'right to repair'.[58] In addition, there are other, more peripheral, regulations that promote sustainable analogue products and services. For instance, initiatives to promote sustainable textiles,[59] a review of the Construction Products Regulation,[60] or actions to address pollution.[61]

[54] ESPR Art 5.1.

[55] Directive (EU) 2024/825 of the European Parliament and of the Council of 28 February 2024 amending Directives 2005/29/EC and 2011/83/EU as regards empowering consumers for the green transition through better protection against unfair practices and through better information.

[56] Directive (EU) 2024/1799 of the European Parliament and of the Council of 13 June 2024 on common rules promoting the repair of goods and amending Regulation (EU) 2017/2394 and Directives (EU) 2019/771 and (EU) 2020/1828.

[57] *Proposal for a directive of the European Parliament and of the Council on substantiation and communication of explicit environmental claims (Green Claims Directive)*, COM/2023/166 final.

[58] European Commission, 'Rules Promoting the Repair of Goods', commission.europa.eu/law/law-topic/consumer-protection-law/consumer-contract-law/rules-promoting-repair-goods_en.

[59] European Commission, 'Textiles Strategy', environment.ec.europa.eu/publications/textiles-strategy_en.

[60] European Commission, 'Review of the Construction Products Regulation', single-market-economy.ec.europa.eu/sectors/construction/construction-products-regulation-cpr/review_en; Commission Delegated Regulation (EU) 2024/2769 of 30 May 2024 supplementing Regulation (EU) No 305/2011 of the European Parliament and of the Council by laying down the applicable systems to assess and verify constancy of performance of construction products in relation to the essential characteristics on environmental sustainability and amending that Regulation as regards the assessment and verification of constancy of performance of construction products based on a modelling approach.

[61] For example, see European Commission, 'Proposal Revision Industrial Emissions Directive', environment.ec.europa.eu/publications/proposal-revision-industrial-emissions-directive_en; Directive (EU) 2024/1785 of the European Parliament and of the Council of 24 April 2024 amending Directive 2010/75/EU of the European Parliament and of the Council on industrial emissions (integrated pollution prevention and control) and Council Directive 1999/31/EC on the landfill of waste. See also European Commission, 'Microplastics Pollution – Measures to Reduce Its Impact on the Environment' (*Have your say*, 18 January 2022), ec.europa.eu/info/law/better-regulation/have-your-say/initiatives/12823-Microplastics-pollution-measures-to-reduce-its-impact-on-the-environment_en.

B. From Analogue to Digital: The Constitutionalising Role of the Declaration

There is therefore an implicit principle of sustainable products and services at EU level. The EU Declaration of Digital Rights and Principles does not declare a new principle from scratch, but it makes a principle that guides EU and Member States policy explicit. The main benefit of that is clarity and transparency as regards to the European strategy and its guiding values. Indeed, a document such as the Declaration has the advantages of being accessible to its addressees because of its short length and conciseness. Moreover, specific actions included in the form of commitments, which may be seen as particular examples of how the principle is to be complied with. The Declaration thus has the capability to turn into a standard for individuals, businesses and Member States. This is in line with the trend noted by Papakonstantinou and Hert, which explains that EU law is making an effort to get closer to the general public within the digital context.[62]

In this sense, the novelty of Chapter VI of the Declaration in EU law lies in making explicit a guiding principle of EU policies in the field of green transition: what we could define a process of normative 'retrofitting'.[63] The Declaration plays a constitutionalising role in the digital realm and thus contributes to the normative movement that has been called digital constitutionalism.[64] It connects the dots between the general principles and values enshrined in EU primary law, and in particular the Charter of Fundamental Rights, and the concrete provisions of the EU regulatory framework and the Commission's policy strategies in the digital field. The Declaration interprets the former to provide a more explicit rationale to the latter in the digital environment.

IV. Questioning the Ambitions of the Declaration: Is it Possible to 'Green' the Digital?

The inclusion of Chapter VI on sustainability in the Declaration is very much in line with current EU policy strategies. In particular, with the emphasis put by the EU institutions on the interaction between the green and the digital transitions,

[62] Papakonstantinou refers to the phenomenon of 'Act-ification', defined as the trend in EU law to publish eponymous regulations in the digital context. As opposed to anonymous regulations, which are numbered, eponymous regulations contain a name in their title. This is the case of 'Acts' published by the EU. See Vagelis Papakonstantinou and Paul de Hert, 'The Regulation of Digital Technologies in the EU: The Law-Making Phenomena of "Act-ification", "GDPR Mimesis" and "EU Law Brutality"' (2022) 2022 *Technology and Regulation* 48.

[63] See Celeste (n 3).

[64] See Edoardo Celeste, 'Digital Constitutionalism: A New Systematic Theorisation' (2019) 33 *International Review of Law, Computers & Technology* 76.

the so-called 'twin transitions'.[65] Notably, the President of the EU Commission claimed that the twin transition was a key priority in the EU in 2020,[66] and it is still considered as such in more recent EU policy strategies.[67] Given the urgency of the climate crisis, the Strategic Foresight Report 2022 argues in favour of digital technologies as the key actor to accomplish the EU goal of climate neutrality, reduce pollution and restore biodiversity.[68] However, the correlation between these two transitions is not clear, and the Strategic Foresight Report also identifies some tensions along the potential synergies.

In light of this, the coherence of the principle of sustainable digital products and services shall be questioned: is it possible for digital products and services to be sustainable? Or is the expression 'eco-digital product or service' an oxymoron? This section discusses whether Chapter VI of the Declaration may effectively reconcile the digital and environmental ambitions of the EU. To do that, it describes the respective aims of the digital transition and of the green transition, as well as its correlation. Then, it positions Chapter VI of the EU Declaration within this framework.

A. The Twin Transitions and the Declaration

The digital transition in the EU puts the focus on businesses and individuals. Indeed, a prosperous digital future is envisioned as human-centred and sustainable.[69] In the 2030 Digital Compass communication,[70] the Commission pointed out the digitalisation degree as a key factor in the economy or society's resilience as well as global influence. Moreover, it identified four cardinal points in the EU's digital transformation: digital skills, digital infrastructures, the digitalisation of business, and the digitalisation of public services. Remarkably, the 2030 Digital Compass proposed to adopt an inter-institutional solemn declaration incorporating digital principles and rights to protect and empower citizens, and it also suggested the approval of a policy programme including an appropriate governance framework in order to implement different strategies in critical areas

[65] See Edoardo Celeste and Goran Dominioni, 'Digital and Green: Reconciling the EU Twin Transitions in Times of War and Energy Crisis' in Federico Fabbrini and Christy A Petit, *Research Handbook on Post-Pandemic Economic Governance & NGEU Law* (Edward Elgar, 2024).

[66] European Commission, 'State of the Union 2020. The EC President's Address', state-of-the-union.ec.europa.eu/state-union-2020_en.

[67] Several programmes within the Horizon Europe – Work Programme 2023–2024 allocate a big amount of funds to the 'Twin Green and Digital Transition'. European Commission, 'Horizon Europe Work Programme for 2023–24 Now Available', cinea.ec.europa.eu/news-events/news/horizon-europe-work-programme-2023-24-now-available-2022-12-07_en.

[68] European Commission (n 23).

[69] European Commission, 'Europe's Digital Decade: Digital Targets for 2030', commission.europa.eu/strategy-and-policy/priorities-2019-2024/europe-fit-digital-age/europes-digital-decade-digital-targets-2030_en.

[70] European Commission, *Digital Compass: the European way for the Digital Decade 2021*, COM(2021) 118 final/2.

of the digital transformation. The former led to the adoption of the Declaration, while the latter has been accomplished with the publication of the Digital Decade Policy Programme 2030.[71]

The EU green transition is mainly driven by the European Green Deal and it aims to achieve an economy which is modern, resource efficient and competitive. Economic growth shall be decoupled from the use of resources, and greenhouse carbon emissions shall be zero by 2050.[72] In addition, such a transition shall be 'just and inclusive'.[73] The Green Deal responds to climate and environmental-related challenges by setting climate targets and, in a similar fashion to the 2030 Digital Compass, it presents a roadmap to implement further key policies and measures. Among other objectives, the European Green Deal sets out climate neutrality by 2050. This commitment has become legally binding through the adoption of the so-called European Climate Law,[74] which includes an intermediate objective: reducing greenhouse gas emissions by at least 55 per cent by 2030.[75]

Digital technologies are identified as key enablers to attain the sustainability goals of the European Green Deal, both in the green and the digital transition policy frameworks. Indeed, the Digital Decade Policy Programme 2030 states that 'digital technologies and new methods and processes are critical enablers for attaining the sustainability goals of the European Green Deal, the Paris Agreement …, and the United Nations' Sustainable Development Goals'.[76] Similarly, the European Climate Law reads as follows: 'Digital transformation, technological innovation, and research and development are also important drivers for achieving the climate-neutrality objective.'[77]

By the same token, while the EU Declaration of Digital Rights and Principles is altogether part of the EU digital transition policy framework, Chapter VI of the Declaration represents in particular the incorporation of the green transition onto it. In other words, it offers a straightforward example of what the EU means by intertwining these two transitions. In this sense, the principle of sustainable digital products and services unfolds as follows: it promotes digital products and services (digital transition), which at the same time shall be sustainable (green transition). However, for this policy to be effective in reconciling the twin transition, it shall be effective in achieving both the aims of the digital and the aims of the green transition. As will be argued below, this remains a challenge.

[71] Decision (EU) 2022/2481 of the European Parliament and of the Council of 14 December 2022 establishing the Digital Decade Policy Programme 2030.

[72] ibid.

[73] European Commission, 'A European Green Deal' (14 July 2021), commission.europa.eu/strategy-and-policy/priorities-2019-2024/european-green-deal_en.

[74] Regulation (EU) 2021/1119 of the European Parliament and of the Council of 30 June 2021 establishing the framework for achieving climate neutrality and amending Regulations (EC) No 401/2009 and (EU) 2018/1999 ('European Climate Law') [2021] OJ L 243/1.

[75] Compared to 1990 levels.

[76] Decision (EU) 2022/2481 (n 71) Preamble, para 6.

[77] Regulation (EU) 2021/1119 (n 74) Preamble, para 11.

B. Rebound Effect, Digital Sobriety and Degrowth

The principle of sustainable digital products and principles responds to the aims of the digital transformation. Indeed, by promoting digital products and services, it fosters a higher degree of digitalisation of the economy and of society. Nonetheless, even if at a first glance the principle seems to be in line with the green transition – as it will bring about a more sustainable economy – the promotion of sustainable products and services may have adverse effects on the environment by increasing greenhouse gas carbon emissions.

Nowadays there is a consensus on the fact that the information and communications technology (ICT sector) has a remarkable carbon footprint, and thus a tangible impact on the environment.[78] Moreover, although the literature claims that measuring this impact is not an easy task since integrated data is difficult to find, three elements may be considered: energy or electricity consumption,; greenhouse gas emissions; and raw materials consumption.[79] Particularly regarding energy consumption and greenhouse emissions, it is claimed that there is no consensus on the effects of ICT. Some studies show that ICT developments result in a reduction of the sector's energy consumption and/or of emissions, others that it results in an increase, and yet others that the correlation is nonlinear.[80] This does not deny the high carbon footprint of the ICT sector. However, it shows a disagreement in how efficiency improvements in the digital may influence it. Whatever the answer to that question is, it is certain that the concerns regarding the digital carbon footprint are increasing.[81]

A recent report from the French think-tank The Shift Project (TSP) considers it illusory to assume that the digital transformation is going to have a primarily positive effect on the energy consumption of services, businesses or nations, or that it is going to have a neutral energy balance.[82] According to TSP, the positive impact of the digital in global emissions is overestimated mainly because it does not consider the so-called 'rebound effect'.[83] Sorrel characterises the rebound effect as 'an umbrella term for a variety of economic mechanisms that reduce the

[78] See Stefano Bianchini, Giacomo Damioli and Claudia Ghisetti, 'The Environmental Effects of the "Twin" Green and Digital Transition in European Regions' (2023) 84 *Environmental & resource economics* 877; Charlotte Freitag et al, 'The Real Climate and Transformative Impact of ICT: A Critique of Estimates, Trends, and Regulations' (2021) 2 *Patterns*, www.cell.com/patterns/abstract/S2666-3899(21)00188-4; and The Shift Project, 'Lean ICT: Towards Digital Sobriety' (2019) 429 *Futuribles*, theshiftproject.org/en/article/lean-ict-our-new-report.

[79] The Shift Project (ibid).

[80] Zhouyi Zhang et al, 'Effects of Heterogeneous ICT on Critical Metal Supply: A Differentiated Perspective on Primary and Secondary Supply' (2023) 83 *Resources Policy* 103690; Huanyu Cui et al, 'Multiple Effects of ICT Investment on Carbon Emissions: Evidence from China' (2023) 30 *Environmental Science and Pollution Research* 4399.

[81] Céline Péréa, Jessica Gérard and Julien De Benedittis, 'Digital Sobriety: From Awareness of the Negative Impacts of IT Usages to Degrowth Technology at Work' (2023) 194 *Technological Forecasting and Social Change* 122670.

[82] The Shift Project (n 78).

[83] See Celeste and Perez Victorio in this volume.

"energy savings" from improved energy efficiency'.[84] In the digital context, this effect demonstrates that even if technology becomes more energy efficient (ie, in theory more sustainable), the energy consumption and thus carbon emissions will still increase since efficiency boosts consumption (ie, making it in practice less sustainable).[85] The TSP report offers a good example of this phenomenon by looking at the frequency with which smartphones are charged. Indeed, even if the average power of smartphone batteries has doubled during the last few years thanks to efficiency developments, the charging frequency of smartphones remains more or less constant.[86]

In light of this trend, TSP argues in favour of 'digital sobriety' to move towards a scenario where digital technologies are wisely managed by taking into account opportunities and challenges.[87] Along the same lines, it is worth mentioning the discussions in the area of technological 'degrowth'. Degrowth is a multifaceted concept, and many argue that it is controversial to give it one single definition.[88] Fournier defines it as a phenomenon that puts together a 'variety of forums' that serves to disseminate ideas and engage in constructive discussions.[89] Most of the degrowth community considers that conventional economic growth – here understood as GDP growth – and sustainability are incompatible.[90] Following this line, the community shows different degrees of enthusiasm and scepticism towards technology.[91]

Returning to Article 23 of the Declaration, we can argue that even if digital products and services are sustainable, their increase may result in greater carbon emissions, mainly due to the rebound effect. Ultimately, and in more general terms, a higher degree of digitalisation may not contribute to a higher degree

[84] Steve Sorrell, 'Energy Substitution, Technical Change and Rebound Effects' (2014) 7 *Energies* 2850, 2850. See also Steffen Lange et al, 'The Jevons Paradox Unravelled: A Multi-Level Typology of Rebound Effects and Mechanisms' (2021) 74 *Energy Research & Social Science* 101982.

[85] For an insight on the rebound effect of digital technologies, see Vlad C Coroama and Friedemann Mattern, 'Digital Rebound – Why Digitalization Will Not Redeem Us Our Environmental Sins', Proceedings of the 6th International Conference on ICT for Sustainability (ICT4S 2019) (RWTH, 2019), www.research-collection.ethz.ch/handle/20.500.11850/387584?show=full; and Ray Galvin, 'The ICT/Electronics Question: Structural Change and the Rebound Effect' (2015) 120 *Ecological Economics* 23.

[86] The Shift Project (n 78) 20.

[87] On digital sobriety, see Péréa, Gérard and De Benedittis (n 81) 4. This phenomenon raises challenges related to the voluntary abandonment or moderate use of IT.

[88] Mario Pansera, Melf-Hinrich Ehlers and Christian Kerschner, 'Unlocking Wise Digital Techno-Futures: Contributions from the Degrowth Community' (2019) 114 *Futures* 102474; Christian Kerschner et al, 'Degrowth and Technology: Towards Feasible, Viable, Appropriate and Convivial Imaginaries' (2018) 197 *Journal of Cleaner Production* 1619; Giacomo D'Alisa, Federico Demaria and Giorgos Kallis (eds), *Degrowth: A Vocabulary for a New Era* (Routledge, 2014).

[89] Valérie Fournier, 'Escaping from the Economy: The Politics of Degrowth' (2008) 28 *International Journal of Sociology and Social Policy* 528, 532.

[90] See Jan Pollex and Andrea Lenschow, 'Surrendering to Growth? The European Union's Goals for Research and Technology in the Horizon 2020 Framework' (2018) 197 *Journal of Cleaner Production* 1863. For a critical position, Hubert Buch-Hansen and Iana Nesterova, 'Less and More: Conceptualising Degrowth Transformations' (2023) 205 *Ecological Economics* 107731.

[91] Pansera, Ehlers and Kerschner (n 88).

of sustainability. Considering too the procedural element of Article 24 of the Declaration, a similar conclusion regarding the effectiveness of the measure in relation to the twin transition is reached. At first sight, Article 24 seems to be coherent with both the digital and the green transitions, since it promotes access to environment-related information about digital products and services by consumers and business. However, just because this information can be accessed does not mean it will be used to make more environmentally friendly decisions. For example, a consumer may be able to access environmental information about product A and product B, and still decide not to access it. Or, even if such information is accessed, it may not be used: the consumer may still buy the product with a higher environmental impact for other reasons, such as price, brand, or other advantages. Thus, even if it is true that the EU commits to incentivise better choices and models,[92] the Declaration ultimately passes the ball to consumers and businesses, on whom its success depends.

The reconciliation between the ambitions of the green and the digital transitions in Chapter VI of the EU Declaration of Digital Rights and Principles is therefore partial. Firstly, because eco-digital products and services may not be adequate to achieve the environmental goals of the policies adopted within the green transition framework. Secondly, because the choices effectuated by consumers may not be aligned with those goals due to other competing factors.

V. Conclusion

Even if the Declaration proposes itself as a quasi-constitutional instrument articulating digital rights and principles for the EU, it does not recognise a right to a healthy environment in the digital context. Nonetheless, since it enshrines the principle of digital sustainable products and services, Chapter VI articulates a procedural element of that right. Although the principle was already implicitly recognised in EU law, the Declaration represents one step forward in the formulation of EU policies. Making the principle explicit not only entails shaping a more apparent strategy and increasing the level of simplicity and clarity, which is relevant to the law-making process and to the further development of EU and national policies in the digital environment. But this also allows individuals and businesses, some of whom are addressed in the Declaration, to have a better understanding of European values. Indeed, because of the fast pace at which digital technologies advance and the need to guide their adoption and use, the digital field is a dynamic environment that witnesses the continuous emergence of new issues and questions the challenge the interpretation of existing fundamental rights.

Ultimately, the Declaration encourages further measures to help the principle of sustainable digital products and principles materialise. Following its focus

[92] Declaration, Ch VI(b).

on individuals, more sustainable choices in the digital environment are incentivised. However, nothing guarantees that they will be taken, as consumers may take into account other factors, such as the impact of the brand or the design. Given the relevance of the green transition, the implementation of, for example, sustainable labels that guide consumer choices, is a rather timid measure. Instead, the implementation of mandatory schemes such as environmental requirements in order to put a product or service in the market may be more effective measures.

Chapter VI of the Declaration is unique as it provides a normative guidance between green and digital policies. It represents an effort to intertwin these two transitions. However, the effectiveness of the principle of sustainable digital products and services may be jeopardised by the energy consumption intensity of digital devices and infrastructures, and more generally by its rebound effect on the environment. This is part of a broader question, which challenges the feasibility of a really 'eco-digital' field, as well as of the discussion promoted by the degrowth community, which objects to the current economic model because of its lack of long-term sustainability. Research in this area presents out-of-the-box thoughts and, although there are many and varied perspectives, its findings may be of interest to both those working in the digital and in the green domains.

13

Digital Sovereignty and ESG Policies: The Role of the EU Banking System

FRANCESCO DIMICHINA*

I. Introduction

This chapter analyses the challenges posed by the European banking system's digital and green transitions while maintaining a global perspective. Indeed, globalisation has increased the size of the capital markets. In the last decade, the size of all banks' cross-border position[1] has also increased. At the same time, the frequency of banking and currency crises grew. These shocks, including the Great Recession, made the enforcement of the international financial architecture all the more urgent. Effectively, it seems that coordination of financial rules and standards has become inevitable in trying to reduce the risk of financial instability at a global level.[2] So, even if the Ukrainian war and the COVID-19 pandemic seem to have undermined the globalisation process, it is not over yet. In this scenario we therefore need to explore what risks and benefits are involved with these transitions for the European banking system.

Section II analyses European integration in a global context. Some recent national judicial decisions have highlighted that the European Union (EU) has demonstrated an excessive tendency to differentiation. However, it seems that, firstly with the Banking Union (BU) and secondly with Next Generation EU (NGEU),[3] the EU is strengthening its integration in spite of the current globalisation slowdown ('slowbalisation').

* The views expressed in the article are those of the author and not the Bank of Italy.

[1] 'Cross-border position' means a 'Position on a non-resident – for example, claim on or liability to a counterparty located in a country other than the country where the banking office that books the position is located', www.bis.org/statistics/glossary.htm?selection=331.

[2] Daniel W Drezner, *All Politics Is Global. Explaining international regulatory regimes* (Princeton University Press, 2007) 119–20.

[3] According to the EU, 'NextGenerationEU is more than a recovery plan – it is a once in a lifetime chance to emerge stronger from the pandemic, transform our economies and societies, and design a Europe that works for everyone. We have everything we need to make this happen. We have a vision, we have a plan and we have agreed to invest €806.9 billion together. Find out how the EU is making Europe

Section III, which looks at the digital transition in the banking system, highlights the necessity to preserve 'digital sovereignty' in the EU, especially because European data are mostly processed and stored by foreign companies.[4] As this risk also concerns the banking system, in November 2022 the European Central Bank (ECB) joined the European Data and Cloud Network Initiative (Gaia-X), a European data infrastructure project, in order to regain its 'digital sovereignty'.

Section IV emphasises risks connected with the green transition of the banking system. Indeed, environment, social and governance (ESG) policies have are increasingly relevant in the exercise of banking activity. In December 2022, the European Banking Authority (EBA) published its roadmap on sustainable finance to highlight some of these challenges.

Section V discusses how to balance preserving the environment with ensuring inclusive growth and equal opportunities, particularly in relation to the use of digital technology. To reconcile both the digital and green ambitions in the EU financial system, we examine the use of artificial intelligence (AI).

Section VI concludes by acknowledging that regulating the green and digital transition will be challenging for European lawmakers: in a global context cooperation is crucial to assure that new domestic rules can be adhered to globally. Subsequently, we refocus the distinction established by Hayek, based on ancient Greek conceptualistions, between *taxis* and *cosmos*, which is applied to the regulation of the digital (*taxis*) and green (*cosmos*) transition.

II. Slowbalisation and European Integration Through the Green and Digital Transition

In the so-called 'global age',[5] people across the world have different experiences of territorialisation. In this context, the EU had to deal with Member States's willingness to reaffirm their own specificities and identities.[6] However, concurrently with that centrifugal force, there is also a centripetal motion highlighted by the strengthening of European integration, especially in the banking system within the BU.[7]

healthier, greener, and more digital, and how you can be part of the change', next-generation-eu.europa.eu/index_en.

[4] Edoardo Celeste, 'Digital Sovereignty in the EU: Challenges and Future Perspectives' in F Fabbrini, E Celeste and J Quinn (eds), *Data Protection beyond Borders: Transatlantic Perspectives on Extraterritoriality and Sovereignty* (Hart, 2021) 211 ff.

[5] Martin Albrow, *The global age: state and society beyond modernity* (Stanford University Press, 1997) 184.

[6] Doreen Lustig and JHH Weiler, 'Judicial review in the contemporary world – Retrospective and prospective' (2018) 16 *International Journal of Constitutional Law* 357. Among others, see BVerfG, Judgment of the Second Senate of 5 May 2020 – 2 BvR 859/15, on the ECB's public sector purchase programme.

[7] As observed, 'the Banking Union is one of the outcomes of the gradual transformation of the EU from a community of benefits to a community of risksharing, where all Member States not only

Today, there is a new global phase characterised by increasing territorialisation. Some scholars have questioned whether the global economy is now driven towards de-globalisation.[8] Indeed, according to Paul Antràs, similar phases have been experienced in the past, for example after the flu pandemic of 1918, the First World War and the Great Depression of 1929. However, since the Great Recession of 2008–2009, one can identify again a general trend towards globalisation.[9] The Recession reignited nationalistic sentiments, as we have witnessed with the war in Ukraine, across the whole European continent. Epiphenomena of this are Brexit and the recent commercial war between the US and China. In recent times, the COVID-19 pandemic has affected global value chains. However, there is no empirical evidence that the global economy has become less global since the turn of the millennium. While there has been a decrease in the importance of capital flow and of transnational economic activities, their levels are closer to those of the early 2010s.[10]

It seems, then, that slowbalisation is only the *pendant* of a phase of hyper-globalisation between the mid-1980s and the first decade of the new millennium, which according to Antràs was practically unsustainable.[11] Once again, this is confirmation of the continuing dialectic of territorialisation and de-territorialisation.[12] However, according to Darvas, the GDP level shows that the EU resisted trade deglobalisation.[13] On the other hand, it seems that – firstly with the BU and secondly with NGEU – the EU is strengthening its integration[14] despite the phenomenon of slowbalisation.

As Cassese observed,

> Global problems require global institutions. To organize Olympic Games and control doping; to fight global terrorism; to control epidemics, world trade, international

share the benefits from integration but also start sharing the risks and potential costs', Pedro Gustavo Teixeira, 'The Legal History of the Banking Union', (2017) 18 *European Business Organization Law Review* 535, 562.

[8] Akvile Bertasiute, Domenico Massaro and Matthias Weber, 'Deglobalisation post COVID-19 could spell trouble for the European Monetary Union' *LSE Business Review* (1 July 2020).

[9] Paul Antràs, 'De-Globalisation? Global Value Chains in the Post-COVID-19 Age' 2021 ECB Forum, 'Central Banks in a Shifting World' Conference Proceedings (2021), scholar.harvard.edu/antras/publications/de-globalisation-global-value-chains-post-covid-19-age; Zsolt Darvas, 'Resisting deglobalisation: the case of Europe' (2020) 1 Working Paper, Bruegel, www.bruegel.org/working-paper/resisting-deglobalisation-case-europe.

[10] Antràs (n 9) 3; Darvas (n 9) 2–3.

[11] Antràs (n 9) 43.

[12] Jürgen Osterhammel and Niels P Petersson, *Globalization. A short history* (Princeton University Press, 2005) 7.

[13] Darvas (n 9) 4; according to Darvas (9): 'hard evidence on deglobalisation, global trade and finance data does indicate that the rapid pre-2008 pace of globalisation has at least stalled or has even gone into reverse. But Europe defies this trend, with both trade and financial claims, especially within the EU, continuing to grow after the recovery from the global economic and financial crisis. Immigration has also continued to grow since the crisis-induced declines.'

[14] According to Federico Fabbrini, 'The Legal Architecture of the Economic Responses to COVID-19: EMU beyond the Pandemic' (2022) 60 *Journal of Common Market Studies* 1, 'NGEU constitutes a turning point in the process of European integration which profoundly changes the constitutional outlook of EMU.'

> finance, the Internet; to protect highly migratory species; or to reduce global warming, one cannot proceed at the national level-one must go global.[15]

There is no doubt that the BU was built to face the European crisis. Indeed, it has been defined as 'the most transformative institutional response to the crisis experienced by the euro area'.[16] In particular, the BU appears as an institutional laboratory built to face the systemic weakness of the euro and to restore trust in banks as well as in the euro. As is known, the BU was built to overcome the close connection between bank and national states that undermine the European financial market.[17]

As has been previously discussed, if the BU was founded in response to the last European financial crisis, the economic emergency following the pandemic is delivering a closer institutional integration by propelling the transition from an external governance to an European industrial policy, whose pillars have become the Temporary framework of state aid and then the Recovery Plan.[18] In fact, NGEU makes it possible for the EU Commission to direct resources for investment in transnational policy priorities, first and foremost in the green and digital transition.[19] Indeed, a series of indicators show that global warming is incumbent and for the sake of the present and future generations can no longer be ignored. At the same time, digitalisation increasingly permeates our way of life.[20] However, through NGEU, the gaps in European fiscal policy were filled.[21]

On the other hand, it was highlighted that Regulation (EU) 2021/241 of the European Parliament and of the Council dated 12 February 2021 establishing the Recovery and Resilience Facility, consolidates the regime of an 'overturned conditionality',[22] because the Union's financial assistance is not related to 'difficulties caused by natural disasters or exceptional occurrences beyond its control',[23]

[15] Sabino Cassese, 'Global administrative law: where do we stand?' in Philippe Cossalter and Gilles J Guglielmi (eds), *L'internationalisation du droit administratif* ([Éditions Panthéon-Assas], 2020) 54.

[16] Guntram Wolff, 'Foreword' in Nicolas Veron, *Europe's radical banking union* (Bruegel, 2015) 5, www.bruegel.org/comment/europes-radical-banking-union.

[17] Marco Macchia, 'Procedural Decision-Making and the Banking Union: The Accountability Mechanisms' (2017) TARN Working paper, 1(4), papers.ssrn.com/sol3/papers.cfm?abstract_id=2948873; Marco Macchia, *Integrazione amministrativa e Unione bancaria* (Giappichelli, 2019) 3–4.

[18] Michela Passalacqua, 'Numquam nega, raro adfirma: *il rinnovato intervento dello Stato nell'economia*' (2021) XXIII *Mercato concorrenza regole* 55, 62.

[19] Danny Busch, Guido Ferrarini, and Seraina Grünewald, 'Sustainable Finance in Europe: Setting the Scene' in Danny Busch, Guido Ferrarini and Seraina Grünewald (eds), *Sustainable Finance in Europe. Corporate Governance, Financial Stability and Financial Markets* (Palgrave Macmillan, 2021) 6.

[20] Klaudia Majcher and Victoria Robertson, 'The Twin Transition to a Green and Digital Economy: The Role for EU Competition Law' (2022) Graz Law Working Paper, 5, 1.

[21] Passalacqua (n 19); see also Federico Fabbrini, *EU Fiscal Capacity. Legal Integration After Covid-19 and the War in Ukraine* (Oxford University Press, 2022).

[22] Michela Passalacqua, *Green deal e transizione digitale verso un diritto eventuale* in Michela Passalacqua (ed), *Diritti e mercati nella transizione ecologica e digitale. Studi dedicati a Mauro Giusti* (Wolters Kluwer, 2022) 6.

[23] Article 122(2) TFEU; see also Art 136(3).

but that 'the Facility shall be to promote' a series of goals[24] in order to support the green and digital transition.

Regarding this, if the BU constitutes a milestone of the European construction,[25] no less important than the euro currency and the balanced-budget constraint, the adoption of an NGEU constitutes another fundamental step in addressing the EU architecture of economic governance and building an arrangement similar to that of federal regimes.[26]

III. Fintech-related Risks for the European Banking System and the Need to Preserve Digital Sovereignty

As previously discussed, NGEU allows the EU Commission to raise resources to invest in transnational policy priorities, first of all the green and digital transition.[27] The concept of FinTech ('financial technology') is crucial in this regard.[28] The Financial Stability Board defines FinTech as 'technologically enabled innovation in financial services that could result in new business models, applications, processes or products with an associated material effect on financial markets and institutions

[24] Article 4(1): 'In line with the six pillars referred in Article 3 of this Regulation, the coherence and synergies they generate, and in the context of the COVID-19 crisis, the general objective of the Facility shall be to promote the Union's economic, social and territorial cohesion by improving the resilience, crisis preparedness, adjustment capacity and growth potential of the Member States, by mitigating the social and economic impact of that crisis, in particular on women, by contributing to the implementation of the European Pillar of Social Rights, by supporting the green transition, by contributing to the achievement of the Union's 2030 climate targets set out in point (11) of Article 2 of Regulation (EU) 2018/1999 and by complying with the objective of EU climate neutrality by 2050 and of the digital transition, thereby contributing to the upward economic and social convergence, restoring and promoting sustainable growth and the integration of the economies of the Union, fostering high quality employment creation, and contributing to the strategic autonomy of the Union alongside an open economy and generating European added value.'

[25] Mario P Chiti and Vittorio Santoro, 'Preface' in Mario P Chiti and Vittorio Santoro (eds), *The Palgrave Handbook of European Banking Union Law* (Palgrave, 2019).

[26] Fabbrini (n 14) 187.

[27] In this sense, we need to remember at least, on the global side, the 2030 Agenda for Sustainable Development, a Resolution adopted by the General Assembly of the UN on 25 September 2015. Then, the Paris Agreement adopted on 12 December 2015 by 196 parties at the UN Climate Change Conference (COP21), that is entitled to hold 'the increase in the global average temperature to well below 2°C above pre-industrial levels' and pursue efforts 'to limit the temperature increase to 1.5°C above pre-industrial levels'. Then, on the European side, we must consider at least European Commission, *Action Plan: Financing Sustainable Growth*, COM/2018/097 final and European Commission, *'Fit for 55': delivering the EU's 2030 Climate Target on the way to climate neutrality*, COM/2021/550 final.

[28] Cambridge dictionary (Cambridge University Press & Assessment 2023), dictionary.cambridge.org. According to the European Commission, 'As digital finance cuts across borders, it also has the potential to enhance financial market integration in the Banking Union and the Capital Markets Union and thereby to strengthen Europe's Economic and Monetary Union' (European Commission, Digital Finance Strategy for the EU, *Communication from the Commission to the European Parliament, the Council, the European Economic and Social Committee and the Committee of the Regions*, COM(2012) 673 final, para 3).

and the provision of financial services.'[29] For example, FinTech is related to crowd-funding and peer-to-peer lending platforms; cryptocurrencies; robo-advisors; smart contracts; the use of blockchain technology for financial purposes; and the use of automatic teller machines.[30] However, the FinTech sector also affects the adequacy of the organisational structure of banks because the digitalisation of the banking system leads to more efficient processes, and simpler commercial relationships and customer profiling, enabling a more measured range of products.[31]

The definition above has been adopted by the EBA, following its 'Discussion Paper on the EBA's approach to financial technology (FinTech)'[32] and its 'Fintech roadmap',[33] in which the EBA highlighted that the pace of FinTech innovation presents a challenge for regulators and supervisors to preserve consumer protection, a level playing field, the integrity of the financial markets and the stability of the financial system.

In 2021, the EU Commission published its call for advice on digital finance and related issues,[34] requesting the European Supervisory Authorities (ESAs) – ie the EBA, the European Occupational Pensions and Insurance Authority (EIOPA), and the European Securities and Markets Authority (ESMA) – to carry out an analysis of the fragmentation of the financial services value chain, the growth of digital platforms and mixed activity groups, and to set out their recommendations in order to ensure that the EU's financial services regulatory and supervisory framework remains fit for purpose.

In response to the EU Commission's request, the ESAs published a report[35] which sets out 10 recommendations[36] with reference to risks and opportunities posed by digitalisation in finance. This advice is related, inter alia, to the need to prevent financial exclusion and to further promote a higher level of digital and financial literacy in order to help consumers make effective use of financial services provided via digital means; to the necessity for the Commission to provide further guidance on the definition of cross-border services in a digital context, due to the

[29] FSB, FinTech, available at www.fsb.org/work-of-the-fsb/financial-innovation-and-structural-change/fintech.

[30] Thomas Lerner, *Mobile Payment* (Springer, 2013) 3.

[31] Rosa Calderazzi, 'Gli effetti della digitalizzazione sugli assetti organizzativi delle banche' in Passalacqua (n 19) 400–03.

[32] EBA, 'Discussion Paper on the EBA's approach to financial technology (FinTech)' (2017), www.eba.europa.eu/sites/default/files/documents/10180/1919160/7a1b9cda-10ad-4315-91ce-d798230ebd84/EBA%20Discussion%20Paper%20on%20Fintech%20%28EBA-DP-2017-02%29.pdf.

[33] EBA, 'The EBA's fintech roadmap. Conclusions from the consultation on the EBA's approach to financial technology (fintech)' (2018), www.eba.europa.eu/sites/default/files/documents/10180/1919160/79d2cbc6-ce28-482a-9291-34cfba8e0c02/EBA%20FinTech%20Roadmap.pdf.

[34] European Commission, 'Request to EBA, EIOPA and ESMA for technical advice on digital finance and related issues' Ref. Ares (2021)898555 (2 February 2021).

[35] ESAs, 'Joint European Supervisory Authority response to the European Commission's February 2021 Call for Advice on digital finance and related issues: regulation and supervision of more fragmented or non-integrated value chains, platforms and bundling of various financial services, and risks of groups combining different activities' (ESA 2022 01) (31 January 2022).

[36] Plus, two which are only related to the insurance market.

fact that digital financial services are essentially borderless; to the need to consider possible ways to strengthen skills and resources available to relevant authorities in order to meet the fast pace of change and complexity observed in digital financial markets; and, finally, to the growing use of social media in relation to financial services and the need to actively monitor it.[37]

These recommendations show that FinTech is a valid and viable resource for banks to improve their capacity to make profits. However, FinTech may also conceal a series of risks for the financial system as a whole. In the above-mentioned risks landscape, there is also a serious risk that the EU would lose its digital sovereignty, especially because European data are mostly processed and stored by foreign companies. Indeed, this risks potential infringement[38] of fundamental rights. In particular, 'digital sovereignty' is an oxymoronic expression that refers to 'a form of control over digital assets, which can be material and immaterial entities, thus potentially "located" in a space that transcends physical boundaries.'[39] Such an expression refers to the control of data as well as the control of network infrastructures or cloud services. It may be relevant to remember that this concept was built by the Court of Justice of the European Union (CJEU) starting with the *Google Spain*[40] case, and then with the *Schrems* case.[41]

In particular, in order to regulate the new digital power in Europe, in contrast to what has occurred in the US, the European Court of Justice (ECJ) has recognised that the European Charters of Rights have a horizontal effect against private operators. According to Pollicino, with the *Google Spain* and *Schrems* cases, the ECJ incidentally made a horizontal application of the EU Charter of Fundamental Rights, in the fields of respect for private life (Article 7) and personal data (Article 8), to recognise digital privacy rights in the face of new digital power. However, this period of judicial activism by the ECJ was then replaced by a new phase of digital constitutionalism, distinguished by a new leading role for the European legislator, first with the General Data Protection Regulation (Regulation (EU) 2016/679).[42] Nevertheless, it is a process that is still ongoing.[43]

Latterly, since non-European digital payment solutions and technologies operating abroad could dominate the European payments market in the near

[37] ESAs (n 35) 6–8.

[38] As early as 1998 it was observed that 'IT revolution is causing a profound transformation in the nature of the world order. A dramatic relocation of power and authority … involving the decline of the sovereign state': Eric Helleiner, 'Electronic Money: A Challenge to the Sovereign State?' (1998) 51 *Journal of International Affairs* 387, 388.

[39] Celeste (n 4) 7.

[40] CJEU, Case C-131/12, *Google Spain SL and Google Inc v Agencia Española de Protección de Datos (AEPD) and Mario Costeja González*, Judgment of 13 May 2014, EU:C:2014:317.

[41] CJEU, Case C-362/14, *Maximillian Schrems v Data Protection Commissioner* ECLI:EU:C:2015:650, and CJEU, Case C-311/18, *Data Protection Commissioner v Facebook Ireland Ltd, Maximillian Schrems* ECLI:EU:C:2020:559.

[42] Oreste Pollicino, 'The quadrangular shape of the geometry of digital power(s) and the move towards a procedural digital constitutionalism' (2023) 29 *European Law Journal* 10, 24–26.

[43] Oreste Pollicino, *Judicial Protection of Fundamental Rights on the Internet. A Road Towards Digital Constitutionalism?* (Bloomsbury Publishing, 2021) 110.

future – the risk of this being raised by the increasing use of payment methods offered by Big Tech companies – there are new concerns about European autonomy and privacy in relation to payments.[44] Regarding this, in order to regain European digital sovereignty in the banking system, on November 2022 the ECB joined the European Data and Cloud Network Initiative (Gaia-X),[45] which seeks to develop a European data infrastructure.

Another fundamental step to preserve European sovereignty will be the introduction of a digital euro, which would enable Europeans to use public money for digital payments throughout the euro area. According to the current governor of the Bank of Italy, a digital euro would also 'protect the singleness of money, monetary sovereignty and the integrity of the financial system', and contribute to European strategic autonomy and economic efficiency.[46] Otherwise, the risk of non-European digital payment solutions and technologies operating abroad controlling our payments market would be increased by the expansion Big Tech payment services, which would profit from their customer base.[47]

IV. Sustainable Banks and Environment, Social and Governance Risks

If the digital transition can provoke the risks summarised above, the green transition can equally play a Janus-faced role vis-à-vis the banking system.[48] According to the European Commission, sustainable finance 'refers to the process of taking environmental, social and governance (ESG) considerations into account when making investment decisions in the financial sector, leading to more long-term investments in sustainable economic activities and projects'.[49]

[44] Fabio Panetta, 'The digital euro and the evolution of the financial system' (15 June 2022), www.ecb.europa.eu/press/key/date/2022/html/ecb.sp220615~0b859eb8bc.en.html.

[45] www.ecb.europa.eu/press/pr/date/2022/html/ecb.pr221117~78120d41f0.it.html. See also Francesca Musiani, 'Infrastructuring digital sovereignty: a research agenda for an infrastructure-based sociology of digital self-determination practices' (2022) 25 *Information, Communication & Society* 785, 787, doi.org/10.1080/1369118X.2022.2049850; Rocco Bellanova, Helena Carrapico and Denis Duez, 'Digital/sovereignty and European security integration: an introduction' (2022) 31 *European Security* 337, doi.org/10.1080/09662839.2022.2101887.

[46] Panetta (n 44).

[47] ibid, but see also Nordine Abidi and Ixart Miquel-Flores, 'Too Tech to Fail?' in Lukas Böffel and Jonas Schürger (eds), *Digitalisation, Sustainability, and the Banking and Capital Markets Union. EBI Studies in Banking and Capital Markets Law* (Palgrave Macmillan, 2023) 41.

[48] Antonio L Riso, 'Which Role for the Prudential Supervision of Banks in Sustainable Finance?' in Danny Busch, Guido Ferrarini and Seraina Grünewald (eds), *Sustainable Finance in Europe. Corporate Governance, Financial Stability and Financial Markets* (Palgrave Macmillan, 2021) 278.

[49] European Commission, 'Overview of sustainable finance', finance.ec.europa.eu/sustainable-finance/overview-sustainable-finance_en. On 27 October 2021, the European Commission adopted the Banking Package 2021 (ec.europa.eu/commission/presscorner/detail/en/ip_21_5401), ie a review of the Capital Requirements Regulation and the Capital Requirements Directive, in order to ensure that EU banks become more resilient to potential future economic shocks, while contributing to Europe's recovery from the COVID-19 pandemic and the transition to climate neutrality. The review consists on a legislative proposal to amend the Capital Requirements Directive (Directive 2013/36/EU) (CRR);

About 60 years ago, in *Capitalism and Freedom*, Milton Friedman stated that in a free society 'there is one and only one social responsibility of business – to use its resources and engage in activities designed to increase its profits so long as it stays within the rules of the game'.[50] Recently, in the same vein, it was stated that 'replacing the Shareholder Value with the Environmental Social goals twist the correct functioning of the market as well as the correct functioning of democracy',[51] on the assumption that in modern democracies the identification of the mission pursued by a given company should be entrusted to parliaments and governments elected according to constitutional rules.[52]

However, as it was recently stated by Maria Rosaria Ferrarese,[53] if national states maintain their monopoly on the use of the force, after internationalisation, the widespread diffusion of privatisation and digital technology, global power is not currently projecting the image of a stable architecture with a specific territorial location. Moreover, 'Globalization is, at the same time, denationalization of State institutions and a cumulative process of expansion of trade, communication, media, migration, crime, terrorism and even fashion. This development has two levels: one is global or universal, the other is supranational.' So, among the main features of the global level there is the 'control of the state by the economy, which replaces state control over the economy'.[54]

a legislative proposal to amend the Capital Requirements Regulation (Regulation 2013/575/EU) (CRR) and a separate legislative proposal, just adopted (Regulation (EU) 2022/2036 amending Regulation (EU) No 575/2013 and Directive 2014/59/EU as regards the prudential treatment of global systemically important institutions with a multiple-point-of-entry resolution strategy and methods for the indirect subscription of instruments eligible for meeting the minimum requirement for own funds and eligible liabilities), to amend the CRR in the area of resolution. As far as we are concerned, with reference to the ESG risks, the aforementioned proposal of the European Commission will require banks to systematically identify, disclose and manage ESG risks as part of their risk management. So it will also become crucial for the banking system to set the balance between the green and the digital transitions.

[50] Milton Friedman, *Capitalism and freedom* ([1962] The University of Chicago Press, 2022) 133; see also Milton Friedman, 'A Friedman doctrine – The Social Responsibility of Business Is to Increase Its Profits' *The New York Times* (13 September 1970), where he stated that: 'Of course, in practice the doctrine of social responsibility is frequently a cloak for actions that are justified on other grounds rather than a reason for those actions. To illustrate, it may well be in the long-run interest of a corporation that is a major employer in a small community to devote resources to providing amenities to that community or to improving its government. That may make it easier to attract desirable employers, it may reduce the wage bill or lessen losses from pilferage and sabotage or have other worthwhile effects. Or it may be that, given the laws about the deductibility of corporate charitable contributions, the stockholders can contribute more to charities they favor by having the corporation make the gift than by doing it themselves, since they can in that way contribute an amount that would otherwise have been paid as corporate taxes. In each of these – and many similar– cases, there is a strong temptation to rationalise these actions as an exercise of "social responsibility." In the present climate of opinion, with its widespread aversion to "capitalism," "profits," the "soulless corporation" and so on, this is one way for a corporation to generate goodwill as a by-product of expenditures that are entirely justified in its own self-interest.'

[51] Concetta Brescia Morra, 'Who will save the planet: the State or the large corporations? ESG: an ambiguous and useless formula' (2022) suppl to no 4 *Rivista trimestrale di diritto dell'economia* 78.

[52] ibid 98.

[53] Maria Rosaria Ferrarese, *Poteri nuovi* (Il Mulino, 2022) 77. See also Cassese (n 16) 55.

[54] Cassese (n 16) 56. See also Brian R Copeland, Joseph S Shapiro and M Scott Taylor, 'Globalization and the environment' in Gita Gopinath, Elhanan Helpman and Kenneth Rogoff (eds), *Handbook of International Economics: International Trade, Volume 5* (Elsevier, 2022) 133.

After all, contrary to Friedman, the ECJ stated in 2012 that 'in a social market economy, a reasonable private investor would not disregard, first, its responsibility towards all the stakeholders in the company and, second, the development of the social, economic and environmental context in which it continues to develop'.[55] Unquestionably, the focus on ESG policies is now sharpening for enterprises, many of which set out among their purposes the pursuit of environmental and social goals,[56] and also for banks all over the world.[57]

In December 2022, the EBA published its roadmap on sustainable finance, building on numerous legislative acts and initiatives: most recently, the European Parliament's legislative resolution of 10 November 2022 on the proposal for a Directive of the European Parliament and of the Council, regarding corporate sustainability reporting, which was recently adopted.[58] According to the EBA, climate change, environmental degradation, social issues and other factors present considerable challenges to the EU economy. These phenomena will continue to cause economic transformations that will affect the financial sector. In particular, environmental and climate-related risks may impact all conventional categories of financial risks in which institutions could be involved in the near future. Moreover, social and governance factors may indirectly influence the financial sector. So, the finance and banking sectors need to put in place resilient solutions. On the other hand, financial authorities are also involved in addressing the efforts required by the ESG risks, in order to preserve the safety and soundness of financial institutions that are engaged in financing the economy towards transition to a sustainable economic system. As stated by the EBA, a 'robust banking sector and overall financial stability

[55] 'The challenges relating to social responsibility and the entrepreneurial context are, in actual fact, capable of having a major impact on the specific decisions and strategic planning of a reasonable private investor. The long-term economic rationale of a reasonable private entrepreneur's conduct cannot therefore be assessed without taking account of such concerns. 83 For that purpose, the payment by a private investor of additional redundancy payments is, in principle, capable of constituting a legitimate and appropriate practice, depending on the circumstances of the case, with a view to fostering a calm social dialogue and maintaining the brand image of a company or group of companies': CJEU, Case T-565/08, *Corsica Ferries France SAS v European Commission* ECLI:EU:T:2012:415.

[56] Guido Ferrarini, 'Redefining Corporate Purpose: Sustainability as a Game Changer' in Danny Busch, Guido Ferrarini and Seraina Grünewald (eds), *Sustainable Finance in Europe. Corporate Governance, Financial Stability and Financial Markets* (Palgrave Macmillan, 2021) 86.

[57] Rosa Calderazzi, '*Sustainability in banking*' (2002) supp 4 *Rivista trimestrale di diretto dell'economica* 168–69. After all, with reference to the Italian legal system, according to the 2022 amendment of the Italian Constitution, 'Private economic enterprise … cannot be carried out in conflict with social utility or in such a manner as may harm health, the environment … The law shall determine appropriate programmes and checks to ensure that public and private economic enterprise activity be directed at and co-ordinated for … environmental purposes' (Art 41 Constitution of the Italian Republic).

[58] Directive (EU) 2022/2464 of the European Parliament and of the Council of 14 December 2022 amending Regulation (EU) No 537/2014, Directive 2004/109/EC, Directive 2006/43/EC and Directive 2013/34/EU, as regards corporate sustainability reporting.

will be key conditions in supporting an orderly transition'; on the other hand, 'Credit institutions also have the technical expertise that is critical for assessing the risks and opportunities attached to sustainable assets, especially during this transition.'[59]

As mentioned above, in December 2022[60] the EBA published its sustainable finance roadmap,[61] which substitutes the EBA's 2019 Sustainable Finance Action Plan. In continuity with the previous action plan, the new roadmap accommodates the necessary adjustments,[62] especially with reference to labelling sustainable products, greenwashing, supervisory reporting and, last but not least, enhancing the risk monitoring framework.[63] Closely related to the ESG risks, the mission of the EBA is to promote the stability, resilience and orderly functioning of the financial system.[64]

In fact, the pursuit of sustainability is challenging for banks due to the complexity of the plurality of interests involved in banking activities, especially in order to achieve a sound and prudent management.[65] First of all, banks need to pursue sustainability during the credit supply phase, by encouraging sustainable companies.[66] In addition, banks need to develop their investment policies to develop strategies that are cohesive with investors' sustainability policies. Then, the operational process needs to be implemented, according to the climate and environmental risks. Finally, banks need to adopt data infrastructures to share

[59] EBA, 'The EBA roadmap on sustainable finance' (2022) 4, www.eba.europa.eu/eba-publishes-its-roadmap-sustainable-finance.

[60] On the basis of the following legislative acts: Regulation (EU) No 1093/2010 (EBA Founding Regulation), Regulation (EU) No 575/2013 (Capital Requirements Regulation) (CRR) and Directive (EU) 2013/36 (Capital Requirements Directive) (CRD), Regulation (EU) 2019/2033 (Investment Firms Regulation) (IFR) and Directive (EU) 2019/2034 (Investment Firms Directive) (IFD), Regulation (EU) 2017/2402 (Securitisation Regulation), Regulation (EU) 2019/2088 (Sustainable Finance Disclosure Regulation) (SFDR).

[61] EBA (n 59).

[62] The previous action plan concerned the following areas of focus: strategy and risk management; key metrics and disclosure; stress testing; scenario analysis and prudential treatment.

[63] EBA (n 59) 5. Today, the EBA's activities on this topic can be classified as follows: a. transparency and disclosures; b. risk management and supervision; c. prudential treatment of exposures; d. stress-testing; e. standards and labels; f. greenwashing; g. supervisory reporting; h. ESG risks and sustainable finance monitoring framework (EBA (n 59) 10).

[64] Involved in this direction are the European Commission, the Basel Committee on Banking Supervision (BCBS) and the Network for Greening the Financial System (NGFS). The European Securities and Markets Authority (ESMA) and the European Occupational Pensions and Insurance Authority (EIOPA) must also be considered to ensure an overall consistency of regulatory actions beyond the EU financial sector. The ECB and other EU and international institutions should also be considered.

[65] Calderazzi (n 57) 169.

[66] As highlighted by R Calderazzi, 'Le Linee Guida EBA sulla concessione e monitoraggio del credito' in Ugo Malvagna and Antonella Sciarrone Alibrandi (eds), *Sistema produttivo e finanziario post COVID-19: dall'efficienza alla sostenibilità. Voci dal diritto dell'economia* (Pisa, 2021) 221, according to EBA: 'Institutions should incorporate ESG factors and associated risks in their credit risk appetite and risk management policies, credit risk policies and procedures, adopting a holistic approach' (EBA, 'Guidelines on loan origination and monitoring' (29 May 2020) 26).

information about their sustainable policies.[67] In the end, as it has been argued, ESG factors become both the start and end point of banks' business activities.[68]

Given the above, and as Copeland, Shapiro and Scott Taylor have stated, 'the climate is a global public good subject to a severe free rider problem, mechanisms to support cooperation may be able to increase the level of cooperation and stringency of climate policy',[69] any effort to support global regulation in this field is also relevant. The EBA highlighted in its roadmap that to work on ESG risks and sustainable finance it is necessary to act at the European and international levels, by attending to numerous ESG initiatives in various EU and international fora, such as the European Commission, the Basel Committee on Banking Supervision (BCBS) and the Network for Greening the Financial System (NGFS); but also by cooperating with the ECB and other ESAs.[70] This cooperation will ensure that, in the field of sustainability, European banking rules have the capacity to become a global model.

V. Reconciling the Digital and Green Transitions in the European Financial System

Sustainability and the need to contribute to the green transition has become one of the three pillars of the European Commission's review of EU banking rules in order to ensure that EU banks become more resilient to potential future economic shocks, while contributing to Europe's recovery from the COVID-19 pandemic and the transition to climate neutrality.[71]

For this reason, it may be useful to highlight what has recently been argued:[72]

> Adopting green policies with exclusive effects is fairly easy. If we require everyone to use renewable energies only, most human beings on the planet will be shut-off from any productivity gain modern industrial technologies have provided to mankind, will be forced to walk, and will most likely starve.

On the other hand, 'Even if we accept some negative environmental impact, it is not so easy to be inclusive: exclusion is often due to risks most incumbent institutions try to avoid in the absence of law and regulation.'[73] So, the matter is how to

[67] Calderazzi (n 57) 182.
[68] ibid 186.
[69] Copeland, Shapiro and and Scott Taylor (n 56) 133.
[70] EBA (n 59) 5.
[71] Banking Package 2021 mentioned in n 51.
[72] At the High-level Panel of the 61st session of the United Nation's Social Commission responsible for the social development pillar of global development.
[73] Dirk A Zetzsche, Douglas W Arner and Ross Buckley, 'Inclusive Green Finance-towards implementation of the United Nation's 2030 Agenda for Sustainable Development' (Oxford Business Law Blog, 20 March 2023), blogs.law.ox.ac.uk/oblb/blog-post/2023/03/inclusive-green-finance-towards-implementation-united-nations-2030-agenda.

balance saving the environment and ensuring inclusive growth and equal opportunities, with reference also to the use of digital technology,[74] according to the above-mentioned recommendations of the ESAs.

Recent studies show that, while the development of environmental technologies reduces greenhouse gas emissions, the spread of digital technologies increases them.[75] In this context, the habits of citizens and companies may be key in reducing the consumption of energy in relation to digital technology. To achieve this goal, according to Ammannati and Canepa, a fundamental challenge lies in the use of AI to fight climate change and to verify the ecological footprint of this technology. While machine learning systems consume large amounts of energy to run their data centres,[76] the increasing use of digital technologies will lead to sharp increase in energy consumption in the near future. However, 'according to some estimates, ICT technologies may reduce 10 times more greenhouse gas emissions than their own footprint'.[77] Finally, the digital transition may generate a series of opportunities, particularly due to AI, which may contribute to the optimisation of energy consumption. However, the intensive use of AI could usher in a series of pitfalls[78] as well.

In this context, the need to mobilise both public and private resources in order to finance the transition to a sustainable economy is clear.[79] In order to ensure the right of choice for private investors, the Commission's Delegated Regulation (EU) 2021/1253[80] establishes that 'Investment firms that provide investment advice and portfolio management should be able to recommend suitable financial instruments to their clients and potential clients and should therefore be able to ask questions to identify a client's individual sustainability preferences.'[81] On the other hand, 'In order to prevent mis-selling and greenwashing, investment firms should not recommend or decide to trade financial instruments as meeting individual sustainability preferences where those financial instruments do not meet those preferences.'[82] However, the increasing use of digital financial services in combination with the Internet and social networks in order to retrieve information

[74] Digital technology may also increase financial inclusion, as shown by Steven L Schwarcz and Robert Bourret, *Fractionalizing Investment Securities: Using FinTech to Expand Financial Inclusion* (2023) 84 *Ohio State Law Journal*, ssrn.com/abstract=4391083.

[75] Stefano Bianchini, Giacolo Damioli and Claudia Ghisetti, 'The environmental effects of the "twin" green and digital transition in European regions' (2023) 84 *Environmental and Resource Economics* 877–918.

[76] Laura Ammannati and Allegra Canepa, 'Towards the ecological transition: State measures and sustainable finance', [2022] supp to no 4, *Rivista trimestrale di diritto dell'economia* 136, 148–49.

[77] AIDA working paper, 'Artificial Intelligence and the Green Deal' (March 2021), mentioned in European Parliament resolution of 3 May 2022 on artificial intelligence in a digital age (2020/2266(INI)).

[78] Ammannati and Canepa (n 76) 149.

[79] ibid 153.

[80] Of 21 April 2021 amending Delegated Regulation (EU) 2017/565 as regards the integration of sustainability factors, risks and preferences into certain organisational requirements and operating conditions for investment firms.

[81] Recital 4.

[82] Recital 7.

presents risks for investors,[83] related to the aforementioned tenth recommendation of the ESAs.[84] According to this point, Ammannati and Canepa questioned whether the road to the transformation outlined by the EU in the Green Deal is viable, considering that the most innovative decision in this field has been taken with the NGEU, which is seen as a transitional model.[85] Regarding this, we can be optimistic because it has been noticed that institutions generally follow a path-dependency approach so that, when a governance or an economic process is put into action, it becomes difficult to change it.[86]

VI. Conclusion

As this chapter has shown, the EU is strengthening its integration, firstly with the BU and secondly with the NGEU, despite the recent globalisation backlash.[87]

Both the digital and green transitions can present some risks for the banking system, which are summarised in the ESA's recommendations and in the latest EBA roadmap on sustainable finance. Among them, a significant question is how to preserve the digital sovereignty of the EU in relation to the banking system. Furthermore, the pursuit of sustainability is challenging for banks. However, the need to convey, through the banking system, both public and private resources to finance the transition to a sustainable economy, is evident. In order to reconcile both the green and the digital transitions, a fundamental challenge lies in the use of the AI in order to fight climate change and to verify AI's own ecological footprint.

Regulating the green and digital transition will also present a challenge to European lawmakers, because, in a global context, cooperation is crucial to ensure that new domestic rules fit for companies from all over the world. In order to reconcile both digital and green ambitions in the EU, it may be useful to highlight the distinction between *taxis* and *cosmos* suggested by Hayek, based on ancient Greek culture:

> A *cosmos* will result from regularities of the behaviour of the elements which it comprises. It is in this sense endogenous, intrinsic .... A *taxis*, on the other hand, is determined by an agency which stands outside the order and is in the same sense exogenous or imposed.[88]

[83] Ammannati and Canepa (n 76) 162.

[84] ESAs (n 37) 8.

[85] Ammannati and Canepa (n 76) 167.

[86] Fabbrini (n 14) 195.

[87] Italo Colantone, Gianmarco Ottaviano and Piero Stanig, 'The Backlash of Globalization' in Gita Gopinath, Elhanan Helpman and Kenneth Rogoff (eds), *Handbook of International Economics: International Trade, Volume 5* (Elsevier, 2022) 407.

[88] Friedrich August Hayek, *The Confusion of Political Language in Political Thought. With some suggestions for remedying it*, 2nd edn (The Institute of Economic Affairs, 1976) 12.

We may view the twin[89] transitions as being the result of a combination of two different arrangements: the digital transition is more related to *taxis*, while the green transition exists in order to pursue *cosmos*. Consequently, we have to note that

> while the complexity of activities which can be ordered as a taxis [in this case the arrangement concerning the digital transition] is necessarily limited to what can be known to the organiser, there is no similar limit in a spontaneous order [ie the arrangement that will result from the green transition].[90]

Ultimately, if both the digital transition and the green transition are human-made, while the digital transition will last as a human-made creation (*taxis*), the green transition is properly involved in a more complex order that we need to learn: the natural one (*cosmos*).

In this sense, we can understand what Pope Francis means when he said that 'Rather than a problem to be solved, the world is a joyful mystery to be contemplated.'[91] Jurists and lawyers are often considered problem-solvers[92] and in the present context, the law, both in the European and global contexts, seeks to implement a set of regulatory provisions to limit the damage to our planet, while also promoting the use of digital technology for this purpose and in the view of a fair balance of interests between present and future generations.[93] But the law remains made by human beings, who need to understand, first of all, the rules of the ecosystem, and these are not human creations. In this context, the verb 'to contemplate' ultimately means 'to spend time considering a possible future action',[94] ie acting in a proactive way, because the green transition logically precedes the digital one.

[89] On this topic see EU Science Hub, 'The twin green & digital transition: How sustainable digital technologies could enable a carbon-neutral EU by 2050', joint-research-centre.ec.europa.eu/jrc-news-and-updates/twin-green-digital-transition-how-sustainable-digital-technologies-could-enable-carbon-neutral-eu-2022-06-29_en.

[90] Hayek (n 88) 13.

[91] Pope Francis, 'Encyclical letter Laudato si', 24 May 2015, §12, www.vatican.va/content/francesco/en/encyclicals/documents/papa-francesco_20150524_enciclica-laudato-si.html. On the contribution of this Encyclical to the legal and political debate, see *ex multis* Lucia Ann Silecchia, 'Laudato Si' and Care for Our Common Home: What Does it Mean for the Legal Profession?' (2016) 6 *Seattle Journal of Environmental Law*, scholarship.law.edu/scholar/956; Massimiliano Montini and Francesca Volpe, 'In praise of sustainability: the Encyclical letter Laudato sì and its legal-economic implications' (2016) *The Italian Yearbook of International Law Online*, 25.1, doi.org/10.1163/22116133-90000118a; and James T McHugh, 'Eternal Law and Environmental Policy: Pope Francis, Laudato Si', and a Thomistic Approach to Climate Change' in Alynna J Lyon, Christine A Gustafson and Paul Christopher Manuel (eds), *Pope Francis as a Global Actor. Palgrave Studies in Religion, Politics, and Policy* (Palgrave Macmillan, 2018).

[92] Paul Brest and Linda Hamilton Krieger, 'Lawyers as Problem Solvers' (1999) 72 *Temple Law Review* 811.

[93] Francesco Capriglione, 'The financial system towards a sustainable transition' (2021) 10 *Law and Economics Yearly Review*, www.laweconomicsyearlyreview.org.uk/Law_and_Economics_Yearly_Review_LEYR_Journal_vol_11_part_1_2022.pdf.

[94] Cambridge Dictionary, dictionary.cambridge.org/dictionary/english/contemplate.

INDEX

www.ingramcontent.com/pod-product-compliance
Ingram Content Group UK Ltd.
Pitfield, Milton Keynes, MK11 3LW, UK
UKHW020801290926
15470UKWH00003B/898